Patterns of Piety

This book offers a new interpretation of the transition from catholicism to protestantism in the English Reformation, and explores its implications for an understanding of women and gender. Central to this is an appreciation of the significance of medieval Christocentric piety in offering a bridge to the Reformation, and in shaping the nature of protestantism in the period up to the Civil War. Not only does this explain much of the support for protestantism, but it also suggests the need to question assumptions that the 'loss' of the Virgin Mary and the saints was detrimental to women.

Patterns of piety are crucial in two senses: devotional trends intersected with the ideas expressed in the lives of godly exemplars. The strength of the idea of the godly woman ensured that the outcome would shape the contemporary understanding of gender. The Reformation undermined the ritual role of the catholic godly woman, but its definition of the representative frail christian as a woman devoted to Christ meant that it was not an alien environment for the weaker sex. Moreover, although scriptural texts could reinforce patriarchy, they were complemented by subtle discussions of the ambiguities of gender and responsibility in the stories of Susanna and Bathsheba. The Christocentric piety of the late medieval parish shaped the Reformation and paved the way for a more subtle understanding of gender.

CHRISTINE PETERS is Lecturer in History, The Queen's College, Oxford.

Cambridge Studies in Early Modern British History

Series editors

ANTHONY FLETCHER
Victoria County History, Institute of Historical Research, University of London

JOHN GUY
Visiting Fellow, Clare College, Cambridge

JOHN MORRILL
*Professor of British and Irish History, University of Cambridge,
and Vice-Master of Selwyn College*

This is a series of monographs and studies covering many aspects of the history of the British Isles between the late fifteenth and the early eighteenth century. It includes the work of established scholars and pioneering work by a new generation of scholars. It includes both reviews and revisions of major topics and books, which open up new historical terrain or which reveal startling new perspectives on familiar subjects. All the volumes set detailed research into broader perspectives, and the books are intended for the use of students as well as of their teachers.

For a list of titles in the series, see the end of this book.

PATTERNS OF PIETY

*Women, Gender and Religion
in Late Medieval and
Reformation England*

CHRISTINE PETERS

PUBLISHED BY THE PRESS SYNDICATE OF THE UNIVERSITY OF CAMBRIDGE
The Pitt Building, Trumpington Street, Cambridge, United Kingdom

CAMBRIDGE UNIVERSITY PRESS
The Edinburgh Building, Cambridge CB2 2RU, UK
40 West 20th Street, New York, NY 10011-4211, USA
477 Williamstown Road, Port Melbourne, VIC 3207, Australia
Ruiz de Alarcón 13, 28014 Madrid, Spain
Dock House, The Waterfront, Cape Town 8001, South Africa

http://www.cambridge.org

© Christine Peters 2003

First published 2003

Printed in the United Kingdom at the University Press, Cambridge

Typeface Sabon 10/12 pt   *System* LATEX 2$_\varepsilon$ [TB]

A catalogue record for this book is available from the British Library

Library of Congress Cataloging in Publication data
Peters, Christine.
Patterns of piety: women, gender, and religion in later medieval and Reformation
England / Christine Peters.
p.   cm. – (Cambridge studies in early modern British history)
Includes bibliographical references and index.
ISBN 0-521-58062-5
1. Christian women – Religious life – England – History.   2. Church
history – England – Middle Ages, 600–1500.   3. Reformation – England.
I. Title.   II. Series.
BR377. P47   2002
274.2′06′082 – dc21   2002067361

ISBN 0 521 58062 5 hardback

CONTENTS

ILLUSTRATIONS

TABLES

ACKNOWLEDGEMENTS

In 1653, as she ventured into print, Margaret Cavendish noted that she had been urged to 'let writing *Books* alone / For surely *wiser Women* never wrote one' and to return to her sewing. In today's society, the attractions of the needle may be less powerful, and the specific problems of female authorship less acute, than in the middle of the seventeenth century, but anyone who has attempted to convert 'the thesis' into 'the book' knows that such an undertaking can often seem far from wise. The acknowledgements of academic and personal support that follow are far from token.

This book is a considerably modified version of my Oxford D.Phil. thesis, 'Women and the Reformation: Social relations and attitudes in rural England *c*. 1470–1570' (1992). To my supervisor, Felicity Heal, I owe a great deal, and much more than I realised at the time of writing my dissertation. I am also most grateful for her continuing support and interest in my work. I owe it to Anthony Fletcher's advocacy that this book was considered by the editors for inclusion in this series. Their comments helped to shape the way in which the book developed ideas that had only been hinted at in the original thesis. I owe a particularly strong debt of gratitude to John Blair, who has been invaluable as a friend, colleague and critic.

My debts to academic institutions are various. The tutors at St Hugh's College offered me the chance to read history at Oxford, and it was in reflecting upon one of my tutorials there that the seeds of this project were sown. The generosity of the Leverhulme Trust in granting me a Study Abroad Studentship to Romania, and of The Warburg Institute in awarding me a Frances A. Yates Fellowship, encouraged me to think about art and religious change in ways which have transformed this text. I am also extremely grateful to the Provost and Fellows of The Queen's College, Oxford for their offer to me of a lecturership in early modern history, and for their further support of the research and writing of this book by granting me periods of sabbatical leave. It is also, of course, a most congenial place in which to live and work.

I would also like to take this opportunity to thank the staff of various libraries in Oxford for their assistance over the years and of Record Offices throughout the country who responded helpfully to my enquiries. David Park also kindly allowed me access to the invaluable Wall Paintings Archive at the Courtauld Institute. For permission to reproduce illustrations, I would like to thank: the Bodleian Library; the British Library; the British Museum; the Burrell Collection; the Courtauld Institute; the National Monuments Record; Norwich Museums Service; The Queen's College; the Victoria and Albert Museum; W. Lack, H. M. Stuchfield and P. Whittemore; S. Rickerby, and for photographic assistance: Ian Cartwright of the Institute of Archaeology, Oxford, and Veronika Vernier.

Members of my family, friends and colleagues have offered invaluable support in many ways for which I am most grateful. Each of them knows the importance to me of their contributions.

ABBREVIATIONS

Am. Hist. Rev.	American Historical Review
Arch. Cant.	Archaeologia Cantiana
Arch. Jnl.	Archaeological Journal
BBOAJ	Berkshire, Buckinghamshire and Oxfordshire Archaeological Journal
Beds. Hist. Rec. Soc.	Bedfordshire Historical Record Society
BIHR	Bulletin of the Institute of Historical Research
CCW	Consistory Court wills
CWA	churchwardens' accounts
EETS	Early English Text Society
EHR	English Historical Review
Hist. Jnl.	Historical Journal
JBAA	Journal of the British Archaeological Association
JEH	Journal of Ecclesiastical History
Jnl. Som. Arch. Soc.	Journal of the Somerset Archaeological Society
N & Q	Notes and Queries
P & P	Past and Present
Proc. Soc. Antiq.	Proceedings of the Society of Antiquaries
RCHM	Royal Commission on Historical Monuments
Rec. Soc.	Record Society
Records of Bucks.	Records of Buckinghamshire
RO	Record Office
Surrey Arch. Coll.	Surrey Archaeological Collections
Trans. . . . Arch. Soc.	Transactions of the . . . Archaeological Society

Trans. Devon Association	*Report and Transactions of the Devonshire Association*
V & A	Victoria and Albert Museum
VCH	*Victoria County History*
Wilts. Arch. & Nat. Hist. Mag.	*Wiltshire Archaeological and Natural History Magazine*
YAJ	*Yorkshire Archaeological Journal*

Introduction

Research for this book began with the deceptively simple question: What was the impact of the Reformation on women? At the time it seemed a straightforward question to answer, and the lines of enquiry well established. In drawing up a balance sheet of the Reformation, the loss of Mary and the female saints had to be weighed against the protestant separation of virginity and sanctity. At the cost of creating a religious environment stripped of saintly female models, the new religion honoured married life and promoted the idea of the godly woman.

But, even at this stage, although the entries in the account book appeared obvious, the appropriate method of accountancy seemed elusive. How could one determine the significance of the psychological and inspirational importance of female saintly role models whose lives not only drew attention to the inadequacies of individual laywomen but also testified to the possibility of female sanctity and pious achievement despite the legacy of Eve? And how to balance this against the retreat from the promotion of the sacred value of virginity which was symbolised on the one hand by the closure of monasteries and nunneries, and on the other by the destruction of those same saint's cults that offered inspiring models of female religious potential? Since marriage was the fate of the majority of women, the answer initially seemed obvious. Surely a religious position that set its face against the christian unease with sex and childbirth and promoted the values of godly marriage must be accounted a positive advance for women, whatever the fate of those virgin saints tortured by pagan persecutors? And yet there was a nagging doubt. Extracts from godly advice literature in collections of early modern writings about women, often edited by crusading feminist historians, suggested that the protestant elevation of marriage heralded the enforcement of patriarchy and the subjection of wives to their husbands.

In the years since the first identification of these conflicting possibilities, striking a balance has often seemed no easier. The rather dismal, but nevertheless initially persuasive, conclusion of Collinson that the period was characterised by continuity rather than change, and that there was no history

1

of the family – nor presumably of gender – in the Reformation, seemed to threaten the very validity of the initial question.[1] But a stress on continuity, though important, risks being too blunt a tool for assessing the gender impact of a process so complex as the Reformation, or indeed of any significant change in ideas and social practice. Granted, it is possible to identify patriarchal assumptions in most periods of English history, but this does not mean that there is no history of gender. What matters is the shifting emphases that create possibilities and opportunities of expression. To take an obvious example, it is important to note that the 'puritan family' was not a Reformation invention, but it is as important to realise that such ideas were much more insistently proselytised, presumably not without some effect, in that period.[2] Moreover, this continuity can be seen as part of the strength of this strand of Reformation culture, which, whilst labelled puritan, was not entirely alien to a broader spectrum of religious opinion.

In religious terms too, this study stresses and defines the importance of continuity, without wishing to negate the significance of the Reformation impact. The altars were stripped, and parishioners were confronted with the need to make choices about maintaining religious traditions that had seemed natural but were now prohibited and derided. But we will not understand this process if we think in terms of the creation of unbridgeable worlds. The government of early modern England lacked the resources of a modern police state to secure speedy outward conformity to its edicts. Moreover, it is clear that neither charting the destruction and concealment of the apparatus of catholic devotion, dramatic though this was, nor drawing attention to early modern laments for the 'merry world' that had been lost with the imposition of the new religion, adequately captures the nature of this transition.

Making windows into men's souls is notoriously difficult, and was not the declared aim of the official Reformation, at least in its period of consolidation in the reign of Elizabeth I. Nevertheless, we need to go further in exploring the devotional psychology and to suggest ways in which people could cope with, and make sense of, a world in which some familiar contours had been erased, but many salient landmarks remained visible. Those historians who have focussed on the contrast between a religion primarily experienced through the image to one primarily apprehended through the word have made an important contribution to this task. Their work has defined the conceptual tools available to those trying to make sense of the new map, and has drawn attention to the permeability of oral and literate cultures in the early modern

---

[1] P. Collinson, *The Birthpangs of Protestant England: Religious and Cultural Change in the Sixteenth and Seventeenth Centuries* (New York, 1988), pp. 60–93.

[2] K. M. Davies, 'Continuity and change in literary advice on marriage', in R. B. Outhwaite (ed.), *Marriage and Society* (London, 1981), pp. 58–80; M. Todd, *Christian Humanism and the Puritan Social Order* (Cambridge, 1987).

period. However, they have implicitly formulated the problem principally in terms of cognitive skills rather than of religious understanding.[3]

Critics of anthropological theories of acculturation pointed out long ago that it is an adaptive process. New ideologies imposed by an elite are not swallowed whole but grafted on to previous understanding.[4] Such arguments carry even stronger conviction in the context of early Reformation England where the laity, despite Duffy's 'traditional' epithet, was far from passive in its religious choices.[5] It supported a burgeoning market in devotional literature, took the lead in organising religious gilds, and adapted and fostered new devotions. Consequently, to understand the 'impact of the Reformation' we must think in terms of devotional transitions rather than leaps. This is complicated by the nature of much of the historiography of late medieval religion. Although convincing in their rehabilitation of the state of catholicism in the parishes of pre-Reformation England, such works largely take their lead from the agenda set by sixteenth-century anti-catholic polemic. Additionally, their concern is to delineate how parishioners' experiences of catholicism were religiously satisfying, catered for the individual and the community, and offered spiritual sustenance and support in dealing with the traumas and uncertainties of everyday life. Neither agenda offers much direct encouragement to understand how late medieval catholics could adapt to protestant surroundings, and yet it is implausible that all protestants and 'parish anglicans' were fearfully obedient conformists prepared to jettison all their previous beliefs.

One of the most noticeable developments in later medieval lay devotional culture was the assimilation of a Christocentric piety that had originated in the world of mystics and the cloistered. Translated into a parish context, it focussed on the passion of Christ, on the cult of his wounds, on the pietà, and on the mercy manifested towards mankind by the crucified Christ at the Last Judgement. Like all devotional developments, this was a strand within later medieval catholicism which was received more enthusiastically by some communities, and some individuals, than it was by others. Nevertheless, the general trend in the fifteenth century of positioning the Doom over

---

[3] P. Collinson, *From Iconoclasm to Iconophobia: The Cultural Impact of the Second English Reformation*, Stenton lecture (Reading, 1986); M. Aston, *England's Iconoclasts: Laws against Images* (Oxford, 1988); T. Watt, *Cheap Print and Popular Piety, 1550–1640* (Cambridge, 1991).

[4] J. Wirth, 'Against the acculturation thesis', in K. von Greyerz (ed.), *Religion and Society in Early Modern Europe, 1500–1800* (London, 1984), pp. 66–78. From a different theoretical perspective, work on hegemony has reached similar conclusions: T. J. Jackson Lears, 'The concept of hegemony: problems and possibilities', *Am. Hist. Rev.* 90 (1985), 567–593.

[5] E. Duffy, *The Stripping of the Altars: Traditional Religion in England, 1400–1580* (New Haven and London, 1992).

the chancel arch, and of emphasising Christ's wounds and the instruments of the passion, suggests that an important aspect of this devotional trend had permeated the understanding of the economy of salvation in most parishes. Such developments had repercussions for the cult of the saints, and of the Virgin Mary in particular, tending to reduce their intercessory role whilst at the same time making them potentially more approachable as human saintly figures.

It is a key argument of this book that this evolving Christocentric devotion offered a bridge to Reformation in terms of religious understanding. Of course, not all its adherents made this transition. Most obviously, the badge of the Five Wounds of Christ was adopted by the defenders of catholicism in the Pilgrimage of Grace in 1536. However, the difficulty faced by historians in determining whether a will preamble expressing the testator's trust to be saved by the merits of Christ's passion and precious blood-shedding should be classified as catholic or protestant illustrates the way in which later medieval Christocentric devotion could facilitate the transition to protestantism. This process was most evident in the first phase of evangelical protestantism, but its strength is further suggested by its fate in the more Calvinist climate of the Elizabethan period onwards. As the image of the deity became more distant and less human, the spirituality of the godly needed to take on a more human, Christ-centred character.

All this, it might be thought, has little relation to gender, and in particular to the impact of the Reformation on women. But, even in terms of our initial list of questions, it is evident that this is not the case. The simple assumption that the protestant attack on the cult of the Virgin Mary deprived women of an inspiring role model and patron seems more questionable in the context of increasingly Christocentric parish religion. Shifting patterns of piety offered new possibilities of identification and emulation, and could alter the extent to which gender was fundamental to this process. A devotional focus on the passion of the adult Christ rather than his infancy had the potential to transform Marian devotion, and if Mary was no longer quintessentially a divine nursing mother, we need to ask how this affected her role as a model primarily for women.

Thanks to the centrality of Christ in the medieval mystical tradition, historians have explored the gender implications of Christocentric piety more extensively than those of Marian devotion. However, we need to be wary about translating these conclusions from the world of the mystic and the cloistered to that of the parishioner. Although the Christocentric emphasis of late medieval devotion came from the former source, it intersected with the devotional needs of parish religion in which mystical ecstasy, and ideas of the individual as the bride of Christ, were less important than the pastorally inspired concerns of moral teaching. In a parish context, gendered notions of the importance of Christian renunciation and divine fusion, which are so central to understanding mystical experience, seem much less obviously relevant. When affective devotion crossed into the parishes it operated in a world with different parameters. For both Marian and Christ-centred devotion, as also for the related cult of the saints, our assumptions concerning the relationship between religion and gender need to be reconsidered. Only then will it be possible to draw conclusions about Reformation impact in terms of gender.

Patterns of piety are crucial to this project in two senses. Neither medieval catholicism nor Reformation protestantism offered a single mode of devotion which was followed by all, whether men or women, clerical or lay. Both were fluid and shifting in their emphases, as they adapted to official stimuli – whether papal encouragement of indulgenced devotions, or changes in official policy that led the Reformation from a Lutheran to a more Calvinist path – and were shaped by the needs and understanding of parishioners. But for an analysis in terms of gender it is important to explore how such patterns of piety intersected with another kind of pious model: the godly exemplar, whether a devout lay person or a canonised saint.

It was a commonplace of early modern thought that women were 'to piety more prone'. Although by their nature such assumptions are hard to prove, they crystallised in the notion of the godly woman, a concept that powerfully shaped contemporary understanding of religion and gender. Moreover, catholicism and protestantism offered significantly different models of the godly woman. Pre-Reformation catholicism identified the mistress of the household as its ritual specialist, whilst in protestantism the godly woman became an emblem of piety, faith and devotion, and a vital counterpart to the potentially sterile understanding of the rational male who could interpret scripture but might lack a living faith.

This redefinition permeated Reformation culture, whether in depictions of the godly woman seated attentively at the preacher's feet, or in the more enthusiastic publication of funeral sermons eulogising the piety of godly women than of those praising godly men. The title page of the 1611 edition of Richard Hooker's *Of the Lawes of Ecclesiastical Politie* summarised this position and raises further questions (Fig.1). Three aspects of the Church were depicted as being illumined by God: the king wielding the authority of the christian magistrate, a cathedral representing the visible Church, and a devout woman as the emblem of the piety of the faithful. Upon closer inspection, the devout woman can be identified as Mary Magdalen. As a substitute for the Virgin Mary as the emblem of the Church, Mary Magdalen seems a problematic model for women. Far from an ideal woman set upon a pedestal, the unchaste Magdalen could be a difficult exemplar in a society in which female honour was defined mainly in sexual terms. Yet, the Magdalen

Figure 1 Detail from the title page of R. Hooker, *Of the Lawes of Ecclesiastical Politie* (1611)

also offered a powerful image of the redemption of the sinner through faith which, in the context of the protestant emphasis on the abject sinfulness of mankind, could make the nuances of gender appear trivial.

The figure of Mary Magdalen also reminds us of a fundamental, but never clearly acknowledged, tension within Reformation protestantism. Despite her scriptural credentials and her inclusion amongst the purged list of saints in the Prayer Book of 1549, this was her last official appearance. In the process that Roston has aptly labelled the 'descent down the ladder of sanctity', protestantism turned away from the ranks of the saints to heroes and heroines drawn from the Old Testament and Apocrypha.[6] Mary Magdalen was an anomaly in this company, but part of the same trend that aimed, at least in part, to avoid the danger of idolatry. Yet it was this process that gave the Reformation its split personality. Such exemplars, despite their conscription into the service of orthodox protestantism, were excluded from the parish church, where the painted scriptural texts and the orderly disposition of the congregation exuded order and uncompromising prescription. In contrast, the accounts and depictions of the most favoured Old Testament and Apocryphal exemplars offered a continuous testing and exploration of the ambiguities of gender and moral responsibility. In accounts of the Fall and the stories of Susanna and Bathsheba, Adam, the elders and godly King David could find their actions subjected to uncomfortable scrutiny.

[6] M. Roston, *Biblical Drama in England from the Middle Ages to the Present Day* (Evanston, 1968), pp. 118, 120.

Despite the prominence of gendered models, and the ability of historians to extract apparently misogynistic quotations from puritan advice literature, the impact of the protestant Reformation on conceptions of gender was therefore a much more complex process. It was, moreover, a process in which little new was invented, but many themes in later medieval catholicism were given greater prominence. For those negotiating the transition, in religious as well as gender terms, it was not a completely uncharted journey, and, from the surviving fragments of the travelogue, it is that journey that this book aims to map.

PART 1

1

Religious roles

In the poem 'How the good wiff taughte hir daughtir', which survives in fourteenth- and fifteenth-century versions, the mother instructs her daughter that it is a wife's duty to go to church, to worship God on holy days and to bid her beads, and suggests that piety is an essential attribute for a young woman wishing to secure a good husband. In contrast, the equivalent male poem, 'How the wise man taught his sonne', contains only a passing reference to the son's religious obligations. Attendance at church is not even mentioned, although the young man is reminded to pray each morning to God that he may not sin. He is also warned not to think too much of amassing worldly goods since wealth is an obstacle to entering Paradise. However, this religious point is linked to the, perhaps more telling, secular one that worldly property is of little use when you die and your wife transfers it on marriage to someone who is not of your kin. These injunctions clearly do not represent a very considerable investment of time or importance on the part of the married man in religious matters. Instead, the implicit message of the two poems seems to be that the pious activities of the wife, and of the female sex in general, are almost sufficient not only for their own religious well being but also for that of the whole household.[1]

Roles outlined in prescriptive literature may not, of course, tell the whole story. Not only may they be directed towards a particular section of society – in this case the mistress of an urban household seeking to guide the conduct

---

[1] Editions of different versions of the poems are as follows: F. J. Furnivall (ed.), *Early English Poems and Treatises on Manners and Meals in Olden Time*, EETS orig. ser. 32 (London, 1868), pp. 36–52 (from Lambeth and Trinity mss); F. J. Furnivall (ed.), *Queene Elizabethes Achademy, A Booke of Precedence etc.*, EETS extra ser. 8 (London, 1869), pp. 44–51 (from Ashmole 61); T. Mustanoja (ed.), *The Good Wife Taught her Daughter, The Good Wyfe Wold a Pylgremage, The Thewis of Gud Women*, Annales Academiae Scientiarum Fennicae B 61/2 (Helsinki, 1948) (from the Emmanuel and Huntington mss). F. Riddy, 'Mother knows best: reading social change in a courtesy text', *Speculum* 71 (1996), 66–86, points out that there is a much stronger tradition of courtesy literature addressed to sons than to daughters. These two poems were not generally paired in collections despite following the same form.

of her daughters – but the prescription could be resisted by the intended pupils.[2] Visiting the tavern, wearing more extravagant dress, talking to men in the street, and selling homemade cloth outside the market for extra profit could seem attractive options, and caused much concern – not only to the author of the Good Wife poem. Nevertheless, although such actions obviously detracted from godliness, it is less clear that their appeal did much to dilute the association of women with religion and the maintenance of ritual, which was reinforced at all social levels. Despite the more rarefied nature of his *Instruction of a Christen Woman*, Vives echoed popular assumptions when he listed 'cure of devotion' amongst female virtues, and asserted that piety was so much a part of female nature that impiety was much more grievous amongst women than men: 'the devotion of holy thynges most agreeth for a woman. Therefore it is a farre worse syghte of a woman that aborreth devotion.'[3] It was also assumed that this natural female aptitude for piety was expressed in daily practice. In popular literature sarcastic comments impugning female piety are rare. Indeed, it seems that of all the virtues for which women were praised, piety alone was not thought by contemporaries to be contradicted in reality. The female virtue of silence was juxtaposed with the image of woman as a gossip; female chastity with the naturally insatiable female sexual appetite; female obedience and wifely submission with the character of the shrew; but female piety was not contrasted with female impiety, or even with religious indifference.[4]

Even the notorious images of women gossiping whilst the devil Tutivullus, who is writing down their words, struggles to keep pace need not be seen as seriously impugning female piety and devotion, although they come closest to it. Such images may simply show that the stereotypical gossip was a woman, and that gossip occurs wherever women gather, whether in the street, alehouse or church. In the Good Wife poems the daughter is instructed to bid her beads in church and not to chatter with relatives and others, but this verse shades into more general advice to be of good tongue and not scornful

[2] Riddy, ibid., 83–6, concludes that the text was directed towards the mistress of an urban household seeking to guide the conduct of her servants rather than of her daughter. However, although the poem is clearly set in an urban household containing servants, it is less evident that servants are envisaged as recipients of its counsel. The advice that daughters should be given in marriage as early as possible, which occurs in most versions of the text, conflicts with life-cycle patterns of servanthood. Moreover, the argument that between mother and daughter such advice would not be needed in textual form applies equally to a mistress guiding her servants. But, of course, this is a text in a female voice, not by a female author. Its first appearance in a friar's collection of *pastoralia* reminds us that this text is, at least partly, an enunciation of a clerical ideal for the behaviour of wives and daughters.

[3] J. L. Vives, *Instruction of a Christen Woman* (London, 1541), f. 32v–34r.

[4] R. H. Robbins (ed.), *Secular Lyrics of the Fourteenth and Fifteenth Centuries*, 2nd edition (Oxford, 1955). For example, 'Of all creatures women be best: / Cuius contrarium verum est', pp. 35–6.

of other people.[5] Wall paintings in English churches based on the Tutivullus
theme do not make the church setting very clear. Their didactic message,
like that of images of Pride or of Warnings to Sabbath Breakers, was appropriate for a church wall but did not necessarily apply only to behaviour in
church.

In texts the Tutivullus theme had two main strands: the devil as a recorder
of idle, and usually female, gossip; and the devil as the gatherer of all the
syllables missed by priests saying their devotions too quickly and in a slap-
dash manner.[6] The former was far more common, but both were seen as
attributes of the vice of sloth, which at this period was largely defined in
terms of neglect of religious duties, and was often viewed as a male failing.[7]
The painting of the deadly sins at Ingatestone (Essex) illustrates it with a
picture of a man lying in bed, and sloth is the main adversary of the male
protagonist in the play *Mankynd*.[8] Nevertheless, in most renditions of the
story the chattering culprits were women. Despite the association of sloth
with men and piety with women, the idea that women were prone to gossip
and vulnerable to the influence of the devil shaped the presentation of this
story in parish culture.

These considerations explain why the medieval plot of the Tutivullus story
was not adopted in late medieval church art, with the exception of a misericord at Ely Cathedral. In this version the deacon spies a devil during mass
who is busily writing down the words of two gossiping women and runs
out of space. To the amusement of the deacon, the devil's attempt to stretch
the parchment makes it burst, causing the devil to hit his head on the wall
and creep away in shame. The comedy here is at the devil's expense, and the
moral lesson occurs as a sobering coda. In later medieval renditions, the emphasis has shifted from uncontrolled human failings and comic devils to the
idea of an influential devil taking advantage of human vulnerability. Thus,
Mirk places the devil on the women's shoulders, has no comic incident, and

[5] Furnivall (ed.), *Manners and Meals in Olden Time*, p. 37; Furnivall (ed.), *Queene Elizabethes Achademy*, pp. 44–5.
[6] The discussion that follows is based on M. Jennings, 'Tutivullus: The literary career of the recording demon', *Studies in Philology* 74 (1977), 10–83.
[7] For example, 'Men and wommen synnyth in sleuthe when they ne kepyth nou ʒt come atte churche upon holy dayes, and when they ne attendeth nat to here bedys-byddynge, in hurynge of masse and matins, and when they ne entendeth nat to here prechynge and techynge. Also sleuthe maketh a man to make noyse and iangelenge in holy churche.' Cited in G. R. Owst, *Literature and Pulpit*, 2nd edition (Oxford, 1961), p. 437; S. Wenzel, *The Sin of Sloth: Acedia in Medieval Thought and Literature* (Chapel Hill, 1967), pp. 68–96, argues that in homiletic and pastoral texts the idea of sloth in God's service predominates, and that occasionally this could be extended to include obligations to this world and society.
[8] M. W. Bloomfield, *The Seven Deadly Sins: An Introduction to the History of a Religious Concept with Special Reference to Medieval English Literature* (Michigan, 1952), p. 198.

ends the story with the two women maintaining that they have been saying prayers during mass, and the bishop ordering the devil to produce the scroll on which their gossip is recorded.[9]

The importance of devilish influence is emphasised in the visual tradition in wall paintings and misericords. At Peakirk (Cambridgeshire) the devil stands on the women's shoulders and holds their heads firmly together (Fig. 2).[10] There is no sign of a recording scroll: what is important is that gossiping women are in the devil's clutches. The devil on the misericord at Enville (Staffordshire) does not have the same tight grip, but he has taken the gossiping women under his protection, sheltering them beneath his wings whilst their prayer book and rosary lie idle.[11] The wall painting at Colton (Norfolk) and the stained glass at Stanford on Avon (Northamptonshire) also depict women beset by devils. Another Norfolk painting, in the church at Stokesby, suggests that not all women succumb to this fate. In the centre of the image a devil holds the heads of two chattering women together, but at the far end of the same bench on which they are seated a pious women sits telling the beads of her rosary and unmolested by a second devil seated at the other end (Fig. 3).[12] At issue is the nature of women's gossip and the possibility of diabolical influence rather than lack of devotion. Women's concern for piety and ritualised acts of devotion was precisely why the church was their meeting place and they felt at home in it. They could act inappropriately by gossiping there, but this was because women were more likely to be vulnerable than men to diabolical influences, as in the case of witches, and of Eve. It was a consequence of women's weakness rather than a negation of their natural affinity with, and reputation for, piety. Moreover, it is notable that all these examples date from the fourteenth century. Later, pastoral concerns could dictate that gossip, as well as lechery, should be viewed as a serious moral offence: when this theme was portrayed in stained glass at Old (Northamptonshire) *c.* 1500, the gossips were men (Fig. 4).[13]

---

[9] T. Erbe (ed.), *Mirk's Festial: A Collection of Homilies by Johannes Mirkus*, EETS extra ser. 96 (1905), pp. 279–80.

[10] F. C. Rouse, 'Wall paintings in the church of St Pega, Peakirk, Northants.', *Arch. Jnl.* 110 (1954), 147–8.

[11] C. Grössinger, *The World Turned Upside Down: English Misericords* (London, 1997), pl. 14.

[12] M. C. Gill, 'Late medieval wall painting in England: content and context (c.1350–c.1530)', Ph.D. thesis, Courtauld Institute of Art (2001), p. 231, corrects Tristram's conclusion that the Stokesby painting refers to conjuring. A misericord at New College, Oxford, similarly contrasts chattering women under the devil's control with a pious female figure.

[13] R. Marks, *Stained Glass in England during the Middle Ages* (London and Toronto, 1993), p. 81; R. Marks, *The Medieval Stained Glass of Northamptonshire*, CVMA catalogue 4 (Oxford, 1998), pp. 160–1.

Figure 2 Warning to female gossips, Peakirk (Cambridgeshire)

<Mural Painting, with fragments of Norman mouldings, as discovered on N.wall, towards the west end of the Church, at Stokesby, Norfolk. July, 1858.

Figure 3 Female gossips and a pious woman saying the rosary, Stokesby (Norfolk)

The concept of the especial fitness of the female sex in matters of piety and devotion also implied a distinct gender division in religious roles. This was clearest within the household, where the role of a woman as housewife and nurturer gave her a specific sphere of responsibility. Women were often identified with the performance of ritual acts designed to procure the well being of members of the family. The author of *Jacob's Well* assumed that it was the responsibility of the mother when her child was sick to go to the church to light a taper in intercession for the child's recovery.[14] The same assumption seems to have been shared by the neighbours of William and Alice Cowper. As Foxe reported, drawing on the accounts of those persecuted for heresy by Bishop Fitzjames of London,

It was alleged against William Cowper, and Alice Cowper his wife, as follows: That they had spoken against pilgrimages, and worshipping of images; but chiefly the woman, who, having her child, on a time, hurt by falling into a pit or ditch, and being earnestly persuaded by some of her ignorant neighbours to go on pilgrimage to St Laurence for help for her child, said, That neither St Laurence, nor any other saint

---

[14] Owst, *Literature and Pulpit*, p. 35; A. Brandeis (ed.), *Jacob's Well, An Englisht [sic] Treatise on the Cleansing of Man's Conscience*, EETS 115 (1900), p. 191, 'þe modyr for here syke chylde makyth a candell, & makyth a vowe in prayere'.

Figure 4 Warning to male gossips, Old (Northants.)

could help her child, and therefore none ought to go on pilgrimage to any image made with man's hand, but only to almighty God; for pilgrimages were nothing worth, saving to make the priests rich.[15]

The same association can be found in the accounts of miracles gathered to support the canonisation of King Henry VI. Many of these stories take the

---

[15] Rev. J. Pratt (ed.), *Acts and Monuments of John Foxe*, 8 vols. (London, 1877), vol. 4, p. 177. Foxe also reports that Robert Cosin of Buckingham and Thomas Man persuaded Joan Norman from near Amersham 'not to go on pilgrimage, nor to worship any images of saints. Also when she had vowed a piece of silver to a saint for the health of her child, they dissuaded her from the same' (p. 214).

form of a miraculous intervention by the king to restore to life a child victim of an accident after a vow had been made to go on pilgrimage to the royal relics. The form of making the vow consists either of bending a penny or, more usually in the case of a child, of measuring the child to establish the size of the taper to be offered at the shrine. In this latter ritual it was always the mother who performed the rite.[16] This demarcation was not a recognition of innate female religiosity. Rather, it reflected the association of women with the rites surrounding birth and death: only women were to be present at the birth of a child, and it was also their task to lay out a body for burial.

The provision of the holy loaf by different households in the parish in turn allowed the public expression of the housewife's role as the representative of the household in ritual provision. It did not represent a distinctive female piety, but it validated a domestic contribution to the religious life of the parish, and of the family. Such actions had enormous symbolic power, and also gave women a theatre of action that could be used as the need arose to ensure the reintegration of the family into the parish community. The case of John and Elizabeth Sharp illustrates this process well. After an acrimonious dispute with the wardens of St Ewen's, Bristol, concerning his arrears of rent, John, a prosperous merchant, made his peace with the parish in 1464 and as a gesture of good will and reincorporation into the parish community paid for his name and those of his wife, his deceased parents and son to be entered on the bede roll. But for the Sharps, or at least for Elizabeth, this gesture still left their ritual incorporation incomplete, and when it came to her turn to provide the holy loaf, she seized her opportunity. Entering the church before matins she '*ful womanly* [my emphasis] bro[gh]t the Cake with Candels in to this Churche, hyr mayden beryng the same after hyr and a fayre twylly towel with werkys at both endys and hool'. Having offered the holy loaf and candles, Elizabeth then announced to the priest and congregation that, as a sign of her great joy that the dispute between her husband and the parish had been settled, she wanted to offer the towel as a houseling cloth to be used by the parish at Easter. Her towel, like the mass in which it would play a part, would symbolise the restoration of mutual charity and unity, especially since the parish had been in the habit of making do by pinning several cloths together for the Easter communion.[17] Such dramas were, of course, not the norm but they serve to accentuate the implications of the commonplace rota for providing holy bread. All that the gift of the houseling cloth symbolised was present also in the routine offering of bread and candles.

Whether Elizabeth's gesture was carried out without consulting her husband cannot be known, but this seems unlikely, even if the presentation of

[16] Father R. Knox and S. Leslie, *Miracles of Henry VI* (Cambridge, 1923).
[17] Duffy, *The Stripping of the Altars*, pp. 127–8.

the houseling cloth may have been originally her idea. Writers of pastoral advice certainly assumed that husbands could control their wives' religious actions when they conflicted with the interests of the household. The author of *Dives and Pauper* laid down that a wife was not to make a vow without her husband's consent, and that vows of pilgrimage and almsgiving made during childbirth were to be commuted so that she would not have to leave home or alienate too much of the family resources.[18] This is particularly striking since, as Karras has pointed out, in his discussion of the sexual double standard the author of this text favoured the position of women more than did many of his clerical contemporaries.[19] Nevertheless, he was unable to countenance the possibility of women's religious choices disturbing the order of the household. Underpinning this was the idea that women's weakness, especially in the traumas of childbirth, required that their wilder gestures be restrained and regulated by a responsible male. Such measures were also encouraged by the desire to safeguard the presence of the wife that was vital to the well functioning of the household economy. This position on women's vows also had scriptural support, even if it was not made explicit. Later, protestant authors would refer to Genesis 3.16 and Numbers 30 to buttress this case, but for them, as for late medieval writers, the crucial factor was establishing a position which was compatible with the maintenance of the household and male authority.[20]

This aim co-existed with an intimate devotional relationship between husband and wife, which went beyond the husband's supervision of his wife's

[18] P. H. Barnum (ed.), *Dives and Pauper*, vol. 1 part 1, EETS orig. ser. 275 (London, 1976), pp. 247–8. 'And þe wyf þat in peril of childynge or of oþir seknesse makith a vouh, alþouʒ she auʒte nout don aʒenys þat vouh be her owyn doom ne withoutyn dom of here sovereyn ʒif she fele here holþyn be þat vouh. Netheles Y trowe pat hir housebonde may unbyndyn here þerfro, and hir confessour also, be changynge into sum oþir good dede, [and namely ʒyf þe kepyng of þe vow schuld turne into preiudyce of þe housbond or lettyng of þe better dede]. For wyvys owyn no gret vouhis make pat schuldyn ben in preiudys and dishese of here housebondis. Ne childryn withynne age schul makyn no vouh withoutyn assent of her fadir or of her tutour, ne þe servant in preiudys ne hynderynge of his lord or of his maystir; and ʒif he do, his lord and his maystir may revokyn it, & so may þe fadir þe childis and þe housebond þe wyvys. Oþer vouhis þat arn no preiudys to þe housebonde þe wyf may makyn, as to seyn certeyn bedys, but of no gret pilgrimage ne of gret abstinence ne of contynence [ne] to ʒevyn gret elmesse, [but ʒyf her housbond be mysdysposyd in his wittys or not rewlyd of custom be resoun. For yf her housbond be unpytous of þe nedy peple sche may make a vowe to ʒeve to þe pore to þe pleasauns of God after her power, savyng her bothe astate].' At York Margery Kempe was asked whether she had a letter of permission from her husband to make a pilgrimage to St William's shrine. Her response makes it clear that not all women travelling independently were required to produce such documentation, and that her husband had given her his verbal permission: S. B. Meech and E. H. Allen (eds.), *The Book of Margery Kempe*, EETS orig. ser. 212 (London, 1940), p. 122.
[19] R. M. Karras, 'Two models, two standards: moral teaching and sexual mores', in B. Hanawalt and D. Wallace (eds.), *Bodies and Disciplines: Intersections of Literature and History in Fifteenth Century England* (Minneapolis and London, 1996), pp. 126–38.
[20] R. C., *A Godly Forme of Household Government: For the ordering of private families according to the direction of Gods word* (London, 1603), pp. 225–6.

actions. Within the household male acts of devotion had a furtive character, and needed to be kept from public view as being somehow incompatible with the authority of the male household head. This unwritten law did not apply to the wife: it was acceptable for her to see her husband arrange crumbs in the shape of a cross during a meal, but not for others.[21] Despite the possibility of the husband having control of his wife's actions, arguably it was within the partnership of marriage that devotional intimacy of the two sexes was most possible. This intimacy could not be advocated strongly when it was felt that the expression of personal devotion at home was unmanly and should be concealed. Yet, paradoxically, when practice could deviate from gender prescriptions, the spiritual intimacy of the couple was further enhanced.

The publicly admissible devotional roles in the household were reinforced by the liturgical and institutional organisation of the pre-Reformation Church. The ecclesiastically administered rites of passage stressed gender distinctions. In the rite of baptism different prayers and exorcisms were read over male and female children and, according to Mirk, the interval between a mother giving birth and being churched was to be forty days in the case of a male child and eighty days for a girl.[22] At death, the number of strokes of the passing bell also depended upon the sex of the deceased. However, as with male devotional activities in the household, the gendered message of the Church was not as clear, nor as stable, as these prescriptions suggest. Lack of detailed parish register evidence before the Reformation makes it impossible to tell whether the different churching intervals after the birth of a boy or a girl were generally observed, but it seems likely that they were not. There is no indication that this practice continued in the later sixteenth and seventeenth centuries, despite the evidence for a strongly conservative attachment to the churching ritual itself. A parallel development, and one that is easier to document, was the gradual transformation of the reasons for preventing women entering the chancel during the later medieval period. This taboo, like the churching distinctions, was based on ideas of spiritual inequality and female impurity. It was also strengthened by a reluctance to associate women with the ministration of the sacraments.[23]

[21] W. A. Pantin, 'Instructions for a devout and literate layman', in J. J. G. Alexander and M. T. Gibson (eds.), *Medieval Learning and Literature* (Oxford, 1976), pp. 400, 421. This Latin text dates from the early fifteenth century, and was to be carried in one's purse.

[22] *Mirk's Festial*, p. 57.

[23] For women to assist as servers at mass was considered scandalous, although not unheard of, as the case against the vicar of Eardisley (Heref.) in 1397 demonstrates. The extensive catalogue of abuses in this case makes it hard to argue that such practice was widespread. M. Aston, 'Segregation in church', in W. J. Shiels and D. Wood (eds.), *Women in the Church*, Studies in Church History 27 (Oxford, 1990), p. 245; Rev. Canon A. T. Bannister, 'Visitation returns for the diocese of Hereford', *EHR* (1930), 447. Lollard arguments and the evidence for lollard women ministering the sacraments are discussed in M. Aston, 'Lollard women priests?', in her *Lollards and Reformers: Images and Literacy in Late Medieval Religion* (London, 1984), pp. 49–70.

The chancel was both the most sacred part of the church and the clerical sphere. The latter association was particularly emphasised in England by the division of responsibility between the laity and the clergy for the upkeep of the nave and chancel respectively.[24] This meant that there could be a general concern about the appropriateness of any lay presence in the chancel, and not only that of women. In the visitations of 1397, it was complained that the laity of the parish of Brunley (Herefordshire) were accustomed to sit in the chancel 'contra ordinacionem ecclesie'.[25] This ordinance of the Church dated from the fourth century, but the concern expressed for the situation at Brunley went against more recent church policy, at least in some dioceses. In 1240 a canon issued for the diocese of Worcester had exempted the patron and people of high status from this ruling, and similar thirteenth-century canons are known from Durham and Lincoln.[26] When members of the lay élite were allowed to be buried in the chancel, this further encouraged the view that access to the chancel, both for the living and the dead, was reserved for clerics and those of high social status. The problem at Brunley may have been less that of lay access than of the social status of the laity who presumed to enter.

Developments in church furnishing in the fourteenth and fifteenth centuries encouraged this process, but it is unlikely that they were responsible for it. The combination of the rood screen and loft enhanced the idea of the chancel as a separate and special chamber to which access could be controlled, even if it is less clear whether the central doors of the screen were usually kept locked. This may explain the relative lack of interest in bequests for the patron saint of the church beyond the token donation to the high altar, compared with the altars and lights in the nave and aisles. The concern to enclose liturgical space also affected gild and chantry chapels, but the desire to multiply intercessory prayers appears to have been stronger than the physical impression of exclusivity. If access to the chancel was largely restricted, this was much less true of the proliferation of altars in the nave and aisles.[27]

Male access was potentially less contentious than that of women, who, since they were unable to minister the sacrament, could also be prevented from coming near the altar when mass was being said. This was first stated

---

[24] Kümin shows that this 'English' differentiation between chancel and nave was not unknown in Europe or always followed in England. B. A. Kümin, *The Shaping of the Community: The Rise and Reformation of the English Parish, c.1400–1560* (Aldershot, 1996), pp. 17–19.

[25] Bannister, 'Visitation returns from the diocese of Hereford', 449.

[26] A. C. Heales, *The History and Law of Church Seats or Pews* (London, 1872), pp. 63–6; F. M. Powicke and C. R. Cheney (eds.), *Councils and Synods with other Documents Relating to the English Church, AD 1205–1265* (Oxford, 1964), part 1, pp. 174, 275, 297, 433.

[27] Pantin, 'Instructions for a devout and literate layman', pp. 399, 421, includes the advice not to go up to the altars as we used to do ('sicut solebamus'), but to pray in a side chapel.

in England in the eleventh-century 'Canons of Eadgar', but this prescription, which is of Carolingian origin, may have borne little relation to English practice even at the time it was issued.[28] Once again, although the late medieval Church was aware of earlier instructions, practice could be less rigid. In 1405 the dean of Salisbury censured the vicar of Lyme Regis (Dorset) for failing to prevent women from approaching the altar of his church.[29] That this criticism could be made shows that the prohibition was not unknown in the fifteenth century; but the action of these women, and the tolerant attitude of their priest, both suggest that local opinion was less convinced of the enormity of the offence.

The response of the parishioners of Lyme Regis may have been facilitated by a new rationale for the prohibition of women's access, which was no longer based on ideas of female impurity or spiritual inequality. Robert Mannyng in his *Handlyng Synne* (1303) stressed that the laity should not enter the chancel, but considered it to be more serious if women did so in service time:

> But ȝyt do wymmen gretter folye
> þat use to stonde amonge þe clergye,
> Oþer at matyns, or at messe,
> But ȝyf yt were yn case of stresse;
> For þerof may come temptacyun
> And disturblyng of devocyun
> For wommens sake þys tale y tolde,
> þat þey oute of þe chaunsel holde
> Wyþ here kercheves, þe devyles sayle,
> Elles shall þey go to helle boþe top and tayle;
> For at hym þey lernë alle
> To temptë men yn synne to falle
> To synne þey calle men, alle þat þey may,
> Why shulde þey ellës make hem so gay?
> For no þyng elles are þey so dyȝt
> But for to blyndë mennës syȝt.
> Certes hyt semeþ, at all endes
> þat many of hem are but fendes.[30]

Although evidently hostile to the female sex, Mannyng's comments may in fact indicate a more positive environment for women: the role of temptress

[28] D. Whitelock, M. Brett and C. N. L. Brooke (eds.), *Councils and Synods, with other Documents Relating to the English Church, 871–1204* (Oxford, 1981), pp. 328–9: 'And it is right that no woman come near the altar while Mass is being celebrated.'
[29] Aston, 'Segregation in church', p. 245.
[30] F. J. Furnivall (ed.), *Robert of Brunne's 'Handlyng Synne', AD1303 with Those Parts of the French Treatise on which it was Founded, William of Waddington's 'Manuel des Pechiez'*, EETS orig. ser. 119 and 123, repr. as one vol. (New York, 1973), pp. 277–80 (lines 8809–14, 8881–92).

may be preferable to that of pollutant. Moreover, the poet went on to
warn clerics to take their duties seriously and not to gaze about looking
at women. It was presumably this attitude, combined with the exceptional
circumstances of the Marian restoration of catholicism, which enabled the
parish of Billingshurst (Sussex) to break the taboo concerning the access of
women to the high altar and to give Joone Fyst a permanent seat in the
church next to the church door for 'her garneschyng of ye aulters'.[31]

Segregation of church seating is often adduced as evidence for the pervasiveness of gender distinctions in the medieval church. The underlying concern in separating the congregation was social propriety rather than a visible
assertion of spiritual inequality. The clearest evidence that ideas of female
impurity were not decisive is that an east–west division of the congregation
was not favoured. In the Orthodox Church this custom is associated with
ideas of purity, and the positioning of women as far west as possible from
the chancel is a natural corollary of the threat of pollution that would be
caused by a woman entering this sphere.[32] However, in the Western Church,
even on the Continent, this reason was less significant. Durandus, writing in
the thirteenth century, recognised that an east–west division of the congregation according to gender was the practice in some areas, but he did not
explain this in terms of the impurity of women. Instead, he asserted that 'the
men are to be in the fore part [i.e. eastward], the women behind: because
the husband is the head of the wife, and therefore should go before her'.[33]
Neither explanation seems to have borne much relation to the situation in
English parish churches in the fifteenth century. One of the earliest seating
plans, that of Ashton-under-Lyne (Lancashire), *c.* 1420, only gives seats for
women, but their position means that the men must have stood further west
than the women.[34] In England it seems that the entire nave was seen as one
unified space without any gradation of sanctity.

It is also far from clear, despite the inferences drawn by many historians
from Langland's description of Wrath cooped up in the pews of wives and

---

[31] W. Sussex RO, CWA, Billingshurst St Mary PAR 21/9/1, p. 65.

[32] E. Friedl, 'The position of women: appearance and reality', in J. Dubisch (ed.), *Gender and Power in Rural Greece* (Princeton, 1986), pp. 43–4. Women are not permitted to go behind the iconostasis, and only male children are carried there during the baptismal ceremony.

[33] Aston, 'Segregation in church', p. 241; Rev. J. M. Neale and Rev. B. Webb, *The Symbolism of Churches and Church Ornaments: A Translation of the First Book of the Rationale Divinorum Officiorum, Written by William Durandus Sometime Bishop of Mende* (London, 1843), p. 37. He also implies that the north–south division was more usual. The work was printed in several editions in the late fifteenth and early sixteenth centuries, but not in England.

[34] The seating plan of the church of Ashton-under-Lyne is discussed in Aston, 'Segregation in church', pp. 266–7, and printed in J. Harland (ed.), 'Custom roll and rental of the manor of Ashton-under-Lyne, 1422', *Chetham Society* 74 (1868), pp. 112–16, and W. M. Bowman, *England in Ashton-under-Lyne* (Altrincham, 1960), pp. 167–8. Bowman suggests that the list must be dated to before the completion of the new church in 1422.

widows, that the separation of the congregation according to gender and marital status was an unquestioned feature of pre-Reformation parish religion. The women's seats at Ashton-under-Lyne were arranged according to tenurial, rather than marital, status. Wealth was similarly the criterion employed at St Mary Woolchurch, London. In 1457 the parishioners drew up an ordinance, instructing the churchwardens to 'set both ryche and poore yn the sayd chyrche in ther pews yt longythe'.[35] The strength of this social segregation is also suggested by the claim in the, admittedly polemical, *Supplication of the Poore Commons* that the Bible would be placed 'in some pew, where poor men durst not presume to come'.[36]

But the arrangement of the congregation according to gender could also seem appealing and appropriate. This was partly because when fixed seating was first introduced it was for women only, as the weaker sex. The subsequent extension of this provision to the whole congregation easily produced distinct blocks of male and female seating. This conservative evolution was also encouraged by concerns for social decency and the avoidance of the profane intermingling of the sexes. However, we need to be careful not to overemphasise the importance of the latter anxieties. It seems likely that, before the introduction of fixed seating and the associated pew rents, separation of the congregation by gender was not normal practice. The thirteenth-century introduction of the pax board to avoid profane behaviour in exchanging the kiss of peace only makes sense in a congregation in which the sexes are undivided. At the same time, this innovation testifies to a growing sensitivity, at least on the part of clerics, that the church should not be an arena for unseemly behaviour. That the pax board originated in England and spread from there to the Continent, where it was in general use by *c.* 1500, lends further support to this interpretation. Continental evidence for the separation of the sexes in church at an early date is stronger than for England, and it seems that here the prevailing practice did not require reform of the kiss of peace.[37]

From these uncertain, and partly incidental, beginnings, it is clear that some parishes wholeheartedly adopted the gender distinction in organising the congregation. For instance, in 1524 the vestry minutes for the London parish of St Christopher le Stocks record the appointment of twelve assessors who were to determine where the parishioners should sit 'as well men to the piews ordained for men as the Women to the piews ordained for Women'. In 1459 the wardens of another London parish, St Michael's, Cornhill, paid for the repairs to the pews of both the men and the women. The difficulties of determining social status in London parishes were notorious and therefore

---

[35] W. J. Hardy, 'Remarks on the history of seat reservation in churches', *Archaeologia* 53 (1892), 99.
[36] S. Brigden, *London and the Reformation* (Oxford, 1989), p. 348.
[37] J. Bossy, 'The mass as a social institution, 1200–1700', *P & P* 100 (1983), 55–8.

gender separation may often have seemed the most appropriate solution. In rural areas social status was more easily defined, and when the introduction of pewing fixed the ambulatory congregation, it is probable that an arrangement according to social status, rather than gender, was more commonly preferred. However, both urban and rural practice was far from being rigidly defined in these terms. In Yeovil (Somerset), where seats were regularly rented for money from 1457 onwards, men usually took places previously held by men unless they were married, when they could occupy seats amongst the women together with their wives.[38]

Whether the arrangement of church seating, or the use of the pax board, responded more to clerical or to lay impulses is uncertain, but it is clear that both could exert influence and that, at least, the detailed implementation of seating policy was, as at St Mary Woolchurch, in lay hands. Clerical voices, when we can hear them, were likely to advocate more extensive gender separation. Thus, Richard Whitforde advised his readers that the segregation of the sexes in the parish church should apply to all social activities:

Assigne you therfore and a poynte you the maner of theyr disportes honest ever and lawfull for a reasonable recreacion and (as moch as conveniently may be) let the sixes be departed in all theyr disportes that is to say: the kyndes men by themselfe and the women by themselfe.[39]

That gender separation, even in the more easily controlled sphere of seating, was not universal, suggests the relative weakness of this clerical agenda in practice. The idea struck a receptive chord in lay culture, but it had to be harmonised with concerns about other social categories and hierarchies of status.

This can be seen most clearly in social activities, or 'disportes', involving the community which took place outside the parish church. Church ales seem to have been organised around the married couple as the basic unit, as shown by the detailed description of procedure in 1536 at Woodbury (Devon). It was noted that the parishioners had agreed

to dyne to gether the tuysdday yn the Whitson weke & the later seynt Swithyn day at the church house of Wodbury & the & ev'y of them to brynge ther meyte and bred w^t them & to paye at every of the seide dayes afore rehersyd for ther drynke at ther dyners yerely for a man and his wyff the sum or summes set on ther names here after folowyng.[40]

---

[38] Hardy, 'Remarks on the history of seat reservation', 99, 101. At Ludlow (Shropshire) in 1540 Richard Langeforde was granted a deceased woman's pew, and this may indicate mixed seating in this parish, although the purchase of the seat for the use of his wife cannot be ruled out (ibid., p. 103).
[39] R. Whitforde, *A Werke for Housholders* (London, 1537), Sig. dii.
[40] Devon RO, Woodbury Malt Book, Woodbury PX1, p. 1.

Unless we are to imagine that the food was pooled, which does not seem a very natural reading of the text, the church ale at Woodbury appears to have been a convivial gathering of couples who ate and drank together, rather than following Whitforde's prescription. As such, the church ale seems to have been modelled on the tenant feast for which the unit of participation was similarly the married couple. The customs of the manor of Ashton-under-Lyne (Lancashire) *c.* 1422 describe the Yule feast, and explain that

the lord shall feed all his said tenants and their wifes upon the Yole Day at ye dinner, if them like for to come; but the said tenants and their wifes, though it be for their ease not to come, they shall send neither man nor woman in their name, but if he be their son other their daughter dwellyng with them unto the dinner.[41]

But not all ritual and social occasions took this form. Gatherings at Hocktide, the practice of hogling, and the groups of wives, maidens and young men who raised money to maintain the church and the lights and altars within it, all show that parish culture accepted the idea of division according to gender and marital status. In part, this was a residue of longstanding tradition, but this was also being moulded by contemporary concerns. Hocktide gatherings, which were usually for the profit of the church, were traditionally made by men and women on Hock Monday and Hock Tuesday respectively. Conceived of as a re-enactment of victory over the Danes, hocking involved capturing members of the opposite sex in the street and exacting a payment or forfeit from them.[42] As such, this practice may be thought to tell us little about contemporary attitudes. However, by the fifteenth and sixteenth centuries modifications to the custom suggest that it was particularly favoured by women. Hocktide collections were increasingly only presented by the wives, as at Bassingbourn (Cambridgeshire), Bramley and Stoke Charity (Hampshire), Lydd (Kent), Shere (Surrey) and St Andrews, Lewes (Sussex). Elsewhere, women typically collected much larger sums than the men, suggesting that the male part of this custom was in decline. For example, at St Lawrence, Reading in 1499 the women gathered 20s, whilst the men only

---

[41] Harland (ed.), 'Custom roll and rental', 94, 121.

[42] Hutton sees this as an invented tradition, based on its appearance in churchwardens' accounts in the last quarter of the fifteenth century, and on the disapproval expressed by the corporation of London in 1406, and by Bishop Carpenter of Worcester in 1450. R. Hutton, *The Rise and Fall of Merry England: The Ritual Year 1400–1700* (Oxford, 1994), p. 60. However, that it was 'wholly a fifteenth-century invention' (p. 59) seems more questionable than Hutton concedes. The London evidence is less significant when set alongside Hutton's observation that the custom is not recorded in most London parishes, but was strongest in market towns (p. 26). Its presence in accounts in the late fifteenth century is presumably part of the same development that saw church ales becoming a regular means of raising parish funds at the same time (p. 59). As Hutton argues for the Elizabethan period, the custom could continue without the link with parish fundraising, but when it did so it was more vulnerable to official and ecclesiastical censure (p. 120).

raised 4s, and at Lambeth in 1518–19 the women collected 8s 3d and the men 3s 9d.[43]

In its full form, with gatherings made by both sexes, the Hocktide ritual can be seen as a classic example of the world turned upside down and then restored. As Hutton reminds us, the women's action 'was a symbolic reversal of their usual position of social subservience', and he sees this as explaining its greater popularity among women. Although this may have been part of the attraction for women, it seems inadequate to explain the decline and cessation of the male part of the ritual. More prosaically, it might be suggested that the generally smaller sums collected by men may have been due less to their lack of enthusiasm than to women having less money at their disposal to give away. After all, it seems reasonable to suggest that there was more than a grain of truth in moralists' criticisms that such occasions encouraged licentiousness. A ritual excuse for grabbing hold of a woman in the street and exacting a forfeit from her should probably be seen as a more powerful encouragement for participation than notions of the symbolic reversal of women's social subservience. Such actions, like those initiated by women, also represented a temporary suspension of the norms of courtship behaviour. This interpretation does of course only make sense of the discrepancy between the amounts collected by men and women. Decisions, like that of the men at St Mary at Hill, London in 1526, to stop the male collection completely require a different explanation. The feminisation of Hocktide should not be seen as a male retreat from communal ritual, but rather as the result of an intensification of gender division in parish ritual customs.

Continuing male participation in seasonal rituals can be demonstrated by the evidence for hogling. This custom has been discussed mainly in relation to Somerset, but the survey of surviving churchwardens' accounts has revealed references to it in fifteen parishes outside Somerset in counties as diverse as Lincolnshire, Sussex and Devon.[44] Detailed work on the Somerset material has discredited the traditional assumption that the derivation of the term 'hoglers' from the verb 'to hoggle', meaning to dig, meant that these were gilds of labourers or miners. Instead, it has been demonstrated that those involved in hogling were frequently members of the parish élite, former churchwardens and drawn from the section of the population leaving wills.[45]

---

[43] Ibid., p. 26.

[44] Launceston (Cornwall); Ashburton, Chagford, Chudleigh, Coldridge, Dartington, Molland, South Tawton, Winkleigh (Devon); Sutterton, Wigtoft (Lincs.); Arlington, Ashurst, Bolney, Rotherfield, Worth (Sussex). Various spellings are employed including hogen' money, hoggenaye, hognel silver and hoglyng.

[45] Bishop Hobhouse (ed.), 'Croscombe churchwardens' accounts', *Som. Rec. Soc.* 4 (1890) Appendix D, p. 251, suggested that hoglers were 'the lowest order of labourer with spade or pick, in tillage or in minerals'. In nineteenth-century Pembrokeshire the practice of lime

The discovery of references to hogling in seventeenth-century church court depositions from Keynsham (Somerset) has shed further light on the nature and organisation of this activity. According to this evidence, which if the stated ages of the witnesses are to be believed dates back to pre-Reformation times, the practice of hogling involved the men of the parish, led by their churchwardens, going around the houses of the dependent chapelries singing and offering entertainment in exchange for food and money to show the benevolence of the chapelries towards the repairs of the church of Keynsham. This gathering made by the men generally seems to have taken place around Christmas, but the 'hogneltym' was defined as lasting from Christmas until Easter since a second gathering, this time by the churchwardens' wives, presumably accompanied by other women, was made at Easter.[46]

This second gathering by women is less well attested than the male one earlier in the year. It is always men who present hogling money in the accounts, and it seems that the process that saw Hocktide gatherings becoming the preserve of women was mirrored in the strengthening of the association of hogling with men. However, in a few parishes there is evidence that the Easter hogling collections by women may still have been maintained. The accounts of Bolney (Sussex) make it clear that 'hogneltym' lasted until Easter, although there is no specific reference to a collection by the wives, and at Croscombe (Somerset) six shillings were received in 1482–3 'of the wyfes dansyng'.[47]

The evidence for both Hocktide gatherings and hogling suggests that, within the guidelines of custom, contemporaries developed a further gender separation of ritual activity. When men abandoned Hocktide gatherings at St Mary at Hill, they left the wives in charge of the festivity and to celebrate alone at a dinner at the parish expense. The quid pro quo was the clearer association of other parts of the ritual year with men, most obviously in the case of hogling, but also in that of the Robin Hood plays. This reorientation is unlikely to have been a conscious bargain; rather, it responded to a general sense in favour of gender division, which can also be seen in the formation of groups of wives, maidens and young men in the parish, who

burners begging from the farmers at New Year was known as hogling. Dr Hobhouse, 'Hogglers and hoglinge money', *Somerset & Dorset N & Q* 20 (1930), 63.

[46] D. M. M. Shorrocks, 'The custom of hogling', *Somerset & Dorset N & Q* 28 (Sept. 1967), 341–2; J. Stokes, 'The hoglers: Evidence of an entertainment tradition in eleven Somerset parishes', *Somerset & Dorset N & Q* 32 (March 1990), 807–15.

[47] W. Sussex RO CWA Bolney f. 2v.; Hobhouse (ed.), 'Croscombe churchwardens' accounts', p. 12. At Wimborne Minster (Dorset) it was the custom for sums to be raised annually by the town wife and the country wife by the sale of cakes. The two wives may have been the wives of the surviving churchwardens, but the connection of this practice with hogling is unclear. C. Mayo, *A History of Wimborne Minster* (London, 1860), p. 86.

organised collections for particular church improvements at other times of
the year and maintained lights in the parish church. In religious terms, such
divisions were due less to the idea of spiritual inequality, and the desire to
prevent licentiousness, than to the belief in the importance of the group in
securing access to divine power, which lay at the heart of the medieval gild
system.

Nevertheless, despite this similarity in conception, these groups rarely seem
to have been given the status of a parish gild. Only one example comes close.
The accounts of Ashburton (Devon) refer to the store of St Mary, which was
also known as 'the wyvyn store'.[48] This is the only instance in which the
term 'store' is used in recording income from a group of wives, and suggests
that they were seen as an organised gild on a par with others in the parish
whose membership was not so clearly defined by gender and marital status.
The reason for this general distinction is not obvious. Most plausibly, groups
of wives, maidens or young men may have been assumed to be open to all
within the parish without the need for any formal process of membership
and payment. Even the 'poor people's gild' at St Austin's, Norwich demanded
a membership fee, which strengthens the view that such payments were a
defining feature of gilds.[49] Instead of recruiting members, the finances of
groups of wives, maidens and young men rested on a different basis. At
Thorpe-le-Soken (Essex) the text on the screen of *c.* 1480 explains that 'This
cost is the bachelors, made by ales theen by ther med.' This, like the church
ale organised by the whole parish, was probably the most common form
of fundraising, although a later tradition records that on St Barnabas' day
(11 June) in South Littleton (Worcestershire) maidens and young girls sold
roses for the profit of the church.[50]

However, in terms of their function, groups of wives, maidens and young
men were analogous to more formalised gilds, even if their contribution was
often economically more modest. Typically, they were concerned to maintain
lights within the parish church.[51] Sometimes these could be identified directly
with the group concerned, as was the case with the 'wyvyn taper' at Morebath
(Devon) or the 'maydens light' at Winterslow (Wiltshire). In other parishes,

---

[48] Devon RO CWA Ashburton.
[49] G. Rosser, 'Communities of parish and gild in the Middle Ages', in S. Wright (ed.), *Parish,
Church and People* (London, 1988), p. 35.
[50] J. F. T. Dyer, *Church Lore Gleanings* (London, 1881), p. 324; E. A. B. Barnard (ed.), 'Churchwardens' accounts of the parish of South Littleton, 1548–71', *Trans. Worcs. Arch. Soc.* 3
(1925–6), p. 74.
[51] The entry for the maidens at Croscombe (Somerset) for the year 1476–7 typifies this type of
organisation: 'Comes the maydence Marget Smyth and Jone Bayle and presents in of old and
new all things lowed 9s 7d herof must be abated for wax and makyng 2s 6d ob. So is cler 7s
ob. delyvered to them ayen 2s 6d.' Hobhouse (ed.), 'Croscombe churchwardens' accounts',
p. 6.

association with a particular light on behalf of the whole parish is clearer: at Stanford-in-the-Vale (Berkshire) the wives maintained the font taper, and in many parishes the groups of young men were responsible for the rood light. Such groups were also able to respond directly to particular needs in their church, which could vary from year to year. In 1488 the accounts of Walberswick (Suffolk) record the gathering of the maidens for the torches, and this seems to have been the standard practice in this parish, but in 1497 part of the money was used to pay for the painting of 'King herry's tabyll' in honour of the uncanonised, but locally venerated, Henry VI. Inscriptions often record the contribution of these groups to large-scale improvements to the church furnishings, such as the windows at St Neot (Cornwall), Hingham (Norfolk) and Dullingham (Cambridgeshire) (Fig. 5). The young men and the maidens contributed to the building of the tower at All Saints, Derby in 1510, and similar co-operation was not infrequent. When a silver chalice

Figure 5 Stained glass with female donors, St. Neot (Cornwall)

was stolen from the church of Morebath (Devon) in 1534, the wardens noted that, 'ye yong men and maydens dru them selffe togethers and with there gyfts and provysyon the bofth (bought) yn another challis with owt ony chargis of ye parysse.'[52]

Such joint action was a response to extraordinary circumstances, but it emphasises the fact that these groups, although separated by gender and marital status, operated in an essentially similar way. Where more detailed evidence survives, it shows that the routine responsibilities of these groups could even be identical. At Heybridge (Essex) the maidens and the young men both maintained the same number of tapers for the Easter sepulchre.[53] Nevertheless, it does not appear to be the case that all parishes contained all three groups. Some had established more subdivisions. At Badsey (Worcestershire) gatherings were made both by the 'maidens' and by the 'lyttul mayds'. Uneven recording makes it difficult to be certain how widespread this practice was, but it seems that Badsey was unusual since groups of young maids seem more likely to be recorded in the accounts than maidens. At Badsey, it was only in their case that the accounts record payment for wax and the making of their taper. It is probable that the maidens also maintained a taper but that, unlike their younger sisters, they did not require the intervention of the churchwardens to secure its purchase.[54] The nature of the sources makes arguing from negative evidence particularly hazardous, but it is nevertheless noticeable that there are more parishes in the sample of churchwardens' accounts containing references to the young men than to the maidens, and some instances of parishes for which only the existence of

---

[52] Rev. W. Symonds, 'Winterslow church reckonings, 1542–1661', *Wilts. Arch. & Nat. Hist. Mag.* 36 (1909–10), pp. 27–47; Berks. RO CWA Stanford-in-the-Vale. The association of the wives with the font taper was not automatic. At St Dunstan's, Canterbury in 1491 the duties of the churchwardens included finding the font and paschal taper from the stock allocated to them annually: J. M. Cowper (ed.), *Churchwardens' Accounts of St. Dunstan's, Canterbury, 1484–1580* (London, 1885), p. 23; Suffolk RO (Ipswich) CWA Walberswick, F C 185/E 1/1, 2 ; G. McN. Rushforth, 'The windows at the church of St Neot, Cornwall', *Transactions of the Exeter Diocesan Architectural and Archaeological Society* 15 (1927), 150–90. At Hingham, according to Blomefield, the east window of the Trinity chapel was contributed by the maidens of the town. At Dullingham a window inscription was visible in 1632 with the words 'Pray for the state of the yeng men and maydens and all the good doiers': C. Woodeforde, *The Norwich School of Glass Painting in the Fifteenth Century* (Oxford, 1950), pp. 72–3; At All Saints, Derby the inscription to the young men and maidens on the tower is thought to indicate that they contributed to its building to that height: J. C. Cox and W. H. St. John Hope, *Chronicles of the Collegiate Church of All Saints, Derby* (London, 1881), p. 49; Bishop Hobhouse (ed.), 'Morebath churchwardens' accounts', *Som. Rec. Soc.* 4 (1890), p. 209. Similarly at South Littleton (Worcs.) in 1555 the small sum of 14d was jointly gathered by the young men and the maidens for the church: Barnard (ed.), 'Churchwardens' accounts of South Littleton', p. 78.
[53] Essex RO CWA Heybridge D/P 44/5 Each group maintained nine tapers at Easter.
[54] Worcs. RO CWA Badsey, 850 Badsey B A 5013/2.

the latter group is known.[55] An entry in the churchwardens' accounts for Bassingbourn (Cambridgeshire) confirms that such groups were not necessarily always present in every parish and could be of recent foundation. In the account for 1503 it was noted that 'Thos Asshewell and John Good singleman hath restyng in ye hands a stocke lately begun of ye syngleman and hath be' in ther hands bi the space of iii yeares next before this present date 12s and 1 quart of barley.'[56] The generally higher profile of the groups of young men was partly because of their association with customs like Plough Monday and with festivities involving Robin Hood and his fellows.[57] However, of more importance was the fact that they frequently took on a responsibility of greater significance within the church: the maintenance of the light before the rood. By 1510 the young men's stock at Bassingbourn was also described as the rood light, and it is probable that this was the purpose for which it was established. Whatever the particular devotional motivations, the evidence from Bassingbourn and elsewhere suggests that gender distinctions were a prominent, but still optional, feature of local parish life.

The impulse towards segregation of communal ritual activity also had an impact on the more formalised world of parish gilds. The spirit of fraternalism identified as being at the heart of the medieval religious gilds has deflected attention away from the principle of separation operating within

---

[55] References to the young men, single men or bachelors occur in churchwardens' accounts at Winkfield (Berks.); Bassingbourn (Cambs.); Chudleigh, Coldridge, Dartington (?), Modbury (grooms), Morebath, South Tawton, Winkleigh (Devon); Great Hallingbury, Heybridge (Essex); Stoke Charity (Hants.); Bishops Stortford (Herts.); Cossington (Leics.); Wigtoft (Lincs.); Shipdham (Norfolk); Culworth (Northants.); Thame (Oxon.); Croscombe (Somerset); Walberswick (Suffolk); Badsey, South Littleton (Worcs.), and in church inscriptions at Dullingham (Cambs.); St Neot (Cornwall), All Saints, Derby, Thorpe-le-Soken (Essex) and Garboldisham (Norfolk).
  References to groups of maidens occur in churchwardens' accounts at Stanford-in-the-Vale (Berks.); Bassingbourn (Cambs.); Stratton (Cornwall); Morebath (Devon); Heybridge, Saffron Walden (Essex); Shipdham (Norfolk); Thame (Oxon.); Croscombe (Somerset); Walberswick (Suffolk); St. Edmunds, Salisbury ('daughters'), Winterslow (Wilts.); Badsey, South Littleton (Worcs.); and in church inscriptions at Dullingham (Cambs.), St Neot (Cornwall), All Saints, Derby and Hingham (Norfolk).
  References to groups of wives (excluding Hocktide references where possible) occur in churchwardens' accounts at Bassingbourn (Cambs.); Ashburton, Morebath (Devon); Croscombe (Somerset); St Andrews, Lewes (Sussex); Sheriff Hutton (Yorkshire) and in a church inscription at St Neot (Cornwall).
[56] Cambs. RO CWA Bassingbourn P 11/5/1 f. 8.
[57] J. C. Holt, *Robin Hood* (London, 1982), pp. 159–60, concludes that Robin Hood was adopted into May games in some parishes in the fifteenth century, but the stories of Maid Marian and Robin Hood were still perceived as distinct by Alexander Barclay writing *c*. 1500 of 'some merry fytte of Maid Marian or else of Robin Hood'. The combination of the two figures is a result of assimilation into the structure of the king and queen of the May games. Robin Hood festivities are mentioned in the churchwardens' accounts of Stratton (Cornwall), Thame (Oxon.) and Croscombe (Somerset). In the latter the accounts are presented by 'Robin Hood and his fellows', suggesting that it was a male-dominated occasion.

them. In reality, at least some parish gilds echoed the structure of the groups of young men, wives and maidens in adopting the pattern of segregation according to sex, although not according to age. This practice can be most clearly demonstrated from the surviving accounts of the fairly wealthy gild of St John the Baptist at Swaffham (Norfolk), which include separate accounts of the 'womanys stoke'. Other gilds in the same town appear to have operated along similar lines, judging from the fact that amounts in the churchwardens' accounts are received at times from the brethren and sisters and at other times from the sisters alone. For example, in 1509 the brethren and sisters of St Peter's gild gave 26s 8d to the repair of the steeple and in the same year the sisters of the gild gave 6s 8d for the same purpose.[58]

It is unlikely that Swaffham was unique in this, but surviving gild records often relate to membership, rather than to details of organisation. In this context, as shown by the lists of the gild of St Katherine in Chagford (Devon), the normal unit of membership was the married couple. The procedures of the Holy Trinity gild in the Cambridge parish of the same name underlined this assumption even more strongly: a single woman joining the gild had to pay the same fee as a husband and wife.[59] These practices reflect familial intercessory structures, which are familiar to the historian from the instructions given in wills of the period and contained in bede rolls. They need not indicate the pattern of internal organisation. Taken together, the evidence for groups of wives, maidens and young men, and the more fragmentary evidence for women's sections in larger gilds, suggest that when the lollards of Coventry established a women's group they were not meeting an unfulfilled need, which could explain the particular appeal of the movement to women, but merely borrowing from the current practice in many parishes.[60]

Attitudes towards segregation by gender and marital status both in patterns of church seating and in parish religious groups were flexible, on the one hand reinforcing separation, and on the other buttressing the authority of the household. These conflicting impulses meant that although parishes could develop groups of young men, wives and maidens, there were no equivalent groups for married men or for widows. Both these categories represent the householders of the community, and their omission suggests that it is the suspension of the importance of the household unit that permits the association of peer groups. In the context of the assembly of the whole community in the parish congregation or the church ale, maintenance of the authority of the household determines the absence of clear-cut gender distinctions.

---

[58] Norfolk RO. Accounts of gild of St John the Baptist, Swaffham P D 52/233; CWA Swaffham P D 52/70–1.

[59] V. Bainbridge, *Gilds in the Medieval English Countryside: Social and Religious Change in Cambridgeshire, c. 1350–1558* (Woodbridge, 1996), p. 47.

[60] S. McSheffrey, *Gender and Heresy: Women and Men in Lollard Communities, 1420–1530* (Philadelphia, 1995), pp. 25–33.

This relationship between the predominantly male position of household head and gender separation in the religious community can also explain the dominant position of males as wardens of stores and of the parish church. Although women were acknowledged to be more responsible for family piety, the system of office-holding focussed attention on the secular hierarchy of male authority. This was particularly the case with the position of churchwarden, which embodied the community at large, but also influenced the selection of wardens of lesser lights and stores. Nevertheless, in contrast to modern Greece, where women are similarly given religious responsibility for the household, the male monopoly of these positions was not absolute. A few women did serve as churchwardens or wardens of lights in English parishes, but this was due less to their role in the practice of piety than to their being involved, unlike modern Greek women, in the organisation of collections for the purchase and repair of specific items for the church.[61]

Female organisational expertise had its limits in diluting the strength of the association of religious office-holding with the authority of the male household head. Women were more likely to serve as wardens of lights than to be elected to the office of churchwarden. This was partly because such office brought them less noticeably into conflict with the authority of male householders and involved no responsibilities outside the parish itself. Of equal importance was the fact that such duties fitted better with recognised female responsibilities. Not only was female piety more focussed on the internal worship of the parish church, but women as widows were often left with the task of carrying out elaborate intercessory provisions for their deceased husbands. The obligation incumbent on the widow of William Marshall of South Littleton (1544) to provide a great taper before the sepulchre and two tapers before the rood for her husband can have differed little from the duties of the warden of a lesser parish gild, which did not have a fixed membership.[62]

That female light wardens were still in a minority partly reflects the strength of ideas of male authority, but it also relates to the importance of secular economic considerations in many, apparently religious, gilds. The duties of the male wardens of the torchlight at Folkestone, as described in the accounts for the year 1488, match the kind of expertise possessed by the widow of William Marshall. The task of these wardens was to supply torches to those wishing to purchase them for the deceased, and then to calculate the cost according to the amount of wax used in burning.[63] Elsewhere, gild wardenship may have involved nothing more than an advantageous leasing arrangement of cattle or land, with the payment of rent in the form of a

---

[61] Friedl, 'The position of women', p. 46. Greek Orthodox women are not elected to the group of lay people who assist the priest in parish affairs.

[62] Worcs. RO CCW, vol. 8, f. 52.

[63] E. L. Holland (ed.), *Folkestone Churchwardens' Accounts* (locally printed, 1934), f. 2r.

taper burning before an image. The example of the brethren of Our Lady at Pluckley (Kent) illustrates this type and the degree of degeneration possible. In this gild the 24 brethren each hired a cow and participated in the annual drinking. By 1536 the moneylending aspect of the gild had become more prominent. In the course of a dispute over the conduct of one of the wardens, it was alleged that 'ye way yerof was usury and no lawful way to obteyn hit for yei payd xiid a yere for ye xis in ye name of ye cow no cow knowen and iiiid to the yevall or drynkyng'. At the same time the annual drinking on Lady day, which had been 'a gud Refresshyng of ye poore wt gud bred dryng and cheese' had sometimes become 'an occasyon of drunkeness, brawlyng, quarrellyng, fayghtyng and vagabondry.'[64] Even when pious purpose was not lost sight of to this extent, such gilds were less likely to appoint female wardens, or even to have female members, because the economic position of women meant that they rarely leased livestock from gilds. At Pluckley, women only appear as widows paying for their husbands' cows, and at Weyhill (Hampshire) only one woman, Mother Fuller, is listed as paying for church sheep.[65]

The nature of record-keeping makes it hard to be certain how common female light wardens were. The sample of churchwardens' accounts contains references to women as wardens of lights and stores in eleven parishes in a wide range of counties:[66]

Cornwall:	Stratton (Our Lady's maidens)
Devon:	Ashburton (store of Our Lady or the wives' store)
	Broadhempston (store of Our lady, store of St Peter)
	Chagford (store of St Mary)
	Woodland (store of Our Lady)
Lincolnshire:	Horbling (light of St Dorothy)
Oxfordshire:	Spelsbury (Trinity light)
Somerset:	Pilton (store of Our Lady)
Suffolk:	Bardwell (light of St Peter)
	Walberswick (gild of St Andrew and gild of St Barbara)
Surrey:	Horley (light of St Katherine)

This is unlikely to be a complete list, even of the activities of women in parishes with reasonably detailed records. The light of St Dorothy at Horbling is only mentioned once in the churchwardens' accounts but was

[64] Kent RO (Maidstone) CWA Pluckley, v275 Q1, f. 10r.
[65] J. F. Williams (ed.), *Hampshire Churchwardens' Accounts*, pp. 156–63.
[66] Churchwardens' accounts from larger urban centres have not been systematically examined for this study, but examples of female light wardens can be found. Our Lady light at Holy Trinity, Cambridge appointed two women guardians annually: Bainbridge, *Gilds in the Medieval English Countryside*, p. 48.

probably not so transient. The fact that half of the known examples of parish stores having female wardens come from Cornwall, Devon and Somerset may indicate a regional pattern, but it may also be a consequence of recording practice. The structure of the accounts and the nature of parish finances largely dictate the extent to which individual stores and their wardens are likely to appear. The form of account predominant in much of the south-west peninsula, in which an annual audit of the profits or increase of the individual stores is made to a body usually known as the 'four men', naturally provides a more comprehensive picture of the existence and organisation of the lights within the parish than is found in other accounts in which stores are only mentioned when they make a particular contribution to the general church fund or to a specific building project.

Despite the probability that the twelve examples of lights with female wardens only represent the tip of the iceberg, we can come to a better understanding of the phenomenon, and of the influences shaping it, by looking at these cases in more detail. Some, such as Ashburton and Stratton, seem to belong more naturally amongst the groups of wives and maidens already discussed, but it seems clear that they were both regarded as more formalised. Detailed accounts of Our Lady's maidens are found throughout the Stratton parish accounts. Only in just over half of the parishes (Broadhempston, Chagford, Woodland, Spelsbury, Pilton and Horley) are women clearly occupying a male sphere of wardenship: in these stores neither the wardenship nor devotion to the particular saint was gender-specific. The remaining examples of Walberswick and Bardwell in Suffolk are harder to interpret. In the former parish there are references in 1463 to a female warden of the gild of St Andrew, and in 1466 of the gild of St Barbara. In Bardwell, women as part of a married couple frequently occupy the office of warden of the light of St Peter. In both these cases it is unclear whether this refers to a section of a gild or to a separate stock within the parish.

The six examples of female wardenship within a mixed context illustrate the limited extent to which women were able to exercise authority in this sphere. Women were wardens of the light of St Katherine at Horley, but they occupied this office only in conjunction with their husbands, and were presumably thought to be acting under their authority. At Pilton a woman was selected on only one occasion to be warden of Our Lady's light. The store of St Mary at Chagford offers the most significant instance of female wardens as in this case a pair of women exercised the office. However, unlike the wardens of all the other stores of the parish, the wardens of St Mary were chosen by the four men who received the accounts of all the stores. At Broadhempston, also in Devon, women were able to name their successors to the office of warden of Our Lady light, but this did not prevent their nomination being overturned in 1530 and the wardenship subsequently passing into male hands. The system of nomination prevailing at Woodland is un-known, but, in view of the Broadhempston evidence, it is striking that in 1531 the wardenship of this gild also passed to men.[67]

The constraints on women exercising authority as wardens of stores within the parish church were greater when it came to appointing churchwardens. In theory, election procedures should not have discriminated against women. The details in most accounts are vague, but all include some measure of choice or election, normally by the 'holl townshippe'. There are no specific references before the Elizabethan period to the selection of churchwardens according to the holding of particular lands in the parish, which may have been detrimental to the chances of most women, if not to a few wealthier widows.

The precise meaning of the phrases 'with the consent of the whole township' or 'chosen by the parishioners' is elusive, but the fact that wardens were often elected for different parts of the parish suggests that the notion of representation was well developed. For example, in Shipdham (Norfolk) in 1528 and in subsequent years four wardens were chosen, two for the east side and two for the west side.[68] But it is less clear who was being represented. It is possible that when contemporaries thought of the parish as a body with powers of election they did not think in terms of a group comprising the total of its inhabitants, or of its 'houseling people', but of its principal householders. It was this group that was expected to assist in organised collections of funds, as is shown by the lists of assessments included in such accounts as those of St Andrew's, Lewes, or St Lawrence's and St Mary's Reading where a church rate for the holy loaf was levied on the principal inhabitant of every tenement or on every householder. Similar arrangements can be found in more rural parishes. At Morebath (Devon), according to the new award made in 1536, every householder was obliged to pay 1d every quarter for the clerk.[69] However, such formal assessments were only one of a number of ways in which the laity contributed financially to their parish church, and this could mean that almost the whole parish could have had a voice in the election. It is noticeable that the phrase 'with the consent of the householders' never appears in the accounts. In practice, the stress on financial participation as a qualification for involvement in the

[67] Devon RO CWA Broadhempston P W 1, pp. 3–4. In 1530 the two outgoing female wardens selected Jone Fawkener and Alsyn Barter as their successors. However, they were either unwilling to serve or were deemed unacceptable. The wardens for the following year were Richard Barter and Roger Hyll. It is possible, although perhaps unlikely, that these two men were the husbands of the women nominated.
[68] Norfolk RO CWA Shipdham P D /337/85.
[69] W. Sussex RO CWA St Andrew's, Lewes; J. Martin, 'The People of Reading and the Reformation 1520–1570: Leadership and Priorities in Borough and Parishes', Ph.D. thesis, University of Reading (1987), p. 180; Hobhouse (ed.), 'Morebath churchwardens' accounts', pp. 222–3.

selection process is probably misleading. Instead, the key factor may be the relationship between authority and representation. This would mean that women and children would be represented by their husbands and fathers, who were deemed to exercise authority over them. In this scheme the position of widows as heads of households appears to pose a significant problem, although one which in the secular world of the manor court was resolved by their virtual exclusion from positions of power.

The search for a definition of the constituency of the decision making body of the parish in these terms, although valuable in illuminating general attitudes, may be irrelevant in practice. In many parishes the idea of the election of the wardens by the parish may have had little more than a nominal significance. In Bethersden (Kent) the practice was for the continuing churchwarden to choose his fellow, and occasionally it was noted in the accounts that his choice was agreed by the parish. Bethersden was unusual in stating this as practice, but it was not alone in reducing the number of parishioners involved in elections.[70] The account for 1547 for the parish of Rotherfield (Sussex) lists the names of those who chose the churchwardens 'for ye behove of the parish'. On this occasion the election was effected by a group of 21 men, not by all the householders, and was headed by the outgoing churchwarden.[71] Clerics could also have an instrumental, although subordinate, role in such elections. At Leverton (Lincolnshire) in 1532 Sir Richard Shepperd, parson of the north part of the parish, recorded that he had called all the parishioners together to hear the account of the last wardens and to choose new wardens whereupon 'for the makyng of the newe churchwardens and at theyr instans I namyd Thos Westland and Wm Wastler'.[72] However, despite this evidence for a narrowing of the voting constituency in practice, we should not assume that this was always to the detriment of women who wished to take part. Sir Richard Shepperd presumably notified his parishioners of the audit and election during a church service when women would have been present. The possibility of women participating in such an election is also suggested by the practice of the gild of St Mary at Beverley, which allowed its elder sisters a voice in the election of aldermen.[73]

Even if women may have had some role in the selection of churchwardens, they normally faced greater hurdles in being elected themselves. Not only were those appointed normally drawn from the wealthier sections of the parish, but the position of churchwarden seems to have been desirable as a stepping stone to higher secular offices which were not open to women.

---

[70] F. R. Mercer (ed.), Churchwardens' Accounts of Bethersden, 1515–73, *Kent Records* 5 (1928).
[71] E. Sussex RO CWA Rotherfield, PAR 465/10/3/1 p. 27.
[72] Lincs. RO CWA Leverton, Leverton 7/1.
[73] J. and L. Toulmin Smith (eds.), *English Gilds*, EETS orig. ser. 40 (London, 1870), pp. 149–50.

In pre-Reformation Reading, Martin has shown by comparing churchwardens' accounts and tax assessments that the churchwardens were drawn from varying levels of wealth, but that this corresponded with the differences in prosperity between parishes. Whatever the prosperity of the parish, its churchwardens were drawn from its highest ranks. In addition, many of those serving as churchwardens subsequently rose to the office of mayor in the town. A similar connection between churchwardenship and the holding of manorial office is evident at Havering (Essex), Halesowen (Worcestershire) and Worfield (Shropshire), and the link between the two spheres is further suggested by the widespread use of the title 'church reeve'.[74]

It is therefore scarcely surprising that female wardens were exceptional. From the sample of churchwardens' accounts, only five parishes appointed women as churchwardens before the death of Henry VIII.[75] The earliest example occurs in the Somerset parish of Yatton in 1496, and the others at Nettlecombe (Somerset) (1524?, 1541, 1542, 1543 and 1544) Trull (Somerset) (1542 and 1544), Halse (Somerset) (1543) and at Morebath (Devon) (1528). The appointment of the widow Lady Isabel Newton to the wardenship at Yatton was presumably due to her exceptional status and involvement with the church at the time. The Newton family of Court de Wyke were evidently the most important family in the parish, and Lady Isabel's wardenship coincided with the final completion of the Newton family chapel in the parish church.[76] However, the wardens chosen elsewhere do not seem to have been of such high status, and parishioners here seem to have accepted the idea that wardens could be chosen from amongst both male and female parishioners of equivalent status.[77]

Religious roles were influenced by gender, and this was a distinction accepted by lay culture rather than simply by ecclesiastics. But the outcome had to accommodate contradictory impulses, which were resolved in ways that allowed for flexibility. The female reputation for piety and responsibility

---

[74] Martin, 'The people of Reading and the Reformation', pp. 185–9; M. K. McIntosh, *A Community Transformed: The Manor and Liberty of Havering, 1500–1620* (Cambridge, 1991), p. 233. Between 1540 and 1563 nearly half of the churchwardens held manor court positions.

[75] The choice of churchwardens in larger urban centres has not been studied systematically. However, the widow Margery Mathew was warden at St. Ewen's, Bristol in 1528: B. R. Masters and E. Ralph (eds.), 'The Church Book of St Ewen's, Bristol, 1454–1584', *Bristol & Gloucestershire Archaeological Society – Record Section* 6 (1967), p. 167, f. 143r.

[76] A. C. Edwards, 'The medieval churchwardens' accounts of St. Mary's church, Yatton', *Somerset & Dorset N & Q* 32 (Sept. 1986), 542–3. The couple were also responsible for the addition of the south porch, which is 'the most highly decorated porch in Somerset'. Their tomb, with recumbent effigies and a relief of the Annunciation, survives in the family chapel. N. Pevsner, *North Somerset and Bristol* (London, 1958), p. 352.

[77] For a discussion of the selection of female churchwardens in the mid-sixteenth century, see below pp. 178–83.

for ritual on behalf of the household was complemented by the male responsibility in the public sphere. On one definition the parish consisted of the
association of household heads. But reality was more complex, and allowed
greater room for manoeuvre. The need for male domestic acts of piety to
be carried out furtively, and out of sight of all save the wife, reinforced the
devotional intimacy of the couple, and counterbalanced the husband's ability to overturn her religious decisions with the support of the priest. Here,
as even more evidently within the parish as a whole, the reasons for gender
separation were increasingly seen as pragmatic rather than innate. Gender
was just one of the ways of dividing up the larger community for the purpose of ritual, intercession and sociability. Thus, tenurial distinctions were
as appropriate as those of gender in seating the congregation decently in the
parish church. Association according to gender and marital status was an
option that could also be actively sought, since it reflected one set of collective identities. The subdivisions of gilds to include a women's stock, the
development of groups of wives, maidens and young men in some parishes,
and the closer connection of hogling and Hocktide with men and women
respectively all testify to the attractiveness of this choice within the parish
community. But this should not be seen as creating a gendered straitjacket.
That women could exercise the authority associated with men as wardens of
a light, and even occasionally as churchwardens, was due in large measure to
their accumulated expertise in these groups, and also to the co-existence of
definitions of religious community in terms of gender and household authority. It was, paradoxically, the appeal of gendered separation that facilitated
the crossing of gender boundaries.

2

Religious choices

According to Michael Gamare, a lollard from Wimborne (Dorset), it was 'a lewde thyng and amadde condition or use occupied in his contree or paryshe that wemen will cum and sette their ca[n]dles atree the Image of Saynt Gyles'.[1] His assumption that such madness was the preserve of women echoed, albeit from an opposing perspective, the views of gender roles contained in catholic prescriptive literature such as the Good Wife poems considered in the last chapter. It is, however, less clear that this represents actual religious choices. The combined stereotype of female foolishness and female religiosity was a gift to the polemicist who wished to denigrate the religious practices of his opponents. Even catholic responses could employ the same assumptions. In response to Tyndale's critique of popular beliefs about images of the Virgin Mary, Thomas More replied in the persona of the 'simplest fool', which he identified as a woman. If even she held correct theological views, then Tyndale's case collapsed.[2] These strategies complicate assessments of gender and religious choices, especially since not all hostile voices were prepared to describe practice in these terms. Another lollard, Alice Hignell of Newbury (Berkshire), stated that 'when devout Cristen people of their devocion be wonte to offre their candles bernyng to the Image of seint Leonard I have called [them] folis'.[3] Alice's description may be influenced by a reluctance to associate her own sex exclusively with what she saw as foolish practices, but lollard men could describe catholic activity in similar terms.[4] Such accounts seem more plausible than those of people like Michael Gamare, which were influenced by the desire for polemical advantage.

---

[1] Cited in A. Brown, *Popular Piety in Late Medieval England: The Diocese of Salisbury, 1250–1550* (Oxford, 1995), p. 215.

[2] W. E. Campbell (ed.), *Thomas More's 'The Dialogue Concerning Tyndale'* (London, 1927), p. 164.

[3] Cited in A. Brown, 'Lay piety in late medieval Wiltshire', D.Phil. thesis, University of Oxford (1990), p. 319.

[4] For example, Roger Parker of Letcombe Regis admitted 'that upon xvj or xvij yeres past, whan I was dwellyng in Bampton in Oxenfordshire, seyng men and women to goo barefote and offer images of wex or money to the reliques of Sainct Bernold ther, I scorned theym

This chapter will assess the way in which male and female individual religious choices actually differed in practice, and the extent to which these patterns of behaviour diverged from the expectations of prescription and polemic. We have already seen, in the last chapter, that gender roles, although clearly expressed, contained a certain amount of flexibility, and that communities could decide upon the degree to which some of these distinctions could be emphasised. Individuals in pre-Reformation catholicism were presented with a great deal of choice in their religious acts. Catholicism offered a menu of options, as people were encouraged to select particular saints for their own personal devotion, and to seek saintly aid by going on pilgrimage, fasting, or lighting candles before an image. This diversity was both a strength and a weakness. It catered for a range of tastes, whilst also making it very difficult to police the boundary between orthodoxy and lollardy: someone who refused to go on pilgrimage could be expressing a principled rejection of the practice, or simply choosing to express devotion in a different approved manner. More importantly, in the context of the present discussion, this diversity encouraged individual choice, which could buttress, or erode, gender distinctions, and sheds light on the importance of gender identity in the religious sphere. Whilst some saints – such as Saint Sythe, the holy housekeeper of Lucca who was resorted to by housewives who had lost their keys – seem to have been especially associated with the female sex, the diversity of the holy company of heaven, and of forms of religious practice, means that such tight gender associations should not be generally assumed.

The historian investigating acts of piety can only glimpse a small part of religious behaviour. The frequency of prayer and saying the rosary, or of ritual gestures like arranging crumbs in honour of the Five Wounds of Christ, remains hidden. Documented acts are those that involve a material investment, and may be partly influenced by more secular concerns of status and display. For both these reasons, women's religious activities are likely to be seriously under-represented. Married women, at least in theory, were not easily able to participate equally with men in acts designed to assist the fate of their own souls. Upon marriage the wife's property became her husband's, and she was only able to make a will with his consent. If these provisions were strictly applied in practice, the ability of most women to participate in the purchase of paradise could be severely limited.

Public representations of pious donation maintained this gender distinction. As Marks has pointed out, women rarely appear in stained glass as individual donors separate from their husbands, although men could be

and called theym foolys in their soo doyng': J. Blair, 'Saint Beornwald of Bampton: Further references', *Oxoniensia* 54 (1989), 401; A. Hudson, *The Premature Reformation: Wycliffite Texts and lollard History* (Oxford,1988), p. 309.

portrayed alone.[5] 'Notions of family hierarchy and order had to be inserted into depictions of donation and devotion, but this produced conventions which did not reflect actual practice. As we have seen, groups of women could pay for stained glass windows, as at St Neot (Cornwall) (Fig. 5).[6] The details of many pious donations apparently made by a couple were implemented, and perhaps designed, by the widow acting as her husband's executrix. Women could also carry out individual acts of donation, even if this role was not visually recognised. That this was so was neither pure misogyny nor the subordination of women's role. For many, donation to church furnishing was principally an intercessory action, as well as being a means to beautify the church and enhance one's standing in the community. As the foundation of chantries and the standard will clauses disposing of the residue for the health of the testator's soul indicate, the understanding of intercession was primarily familial. This may have been especially important for women. Studies of bequests to individuals in wills consistently show that women recognised a wider range of kin than men did, and this also fits with a strong anthropological tradition which observes that women have a special role in maintaining kin networks. The lone female donor, like the lone female figure on a memorial brass, did exist, but was more likely to be associated with her husband or family.

Despite the strength of these conventions, it is still worth asking whether men and women responded differently in their personal devotional preferences. Wills are the most obvious source for this question, and studies of late medieval piety have naturally focussed on the religious requests contained in them, whilst recognising that deathbed acts might not be wholly representative of priorities during the rest of the testator's life.[7] It has also been pointed out that, although wills can be found in which the testator's goods were considerably less than the £5 threshold at which probate was required, this source is heavily skewed towards the wealthier sections of society. The sample is also predominantly male, partly as a result of this economic profile, but more decisively because married women were unable to make wills without the consent of their husbands. Less than 10 per cent of the wills proved

---

[5] Marks, *Stained Glass in England*, p. 11. Donor figures are much less frequent in paintings on walls and rood screens, probably because a different pattern of patronage prevailed which involved individuals of lower social status and recourse to general parish funds. Nevertheless, representations of donation in both media correspond with Marks's conclusions for stained glass. E. Duffy, 'The parish, piety and patronage in late medieval East Anglia: The evidence of rood screens', in K. L. French, G. G. Gibbs and B. A. Kümin (eds.), *The Parish in English Life, 1400–1600* (Manchester, 1997), pp. 133–62.

[6] See above p. 29.

[7] C. Burgess, 'Late medieval wills and pious convention: testamentary evidence reconsidered', in M. Hicks (ed.), *Profit, Piety and the Professions in Later Medieval England* (Gloucester, 1990), pp. 14–30. Burgess's main focus is chantry provision. For arguments that the lack of continuity, at least as regards the cult of saints, may have been overstated see below pp. 100–1.

in the Consistory Court of Norwich, 1370–1420, were made by women, and in the fifteenth century 15–18 per cent of the testators were female. In wills proved in the Exchequer Court of York in the second half of the fifteenth century about one fifth of testators were women.[8]

Churchwardens' accounts provide a more comprehensive picture of male and female acts of donation. Despite the inaccuracies of accounting, wardens had no strong reason to discriminate against the recording of gifts and bequests from women. Nevertheless, examination of eight detailed accounts from the late fifteenth and early sixteenth centuries shows that in all of them a minority of bequests were made by women.[9] Typically, female bequests comprised between one fifth and two fifths of the total. The lowest percentages (19%) are found at Leverton (Lincolnshire) and Bassingbourn (Cambridgeshire), and the highest (43%) at Halesowen (Worcestershire). This variation can probably be explained demographically: in all the eight parishes the majority of female donors appear to have been widows. In Bassingbourn (Cambridgeshire), for example, only one of the 22 female donors in the period 1498–1538 is described as a wife (Alice, the wife of George North who left 6s 8d in 1498). The accounts of Chagford (Devon), which consistently contain details of gifts and legacies to the church and the stores within it for the period 1480–1546, reveal a similar pattern. Of the 49 female donors, only four appear to have been wives. Parishes that produced higher proportions of female donors, such as Halesowen, do not seem to have had significantly greater numbers of wives making bequests. In this parish four of the 21 female donors are known to have been wives. However, in one case it appears that the intended bequest was never carried out: the bequest of a ring to the church by the wife of William Grove in 1512–13 was subsequently deleted from the churchwardens' accounts.

The preponderance of male bequests can therefore be attributed principally to the difficulty of married women in gaining control over the disposition of material goods. This situation also explains the prominence in areas like Devon and Somerset of female bequests in the form of kirtles and rings. Furthermore, even in cases where wives, presumably with the consent of their husbands, did leave goods to the church, it is sometimes possible to detect a reluctance on the part of male family members to allow the items to pass outside the family circle. Two cases from Woodbury (Devon)

---

[8] S. Sutcliffe, 'Women's religion in the diocese of Norwich, 1350–1500', paper given in Oxford 8/6/92; P. J. P. Goldberg, *Women, Work and Lifecycle in a Medieval Economy: Women in York and Yorkshire, c. 1300–1520* (Oxford, 1992), p. 267. In the period 1445–69 23.0% of testators were female, and in 1470–1550, 19.9%.

[9] The eight accounts used are Bassingbourn (Cambs.), Leverton (Lincs.), Halesowen (Worcs.), Bramley (Hants.), Ashburton (Devon), Chagford (Devon), Woodbury (Devon) and Ecclesfield (Yorks.).

illustrate this point. In 1543 Joan Pyne bequeathed a kirtle to the church, which was immediately bought back by her husband Thomas. Three years later, a ewe bequeathed by Alice Martyn, the wife of John Martyn the younger, was sold to a certain William Martyn, who was presumably a relation. Wealthier parishioners could also react in the same way. At Morebath, also in Devon, Cecily Tymwell at Hayne bequeathed her best gown to the church in 1534, and the accounts record that 'for the wyche gowne her husband Nicholas at Hayne brotsch [brought] yn to this churche a awter clothe of sylke the prisse xiiis iiiid.' Married women, more than their widowed sisters who had clearer control over material goods, were normally associated with personal acts of piety during life, and not with material acts of deathbed donation.

That age, marital status and gender influenced the type of religious provision which was seen as appropriate is also borne out by the evidence of the payments for months minds and anniversaries at Sutterton (Lincolnshire) from 1461 to 1499.[10] The detailed lists in the churchwardens' accounts of the expenditure on candles at burial, the seventh day, thirtieth day and the year day reveal a clear stratification. Children received no commemoration except on the day of burial, and were usually buried with the minimum expenditure on wax, a penny candle. The highest average per capita expenditure on wax was for men, and this was the only group which made additional legacies to the church or to the various lights within it. There was also a greater concern that the observances for men's souls should continue for longer after their deaths than was the case for women. Only four year days are mentioned for women in the period compared with 18 for men. Two of these four are for wives, and in one case the anniversary is shared with her husband.[11]

The provision for wives and 'widows' also differed. Wives form about one third of the women listed and the average expenditure on wax for this group is just over two pence more than for the 'widows'.[12] These averages conceal a greater variation between the two groups. Of the 'widows', 42% were buried with only a single penny candle whereas only 17% of wives were so buried. This discrepancy cannot be entirely attributed to the probable difference in wealth between the two groups, since in all cases the sums involved are small. Instead, the evidence suggests an acknowledged differentiation between what was appropriate for wives and for widows which reversed that which was

---

[10] CWA Sutterton, Bodl. Ms. Rawl. D. 786.
[11] A similar pattern can be seen at Seend, a rural chapel of Melksham (Wiltshire). A list of stocks supporting anniversaries which was drawn up *c.* 1500 reveals that 16 people were commemorated of whom four were women. Brown, 'Lay piety in late medieval Wiltshire', p. 81.
[12] Individuals not described as wives have been assumed to be widows.

expected when women themselves were the actors. The grief of a husband at what must have often been the unexpected death of his wife seems to have made an increased commemoration socially acceptable.

The distinctions observable at Sutterton can also be traced in funeral provisions in gild statutes. In 1504 a clause added to the statutes of the Assumption gild at St Mary's, Ely prescribed that trentals were only to be said for brothers and sisters of the gild over the age of 16 years. It was the custom at All Saints gild in the Cambridge parish of that name for five priests to sing dirige and mass on the death of a brother, but only two for a sister. Other Cambridge gilds practised economic differentiation. Poor brethren of the Assumption gild at Holy Trinity, and poverty-stricken widows of brethren of the Purification gild at Great St Mary's, were denied burial at gild expense.[13] These distinctions might reflect the economic contributions of members to the gild, but this seems slightly surprising given the ideas of mutual support and charity that were supposed to underpin such organisations. Whatever the reasoning, gild procedures helped to set, and to reinforce, the pattern of appropriate commemoration that was followed by individual parishioners.

The consistency of provision suggests that common expectations were more significant in this respect than the assertion of varying socio-economic status, which may have been displayed in other aspects of the funeral rites, such as the accompanying procession, which were less narrowly connected with intercession. For both parishioners and gild members, what was considered appropriate largely matched a scheme of spiritual status, which was the converse of the social hierarchy. The reputation of women, and especially widows, for piety, meant that less expenditure on intercession at their deaths could be justified. Similarly, the fact that children had had the least time since their baptism to sin and succumb to worldly temptations meant that there was seen to be less need to invest in intercession on their behalf. However, the more substantial provisions for wives suggest that the female reputation for piety was less significant than the belief that it was more acceptable for men to dispose of family property than it was for women, but it is notable that, even when the husbands were perceived as the actors, this did not usually extend to including elaborate trentals or intercessory provision.

These conclusions should influence the way we read the religious provisions contained in women's wills. A study of all of the female Consistory Court wills from the diocese of Worcester and a male sample from the deaneries of Kidderminster and Powick and the peculiar of Evesham suggests that such considerations strongly shaped testators' behaviour. A comparison of two categories of religious bequests can be particularly instructive: those to lights, altars and the service of individual saints (other than to the

---

[13] Bainbridge, *Gilds in the Medieval English Countryside*, p. 89.

Table 2.1. *Bequests to lights and altars (excluding the high altar)*
and for masses and trentals in Consistory Court wills in the diocese
of Worcester, 1509–47

Sample	No. of wills	Lights, altars	Masses, trentals
Female all diocese	337	78 (23.1%)	82 (24.3%)
Female Kidderminster	25	12 (48%)	5 (20%)
Female Evesham	22	8 (36.4%)	10 (45.5%)
Female Powick	31	2 (6.5%)	7 (22.6%)
Male EPK	373	131 (35.1%)	57 (15.2%)
Male Kidderminster	132	59 (44.7%)	18 (13.6%)
Male Evesham	121	56 (46.3%)	47 (38.9%)
Male Powick	120	16 (13.3%)	16 (13.3%)

parish church and high altar), and requests for dedicated intercessory masses,
trentals and anniversaries (Table 2.1). The proportions of female wills in the
diocese including bequests for lights and for masses are strikingly similar
(23.1% and 24.3%), whilst male wills show a clear preference for lights
rather than masses (35.1% and 15.2%). Of course, these samples are not directly comparable. As other historians working on will material have noted,
regional variations in pious provision are generally more marked than those
based on gender, and the diocese of Worcester is no exception.[14] The male
wills from the three areas reveal different patterns of bequests, and also of
choice of will preamble. However, it is notable that when these figures are
compared with the female wills from the same areas, it is always the case
that a higher percentage of women than men include requests for masses.
Viewed in isolation, it would seem natural to interpret this as evidence for a
greater female commitment to intercessory masses, and as a natural corollary of their association with piety. This might seem even more likely when
it is remembered that a gift of a few pence for a taper at every altar in the
parish church would probably cost the testator less than a shilling, whereas
the standard charge for a trental was ten shillings (or five shillings for half
a trental) and even larger sums were required for more elaborate months
minds and anniversaries. However, the evidence from Sutterton and elsewhere discussed above suggests an alternative reading: the social reluctance
to see extensive post-mortem intercessory provision for women as normal
encouraged female testators to make such demands explicit in their wills.
Men, relying on their widows and prevailing convention, had less need to be
specific and were more likely to see a general instruction to their executors
to 'dispose for the health of my soul' as an adequate safeguard.

[14] For example, C. Litzenberger, 'Local responses to changes in religious policy based on evidence from Gloucestershire wills (1540–80)', *Continuity and Change* 8/3 (1993), 417–39.

But if wills do not reveal gendered patterns of commitment to intercessory masses, can they at least tell us something about different devotional preferences in the cult of saints? Intuitively, we might expect that such choices would be gendered. It would seem logical, for example, for women to favour female saints over male saints, especially as female saints were so commonly called upon by women to intercede for them during childbirth. However, this does not seem to have been the case. In the diocese of Worcester, 1509–59, the saints mentioned by all the female testators whose wills were proved in the Consistory Court were predominantly male. Only three of the nineteen saints selected were female: St Katherine, St Anne and St Sythe. Analysis of the wills of 125 parishes in Sussex for the same period similarly shows that female testators had no marked preference for female saints.[15] In Sussex, as in Worcester, only a minority of wills included bequests to saints apart from the Virgin Mary. In the total sample there were only 78 male and nine female bequests to saints, and in both groups these were directed overwhelmingly to male saints. Only eight of the 78 male bequests were to female saints, and these were mainly to St Katherine (five) with the remainder being in favour of St Anne and St Margaret. St Katherine was the only female saint to attract a bequest from a woman. Bequests to the high altar, rood light and to the Virgin Mary were much more frequent and the pattern of bequests suggests that the devotional priorities of both sexes were almost identical. In all these three categories women account for a low proportion of the bequests, owing to the smaller number of female testators in the sample, but they consistently account for 13–14 per cent of the total.

This evidence suggests the possibility that, especially in testamentary acts of piety, women felt constrained to conform to a male model of pious activities. However, the adoption of male norms to secure acceptance of female post-mortem provisions may have been less important than the male emphasis in parish religious culture. With the obvious, and somewhat ambiguous, exception of the Virgin Mary, male saints were predominant in paintings on the walls of the parish church, whilst female saints were more likely to be relegated to being part of the holy company of heaven on the lowest panels of the rood screen. In such a position their individual identity tended to be eroded. Their role in the grand scheme of the screen supporting the rood group, and dividing the secular sphere of the nave from the clerical sphere of the chancel, was to testify to the possibility of the human achievement of saintliness, rather than to provide a means of intercession with the divine.[16]

Nevertheless, it would be mistaken to assume that in these acts of piety women were simply reproducing the dominant male devotional culture. Studies of individual parishes and of the larger will samples demonstrate

[15] R. G. Rice (ed.), Transcripts of Sussex Wills, *Sussex Rec. Soc.* 41–4 (1935–41).
[16] For a fuller discussion, see below pp. 105–8.

that within this male framework women developed particular priorities in their religious bequests. In general, they tended to focus their acts of piety more closely on particular altars and gilds within the church and were less concerned with the maintenance of the parish church as a whole. Thus, for example, at Worfield (Shropshire), where the parallel accounts of the parish church and the chantry of Our Lady permit close comparison, women were much more likely to make a bequest to the chantry only, whereas men tended to combine this with a bequest to the church. In the churchwardens' accounts of the nearby parish of Halesowen (Worcestershire) a similar pattern is apparent: men include bequests for the maintenance of the church fabric, whereas women concentrate on the light of St Katherine.[17]

This contrast between the religious priorities of men and women is also supported by the evidence of the churchwardens' accounts of Chagford (Devon), which include accounts of a wide range of stores.[18] Here, the flourishing store of St Katherine attracted bequests from 71 per cent and 81 per cent of male and female donors respectively. The saint had obvious appeal in this stannary town as the patron saint of tinners, in addition to her more usual role as protectress of the dying. The rough equality of male and female gifts may be explained by the fact that membership of the gild seems to have consisted chiefly of married couples. The undated, but early sixteenth-century, list of the brothers and sisters of the fraternity has a total of 231 names of which the majority are couples. Two women and fourteen men were listed as members individually, but the later deletions and the changes made to the names of wives suggest that the normal unit of membership was the couple. The evidence for the bequests to the store of the Virgin Mary further underlines the homogeneity in male and female behaviour, and also suggests that the structure of the gild or store may have had little influence. Although from 1500 onwards the wardens of this store were almost entirely female, bequests were received from strikingly similar proportions of men and women: 25 per cent and 26 per cent respectively.

At Chagford an obvious discrepancy between male and female behaviour is only evident in the case of bequests to St Michael. This store was in effect the store of the parish church, although overall supervision of all the stores rested with the 'four men'. The proportions leaving bequests to St Michael (43.5 per cent of men; 10.6 per cent of women) contrast with the figures for St Katherine and Our Lady, and are in line with the evidence from Worfield and Halesowen. The paucity of female bequests to this store cannot be explained by women making a more limited range of bequests than men since the difference in the average number of bequests is actually quite small

---

[17] H. B. Walters (ed.), 'Churchwardens' accounts of the parish of Worfield', *Transactions of the Shropshire Archaeological and Natural History Society* 3rd ser. 3–9 (1903–9); F. Somers (ed.), Halesowen Churchwardens' Accounts, 1487–1582, *Worcs. Hist. Soc.* 40 (1952–7).
[18] Devon RO CWA Chagford, pw 1–4.

(1.5 for men; 1.3 for women). Instead, the reluctance of women to make bequests to this store fits with the tendency of women not to give to the parish church as a whole. In contrast, the strength of male concern for the fabric and finances of the parish church is shown by its extension to other churches in the neighbourhood: in wills from the diocese of Worcester male testators frequently make bequests of equal sums of money to a large number of local parish churches, but there are no examples of women doing the same.

The closer focus of female testators on their parish church, and especially on the lights and altars within it, suggests that acts of female piety differed from male piety in scope if not in substance. This may be explained by women's use of religious acts as a focus of their devotion, rather than as an opportunity to display worldly influence or prestige. Such behaviour was part of the same set of ideas that ensured a male near-monopoly of the office of churchwarden. Throughout the later medieval period, piety was seen as a particular attribute of the female. The emphasis on the role of women as the nurturers of their families meant that they were identified more closely with the observation of religious rites during life. The legal position of married women reduced their capacity to invest in rituals for the purchase of paradise. However, these structures of ideas and constraints did not produce a specifically female piety. In their choice of bequests to saints, women followed the male pattern of selecting, with the exception of the Virgin Mary, a predominantly male group of saints as intercessors. Women may have been the models of piety, but the limitation of their religious activities to the domestic sphere of household and parish prevented a selection of devotional subjects that could have formed the substance of a specifically female pattern of piety.

The close association of women with the domestic sphere did, however, have one important consequence for the nature and meaning of their religious contribution in the parish church. As we saw in the last chapter, illustrated by the case of Elizabeth Sharp and her use of the customary provision of the holy loaf, the domestic and parochial could intersect, and in so doing enrich women's contribution. The same was true for less structured individual acts of piety, which may not have been motivated by the same desire for reconciliation which prompted Elizabeth's presentation of a houseling cloth. A number of women responded in the same way as Edith Holder of Tiddington (1537) and Joan Malboche of Wellesbourne Mountford (1540), who each bequeathed a sheet to the church to serve as an altar cloth. Items of clothing were also envisaged as playing a hallowed role in the mystery of the mass. Women like Emma Meredyth of Peopleton (1543) and Helen North of All Hallows, Evesham (1544) gave their kerchiefs to make corporas cloths. More unusually, Margaret Broke of Norton (1545) bequeathed her best coverlet to lie before the high altar.[19]

---

[19] Worcs. RO CCW 62 p. 87; 75 p. 102; 236 p. 108; 20 p. 104; vol. 5 54 p. 18.

The same intimacy is found in female bequests to the images within their parish church. Agnes Llewellyn of Pucklechurch (1537) requested that her best kerchief be 'set about' the image of Our Lady of Pity, and Jone Grene of Bretforton (1530) gave her best gown to Our Lady of Bretforton.[20] Girdles and sets of beads were also offered to images of saints and were probably often intended to be worn by the statues of the saints.[21] Wills of higher social status occasionally make this practice explicit. Katherine Robins of Morebath (Devon) (1531) bequeathed beads of coral and amber set with silver Pater Nosters and specified that 'the which beads must hang upon the new image of Our Lady every high day'.[22] An even more elaborate example is the will of Dame Joan Chamberlayn of York (1502), which includes the provision,

Also I wit my weddynge ring of golde, a gyrdill the tushoye theroff of gold of Vynes harnest with sylver and gylt, and a payr of corall baydes gaudiett wt sylver, unto ye blessid ymage of Saynt Anne wt in the said monystorie of our Lady: and I wyll that the rynge the day of my bureall, be put on hir fynger, the gyrdyll abowt hir, and the baydes in hir hand.[23]

St Anne's intercession for Joan's soul was to be secured by causing the saint's image to impersonate the living figure of Joan during her funeral. Similarly, every time an image wore a testator's clothes or jewels, the saint was not simply being glorified by being lavishly adorned. At the same time a kinship was established between the living, the dead and the community of the saints.

In view of this, it is scarcely surprising that wedding rings had a special religious significance for women and were often included among their pious bequests. Rings were often kept on sets of beads, which could also be used as rosaries. The presence of a wedding ring on a woman's rosary may therefore have enhanced the perception of its association with the sacramental nature of marriage. In donating their wedding rings to the church, and especially to the mother church, women symbolised their transformation at their deaths into brides of Christ. It is striking that, although Joan Chamberlayn could bequeath a ring to St Anne, this choice was unusual: in the will sample from the diocese of Worcester all religious bequests of rings and wedding rings were made to the mother church, which represented the Church in a way that the familiar parish church could not.

---

[20] Worcs. RO CCW 81 p. 87; vol. 3 18 p. 6.
[21] This was not always the case. On occasion such gifts were meant to be converted to other uses. For example, Elizabeth Gonderton of Upton Snodsbury (1546) donated all the silver and gilt of her best girdle to the gilding of the crucifix if the parishioners decided to buy one. Worcs. RO CCW vol. 5 407 p. 161.
[22] R. Whiting, *The Blind Devotion of the People: Popular Religion and the English Reformation* (Cambridge, 1989), p. 54.
[23] J. Raine (ed.), *Testamenta Eboracensia*, Surtees Society 53 (1868), pp. 200–2.

Figure 6 Assumption of the Virgin, with St Thomas receiving Mary's girdle, Beckley (Oxon.)

The selection of the girdle as the object of a religious bequest was partly due to the fact that they were frequently decorated and of comparatively high value, but such gifts may also have had a symbolic significance for women. Girdles were usually bequeathed to the Virgin Mary. Thus, for example, Ellyn Taylour of Chipping Sodbury (1519) left her best girdle to Our Lady of Wickwar; Agnes Holder (1511) and Agnes Wade (1513), both of Tewkesbury, bequeathed girdles to the image of Mary in the Jesus chapel.[24] This association with Mary suggests a connection with the story of the Assumption. The proof of Mary's Assumption is the girdle she threw from heaven to doubting Thomas on earth (Fig. 6). In reversing the gesture by

[24] Worcs. RO CCW 65 p. 82; vol. 2 p. 52.

bequeathing her girdle to Mary, the testator symbolically affirmed her faith in Mary's special status.

The evidence of female bequests in wills may only be an incomplete record of individual religious activity, but it does remind us that this piety was characterised above all by the intimate relationship of the woman with the articles she gave. The paucity of women's devotional equipment was counterbalanced by the fact that so many of their other possessions had the potential to be put to holy use. Tablecloths and sheets could be given as altar cloths and towels for the priest to wipe his hands on during the mass. Female garments too could be sanctified. Images of saints frequently received kerchiefs, girdles and sometimes gowns. The pursuit of good housewifery, and the careful hours spent in sewing and embroidery, not only had a significance in the maintenance of a good household but could also be works in the service of the divine. Many of the items bequeathed by women may not have had the symbolic value of the wedding ring or girdle, but their significance lay in the ease with which the mundane and domestic could be transformed into the hallowed.

Male pious bequests from the Worcester sample show a different pattern. Gifts of household linen and of garments are rare. Instead, men focus on giving legacies in the form of cash and corn, which could be employed to profit by holding an ale. Such gifts were also the products of the testator's skill in his contribution to the household economy, but their form meant that once donated they soon lost any specific identity and association. In part, of course, this reflects the different resources available to men and women, but this cannot be the whole story. There was nothing to stop men making religious gifts of clothing, and yet they chose not to do so. Instead, the choice of bequests reflected and reinforced a gender distinction in the relationship of people to their parish church. In the type of bequests, as well as in their scope, women had a more intimate emotional involvement with the devotional and liturgical life of the parish.

The spiritual functions of ritual piety and almsgiving were identical, but the latter was more intimately associated with the produce of the household and traditions of hospitality.[25] That such acts were not prescribed, but rather chosen, increased the possibility that ideas of gender would shape the practice of charity. The lives of popular saints, like St Anne or St Sythe, elaborated the importance of charity in the context of female piety, but also hinted at potential conflict with the household (Fig. 25, p. 99). The former assigned one third of her income for the support of widows

---

[25] Occasional dissenting voices could be heard. A Franciscan preaching at Herne Bay (Kent) on Passion Sunday, 1535, got into trouble for maintaining that 'whoever offered one penny to St. Thomas's shrine, it was more meritorious than to give a noble to poor people; for one is spiritual and the other corporal'. Cited in D. Webb, *Pilgrimage in Medieval England* (London and New York, 2000), p. 246.

and orphans, whilst the latter gave away bread to the poor against her employer's wishes. Charity, like ritual piety, intersected with a gendered understanding of control over property. The injunction to charity, especially in its domestic form of hospitality, provision of food and succour of the sick, could clash with the demands of household management. As the author of *Dives and Pauper* stated, 'Oþer vouhis þat arn no preiudys to þe housebonde þe wif may makyn, as to seyn certeyn bedys, but of no gret pilgrimage ne of gret abstinence ne of contynence [ne] to ʒevyn gret elmesse'. The wife was not allowed to make a vow to give 'great alms', but in at least one version of the text it was felt necessary to add that the husband's hardheartedness towards the poor licensed his wife to act charitably upon her own initiative:

but ʒyf her housbond be mysdysposyd in his wyttys or not rewlyd of custome be resoun. For ʒyf her housbond be unpytous of þe nedy peple sche may make a vowe to ʒeve to þe pore to þe plesauns of God after her power, savyng her bothe astate.[26]

But, even then, her ability to do so was not unlimited: she was not to give beyond her means, and those of the household. Such instructions suggest that issues of property imposed similar constraints on women in both their ritual and their charitable activities. The personification of Charity as female may have encouraged the weakening of these restrictions, but depictions of the Works of Mercy in wall paintings and stained glass included male and female protagonists, and may have been less effective in sanctioning charitable giving by women (Fig. 7).[27]

W. K. Jordan's conclusion that women were much more concerned with the succour of mankind in the form of bequests to the poor, rather than with projects such as road building or religious bequests for the church and its services, seems plausible in the context of the patterns of piety explored so far in this chapter.[28] It fits well with arguments for the domestic and personal focus of women's religious activity, and raises the question of ritual and charitable priorities. Jordan's study has, of course, been much criticised but the concerns raised have been mainly methodological. His reliance on wills proved in the PCC means that these results relate more to the social elite than to a cross-section of society. More misleadingly, the use in his calculations of the total value, rather than the number of bequests, introduces a distortion. In their published form Jordan's data do not permit reinterpretation, but the validity of his proposition can be tested using different will samples. An analysis of Consistory Court wills from the diocese of Worcester shows that

---

[26] Barnum (ed.), *Dives and Pauper*, pp. 247–8.
[27] Marks, *Stained Glass in England during the Middle Ages*, pp. 79–80; M. C. Gill, 'Late medieval wall painting in England: content and context', Ph.D. thesis, Courtauld Institute of Art (2001), pp. 283–7.
[28] W. K. Jordan, *Philanthropy in England, 1480–1660* (London, 1959), pp. 354–5.

Figure 7 Detail from the Works of Mercy, Potter Heigham (Norfolk)

Table 2.2. *Bequests to the poor and for the maintenance of highways in the diocese of Worcester, 1509–47*

Sample	No. of wills	Poor	Highways
Female all	337	54 (16%)	20 (5.9%)
Female EPK	78	9 (11.4%)	4 (5.1%)
Male EPK	373	33 (8.8%)	20 (5.4%)

Table 2.3. *Types of bequests to the poor in Consistory Court wills in the diocese of Worcester, 1509–47*

Type of bequest	Female all	Female EPK	Male EPK
At funerals/obits	22 (40.7%)	7 (77.8%)	10 (30.3%)
To parish/resident poor	9 (16.7%)	1 (11.1%)	8 (24.2%)
To poor in institutions	4 (7.4%)	–	–
To poor man's box	–	–	2 (6.1%)
To named poor	2 (3.7%)	–	–
Of money	32 (59.3%)	7 (77.8%)	19 (57.6%)
Of bread	5 (9.3%)	1 (11.1%)	4 (12.1%)
Of bread or money	3 (5.6%)	–	–
Of corn/malt	4 (7.4%)	–	5 (15.2%)
Of clothing, bedding	6 (11.1%)	1 (11.1%)	–
Of wood	–	–	2 (6.1%)
Total wills with bequests to poor	54	9	33

this group at least did not behave as Jordan thought (Table 2.2). In the Henrician period the proportion of testators of both sexes making bequests to the poor, and especially to the maintenance of highways, was similar, and such bequests were considerably less frequent than ritual ones.

In the Worcester sample, the influence of gender was evident less in the decision to make a bequest to the poor, than in the form which it took (Table 2.3). These differences largely reflect those which we have already seen for ritual bequests. Thus, women gave clothing and bedding to the poor, but men do not seem to have done so. However, even for women this was not a particularly popular form of charitable bequest, accounting for just over ten per cent of their gifts, even if in some wills the charitable redistribution of the residue of the testator's clothing is strongly implied.[29] It is also possible

[29] Thus, for example, Elizabeth Browne of Suckley (1556) charged her executors to distribute the residue of her raiment 'as they shall think need'. Similarly, Elizabeth Golde of Upton

that women were more likely than men to specify that their generosity to the poor should be distributed at their funerals. Overall the differences are not that great (40.7 per cent of women and 30.3 per cent of men), but, given the importance of regional patterns, it may be significant that of the nine women making bequests to the poor in the area of the male sample, seven specified that this was to take place at their burial.

However, if female charity was distinguished by the indiscriminate giving of the funeral dole, it was also characterised by a high degree of specificity. Bequests, such as that of Agnes Penne of Bidford (1557), who gave a sheet to the lame beggar, or Joanne Smith of Leigh (1556), who gave her old red petticoat to 'an old woman who useth to beg on the bridge' and Joanne Smith of Great Malvern (1547), who gave 6d to Sibyl Reed, 'the poor woman', demonstrate women meeting a particular social need.[30] Bequests to named individuals form only a very small part of the total female bequests to the poor, but it is probable that this type of charity was often subsumed in the long and very detailed lists of gifts of items of clothing and household linen, which are such an obvious feature of women's wills.

Male bequests to the poor never specify named individuals and never take the form of gifts of clothing or bedding. Instead, their legacies are in the form of money, bread or corn, and wood. Despite the frequency of gifts of clothing, female bequests to the poor are predominantly in cash, although it is often unclear whether the sum is meant to be converted into food and drink in the context of a funeral dole. That women were less likely to make gifts of grain than men were suggests that access to surplus grain was more difficult for them. This interpretation is strengthened by the fact that women were most likely to make bequests of grain in the reign of Mary I. The high mortality of this period may have left more widows in full charge of their husbands' estates at the time of their own deaths.

Despite these nuances, in general the evidence from the diocese of Worcester suggests that there was no fundamental difference along gender lines in attitudes towards the relief of the poor. Similarly, the evidence suggests that both sexes attached broadly the same degree of importance to the maintenance of bridges and highways in their localities. In both these categories of charitable activity, the significant difference was not in patterns of behaviour but the greater intensity of female commitment to it. It was in the strength of attachment that female stereotypes of Charity appear to have had the most impact.

This broad similarity in male and female ritual and charitable activities for the purchase of paradise, which has been a theme of this chapter, suggests

(1557) and Joan Holle of St Nicholas, Droitwich (1551) bestowed the residue of their apparel upon the poor. Worcs. RO CCW PG601 9 p. 138; PG608 573 p. 161; PG603 186 p. 146.
[30] Worcs. RO CCW PG602 118 p. 144; 214 p. 152; vol. 5 p. 298.

Figure 8 Brass of Roger Harper, wearing a short rosary, and his wife Joan, Axbridge (Somerset), 1493

the need to question the strength of gender stereotypes. Also, and as an illustration of this, it points the way towards understanding a puzzling feature of memorial brasses of the period. The association of women with piety of a ritual kind which did not require significant expenditure would lead us to expect that women rather than men would be depicted wearing a rosary. The author of *Dives and Pauper*, it will be recalled, saw saying beads as a domestically unproblematic form of female piety. Moreover, the conventions which inhibited the portrayal of women as donors in their own right should not have affected the portrayal of women with such unthreatening attributes of piety. However, memorial brasses featuring rosaries occur in two main types clearly separated in time.[31] The first, which was popular in the closing decades of the fifteenth century, depicted the man wearing a short

[31] These conclusions are based on the Monumental Brass Society's volumes so far published for the following counties, edited by W. Lack, H. M. Stuchfield and P. Whittemore: Bedfordshire, Berkshire, Buckinghamshire, Cambridgeshire, Cheshire, Cornwall, Cumberland and Westmorland, Derbyshire and Devon; C. T. Davis, *The Monumental Brasses of Gloucestershire* (1899, repr. Bath, 1969); A. B. Connor, *Monumental Brasses in Somerset* (Bath, 1970); and M. Stephenson, *A List of the Monumental Brasses in Surrey* (1921, repr. Bath, 1970).

Figure 9 Brass of William Gardyner and his two wives, Elizabeth and Cecily, wearing long rosaries, Chalfont St Giles (Bucks.), *c.* 1540

rosary hanging from his belt, sometimes accompanied by a purse. Women of this period were not depicted with rosaries, although their piety, like that of their husbands, was indicated by the portrayal of their hands in an attitude of prayer (Fig. 8). The second type, which became fashionable in the 1520s and increasingly popular by the 1540s, reversed this pattern. It was now the women, rather than the men, who were portrayed wearing rosaries, but this was not the short form favoured in the earlier period, but rather a long rosary of many decades hanging down from their girdles almost to their feet (Fig. 9).

The reason for this change is not clear, but fashion probably provides the best answer, if not a complete explanation. Like the tiny girdle books which became popular amongst ladies at court in the last years of the reign of Henry VIII, the long rosary was an accessory as well as a devotional aid.[32] In terms of gender, though, what is significant is that the vagaries of fashion could cut across gender stereotypes. If the rosary is an emblem of special piety, then men and women at different times could be considered representatives of this. However, such flexibility had its limits: men were associated with the short rosary, which in Germany was even known as the 'Mannsbeter' or 'Mannspaternoster', whilst the long rosary of many decades was the attribute of women.[33] Both the rosaries and the examples of religious choices discussed in this chapter indicate that, although male and female piety overlapped to a greater extent than the stereotypes suggest, the association of piety with women was reflected more subtly in distinctively female priorities.

[32] P. Collinson, 'Windows in a woman's soul: questions about the religion of Queen Elizabeth I', in his *Elizabethan Essays* (London, 1994), pp. 91–3.

[33] E. Wilkins, *The Rose Garden Game: The Symbolic Background to the European Prayer Beads* (London, 1969), p. 54.

3

The Virgin Mary and Christocentric devotion

The petition 'Jesus mercy, lady help', commonly found on funeral monuments, summarises the roles of Mary and Christ in late medieval religion. It places them firmly in the context of every christian's search for salvation, and illustrates the priorities of the laity in the fifteenth and early sixteenth centuries. It also draws attention to their partnership of clearly defined roles: Mary is the one who will respond to devout intercession and will aid by interceding for the seeking soul; Christ is the one who offers help in the form of mercy rather than supplication. The sharpness of this focus on the roles of both Mary and Christ in achieving salvation was, however, the outcome of an evolving process. It was part of the distinctiveness of the late medieval devotional context, and served to facilitate and encourage a religious culture in which gender boundaries, although not insignificant, did not clearly demarcate religious experiences and preferences.

The integration of the cults of Mary and of Christ into the concern for the salvation of the soul was, of course, not complete, even at the close of our period, but it increasingly permeated religious understanding. When an unknown woman at Horwood (Devon) was portrayed on her tomb as the Madonna of Mercy sheltering souls beneath her cloak, she was not appropriating for herself the intercessory role of Mary in the scheme of salvation, but modelling her care and protection for her children on the concern of that model mother for the children of the world (Fig. 10).[1] What is significant here is less that the concept could operate on different levels of cosmic significance, than that the language for the familial was that of the role of Mary in the economy of salvation. Such priorities in adopting Mary as a model were less likely to have seemed appropriate in the twelfth, thirteenth, or probably even the fourteenth centuries, when the most common image

---

[1] A. Gardiner, *English Alabaster Tombs of the Pre-Reformation Period in England* (Cambridge, 1940), pls. 226–7. A similar early sixteenth-century example in alabaster survives at Stourton Caundle (Dorset). G. Dru Drury, 'Three Dorset effigies with unusual individual details', *Proceedings of the Dorset Natural History and Archaeology Society* 75 (1953), 89–90, pls. 4 & 5.

Figure 10 Effigy of an unknown woman as the Madonna of Mercy, Horwood (Devon)

of the Virgin was that of mother and child, and the intimate family was the dominant reference point for Mary's role. That such changes were possible underlines the need to avoid simple and universal conclusions about the cult of the Virgin Mary and her significance in terms of gender. To the extent that Mary was inscribed in the economy of salvation in the later Middle Ages, the distinctiveness of her appeal to both men and women was modified accordingly. Moreover, such developments only arose from the intersection of the Marian cult with the developments of Christocentric piety that, amongst other things, shifted the devotional focus from the infant to the adult Christ. Whether the nature of religion seems best summed up in images of the Virgin and Child or in the phrase 'Jesus mercy, lady help', an understanding of the gender implications of late medieval religion can be reached only by considering the relationship between Christocentric and Marian devotion.

One of the fullest surviving schemes of wall paintings illustrating the lives of Mary and Christ survives in the chancel of the parish church at Chalgrove (Oxfordshire). This narrative sequence dates from the early fourteenth century, and was apparently the product of lay patronage. On the east wall, evidently the most important position, the Assumption and the Coronation of the Virgin are portrayed and are given equal emphasis with Christ's Resurrection, Ascension and Descent into Hell.[2] These images graphically illustrate the extent to which Mary and Christ could be seen to have parallel lives. But they also illustrate an understanding of these parallels that was increasingly eroded during the later fourteenth and fifteenth centuries. Although the divinity of Christ was central to late medieval religiosity, the Resurrection was seen as less remarkable than the fact that Christ became man.[3] This same period also saw a re-evaluation of the meaning of Mary's Assumption and Coronation that questioned the significance of her maternal role whilst redefining her powers of intercession. The changing nature of Mary's intercessory powers, and the evolving focus on the passion of the incarnate Christ, provide the key to understanding the way in which later medieval religious culture offered possibilities for men and women which differed substantially from those previously available.

Of all the Marian feasts, the Assumption was considered the most important, and it attracted the most fulsome descriptions of the Virgin's powers. Writing in the fifteenth century, Mirk informed his readers that this was 'the highest holy day of Our Lady', and recommended that on the eve of the feast every man and woman over the age of twelve be ordered to fast, and on the feast itself to come to the church and worship Our Lady with all their 'myght and conyng'. In keeping with these demands, Mirk's sermon on the Assumption described Mary's power in terms that greatly exceeded that of any other saint, and even rivalled that of Christ. He explained that, after her Assumption, Mary was crowned not only Queen of Heaven and Lady of the World, but also Empress of Hell, and was granted the power to command the obedience of the demons. As a result her powers were extensive:

---

[2] R. W. Heath-Whyte, *A Guide to the Medieval Wall Paintings of St. Mary the Virgin Church, Chalgrove* (1985). Although the paintings are in the chancel, the presence of donor figures suggests lay patronage.

[3] E. M. Ross, *The Grief of God: Images of the Suffering Jesus in Late Medieval England* (Oxford, 1997), p. 137.

Al that byn in Hevyn byn buxom to hur and redy at hur commaundement, and don hur worschyp in honowre, as they owyn forto do to hor Lordis modyr and hor qwene; and ys ther of on wyll and one love with the holy Trinyte that grauntyth hur what that ever sho askyth, and at hur prayer rewardyth all hur servauntes.[4]

Giving Mary powers of salvation on this scale was a comparatively recent phenomenon, connected with the development of her cult since 1100. In Anglo-Saxon descriptions Mary, St Michael and St Peter jointly intercede for the souls of those in hell, and each is granted successively a third of the souls still languishing in hell whilst the final remainder are condemned to eternal damnation. Mary's claim is based on her divine maternity, St Michael's on his lordship over heaven, and St Peter's on his possession of the keys of both heaven and hell.[5] Vestiges of this original scheme remain in late medieval portrayals of the Last Judgement: St Peter holds the keys and admits souls to the heavenly city of Jerusalem; St Michael appears in the Soul-Weighing scene. However, by this date both figures have suffered a loss of power over the fate of human souls. St Peter merely admits souls selected by Christ. St Michael, holding the balance and wielding his large sword, has become the personification of justice. Typically he is depicted looking directly at the viewer rather than towards the soul awaiting judgement: his inflexibility suggests the futility of intercession and his personal powerlessness over the fate of the souls in the balance. Similarly, the apostles, when they appear in the Last Judgement, take on the aspect of a jury rather than intercessors on the part of the defence.

In contrast to the fates of St Peter and St Michael, the flowering of Marian devotion in the twelfth and thirteenth centuries, and the intimate relationship of Mary with Christ, ensured that Mary would have a more complex history and would retain, and indeed increase, her prominent intercessory function. The precise nature of Mary's role depended, however, on the importance attributed to her Assumption and Coronation, since both episodes could be seen as crucial moments in determining the nature of Mary's intercessory powers. In the thirteenth century when Voragine wrote his *Legenda Aurea* (*Golden Legend*), the primacy of the Assumption seemed clear. In his account, the reverence owed to Mary is not the result of powers granted to her at her Coronation, which is not mentioned, but the consequence of her motherhood of Christ. The stress is on her bodily assumption, made possible

---

[4] Erbe (ed.), *Mirk's Festial*, pp. 221–30.
[5] M. Clayton, *The Cult of the Virgin Mary in Anglo-Saxon England*, Cambridge Studies in Anglo-Saxon England 2 (Cambridge, 1990), pp. 253–5. The story is found in the Last Judgement text Vercelli xv, and derives from the 'Apocalypse of Mary', although this source describes events immediately after Mary's Assumption. The idea that saints could intercede for the damned in this way was criticised by Aelfric, but his views were unusual and did not come to predominate.

Figure 11 The Coronation of the Virgin Mary by Christ, alabaster *c.* 1400

because Christ took of her flesh, and on her special position as the one chosen to be the mother of Christ. By contrast, as we have seen, in the early fifteenth century Mirk focussed on the specific powers granted to Mary at her Coronation, and placed relatively little stress on Mary's inherent qualifications for her Assumption and Coronation.

This change in emphasis was most marked in religious imagery. Fourteenth-century depictions accorded with Voragine's interpretation in connecting Mary's claim to this honour with her maternal relationship with Christ. In both alabasters and wall paintings, Christ and Mary were depicted seated side by side on a bench as Christ blessed his mother, who was usually already crowned (Fig. 11). In the later fifteenth century, Mary's role in the scene changed dramatically from one of near equality with Christ to that of recipient of the favour of the Trinity (Fig. 12). Now, whether in wall

Figure 12 The Coronation of the Virgin Mary by the Trinity, fifteenth-century alabaster

paintings, stained glass or alabaster, it was the act of crowning by the Trinity that was normally shown, and Mary assumed the aspect of a mere mortal upon whom a great favour was being bestowed.[6]

---

[6] Developments in the iconography of the Coronation in alabasters are detailed in F. Cheetham, *English Medieval Alabasters, with a Catalogue of the Collection in the Victoria and Albert Museum* (Oxford, 1984), pp. 206–16. A notable example of the former type in stained glass is the panel from All Saints, Wing (Bucks.) and of the latter the window at Holy Trinity, Goodramgate, York. S. Crewe, *Stained Glass in England, 1180–1540* (RCHME, 1987), pp. 39, 50. There is also a small transitional group of alabasters, dating from the late four-teenth century, which adopt a hierarchical arrangement of Christ and Mary, with the latter

Homiletic descriptions did not quite keep pace with these iconographical developments, suggesting perhaps that the impulse for such shifts came more from the logic of trends in parish devotion than from clerical initiatives. Sermon writers, even those as in touch with their congregations as Mirk or the author of the early fifteenth-century *Speculum Sacerdotale*, remained heavily reliant on their source texts, especially the *Golden Legend*, and may also have been influenced by the scriptural references that underpinned these earlier writings. Thus, although Mirk's sermon identifies the Coronation as decisive in granting Mary powers of intercession, he describes this event in terms that match the earlier iconography. In his version, on the third day after the funeral of Mary, Christ came out of heaven accompanied by a great multitude of angels, prophets, patriarchs and saints, and summoned Mary, who was borne body and soul into heaven where Christ seated her beside him on his throne and crowned her. It may be no coincidence that this description could also claim scriptural and typological sanction. The Old Testament type of the Coronation occurs in the story of Solomon (1 Kings 2.19): 'And the king rose up to meet her, and bowed himself unto her, and sat down on his throne, and caused a seat to be set for the king's mother, and she sat on his right hand.' In the early fifteenth century Mirk, whilst accenting the Coronation, retained this Solomonic framework. The author of the *Speculum Sacerdotale*, a work that bears strong similarities to Mirk's *Festial*, adopted a more evasive solution. Aware, perhaps, of the visible discrepancy between parish imagery and his source, he used the first part of Mirk's sermon on the Assumption which details the miraculous arrival of the apostles and the events of her funeral, but chose not to include the second part describing Mary's reception in heaven.

All these texts continued to circulate during the fifteenth century, and the *Golden Legend* and *Festial* were even produced in print by Caxton, but their reservations could not prevail. The hierarchical version of the Coronation retained its place in the visual culture of the parish in the fifteenth and early sixteenth centuries. By this period, the logic of Mary's powers made other descriptions seem less appropriate. The extent of her powers meant that they were compatible only with a process of delegation, and the emerging devotion to the Trinity made this form of bestowal a natural solution.

A disjunction between texts and parish imagery was also a feature when Mary's intercessory powers were envisaged in action. Her ability to determine the fate of souls, and to intercede on their behalf, was illustrated in portrayals of the Doom, or Last Judgement, and of St Michael weighing the souls that were probably to be found painted on the walls of every

kneeling (Cheetham, *English Medieval Alabasters*, p. 208). Wall paintings of the first type include those in the churches of St Olave's, Chichester (Sussex), Lower Halstow (Kent), Chilton Cantelo (Somerset) and Chalgrove (Oxon.). Pickering (Yorks.) has the Virgin crowned by the Trinity, but the composition is less clearly hierarchical than those in stained glass and alabaster.

parish church. The latter image was particularly striking in its assertion of the powers of Mary, who is shown in most paintings intervening in favour of the soul by placing her rosary in the balance (Fig. 13). This detail may be a result of Dominican influence, although many of these images pre-date the resurgence of interest in rosary devotion on the Continent in the 1470s, and it does not appear to have been adopted there.[7]

Despite the influence of Voragine, in England, and also in Wales, a concern to accent the importance of devotion to the Virgin more than her innate qualities seems to have led to this distinctive solution. With the possible exception of Catherington (Hampshire) no English wall painting depicted Voragine's description in which Mary puts her hand to the side of the balance containing the soul's few good deeds. Similarly, it is only at St Martin's, Ruislip (Middlesex) that Mary places the end of her robe in the scale. Such depictions emphasised the importance of contact with Mary and of powers inhering in her. In contrast, the presence of the rosary in the Soul Weighing symbolised the saving power of devotion to the Virgin. This visual rewriting indicates the priorities of parish culture, and represents a creative and selective use of the source texts: it was, after all, the power of Marian devotion which was emphasised in exempla included in compilations such as *The Golden Legend* and Mirk's *Festial*.[8]

Interpreting Mary's presence in the Soul Weighing in this way also helps to explain the change in the location of this image, which initially appears very puzzling. In the thirteenth and fourteenth centuries the Soul Weighing was frequently included in the Last Judgement. In this position, Mary's power to effect the ultimate salvation of souls was clear, but from the fourteenth century onwards it became less common to include this scene in the Doom. This may have been partly the result of the trend, which became pronounced in the course of the fifteenth century, of painting the Doom over the chancel arch, but this practical explanation does not sufficiently explain the completeness of the change.[9] In some churches the lack of height above the apex of the chancel arch made it difficult to depict both Christ in Majesty and

---

[7] The Dominican 'invention' and propagation of the rosary in Marian devotion is discussed in M. Warner, *Alone of all her Sex: The Myth and the Cult of the Virgin Mary* (London, 1976), pp. 306–9; L. Rothkrug, *Religious Practices and Collective Perceptions. Hidden Homologies in the Renaissance and Reformation*, Reflexions Historiques 7/1 (1980), pp. 95–99. For the distinctiveness of English and Welsh iconography see A. Breeze, 'The Virgin's rosary and St. Michael's scales', *Studia Celtica* 24–5 (1989–90), 91–8.

[8] F. S. Ellis (ed.), *The Golden Legend, or Lives of the Saints as Englished by William Caxton*, 7 vols. (London, 1928), vol. 4, p. 252.

[9] J. E. Ashby, 'English medieval murals of the Doom', M.Phil. thesis, University of York (1980), pp. 22, 107, 166–7. Ashby states that from the middle of the fifteenth century the Doom was normally placed over the chancel arch. In her sample of 65 complete Dooms from the fifteenth and early sixteenth centuries, 52 are found over the chancel arch and a further eight are on wooden tympana filling this position. This location began to be popular in the fourteenth century.

Figure 13 St Michael weighing a soul with the Virgin Mary interceding, Swalcliffe
(Oxon.)

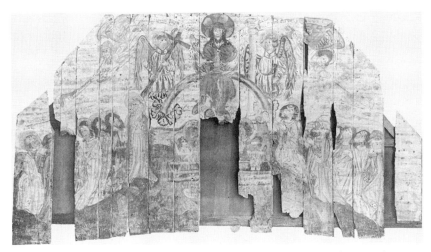

Figure 14 The second version of the Doom painting at Penn (Bucks.) emphasising Christ's passion

the Soul Weighing, but the option of adding a tympanum to extend the picture space was always available.[10] More significant was the new rationale that prompted the general move of the Doom to the chancel arch. Not only was this the focal point for the laity in the congregation, but also in this position the Doom was more clearly related to the rood group.[11] By linking the graphic portrayal of the fate of human souls to the suffering of Christ on the cross, the new arrangement reinforced the message of the developing Christocentric piety.

That this was so is demonstrated by the paintings at Penn (Buckinghamshire). Here, two versions of the Doom were painted over the chancel arch in the course of the fifteenth century. The first, dating from the early fifteenth century, included a depiction of St Michael weighing the souls assisted by the Virgin Mary, but the later painting, *c.* 1500, omitted this scene and focussed more closely on the passion of Christ, emphasised by the portrayal of angels bearing the instruments of the passion and the vivid depiction of the blood issuing from Christ's wounds (Fig. 14).[12]

Penn is unusual in providing an opportunity to distinguish clearly between successive layers of painting, and also in the initial inclusion of a Soul

[10] This solution can be seen, for example, at Pickworth (Lincs.), where the roof was lowered in the late fifteenth century. E. C. Rouse, 'Wall paintings in St. Andrew's church, Pickworth, Lincolnshire', *JBAA* 3rd ser. 13 (1950), 28.

[11] In some instances the standing figures of the rood group may have been incorporated into the painted scene of the Doom as, for example, at Wenhaston (Suffolk).

[12] E. C. Rouse, 'The Penn Doom', *Records of Bucks.* 17/2 (1962), 95–104.

Weighing in a Doom painted over the chancel arch. Generally, fifteenth-century Soul Weighings were separate scenes.[13] This change affected the view of Mary's intercessory powers, but was driven less by trends of Marian devotion than by a desire to define more closely the place of purgatory in the scheme of salvation.[14] In isolation, the Soul Weighing could be taken to refer only to the admission of souls into purgatory, and not to the Last Judgement, which involved the reunification of body and soul and the permanent entrance of both to the full bliss of heaven or the torments of hell.

It has often been noted that, despite the emphasis on purgatory in the proliferation of indulgences and intercessory masses, purgatory itself had little visual presence in late medieval religion.[15] The wall painting at Swanbourne (Buckinghamshire) has seemed to be a curious exception, an erudite rendition out of the mainstream of parish devotion (Fig. 15). However, the idea underpinning it seems to have had greater resonance. The painting portrays in three tiers the fate of different categories of souls: those who go straight to heaven, those accompanied by their good angel to purgatory, and those consigned to hell immediately after death. Such a scheme renders the Last Judgement redundant in terms of decision-making, since souls in purgatory can be confident of their eventual salvation. Instead, it marks the final reunification of body and soul at the general resurrection.[16] In this framework, if

---

[13] In the fifteenth century only one other surviving Doom, at Broughton, also in Buckinghamshire, included the scene, although here Mary was portrayed as the Madonna of Mercy sheltering souls within her cloak. The two examples from the early sixteenth century, Wenhaston (Suffolk) and Waltham Holy Cross (Essex), also have unusual Last Judgement iconography. This also suggests the dangers in using later sixteenth-century statements to summarise the immediate pre-Reformation situation. Lord Bacon, writing to Elizabeth I when she was uncertain whom to appoint, commented 'that hee had heard that in old time there was usually painted on the churche walls the Day of Doome, and God sitting in Judgement, and St. Michael by him with a paire of balance, and the soule and the good deeds in the one balance, and the faults and the evil deeds in the other, and the soules ballance went up farre too light: then was our Ladie painted with a great paire of beads, casting them into the light balance to make up the weight: so place and authoritie, which were in her hands to give, were like our Ladies beads, which though men, through diverse imperfections were too light before, yet, when they were cast in, made weight competent.' Cited in P. Slater, 'Ancient mural painting now discovered in Lindfield church', *Sussex Archaeological Collections* 2 (1849), 131.

[14] For changing perceptions of purgatory in the medieval period, and the development of a view of purgatory as a place of hope distinct from hell, see T. Matsuda, *Death and Purgatory in Middle English Didactic Poetry* (Cambridge, 1997).

[15] P. Binski, *Medieval Death: Ritual and Representation* (London, 1996), pp. 181–99, addresses the question of the non-representation of purgatory outside liturgical books, and suggests that this reflects the difficulty of adapting visual conventions from a binary to a ternary system.

[16] J. Slatter, 'Description of the paintings discovered on the north wall of Swanbourne church, Buckinghamshire', *Records of Bucks.* 3 (1870), 136. This is also the interpretation offered in the Judgement play in the Chester cycle in which souls know from their experience in purgatory or hell whether they are damned or saved. Christ does not judge, but explains the limits of his mercy. Dr Matthews (ed.), *The Chester Plays, part 2*, EETS extra ser. 115 (London, 1916), pp. 427–53.

Figure 15 Drawing of the wall painting of purgatory, Swanbourne (Bucks.)

the image of the Last Judgement is conceived as a single historical moment, then the Soul Weighing can have no place within it.

The Soul Weighing depicted separately from the Last Judgement can therefore be seen as visualising the decisive moment shortly after death when the fate of the soul is determined. This involved a significant reorientation of ideas. It brought Mary's role back more closely to the Apocalypse of Mary source text, and, more importantly, allowed the idea of purgatory to be incorporated in depictions of the economy of salvation in the parish church. The Virgin could still be attributed a significant role in this event, but this was understood in such a way as to reinforce the view that her powers were delegated. This was largely due to the importance of Christ's passion in parish religion, as underlined by the change in the iconography and position of the Doom. It is no accident that the mystery plays had no place for the Soul Weighing, or for an exposition of how one could enter purgatory. Taking as their theme the cycle of christian history from the Fall to the Redemption and the Last Judgement, what was important was the role of Christ's passion, as emblematised by his wounds.[17] The later medieval revision of the iconography of the Doom shared the same concerns.

The appropriate roles of Mary and Christ in this understanding were most clearly delineated in texts describing visions of purgatory. A particularly good example is the late fourteenth-century *Gast of Gy*, which exists in several manuscripts, and takes the form of a dialogue between a friar and a spirit in purgatory who visits his former home.[18] The narrator does not provide a visual description that matches the parish iconography, but the procedures he outlines fit this closely and accord with the Swanbourne scheme.[19] When asked by the prior about the fate of the soul at death, the spirit of Gy explains that those who die in deadly sin, unshriven and without any sorrow or contrition, will be reminded of Christ's passion by a good angel and then carried away to hell by the fiends. Those who have died with the last rites, but have not made full satisfaction of their sins, will be defended by the good angels from the fiends. The devils' case that the deceased has sinned and therefore belongs to them will be countered by the argument of the angels: the merits of Christ's passion and of his wounds are a shield between the deceased and the fiends and will wash away his sins so that he will experience the transitory pains of purgatory rather than those of everlasting damnation.

In this scheme, the Virgin Mary's role is clearly subordinated to a Christo-centric framework. All those who die shriven receive the assistance of Mary, but, although her list of titles is impressive ('I am mayde and mother of ihesu crist, queene of hevene, and lady of þe world and emperice of helle'), her role is to pray to Christ, who is her son and also king of heaven, 'þat he iugge þys mannus soule to þe stede of purgatory'. Also, as Mary goes on to explain, it is 'þurow þe wille of my swete sone' that almsdeeds and masses will alleviate the suffering of the soul. In fact, the only specific power Mary has is to stop the fiends annoying the soul of one who has received the sacrament, but here Mary is policing a clear-cut rule, rather than exercising judgement in

---

[17] See, especially, the prominence of the wounds in the Towneley play. A. W. Pollard (ed.), *The Towneley Plays*, EETS extra ser. 71 (London, 1897, repr. 1952), pp. 367–87.

[18] R. H. Bowers (ed.), *The Gast of Gy: A Middle English Religious Prose Tract Preserved in Queen's College, Oxford, MS. 383*, Beiträge zur englischen Philologie 23 (Leipzig, 1938).

[19] The narrator is concerned that the experience of his protagonist should not be confused with superstitious ideas about ghosts whose outward form can be seen with the bodily eye, and this may explain why he avoids graphic visual descriptions of purgatory.

determining the soul's fate. Although both Mary and Christ are considered merciful, the text 'Jesu mercy, lady help' largely summarises their division of labour.[20]

Of course, such precise nuances were not always honoured. A later passage in *The Gast of Gy* seems to imply that devotion to Mary causes her to secure salvation for the soul.[21] For many though, perhaps especially amongst the clergy, the idea that Mary could act independently was seen as a risk to be circumvented. It is striking that, despite its presence in the *Golden Legend*, the Soul Weighing is not very developed in fifteenth-century texts. Both Mirk and the author of the *Speculum Sacerdotale* can produce sermons for St Michael's day without mentioning his role in the Soul Weighing directly. Their principal aim is to show Michael as the most trusted executant of God's will and the most capable fighter against the forces of darkness.[22]

Thus, although the image of St Michael weighing the souls with the Virgin interceding was a frequent one, it raised some concern lest too great powers should be attributed to Mary. The rosary was therefore employed to emphasise the importance of devotion rather than her person, and some artists were concerned to make the connection between Mary and the Soul Weighing less direct. The solution at Cullompton (Devon) in which the Madonna of Mercy is portrayed below the Soul Weighing is more plausibly viewed as an iconographical strategy than as a simple response to a problem of space: artists elsewhere were not averse to solving spatial problems by discrepancies of scale. The painter at Bovey Tracey, also in Devon, adopted an unusual linear composition to associate the Soul Weighing, the Virgin Mary and the Lamb of God in a manner that would have met the approval of the author of *The Gast of Gy*.[23] For some later fifteenth-century artists, it was clearly going too far to say, as Mirk had done, that Mary was 'of on wyll and one love with the holy Trinyte that grauntyth hur what that ever sho askyth, and at hur prayer rewardyth all hur servauntes.'[24] The idea of Mary's extensive intercessory powers survived the transition from the Last Judgement to purgatory, but the very success of this development prompted theological concerns at parish level. In this view, the powers delegated to Mary at the Coronation gave her considerable influence, but to identify her will with that of the Trinity was inappropriate.

[20] Bowers (ed.), *The Gast of Gy*, pp. 25–6.   [21] Ibid., p. 36.

[22] Erbe (ed.), *Mirk's Festial*, pp. 257–60. The intervention of the Virgin shortly after death, but not the Soul Weighing, is delineated in Mirk's sermon 'In die sepulture' (p. 297); E. H. Weatherly (ed.), *Speculum Sacerdotale*, EETS orig. ser. 200 (London, 1936), pp. 210–15.

[23] P. C. Delagarde, 'A supplement to an account of the church of St Andrew, Cullompton', *Transactions of the Exeter Diocesan Architectural and Archaeological Society*, 1st ser. 3 (1849), 264 pl. 34; 'Quarterly Report', *Transactions of the Exeter Diocesan Architectural and Archaeological Society* 1st ser. 6 (1861), 310–11, pl. 53.

[24] See p. 63.

The removal of the Soul Weighing from the Last Judgement was not the only change to the portrayal of Mary's intercessory role. The Virgin Mary and St John were customarily depicted kneeling in prayer on either side of the central figure of Christ, and this continued to be the case throughout the period. However, Mary's intercessory role was gradually assumed to have a different basis that matched the shift from a Voragine-style to a Mirk-style interpretation of the origins of her powers. During the fifteenth century it became unusual for the supplicating figure of Mary to be shown baring her breasts.[25] The weakening of maternal ties, and especially of the emphasis on the mother's nursing role, in conceptions of Mary's ability to intercede was part of a general trend in devotion in late medieval England that emphasised the adult Christ at the expense of the infant.

Thus, although in France the Infancy cycle was still commonly used to illustrate Books of Hours, in England the Passion cycle became more popular in the fifteenth century.[26] In wall paintings in English parish churches, scenes of the Nativity became less frequent, especially as cycles of the life of Christ and of Mary became less common. The later development of the Nativity scene, inspired by the vision of St Bridget of Sweden in which the Christ Child was portrayed in a mandorla of light adored by the Virgin Mary, does not appear to have been adopted in wall painting, despite its occasional use in the more élite media of stained glass and jewellery. Where detailed narrative Christological series were still attempted, as at South Newington (Oxfordshire), their focus was the events of his passion, rather than his life as a whole, and they were combined with emblematic and abstract images of the cult of the Five Wounds and the instruments of the passion (Fig. 22). Also illustrative of this shift away from Christ's infancy was the decision taken at Beckley (Oxfordshire) to paint a separate Soul Weighing over the delicate fourteenth-century image of Mary suckling the Christ Child (Fig. 16).

The increasingly Christocentric focus of late medieval piety, with its emphasis on the suffering Christ of the Crucifixion, promoted a re-evaluation of the role of Mary: she became primarily a witness who was intimately involved with the sufferings of Christ, and well placed to communicate her anguish to the human race. It was this understanding, rather than the claim of biological maternity, which underpinned her ability to intercede on behalf of those devoted to her. The image of Our Lady of Pity (Pietà), which had a

---

[25] Of the 36 fifteenth- and early sixteenth-century Dooms with complete Judgement groups listed in Ashby's catalogue, only two examples show Mary baring her breasts. The Doom at Chesterton (Cambs.) dates from the late fifteenth century and has unusual iconography. The supplicating figures are small and on the arms of the rood. The painting at Oddington (Glos.) is dated to the early fifteenth century.

[26] F. Lewis, 'From image to illustration: The place of devotional images in the Book of Hours', in G. Duchet-Suchaux (ed.), *Iconographie médiévale – Image, texte, contexte* (Paris, 1990), pp. 31–2.

Figure 16 Two layers of wall painting at Beckley (Oxon.): the Virgin suckling the Christ Child and the Soul Weighing with the Virgin interceding, surrounded by the torments of souls in purgatory

Figure 17 Early fifteenth-century alabaster Pietà

prominent place in, probably, every parish church, confirmed this reorientation of Mary's maternal role (Fig. 17).[27] In depicting the Virgin holding the

[27] E. Waterton, *Pietas Mariana Britannica: A History of English Devotion to the Most Blessed
Virgin Marye* [*sic*] *Mother of God* (London, 1879), p. 240, asserts that a statue of the Pietà
would be found in every church. The evidence for this cannot be conclusive, although the
frequency of references in churchwardens' accounts and wills suggests that such images
were widespread. F. P. Tudor, 'Changing private belief and practice in English devotional

body of Christ after it has been taken down from the cross, the link between Mary and other mothers was not the shared experience of childbirth and care for an infant, but the difficulty of accepting the death of one's child. This is elaborated in the mid-fifteenth-century poem 'The Complaint of Mary to other Mothers', which was inspired by the sight of an image of the Pietà. In each verse women are asked, in contemplating their own children, to imagine the sufferings of Mary at the loss of her son. The first verse conveys the flavour of the poem:

> Of all wemen that ever were borne,
> That bere childer, abide and see
> How my sone lyeth me beforne,
> Upon my skirte, taken from the Tree.
> Youre children ye daunce upon youre knee,
> With laghyng, kissing and mery chere:
> Beholde my childe, beholde wele me,
> For now lyeth dedd my dere sone, dere.[28]

In such an appeal there is no sanctification of the virtues of motherhood. Although the image of Our Lady of Pity appealed to a maternal instinct, the connection with the birth of Christ was attenuated. Mary's concern was a parental one, which, unless we think that late medieval fathers were not attached to their children, was not gender specific. Mary's grief, far from striking a chord amongst mothers alone, was more commonly understood to stand for the general grief of mankind for the necessity of Christ's sacrifice. As an object of devotion, the image of Our Lady of Pity appealed to both male and female parishioners. Although the poet addressed mothers, Mary's sorrow, illustrated poignantly in the tear she sheds in the painting of the Pietà at Thame (Oxfordshire), formed the focus of affective piety for the laity as a whole (Fig. 18).

Mary's qualifications for this role were only partly those of a mother. Of greater importance was her ability to provide an impassioned testimony to the final stages of Christ's life on earth. Her relationship with her son, whose sacrifice redeemed the sins of the world, was limited to that of a human, maternal mourner. But she was more than an uncomprehending observer. Not only does she lament the sufferings of her child, she also assumes the task of confronting erring mortals with the horror of their blasphemous deeds. Her parental concern for her son is coupled with a parental concern

literature, c. 1475–1550', D.Phil. thesis, University of Oxford (1984), p. 108, notes that many printed and manuscript primers contain short prayers to be said before a crucifix on rising, on entering a church and before an image of pity. See also R. Woolf, *The English Religious Lyric in the Middle Ages* (Oxford, 1968), Appendix F – 'The history of the Pietà', pp. 392–4.

[28] R. T. Davies (ed.), *Medieval English Lyrics* (London, 1963), pp. 210–12.

Figure 18 Detail of Mary weeping tears of blood from the Pietà at Thame (Oxon.)

to admonish God's children on earth. Thus, in a story included in *Dives and Pauper*, a righteous justice, who was given to much swearing, is confronted by Mary holding a wounded and bloody child, and is asked to prescribe a penalty for the offender. When he replies that hanging and eternal damnation would be a fit punishment, Mary explains that he is the guilty man:

Thu art the same man, for Y hadde nevyr child but this alone whiche was borne of my body for savacion of al mankende, and thu, as mychyll as is in the, hast put out his eyne when thu swore by Gods eyne. Thu rentist out his herte whan thu swore be Godis herte. Thu hast al torent hym with thin foul othis. And therfor ament the or thu schalt han the same doom that thu hast gevyn and hangyn be by the nekke in the feer of helle withoutyn ende.[29]

The extent to which admonition, coupled with an emotive concern for the injuries sustained by Christ, was internalised in the laity's view of Mary's role is demonstrated by the striking images of the Warning to Swearers in wall paintings and stained glass. The iconography of the

[29] Barnum (ed.), *Dives and Pauper*, pp. 240–1. Slightly different versions of this story occur in other texts. For example, Robert of Brunne's *Handlyng Synne*, unlike its French source, gives the story of a rich man who sees the same vision. This account lacks the element of unwitting self-accusation, but emphasises Mary's frustration: she wants to pray for mankind, but wonders why she should when such oath-swearing pains Christ more than the action of the Jews at the Crucifixion. Furnivall (ed.), *Handlyng Synne*, pp. 25–8.

window formerly at Heydon (Norfolk) can be taken as typical. Many young swearers, drunkards and dice players, together with a representation of hell, were depicted arranged around an image of the Virgin holding the body of Christ. A scroll gave the text of the Virgin's lamentation, 'Alas my child, have they the[e] thus dyth. The cursed swearers, al be hys lemys be rent asunderyth.' In wall painting, the best-known surviving example is at Broughton (Buckinghamshire) and is a similarly dramatic portrayal, whilst the painting at Corby Glen (Lincolnshire) broadens the scope of this theme to incorporate the Seven Deadly Sins more directly (Fig. 19).[30]

Given her didactic role, albeit one tempered with compassionate emotion, Mary cannot be seen as a 'soft touch'. Despite the initial impression that a few conventional gestures of Marian devotion, like saying the rosary, will awaken an endlessly compassionate maternal instinct to ensure salvation for the individual, a fuller view has to incorporate an understanding of Mary as a parent aiming to discipline her children and to influence all aspects of their everyday behaviour. It is therefore mistaken to assume, as many psychologists of religion have done, that emotion and discipline characterise female and male religious role models respectively.[31] Recognising this, although vital for our understanding, does, of course, complicate an assessment of the meaning of figures like Mary in terms of gender. However, it would be equally wrong to conclude that in such a framework Mary is completely stripped of gender significance. Marian meanings fluctuated both chronologically and according to context. Before the fifteenth century, in an era of Virgin and Child imagery when images of the deadly sins were separated from any direct Christocentric and Marian association, Mary's admonitory role was not so pronounced. Additionally, as McMurray Gibson has pointed out, different ritualisations of the same scene from the Virgin's life could simultaneously have more and less gendered resonances. Taking the Purification of Mary as her example, she contrasts its dramatisation in the all-female context of the churching ceremony with its use in much less clearly gendered civic ceremonial.[32]

In attempting to assess the significance of the late medieval emphasis on Mary's role as the parent of an adult child, it is also necessary to reflect more clearly on the nature of the appeal of the earlier Virgin and Child imagery

[30] M. R. James, 'The iconography of Buckinghamshire', *Records of Bucks.* 12 (1932), 289, cites Blomefield's description in his *History of Norfolk* (1769, vol. 3, p. 537) of the window formerly at Heydon; E. C. Rouse, 'Wall paintings in the church of St. John the evangelist, Corby, Lincs.', *Arch. Jnl.* 100 (1943), 160.

[31] B. Beit-Hallahmi and M. Argyle, *The Psychology of Religious Behaviour, Belief and Experience* (London, 1997), esp. Ch. 6, summarises relevant research findings.

[32] G. McMurray Gibson, 'Blessing from sun and moon: churching as women's theater', in B. Hanawalt and D. Wallace (eds.), *Bodies and Disciplines: Intersections of Literature and History in Fifteenth-Century England* (Minneapolis and London, 1996), pp. 139–54.

Figure 19 Warning to swearers, Broughton (Bucks.)

that this largely replaced. The easy assumption that such images represented
an elevation and sanctification of motherhood, and thus appealed especially
to women and provided them with powerful and comforting role models
in the religious sphere, may be part, but certainly is not all, of the story.
Bynum's work on the importance of the idea of nurturing, and on the interchangeability in religious terms of milk, blood and the eucharist as sustaining metaphors, reminds us that such images will be more complex than
a straightforward transcription of domestic circumstance. In the same way
as we have learnt to see the images of St Anne teaching the Virgin to read
as more than intimate portrayals of the learning process in the context of
the family, Virgin and Child imagery needs to be considered in a broader

framework.[33] By doing so, we can also remove the apparent anomaly of the presence in the male-dominated (at least in terms of patronage) parish church of imagery relating only to female concerns. As Ashley and Sheingorn have pointed out in their consideration of the cult of St Anne, such figures were, following the anthropological analysis of Turner, 'polyvalent or polysemic symbols'. St Anne could stand for fruitful maternity, and thus be held in regard by both barren and fertile women, or she could stand for the 'genderless idea of lineage and dynasty'.[34]

An important, and frequently neglected, question is how men responded to representations of the Virgin Mary. Historians of the Middle Ages have suggested that Mary was, in fact, more central to male than to female religious experience. Simone Roisin, for example, concludes an analysis of thirteenth-century visions with the observation that the Virgin Mary appeared more often to men than to women.[35] Intuitively this seems surprising, but this is because we are confusing the role of such figures as social models (a woman who gives birth) that are assumed to involve gender correlation, and the role of such figures as models of aspired-to religious attitudes (a woman as an exemplar of christian humility). To the extent that christian virtues were equated with ideal female characteristics and that Christianity involved renunciation and reversal, the model for the religious man had to be a woman, and especially the Virgin Mary, but following the Virgin could not entail a satisfactory renunciation for women. As Bynum explains,

The male writer who saw his soul as a bride of God or his religious role as womanly submission and humility was conscious of using an image of reversal. He sought reversal because reversal and renunciation were at the heart of a religion whose dominant symbol is the cross – life achieved through death. When a woman writer (often but not always a virgin) spoke of herself as either bride or knight, each image was in a sense a reversal. But neither was as highly charged as the notion of the male as bride or woman, for neither expressed renunciation. Because women were women they could not embrace the female as a symbol of renunciation. Because society was male-dominated, they could not embrace the male as a symbol of renunciation. To become male was elevation, not renunciation, and elevation was a less significant reversal given the values at the heart of medieval Christianity.[36]

This understanding goes a long way towards explaining the capacity of the Virgin Mary to appeal to the opposite sex, but it is of little help in clarifying

[33] W. Scase, 'St Anne and the education of the Virgin: literary and artistic traditions and their implications', in N. Rogers (ed.), *Harlaxton Medieval Studies III: England in the Fourteenth Century* (Stamford, 1993), pp. 81–96; P. Sheingorn, 'The wise mother: the image of St. Anne teaching the Virgin Mary', *Gesta* 32/1 (1993), 69–80.
[34] K. Ashley and P. Sheingorn (eds.), *Interpreting Cultural Symbols: Saint Anne in Late Medieval Society* (Athens, Georgia, and London, 1990), p. 5.
[35] Cited in C. W. Bynum, *Fragmentation and Redemption: Essays on Gender and the Human Body in Medieval Religion* (New York, 1991), p. 153.
[36] Ibid., p. 171.

the significance of different emphases in the representation of her, since it views the Virgin as an isolated emblem of feminine christian virtues. Put simply, does an image of the Virgin suckling the Christ Child work in the same way as a Pietà? In the former, from the perspective of the child or the human soul, Mary represents a haven of security, a source of nurture that is both comforting and essential to development and well being. It is, moreover, an image that has the potential to awaken the child within, whilst possibly carrying erotic overtones. Though much of this may be unacknowledged, its influence cannot be completely discounted. In contrast, the image of the Pietà is self-evidently a less comforting one. Powerless maternal grief has replaced maternal succour. The attractive vulnerability of the child, made possible by the fact that its wants are cared for, is now the suffering of a man who is an instrument of his father's will and whom his mother cannot assist.

Of course, since the child can represent the human soul, much of this could apply equally to the female viewer, although complicated by the possibility of a stronger identification with the mother's role. However, even viewed from this perspective, the image of the Pietà portrays a woman who is less able to cope with the demands placed on her as a mother than is the case in images of the Virgin and Child. Whatever the viewpoint, the later emphasis on the Pietà seems to involve the absence of reassuring, and secure, roles that define the relationship of both men and women with Mary. In the same way as intercession combined with admonition creates a confusion of roles, so the helpless mother is seen as losing control and her function as a source of comfort. Both the changes in the way in which Mary was perceived to intervene on behalf of the christian, and the new emphasis on her relation with the adult crucified Christ, served to diminish the clarity of her gender significance. Whether viewed in psychological or theological terms, Mary has become the witness, representative and tutor of mankind, largely drained of her maternal attributes. In later medieval Christocentric religion, Mary is neither the aloof ideal of the perfect woman mounted on a pedestal nor reassuringly maternal, and it is no coincidence that Mary was no longer more central to male than to female religious experience.[37]

The emphasis on Christ's passion was not only significant in terms of its impact on the role of Mary, it also affected the importance of gender in the relationship of the laity to Christ. It opened up possibilities that differed significantly from earlier medieval experience, and also from the understanding of mystical writers that had stimulated these developments. The close association of the Doom with the rood group, and the popularity of the image of the Pietà, emphasised the wounds and passion of the incarnate Christ,

[37] See p. 47.

and also served to alleviate the severity of his judgement (Figs. 14 and 20). Christ's incarnation and mortal death involved an understanding and acceptance of human frailty, and the mercy of Christ's sacrifice was carried through to the mercy of Christ in judgement. This message, underlined by the angels who appear in many fifteenth-century Dooms carrying the instruments of the passion, received its supreme rendition in a detail in the Last Judgement at Wymington (Bedfordshire). Here, above the entrance gate to the city of Jerusalem through which St Peter leads the saved, is a small shield emblazoned with the Five Wounds of Christ (Fig. 21).

The cult of the Five Wounds of Christ, like the cult of the Name of Jesus, grew in popularity in the later Middle Ages. Developed amongst mystics and the cloistered, both became dominant features of parish religion, being enshrined in the liturgy and buttressed by papal grants of indulgences. Masses of the wounds first occurred in the early fourteenth century, and during the course of that century Pope John XXII and Pope Innocent VI granted seven years' indulgence to those looking at, wearing or kissing a representation of the side wound, from which eucharistic water and blood was thought to have flowed.[38] By the fifteenth and early sixteenth centuries, the cult of the Five Wounds seems to have been as popular as that of the side wound, perhaps as the connection with the eucharist became less direct. It spread from Books of Hours and became a common choice in decorating bench ends, fine examples of which still survive in many Cornish and Devon parish churches. Lewis, considering the relative popularity of a group of devotional images of the passion in Books of Hours, concludes that in this medium depiction of the wounds enjoyed less popularity than the Veronica, the *arma Christi* or the man of sorrows. For this she offers no explanation, although her further comment that the wounds were more frequent in prayer rolls may point us in the right direction.[39] The wounds, more than the other images, seem to have had a stronger amuletic quality, as illustrated most clearly by the concern to ascertain the precise measure of the side wound or the number of drops of blood.

The belief that a parchment inscribed with the measure of the wounds, and an appeal to Longinus the centurion who pierced Christ's side with his spear, would stop the wearer's flow of blood provides an obvious example of religious faith in mimetic healing, but it scarcely accounts for the strength

---

[38] M. Rubin, *Corpus Christi: The Eucharist in Late Medieval Culture* (Cambridge, 1991), pp. 303–4. The significance of indulgences in promoting late medieval devotions is, however, less clear. Although frequent in manuscripts, they rarely appeared in Books of Hours printed for the English market and do not seem to have been a strong selling point. F. Lewis, ' "Garnyshed with gloryous tytles": indulgences in printed Books of Hours in England', *Transactions of the Cambridge Bibliographical Society* 10 (1995), 577–90.

[39] Lewis, 'From image to illustration', p. 43.

Figure 20 Indulgenced Pietà with instruments of the passion

Figure 21 The entrance to heaven with the shield of the Five Wounds at
Wymington (Beds.)

of the cult of the wounds.[40] In fact, their emblematic, rather than amuletic, qualities were of much greater significance. As summarised by the English version of the host salutation,

> Through virtue of your wounds v.
> That ʒsuffryd in ʒoure lyve
> Have mercy on me. Amen,

the Five Wounds encapsulated the passion and crucifixion of Christ in a way that was more powerful than a simple description of a body hanging on the cross.[41] In part this was because they fitted in with the need for numerical structures in repetitive prayers, but more important was the need to distance the passion of Christ from a human drama of suffering. Although the incarnation was central to the understanding of late medieval religion, this was informed by a sense that such a miracle was almost beyond human comprehension. As such, it could seem inappropriate to assimilate the figure of Christ on the cross to any other human. Thus, despite the apparently human fascination with the blood-bespattered body of Christ, this was only comprehensible by a process of emblematisation. Any other route, as the experience of Mary in the Pietà illustrated, would founder with the use of inappropriate tools of comprehension, even if the sight could stir contrition. Such concerns make sense of the paintings in the nave at South Newington (Oxfordshire) where narrative scenes of Christ's passion are interspersed with shields of the Five Wounds and instruments of the passion suspended from trefoil trees, perhaps an abstract allusion to the Trinity (Fig. 22).

The cult of the Five Wounds therefore needs to be understood as a product of the same religious viewpoint that produced the parallel devotion to the instruments of the passion, which had no strong independent existence in Books of Hours. From the fourteenth-century wall painting of the instruments of the passion in separate roundels at Smarden (Kent) to their frequent inclusion on bench ends in the fifteenth and sixteenth centuries, and in the Last Judgement, the English concern for them differed significantly from that on the Continent. There they were much more likely to be depicted as the backdrop to an image of Christ as the Man of Sorrows, and in this context, although abstracted, the instruments evoked a much tighter narrative connection. In contrast, the English instruments allowed contemplation of the passion that was separated, as far as possible, from the human experience of Christ.

Two other devotions, which enjoyed significant popularity in the later medieval period, also support this interpretation of the nature of late medieval

[40] Rubin, *Corpus Christi*, p. 305.   [41] Ibid., p. 304.

Figure 22 Shield with the instruments of the passion, South Newington (Oxon.)

Christocentric devotion in England: the pelican in her piety and the head of St John the Baptist. Both these devotions could be seen as prefigurations of Christ's passion as well as being emotive emblems. The pelican, a bird that, it was thought, pierced its breast to feed its young with its own blood, was an obvious type of Christ's passion, and the severed head of John the Baptist on a platter was seen as a prefiguration of the eucharist. But in developing these cults, late medieval piety was continuing the process of displacing affective devotion from the person of Christ. Piety, although strongly Christocentric, developed a symbolic language to ensure a distance from Christ that became more important to maintain as devotion became more centred upon Christ.

All this suggests that the mystic's desire to hide in the wounds of Christ was far from the experience of most of the laity.[42] For them, the wounds may have been less clearly entrances or apertures than vivid testimony to the passion of Christ and the attendant promise of salvation offered to fallen humanity. The instruments of the passion were almost as important as the wounds. This needs stressing because much of the commentary on late medieval Christocentric piety has assumed that the gradual diffusion of these cults from the world of mystics and the cloistered occurred without any significant change of content. Of course, there is some basis for this case. Mystical writings did enjoy some circulation, and these ideas could filter into collections of prayers. However, the specific selection and integration of these ideas into a parish context was not a precise transcription. Just as parish iconography offered no place for the theme of mystic marriage with Christ,[43] so the mystical understanding of the wounds was less central to ordinary parishioners.

For such people, Christ's body was still an 'organising metaphor'.[44] The idea of the body politic underpinned notions of society, and partaking of Christ's body in the form of the eucharist required members of a community to be in charity with each other. But beyond this unifying ideal, the devotional implications are less clear. Rituals of unity are attempts to conceal underlying social fragility – parishioners who are supposed to take communion together may not always be in charity with each other – but we need to question whether this creates, as Beckwith argues, a devotional fascination with the 'borders and boundaries of Christ's body'. In her view

> It is precisely because of the failure of Christ's body to function as an image of unity, the impossibility of that project, that in late medieval crucifixion piety it is the borders and boundaries of Christ's body . . . that become the object of obsessive interest and attention. Late medieval crucifixion piety is a curiously literal embodiment of a drama of exclusion and participation in that body. For affective piety is obsessed with belonging, with the fantasy of fusion and the bitter reality of separation, and so with the entrances to Christ's body.[45]

For most of the laity, however, the entrances of Christ's body did not feed a 'fantasy of fusion'. The reality of separation was not bitter, but rather the heart of the mystery of redemption, and the only way in which the amazing

---

[42] For a discussion of the gender implications of this desire in texts written principally for the female religious see F. Lewis, 'The wound in Christ's side and the instruments of the passion: gendered experience and response', in L. Smith and J. H. M. Taylor (eds.), *Women and the Book: Assessing the Visual Evidence* (London and Toronto, 1996), pp. 204–29.

[43] See pp. 113–15.

[44] S. Beckwith, *Christ's Body: Identity, Culture and Society in Late Medieval Writings* (London and New York, 1993), p. 1.

[45] Ibid., p. 42.

events of the incarnation and crucifixion could be conceptualised. There was a concern with the entrances to Christ's body, but not as apertures. Rather they were the sites of interaction of human and divine behaviour, signalling their incompatibility and interconnectedness. The wounds on Christ's body inflicted by blasphemers or Sabbath breakers, as depicted in the vivid paintings of these themes on the walls of parish churches, were far removed from a fantasy of fusion. Participation in that body was unwitting, and subsequently a cause for regret. Such images also encapsulated the understanding of the wounds of the crucified Christ. The prominence of the instruments of the passion can be understood in the same way as that of the tools used on the Sabbath: both were graphic illustrations of man's misguided actions.

Very little parish-focussed imagery explored the possibility of Christ's wounds as entrances. The exception is the portrayal of the resolution of Thomas's doubt in which Thomas's hand placed in the wound in Christ's side convinces him of the Resurrection. The fifteenth-century innovation, in what was never a very frequently chosen image, was to make it Christ who placed Thomas's hand into the wound (Fig. 23).[46] This revision was clearly part of the same distancing strategy mentioned earlier: it was now seen as too presumptuous for Thomas to take the initiative in entering Christ's body. But in terms of mystical aspiration, St Thomas was always a rather unsatisfactory model. His physical intimacy with Christ was the result not of spiritual ascent, but of faith shot through with doubt. In the process, he learned a lesson rather than experiencing the mystic's ecstasy. His experience, and probably the horizons of most of the laity, was similar to the sermon exemplum in which a woman who refused to make confession of a dark sin encounters Christ in a vision; Christ places her hand in his side wound so that she can feel his intestines, and then tells her that just as he has shown her the hidden parts of his body, so she should confess her concealed sins.[47] The wounds on Christ's body were, therefore, marks of human failure and of divine assistance. Although welcomed by the laity as emblems of hope, they chastised as well as comforted, and did not generally stimulate aspirations of fusion.

In this context, despite the hostile reception she gained in some places on her travels, Margery Kempe is a better guide to lay response than mystics

---

[46] G. McMurray Gibson, *The Theater of Devotion: East Anglian Drama and Society in the Late Middle Ages* (Chicago, 1989), pp. 16–18. This interpretation was already present in texts of the fourteenth century, occurring in Langland's *Piers Plowman*. It was also adopted by the cycles of mystery plays, and developed further in those plays with a strong emphasis on Christ's wounds, the Cornish *Origo Mundi* and the York plays.

[47] W. O. Ross (ed.), *Middle English Sermons Edited from BM MS Royal 18B xxiii*, EETS orig. ser. 209 (London, 1940), pp. 216–17. The story also appears in the *Speculum Laicorum* and in the sermons of Mirk and Bromyard.

Figure 23 Fifteenth-century alabaster panel depicting Christ placing St Thomas's
hand in his side

like Julian of Norwich.[48] Although far from a typical laywoman, Margery's
encounter with the world of the mystics, and yet her failure to absorb many of
its key characteristics, strengthens the case for the reading of lay experience

[48] There are numerous studies of Margery Kempe. These include C. W. Atkinson, *Mystic
and Pilgrim: The Book and the World of Margery Kempe* (Cornell, 1983) and K. Lochrie,
Margery Kempe and Translations of the Flesh (Philadelphia, 1991).

so far outlined. Margery's 'material mysticism' involves an overwhelming affective Christocentric piety, which is focussed on Christ's passion and on his wounds, and often manifested quite literally in floods of tears provoked by the sight of an image of Christ on the cross.[49] But her experience does not involve a real 'fantasy of fusion'. Her religious self-conception is more strongly rooted in the world of parish piety than in that of the mystics, despite her acquaintance with the latter and with their writings. An anchorite whom she consults turns her experience into the language of physically intimate mysticism, but the idea that she is 'sucking at Christ's breast' is a notion that is foreign to Margery's own understanding, and is not applied by her to her own experiences anywhere in the text.[50]

Christ can be Margery's love, as the inscription 'Ihesus est amor meus' on her ring testifies, and she can undergo a wedding ceremony with God according to the liturgical conventions of the Sarum Use, but this is not conceptualised in terms of a mystical physical intimacy.[51] Following the wedding, God explains its significance in terms of cementing his commitment to care for her and to guide her as a patriarchal husband, and of her meek and submissive obedience. Physical intimacy with the Godhead cannot be easily imagined. It is upon Christ that Margery continues to rely, and to Christ that she continues to direct her love. Despite Margery's modelling of herself on the saints, resulting most notably in her anxieties about virginity and chastity, and the model of the saint as the bride of Christ, Margery cannot envisage a mystical marriage with Christ. He may sit in her soul, but her soul is a chamber that she and the saints can decorate with flowers and spices to encourage him to visit. The image of Margery setting out three coloured cushions in her soul for God, Christ and the Holy Spirit to sit on underlines how far Margery's mystical meditations are from fusion.[52]

Christ in Margery's account consistently addresses her as his daughter, and where wifely metaphors are used they appear in conjunction: Margery is daughter, wife and mother. Such usage parallels addresses to the Virgin Mary in medieval devotion which suspend the normal laws of familial relationships to underline the extraordinary truth of Christ's incarnation and provide comprehensive models of the christian's love for Christ. When Christ uses wifely metaphors to instruct Margery, he does so in terms of a wife's uncertainty about the love of her husband, and her preparations to receive him after

[49] S. Beckwith, 'A very material mysticism: The medieval mysticism of Margery Kempe', in D. Aers (ed.), *Medieval Literature: Criticism, Ideology and History* (Brighton, 1988), pp. 34–57.

[50] S. B. Meech and E. H. Allen (eds.), *The Book of Margery Kempe The Text from the Unique Manuscript Owned by Colonel W. Butler-Bowden*, EETS orig. ser. 212 (London, 1940), p. 18: 'Dowtyr ȝe sowkyn evyn on Crystys brest'.

[51] Meech and Allen (eds.), *The Book of Margery Kempe*, pp. 78, 86–9.

[52] Ibid., pp. 210–11.

an absence. The reception that is envisaged is not the delights of the marriage bed, but the reception of Christ's body and blood in the form of the
eucharist.[53] Being the wife of Christ, just like being his daughter, is a way
of understanding the nature of Christ's love and of the appropriate love
of the individual for Christ. Even when the bounds of intimacy are most
clearly crossed, when Christ gives Margery permission to kiss his mouth,
head and feet in her soul, she is given the composite role of daughter, wife
and mother.[54] The divine love that is given to her is carefully measured. If it
were not, Christ informs her, it would be too overwhelming for her to cope
with. Moreover, its withdrawal is also necessary so that she can begin to
recognise its value and its divine origin, even if she will not fully appreciate
what she has been granted until she can review this in heaven.[55] But being
in heaven holds out the prospect not of closer union with the divine, but
simply of freedom from the doubts incurred in expressing the grace of love
for Christ in an uninhibited manner in the world. When Margery is incorporated into heaven, Christ and Mary will take her by the hand and dance
with her and the saints.[56]

The process of spiritual development outlined in Margery's *Booke* is not an
ascent towards mystical physical intimacy. Love is manifested towards her
in two forms: the grace to intercede on behalf of sinners, and her capacity to
witness that grace and her love of Christ to the world by her uncontrollable
devotional weeping and by miracles. That her weeping, and commitment
to wearing white clothes despite being a married woman, cause her to be
shunned by many of her fellow travellers, or to be accused of heresy, reveals the paradoxical nature of Christ's love and love of Christ. It involves
a rejection of worldly shame: if Margery is scorned it is the Christ in her
that is scorned, and her public actions that demonstrate her love for Christ
are testimony to the divine grace that she has been granted. Union with
Christ does not in Margery's terms inspire the spiritualised eroticism of the
'fantasy of fusion'. Instead, Christ being in her like a 'hidden God' in her
soul meant, as it would also mean for the Quakers later, being scorned by the
world as Christ had been.[57] Alongside this, assuming Christ's identity had a
more distinctly late medieval resonance: when her neighbours blasphemed
or took the name of Christ in vain, Margery experienced pain as if she were
the wounded figure of Christ painted on the walls of parish churches as a
warning to swearers. The strength of her love encouraged her to see herself
as a surrogate for Christ when wounded by someone's swearing or crucified
by the Jews.[58]

---

[53] Ibid., p. 213.   [54] Ibid., p. 90.   [55] Ibid., pp. 157, 205.   [56] Ibid., p. 52.
[57] Ibid., pp. 30, 158, 205.
[58] Ibid., pp. 85, 160: 'Forþermor, I thank þe, dowtyr, specyaly for thou mayst suffyr no man
to breke my comawndementys ne to sweryn be me but ȝif it be a gret peyne to þe and for
þu art alwey redy to undyr-nemyn hem of her sweryng for my lofe.'

For Margery, as for her neighbours to a less intense degree, the idea of divine fusion was translated into an un-gendered identification with the sufferings inflicted upon Christ rather than a spiritualised eroticism that required the definition of gendered roles. It is this that explains why Margery's principal role had to be that of a daughter of Christ rather than his spouse, and why, although accused by some as a heretic or as possessed by a devil, she could convince many others of her intense devotion and orthodoxy. Her extraordinary career testifies to the inapplicability of models culled directly from the world of mysticism to understanding parish religion and its significance for gender.[59]

If notions of mystical fusion need modification when applied to the parish context, so too does the related understanding of the religious strategies of men and women in terms of renunciation and reversal. For Bynum, as has been mentioned, these strategies were available to men, but not to women. Consequently, since 'becoming male' was incompatible with christian values, the only option for women lay in the idea of humanity, a genderless idea of physicality and otherness from God implicit in the theology of redemption. For women, gender differences become insignificant 'in the blinding light of the ultimate asymmetry between God and creation'.[60]

However, whilst such structures may have had overriding significance for the writers discussed by Bynum, it is less clear that they did so for the majority of the laity. Most obviously, as far as women were concerned, following the female virtues could fulfil the criteria of renunciation, not by denying femaleness, but by successfully avoiding the temptations to vice and weakness to which women were assumed to be naturally susceptible. At issue was not the religious inadequacy of becoming male, but two competing definitions of the female, broadly corresponding to the stereotypical division between the figures of Mary and Eve. In such an understanding, the lactating Virgin offered enormous potential. She enshrined female virtues and validated the domestic and familial, particularly when the awkward fact of her virginity was reinterpreted to distinguish between physical and spiritual definitions.

---

[59] Extracts from Margery's *Booke* were printed in 1501 by Wynkyn de Worde and in 1521 as part of Henry Pepwell's *The Cell of Self Knowledge*. These omitted Margery's tribulations whilst on pilgrimage, her Marian visions, her worries about virginity, and all hint of mystical marriage. The emphasis is on love for Christ rather than mechanical prayers and almsdeeds, and on compassion for Christ's sufferings stimulated by the sight of a leper covered in sores, or a beaten animal. Margery, despite being elevated now to the position of 'devout ancress', is even less entitled to be called a mystic than in her *Booke*, and even closer to the piety of the parish. See S. E. Holbrook, 'Margery Kempe and Wynkyn de Worde', in M. Glasscoe (ed.), *The Medieval Mystical Tradition in England*, Exeter Symposium IV, Papers Read at Dartington Hall, July 1987 (Woodbridge, 1987), pp. 27–46; Lochrie, *Margery Kempe and Translations of the Flesh*, pp. 220–3; E. G. Gardner (ed.), *The Cell of Self Knowledge: Seven Early English Mystical Treatises Printed by Henry Pepwell MDXXI* (London, 1910), pp. 51–9.

[60] Bynum, *Fragmentation and Redemption*, p. 179.

The late medieval context was significantly different. The reduced emphasis on the maternal and nurturing characteristics of Mary, and the diminished visibility of Eve, rendered the struggle between female virtues and vices less dominant. As part of this trend, didactic and pastoral concerns foregrounded pride, a vice that, although gendered, was much less stable than lust in its gender associations.[61] Even more importantly, the developing Christocentric focus on the passion stressed both the mystery of the incarnation and the gulf between man and the divine. In this period, it was not only for women that 'in the blinding light of the ultimate asymmetry between God and creation' gender differences became insignificant.

Paradoxically, the late medieval devotional context, characterised in Gibson's apt phrase by an 'incarnational aesthetic', reduced the religious significance of gender. Despite the traditionally gendered associations of body and flesh, the tendency 'to objectify the spiritual even as the Incarnation itself had given spirit a concrete form' and hence to see the world as 'saturated with sacramental possibility' did not weaken the traditional christian opposition of the spirit and the flesh.[62] This was largely because the strongly incarnational religiosity was not concerned to narrow the gulf between human and divine, but rather to stress its amazing breadth. As we have seen, the development of emblems served to distance believers from the actual humanity of Christ, and Mary was no longer pre-eminently the lactating, nursing mother. But there was one aspect in which a Christocentric emphasis could encourage a more positive reading, as shown, for example, by the fifteenth-century 'Disputacion Betwyx the Body and Wormes' (Fig. 24).[63] In this poem Body is female and boasts about her corporeal descent from Eve, but the poem does not end with the victory of Death as worms feast on Body. Instead, the poet argues for victory over Death, not by denying the horrors of decay, but by identifying corruption with the suffering of Christ on the cross. The poet is able to assimilate body to Christ, and thus give it a positive value, but he has nothing to say about the more troublesome, and primarily sexual, problems of the flesh.

Later medieval religion, therefore, sanctified the carnal, whilst advocating a struggle against the flesh. In this scheme the distinction between the body

---

[61] See pp. 141–4.
[62] McMurray Gibson, *The Theater of Devotion*, Ch. 1, esp. pp. 6–8.
[63] Bynum, *Fragmentation and Redemption*, p. 237; M. M. Malvern, 'An earnest "Monyscyon" and "thinge Delectabyll" realized verbally and visually in "A Disputacion Betwyx the Body and Wormes", a Middle English poem inspired by tomb art and northern spirituality', *Viator* 13 (1982), 415–43. T. Matsuda, *Death and Purgatory in Middle English Didactic Poetry* (Cambridge, 1997), pp. 158, 163–167, notes that this poem is also unusual amongst medieval body and soul dialogues in having the more optimistic concept of purgatory as its background instead of the starker options of heaven and hell. Within a Christocentric framework, Body can learn to accept fleshly decay and the gnawing of worms as essential and purgatorial characteristics of man's destiny, and to look forward to final bliss through the mediation of Christ.

Figure 24 Drawing of Body's tomb in 'A Disputacion betwyx the Body and Wormes'

and the flesh was sharpened. At issue was the control of the carnal rather than the complete denigration of the physical in favour of the spiritual. The humanising tendencies of both Marian and Christocentric devotion, despite their limitations, encouraged the acceptance of the carnal life of the devout laity and lessened the importance of virginity as a religious aspiration. However, since women were usually assumed to be inherently more lustful and less able to exercise self-control than men, the clearer distinction between body and flesh in terms of the exercise of proper control could accentuate the negative association of flesh with the female. Such conclusions were tempered by pastoral considerations, but, compared to the earlier medieval mystical interpretations discussed by Bynum, the concern for the incarnate Christ, and the resulting identification with nurturing and physical suffering, was less far-reaching and less effective in validating female physicality. These trends were therefore a weaker antidote to ideas of the female body in terms of flesh, lust and earthly sensuous vanity.

The incarnational aesthetic could not significantly narrow the distance between the human and the divine. In the context of an evolving Christocentric piety, which focussed on the adult rather than the infant Christ, the development of the cult of the Virgin Mary and the attribution to her of greater intercessory powers had to be curtailed. There was a need to bring the Queen of Heaven back to earth, and to re-style her more as the representative of grieving humanity, albeit a figure possessed of greater knowledge and powers of admonition. In this new climate, which stressed the human and parental more than the maternal and divine, gender was of less importance in shaping devotional choices and religious identities. Gendered strategies of renunciation and identification made less sense when the focus was on human frailty and the gulf between the human and divine. The cult of Christ's wounds, and the general devotional focus on his passion, tempered this apparently austere situation with divine mercy. But it also preserved the distance between Christ and the believer, and did more to impose a sense of moral obligation than to encourage notions of empathetic fusion. By defining Christ as an emblematised suffering redeemer, and the Virgin Mary as a representative grieving christian and admonishing parent, late medieval devotion created a religious framework that related to individual parishioners more than to men and women.

4

The saints

The presence of large numbers of female saints in the devotional round of medieval catholicism is frequently seen as a positive factor in the religious experience of women, and their removal at the Reformation as detrimental.[1] Such assumptions, as we have seen in the case of Mary, usually rest on oversimplified views of role models and gender. Female saints are tokens that female sanctity is attainable, but the possibilities of identification and aspiration are much more complex: female and male saints do not simply speak to women and men respectively, any more than virgin martyrs speak only to virgins. Saints, like their images, are 'polysemic symbols'. As Ashley and Sheingorn remind us, a saint like Anne can represent motherhood but also the 'genderless idea of lineage and dynasty', and virginity, so central to the stories of many saints, 'could be a gendered or genderless issue in medieval culture'.[2] Even if such views overstate the extent to which these processes could be completely genderless, they provide a valid criticism of biological essentialism in defining responses to saints. It follows that to understand the gender significance of saints, we need to consider more closely their nature and changing role in late medieval lay devotion. Characteristics, such as virginity or the role of the saint as the bride of Christ, were subject to evolving interpretation and could become more or less prominent. These changes were necessarily part of wider religious conceptions concerning the powers of the holy company of heaven and how this related to the developing Christocentric piety discussed in the previous chapter.

Two aspects of the cult of saints will be of particular importance in this discussion: their role as intercessors, and the process of their humanisation. Both could exert a significant influence on the way in which saints were seen as exemplars by the laity, and both were undergoing re-evaluation in

---

[1] For example, M. Kinnear, *Daughters of Time: Women in the Western Tradition* (Ann Arbor, 1982), pp. 69, 88.

[2] Ashley and Sheingorn (eds.), *Interpreting Cultural Symbols*, p. 5.

this period. Partly due to protestant rejection of it, intercession is often seen as the primary function of saints in late medieval religion, and one that overshadowed the instructive role of the details of their holy lives. The holy company of saints in heaven, to whom most catholic testators bequeathed their souls, were seen as heavenly courtiers who glorified the kingdom of heaven and provided a means by which the requests of humble subjects could be brought to the attention of the almighty ruler. But the strength of this parallel of the heavenly and earthly courts was weakened by trends in late medieval piety, which modified the role of saintly intercession and envisaged a more direct relationship between the individual believer and Christ. In this new framework saints came to be viewed less as intercessors, and increasingly as merely minor powers who could cure ills as a consequence of their christian life on earth.

This development was made possible by the crucial shift to a focus on Christ and the saving merits of his passion, but it was also facilitated by the existing structure of medieval devotion to the cult of the saints. Medieval people assumed that the social hierarchy they observed here on earth would be mirrored in heaven. It was this literal imagination that produced depictions of the holy company of heaven segregated by gender, and less orthodox beliefs in the existence of three heavens relating to social status on earth.[3] From such conceptions a belief in a hierarchy of saints, to whom one should have recourse according to the gravity and nature of the circumstances, arose naturally. This process is implicit in the specialised functions of different saints, whether it is the power of St Apollonia to cure tooth ache or of St Sythe to find the housewife's lost keys, and is shown by the adoption by particular groups of their own patron saints (Fig. 25). The consequence of this situation, as christian's study of sixteenth-century Spain illustrates, was that lesser and more local saints, or those with particular specialisations, would be called upon for help with personal problems, whereas the assistance of saints from major shrines, typically of Our Lady, would be sought for major difficulties and as a last resort.[4] This hierarchy in the power and functions of the saints meant that changes in the importance of their intercessory roles could be achieved without seriously disturbing belief in their capacity to assist with the problems of everyday life. It was quite possible to call upon the help of a specialised saint like St Margaret in childbirth, yet to view Christ as the only mediator in the vital question of the salvation of one's soul. However, as Christocentric devotion grew stronger, the intercession of the saints could

---

[3] The woodcut for Caxton's edition of Voragine's *Golden Legend* shows the segregation of male and female saints in heaven.

[4] W. A. Christian, *Local Religion in Sixteenth Century Spain* (Princeton, 1981), pp. 64, 98. Major saints, unlike lesser ones, were also not thought to inflict harm on human communities and were therefore seen as less human.

Figure 25 Drawing of the wall painting of St. Sythe, Shorthampton (Oxon.)

be seen as an irrelevant distraction from true devotion, seriously reducing their role in popular piety.

This suggests the need for caution in assuming, as some historians do, that the late medieval cult of saints was primarily concerned with intercession.[5] The statutes of the London fraternities show that securing saintly intercession for the souls of the departed became less prominent after 1400 when it was just one amongst twenty or thirty clauses.[6] In the later period the

[5] E. Duffy, 'Holy maydens, holy wyfes: The cult of women saints in fifteenth and sixteenth century England', in W. J. Shiels and D. Wood (eds.), *Women in the Church*, Studies in Church History 27 (Oxford, 1990), pp. 189–90.

[6] C. M. Barron, 'The parish fraternities of medieval London', in C. M. Barron and C. Harper-Bill (eds.), *The Church in Pre-Reformation Society: Essays in Honour of F. R. H. Du Boulay* (Woodbridge 1985), pp. 25–8. The similarity of these highly organised urban fraternities

co-operative religious and convivial activities of the living were predominant. The function of the fraternity was more the realisation of the concept of the community of the living faithful in charity with one another than 'a cult of the living in the service of the dead'.[7] It is also clear that in the fifteenth century only a small proportion of testators made specific bequests to images and lights of saints in the parish church. It was also rarely stipulated that masses on behalf of the soul of the deceased should take place at the altar of a particular saint, or that burial within the church should take place in front of particular images or altars.[8] Even chantries were increasingly known by the names of their founders, who may have been as interested in enhancing the liturgical provision in their parish churches as in securing the intercession of saints for the salvation of their own souls.[9] From this evidence it is hard to escape the conclusion that it was the saving power of the mass and of the passion of Christ that was seen as efficacious, rather than the intercessory powers of an individual saint.

Of course, this lack of emphasis on the powers of the saints to intercede for the salvation of one's soul may not have been matched by popular religious attitudes during life. It has become a commonplace in the use of will material to add the disclaimer that pious provision on the deathbed need not reflect previous pious practice. On the testimony of contemporaries, however, a closer correlation between the two than is generally allowed seems likely, especially in the case of devotion to particular saints. The anonymous author of *The ordynarye of crysten men* (1506) asserted that masses for souls were

to the experience of fraternities in rural England does, of course, remain an open question, although village gild accounts do provide a lot of detail of the expenditure and organisation of gild feasts.

[7] The importance of members of the christian community being in charity with one another on the eve of the Reformation is described in S. Brigden, 'Religion and social obligation in early sixteenth-century London', *P & P* 103 (1984), 67–112, and in J. Bossy, 'Blood and baptism: kinship, community and Christianity in Western Europe from the fourteenth to the seventeenth century', in D. Baker (ed.), *Sanctity and Secularity: The Church and the World*, Studies in Church History 10 (Oxford, 1973), pp. 138–9, who, using anthropological parallels, claims that systems of formal friendship imply systems of formal hostility and the definition of a group with whom the members were in a state of enmity. However, this would seem to be rather overdrawn. The quotation is taken from A. N. Galpern, 'The legacy of late medieval religion in sixteenth century Champagne', in C. Trinkaus and H. A. Oberman (eds.), *The Pursuit of Holiness in Late Medieval and Renaissance Religion* (Leiden, 1974), p. 149.

[8] Worcs. RO CCW. The few exceptions involve St Katherine and the Virgin Mary, who are distinguished from the general company of saints. St. Katherine as protectress of the dying was clearly a specialised saint in this context, and Mary possessed extensive delegated powers, as illustrated in the Soul Weighing scenes.

[9] C. Burgess, ' "For the increase of divine service": chantries in the parish in late medieval Bristol', *JEH* 36/1 (1985), 46–65. A. Kreider, *English Chantries – The Road to Dissolution* (Cambridge, Mass., 1979), pp. 38–68, also draws attention to the importance of chantry priests for the cure of souls and for education, but views these aspects as clearly secondary motives in foundation.

more efficacious if they were directed towards saints to whom the deceased had been devoted in life.[10] This basic principle also underlies many of the miracle stories included in sermon collections, such as that of Mirk, in which the Virgin Mary saves the souls of those who have performed some act of devotion to her during their lives.[11]

If such beliefs in the benefits of continuity were widespread, the low profile of saints in the testamentary material might seem to suggest that saints were unimportant in the religion of the laity during life. More plausibly, it indicates that they could be viewed as fulfilling different functions. Although all saints might assist in minor concerns, not all were privileged with equal powers of intercession in the vital matter of the salvation of the individual's soul. A clear hierarchy of power and influence was envisaged, and even those saints who were thought to be particularly close to Christ had limited influence, as the appeal to St Anne at the end of Mirk's sermon for her feast day illustrates:

Wherfor ye schul now knele adowne, and pray Saynt Anne to pray to her holy doghtyr, oure lady, that scho pray to her sonne that he gyve you hele yn body and sowle, and grace to kepe your order of wedlok, and gete such childyrn that byn plesant and trew servandys to God, and soo com to the blys that Saynt Ann ys yn.[12]

St Anne's special position as the mother of the Virgin Mary enabled her to exercise intercessory power, but only at several stages removed. Even St Mary Magdalen, who was seen as having a specially intimate relationship with Christ, was not considered to possess personal intercessory powers. Her role, according to Mirk, was as a model to spur the believer to ask God for forgiveness, 'Wherfor ye schul now knele downe and pray to God as he forgaf Mary Maudelyn her synnys, so he forgeve you your synnys, and grant you the blys that he boght you to.'[13] Lesser saints were normally relied upon to preserve the christian from sins and disasters during life. Such assistance may aid the soul on the road to salvation, but has no place at the Last Judgement. Furthermore, this assistance could extend to human ailments and concerns which had no link with salvation. It was believed, for example, that in any house in which St Dorothy was honoured no woman would have a miscarriage, there would be no danger of fire and no one would die without the last rites. This function, as well as their reputation for capriciousness, finally determined their lower religious status. As Sir Thomas More commented, 'Saincte Apoline we make a tooth-drawer, and may speke to her of nothing but sore teeth. St. Sythe women get to seke their keys. Sainte

---

[10] *The ordynarye of crysten men* (1506) (Bodl. Douce O 164 unpaginated). The preface states that the book was begun in 1467. The work appears orthodox, although it contains a strong emphasis on the Ten Commandments. The author asserts that after masses, fastings and almsdeeds a man may still be damned, but if he obeys the Commandments he cannot fail to be saved.

[11] Erbe (ed.), *Mirk's Festial.*   [12] Ibid., p. 216.   [13] Ibid., p. 208.

Roche we set to se to the great sykenes bycause he had a sore.'[14] Debate about whether late medieval saints were primarily defined as intercessors therefore needs to incorporate awareness of these two types of intercessory function which do not correspond neatly to deathbed and lifetime concerns, despite the importance of salvific intercession, but rather to a strong hierarchical awareness.

Duffy, assuming a strong emphasis on intercession, argues that the role of saints as intercessors made them almost insignificant as exemplars. Although some texts asserted the importance of the saints as models of virginity, this, in his view, had little impact on contemporary lay society. Virginity was seen more as a source of sacred power than as a social aspiration.[15] This conclusion overstates the case. The potential role of saints as exemplars clearly embraced a wider range of attributes than virginity, however broadly that concept should be understood. Moreover, since physical virginity was obviously incompatible with the lives of most laypeople, we should expect the ability of saints to act as role models in this respect to be relatively weak, whatever the strength of their status as intercessors. It is also unclear in general that a strong reputation for intercession obscures the social characteristics of the saints, and that its weakening makes them more visible. The power of intercession can validate the qualities of the saint as a means of access to divine favour, and its reduction can render saints little more potent as exemplars than ordinary frail mortals. The importance and nature of intercession does not indicate the significance of saintly lives as models for imitation. It was not due to their role as intercessors, or to a desire to gain intercessory powers herself, that Margery Kempe saw her lack of virginity as an obstacle in reaching the place of St Katherine, St Margaret and St Barbara. Rather, she aspired to their status of faithful followers beloved by God. The powers of intercession granted to these saints, and to Margery Kempe, were merely tokens of God's love towards them that was manifested more importantly in other ways.

Margery's resolution of her agony about virginity came through a developing conviction that such demands should be seen in a spiritual, rather than a social, sense. The saint was a spiritual, not a fleshly, model. Nevertheless, such beliefs co-existed, and were compatible, with an understanding of the saints that increasingly saw them as ordinary human figures. The physical virginity of the few was less important in marking them out for special sanctity. In religious terms this humanisation has usually been seen as a negative trend. Long ago, Huizinga asserted that the cult of saints in the late medieval period was doomed as a result of their increased assimilation of contemporary

[14] W. E. Campbell (ed.), *Thomas More's 'The Dialogue Concerning Tyndale'* (London, 1927), p. 160.
[15] Duffy, 'Holy maydens, holy wyfes', pp. 189–93.

human attributes.[16] However, whilst this process necessarily reduced the gulf between saints and ordinary mortals, it is less clear that it impoverished the role of the saints as exemplars of religious achievement. The increased humanisation of the saints could accentuate their social significance as models of christian conduct and spiritual development.

The emphasis on the human attributes of the saints manifested itself in many ways. Most notably, there was the tendency for different images of saints to be both localised and individualised. This was notoriously the case with images of the Virgin Mary: women could be observed discussing the relative merits and virtues of Our Lady of Ipswich and Our Lady of Walsingham as if they were distinct contemporary ladies.[17] The extent to which this individualisation of images of universal saints was found throughout the hierarchy of the holy company of heaven is more difficult to ascertain. In the seventeenth century this view could be thought to have extended to lesser saints. In a humorous anecdote, which he claimed to have heard in the course of his travels, John Taylor, the 'Water Poet', told the story of a man worshipping the image of St Loy:

A Poore Country may [man] praying devoutly superstitious before an old Image of S. Loy, the image suddenly fell downe upon the poor man, and bruised his bones sorely, that hee could not stirr abroade in a moneth after; in which space the cheating priests had set up a new Image: the Country man came to the Church againe, and kneeled a farre off to the new Image, saying, Although thou smilest and lookest faire upon mee, yet thy father plaid me such a knavish pranke lately, that Ile beware how I come too neere thee, lest thou shouldst have any of thy Fathers unhappy qualities.[18]

Notions of localised individuality were implicit in the attribution of genealogy to imagery.

The reality of beliefs which lay behind the remarks of Tyndale and the anecdotes of the Water Poet is more subtle. Protestant polemic and seventeenth-century popular humour cannot be completely accurate guides to pre-Reformation catholic popular religious beliefs. Fortunately, the texts of the controversy between William Tyndale and Sir Thomas More permit a more reasoned assessment of the situation. Replying to Tyndale's example of the individualisation of images of the Virgin, More accepts that Tyndale could have overheard the alleged discussion, but asserts that such comments

---

[16] J. Huizinga, *The Waning of the Middle Ages: A Study of the Forms of Life and Art in France and the Netherlands in the Fourteenth and Fifteenth Centuries* (London, 1955), pp. 168–78. The extent to which there was an actual increase in the humanisation of saints in this period depends on the type of saint considered. Local, rather than universal, saints had probably always been viewed in this way.

[17] Aston, *England's Iconoclasts*, p. 107n. ' "Of all our ladies", saith one, "I love best Our lady of Walsingham." "And I", saith the other, "our lady of Ipswich." ' Campbell (ed.), *Thomas More's 'The Dialogue Concerning Tyndale'*, p. 62.

[18] Watt, *Cheap Print and Popular Piety*, p. 321.

are part of a more sophisticated and orthodox understanding than he admits. The comparison between images is only in terms of their relative reputations for the incidence of miracles, and does not imply a multiplicity of Virgin Marys. If you were to ask even the most foolish woman which of these images stood by the cross at the Crucifixion, your question would be greeted with incredulity and receive the orthodox reply that it was none of these images but Our Lady herself.[19]

More's answer may simply reflect a defensive theologian's hopeful rationalisation of popular belief, but it is not implausible that the laity, like More's 'simplest fool', knew the difference between an image and its prototype. That different images could gain reputations for being more efficacious was not incompatible with this. The idea of exorcism entailed a belief that objects could be imbued with power. As the author of *The ordynarye of crysten men* (1506) explained, discussing the need for exorcism in baptism, the power or 'domynacion' of the devil is in all things as a consequence of original sin, but by exorcism objects can be freed from this 'domynacion', and are presumably imbued with divine power.[20] These ideas could be transferred to the images of saints. The power of Our Lady is in every image of her, but each image can gain a different reputation for miracles, since its particular efficacy, despite the apparently capricious nature of some saints, depends principally on the devotion of the pilgrims visiting the shrine. Ideas of the particular nature of individual images were therefore embedded in theologically orthodox belief, even if some of its alleged manifestations, such as the idea of the mortality and the regeneration of the image of St Loy, went beyond the bounds directly sanctioned by orthodoxy. This individualisation and humanisation of the images of the saints was, however, accompanied by a strong idea of the saints as a collective group, who both glorified heaven and offered reassurance of the possibility of human sanctity.

The way in which saints were arranged in the parish church reflected these two ideas of their roles. Historians, despite eagerly attributing significance to the patterns of pewing arrangements, have reflected relatively little on the implications for lay devotion to saints of the religious geography within the parish church.[21] The elaborate, and probably overinterpreted, conclusions

---

[19] Campbell (ed.), *Thomas More's 'The Dialogue Concerning Tyndale'*, p. 164; Aston, *England's Iconoclasts*, p. 32. 'Take the simplest fool that ye can choose, and she will tell you that Our Lady herself is in heaven. She will also call an image an image, and she will tell you a difference between an image of an horse and an horse indeed.'

[20] *The ordynarye of crysten men.*

[21] Aston, 'Segregation in church', pp. 274–5 is the only exception. She suggests that the position of Mary and John in the rood group was reflected in the male–female division of the congregation. The idea that the same pattern was respected in the gender of saints chosen for the side altars is less easily sustained and is unlikely, due to the fact that saints attracted devotion from the laity of both sexes.

of scholars like Durandus in the thirteenth century may be inappropriate for the late medieval lay mentality, but we should not lose sight of the importance of spatial messages in a visual culture.[22] The image's sacred power, and the parishioner's response to it, was influenced and defined by its position.

In view of this, it is unfortunate for a full understanding of the cult of saints that one important category of images, three-dimensional statues, has barely survived Reformation image destruction. Obliteration with white-wash preserved many paintings, but fragments of statues survive only when they were successfully concealed in wall cavities or beneath the floor. Thus, although it is likely that a statue of the Pietà could have been found in most parish churches on the eve of the Reformation, the example from Battlefield (Shropshire) is a rare survival.[23] Consequently, paintings on the rood screen and the walls of the church must form the basis of the discussion of the roles of saints in late medieval parish religion. The saints chosen in these two positions differ significantly, and reinforce the suggestion of the importance of spatial meanings.

Of the two, the rood screen has received more attention from church historians, who have pointed to its close association with the rood group and yet its evolutionary independence from it. Bond and Camm saw the figure-painted rood screen as the most convincing testimony to the strength of the cult of the saints.[24] This conclusion is most appropriate for the early phases of the development of the rood screen, although even then it underestimates the undoubtedly important function of the screen, as a barrier between nave and chancel, in enhancing the mystery of the mass. In the later Middle Ages, the clear iconographic links between the rood group, the screen panels and the painting above the chancel arch mean that a composite interpretation is necessary, despite their earlier separate evolution. The rood screen may be devoted to the glorification of the holy company of heaven, but it also clearly situates that group in the context of Christ's passion. The fifteenth-century fashion for placing the Doom over the chancel arch further strengthened the connections between the rood screen and the Last Judgement. The iconography of the Doom clearly related to the passion of Christ: the depiction of

---

[22] C. Brooke, 'Religious sentiment and church design in the later Middle Ages', in C. Brooke (ed.), *Medieval Church and Society* (London, 1971), pp. 162–82.

[23] N. Pevsner, *Shropshire* (London, 1958), p. 70. A wooden Pietà, dating from the late fourteenth century, was discovered at Breadsall (Derbyshire) in 1877: N. Pevsner, *Derbyshire*, 2nd edition (London, 1978), p. 108.

[24] F. Bligh Bond and Dom. Bede Camm, *Roodscreens and Roodlofts* (London, 1909), pp. 82–3, suggest that the early fourteenth-century introduction of the rood loft was partly due to an increased emphasis on the cult of saints. In their view, the devotion to the rood was of lesser significance, since structurally the rood was originally associated with the rood beam, not the rood loft.

Christ's wounds and of the instruments of the passion emphasised the dual role of Christ as suffering saviour and as judge.[25]

The images selected for the rood screen also stress the connection with the passion of Christ and salvation. Most notably, the portrayal of the prophets and, especially in Devon, of the pagan Sibyls bearing the instruments of the passion demonstrate the symbolic role of this group and its association with the Crucifixion and salvation.[26] The apostles, often depicted alternately with the prophets and carrying scrolls with the words of the Apostles' Creed, point to the link between human faith and salvation. It is in this context that the portrayal of seemingly random selections of saints can be understood. On the rood screen, the saints are testimony to the possibility of human sancti- fication and salvation through the merits of Christ's passion. Situated on the barrier between the secular and spiritual zones of nave and chancel, they rep- resent the possibility of ordinary mortals moving between the two spheres.[27]

Sometimes the relationship of the figures on the rood screen to the laity in the congregation was made even more explicit by the division of the saints into male and female groups, corresponding both to the male and female sides of the congregation and to the figures of Mary and John in the rood group. An example of this arrangement can be seen at North Elmham (Norfolk), but it remained, especially in the West Country, a comparatively rare pattern. Examples of screens, such as Eye (Suffolk), in which male and female saints are depicted alternately demonstrate that, even when the artists were working to a particular pattern, they did not see a reflection of the gender division of the congregation as necessarily appropriate.[28] It may have been the existence

---

[25] See pp. 82–3.

[26] C. E. Keyser, 'On the panel paintings of saints on the Devonshire screens', *Archaeologia* 56/1 (1898), 189. Sibyls occur on many Devon screens including Bradninch, Heavitree, Ipplepen and Ugborough. The popularity of these pagan prophetesses, who were thought to have foretold the Crucifixion, may be due to French contacts. The emblems of the Sibyls on the screens are similar to those of a French prayer book of 1514. The fortunes of the Sibylline texts in the medieval period are traced in B. McGuinn, 'Teste David cum Sibylla: The significance of the Sibylline tradition in the Middle Ages', in J. Kirshner and S. F. Wemple (eds.), *Women of the Medieval World: Essays in Honour of John H. Mundy* (Oxford, 1985), pp. 7–35.

[27] The practice of hearing confessions by the rood screen would also have enhanced the liminal significance of this position: P. Marshall, *The Catholic Priesthood and the English Reforma- tion* (Oxford, 1994), p. 6.

[28] The only Devon example of the male–female division of saints is at Kenn. Keyser's view that this was the 'correct arrangement' of saints on rood screens therefore seems mistaken. Bond and Camm, *Roodscreens and Roodlofts*, p. 242; Keyser, 'On the panel paintings of saints on the Devonshire screens', 183–222. Identification of the sequence of paintings on the panels of screens is often complicated by nineteenth-century restoration and rearrangement. At North Elmham (Norfolk) the presence of inscriptions identifying the saints on the female panels and the lack of such scrolls on the male panels suggest that the present arrangement is not original. Certainly, the first four male panels are no longer in their original frames. I am grateful to Dr J. Blair for a detailed study of this screen. The arrangement of the panels of some screens

of the holy company of heaven, rather than the gender distinctions within it, which was of the greatest importance to the laity as a whole.

In contrast, the paintings of the saints adorning the walls of parish churches were more likely to attract individualised devotion. Although their association with altars generally remains unproven and an attempt to match surviving wall paintings with bequests in wills in Yorkshire failed to produce a convincing correlation, the scale and selection of these images suggest that they reflected and stimulated patterns of lay devotion to particular saints.[29] The saints selected for the wall and the rood screen might correspond to the specific devotional preferences of individual patrons, but the siting of the images conveyed subtly different messages. The large-scale image in the nave could be seen as a source of access to divine power, whilst those on the screen have more of the character of a representative group. In many cases even the portrayal of their attributes is insufficient to secure a definite identification. Frequently, the addition of scrolls naming the individual saints points up the inadequacy of identification by attributes alone.[30]

That different saints were chosen for walls and rood screens reinforces the idea of different spatial functions, especially since in both positions patronage was both individual and communal.[31] Using Keyser's list as a reasonable, although imperfect, sample, it appears that female saints were more likely to be chosen for rood screens than for wall paintings (Tables 4.1 and 4.2).[32]

(e.g. Ranworth, Norfolk) was also affected by the presence of altars against the rood screen. However, by the fifteenth century, altars in this position seem to have been less common as altars were increasingly moved into the side aisles: Bond and Camm, *Roodscreens and Roodlofts*, p. 81.

[29] S. Sutcliffe, 'Piety and the cult of saints in fifteenth century Yorkshire from testamentary evidence and surviving church art', MA thesis, University of York (1990), pp. 64–5. The size of the will sample means that the negative correlation is not conclusive. For example, there are seven recorded images of St Katherine, including two narrative cycles, but the wills mention only one altar and one image. Wall paintings are known from 19 parishes in the county for which 260 surviving wills were studied mainly dating from the fifteenth century. This produces an average of 14 wills per parish, although in fact the numbers of wills drawn from Beverley and Scarborough are significantly larger.

[30] For example, representations of St Sythe with her keys and flowers are easily confused with those of other female saints like St Petronella, St Cecilia and St Dorothy.

[31] E. Duffy, 'The parish, piety and patronage in late medieval East Anglia: the evidence of rood screens', in K. L. French, G. G. Gibbs and B. A. Kümin (eds.), *The Parish in English Life, 1400–1600* (Manchester, 1997), pp. 133–62.

[32] The Virgin Mary, the apostles, prophets and church fathers are excluded from these figures, since they constitute significantly different categories. Most painted rood screens date from the mid-fifteenth to early sixteenth centuries. The wall painting sample used covers a longer medieval time span, although many of the earlier paintings would still have been visible on the eve of the Reformation. Some wall paintings have, of course, been discovered since Keyser compiled his list in 1883, although the majority of known paintings were uncovered during nineteenth-century refurbishment of churches. Many of the paintings discovered in this period no longer survive and Keyser's list therefore provides the largest and most easily accessible sample. Comparison in random counties suggests that later discoveries do not

Table 4.1. *Most frequent saints in wall
paintings*

St Christopher	175
St George	51
St Katherine of Alexandria	33
St Thomas Becket	31
St Mary Magdalen	26
St Michael (weighing souls)	25
St John the Baptist	20
St Margaret	17
St Edmund	16
St Nicholas	15

They account for three quarters of the most frequent images on rood screens, but for only three of the ten most popular subjects in wall paintings.[33] On the rood screen, female saints seemed most appropriate to patrons of both sexes: as representatives of the weaker vessel, they symbolised most effectively the possibility of the sanctification of the poor mortal.

The lower profile of female saints in contexts associated with intercession is confirmed by the evidence of wills and by the dedications of gilds. Study of all the surviving wills from Sussex before 1559 reveals a pattern of bequests in which the rood and Our Lady are the dominant recipients and bequests to other saints are quite infrequent. Among those who are selected, however, male saints predominate.[34] Similarly, the evidence of parish gilds recorded in fifteenth- and early sixteenth-century churchwardens' accounts shows a preponderance of gilds and lights in honour of male saints. Female saints are noticeably lacking, with the exception of the Virgin Mary, St Katherine and St Margaret (Table 4.3).[35]

seriously affect the frequency of the most popular images. C. E. Keyser, *A List of Buildings Having Mural Decorations* (London, 1883).

[33] Duffy, considering the top twenty images on rood screens in East Anglia and Devon, finds that 15 out of 26 (58%) are female: Duffy, 'Holy maydens, holy wyfes', pp. 178–9.

[34] R. G. Rice (ed.), transcripts of Sussex wills, *Sussex Rec. Soc.* 41–4 (1935–41). In the wills of 319 parishes saints attracting bequests in more than five parishes were as follows: Our Lady 31.7% of parishes, rood light 30.7%, St Nicholas 6%, St Katherine 5.3%, Trinity 3.8%, St John the Baptist 3.5%, St Peter 3.2%, St George, St Margaret and St Michael 2.2%, All Hallows, St Anne, St Erasmus 1.9%, St Anthony, St James, St Sunday and St Thomas 1.6%.

[35] The churchwardens' accounts of 47 parishes give sufficient details: Brightwalton, Winkfield (Berks.); Wing (Bucks.); Bassingbourn (Cambs.); Stratton (Cornwall); Ashburton, Braunton, Broadhempston, Chagford, Chudleigh, Coldridge, Dartington, Iddesleigh, Modbury, South Tawton, Tavistock, Woodbury, Woodland (Devon); Broomfield, Great Dunmow, Great Hallingbury, Heybridge, Saffron Walden (Essex); Andover, Bramley (Hants.); Horbling, Leverton (Lincs.); Denton, North Elmham, Shipdham, Snettisham (Norfolk); Culworth (Northants.); Thame (Oxon.); Worfield (Shropshire); Banwell, Nettlecombe,

Table 4.2. *Most frequent saints on rood screens*[1]

St Barbara	25
St Mary Magdalen	25
St Katherine of Alexandria	23
St John the Baptist	23
St Edmund	20
St Margaret	19
Edward, king and confessor	18
St Dorothy	17
St Helen	17
St George	16
St Agnes	15
St Apollonia	15

[1] Sets of images on rood screens are incomplete due to the loss of the rood loft which could carry elaborate series of images. At Mere (Wilts.) images of the twelve apostles were painted on the face of the rood loft. The loft at Yatton (Somerset) contained 69 images which had been purchased in 1454–5 at a cost of £3 10s 4d, and at Leverton (Lincs.) the bequest of William Frankyshe (1526) paid for 16 images of alabaster in the 'fore syde of ye rode loft'. The 1567 visitation of the diocese of York also discovered that painted pictures upon the rood loft remained undefaced at Hombleton and Garton. It is unclear whether these were additional to paintings on the lower panels of the screen. At Mere, where the reference is to defacing the images, there do not seem to have been any other paintings on the screen. This choice may explain the geographical distribution of surviving figure painted screens: Baker (ed.), 'Churchwardens' accounts of Mere', 31; Hobhouse (ed.), 'Churchwardens' accounts of Yatton', 98; Lincs. RO CWA Leverton, Leverton 7/1 f. 21v–22r; J. S. Purvis (ed.), *Tudor Parish Documents of the Diocese of York* (Cambridge, 1948), p. 32.

The ranked frequency of saints appearing on rood screens differs slightly from that given by Duffy, who considers the evidence of 160 painted screens in Norfolk, Suffolk and Devon. Duffy's ordering is (1) St John the Baptist, St Dorothy, (2) St Barbara, St Mary Magdalen, (3) St Apollonia, St Katherine, (4) St Stephen, (5) St Lawrence, (6) St Agnes, (7) St Margaret, (8) St Edmund (East Anglia only), (9) St George, (10) St Helen: Duffy, 'Holy maydens, holy wyfes', pp. 178–9. Figure painted screens do survive from other counties: Rev. W. W. Lillie, 'Medieval paintings on the screens of the parish churches of mid and southern England', *JBAA* 2nd ser. 9 (1944), 33–47.

In general, the saints were easily reduced to members of a holy group and became to some extent interchangeable. Of course, individual saints did have their own feast days and gained a reputation for giving assistance in the face of particular calamities. However, in the scheme of salvation the

Pilton (Somerset); Boxford, Brundish, Cratfield, Dennington, Walberswick (Suffolk); Horley (Surrey); Arlington (Sussex); Solihull (Warw.); Halesowen (Worcs.); Ecclesfield (Yorks.).

Table 4.3. *Most frequent dedications of parish gilds and lights in 47 parishes*

Virgin Mary	32
St Katherine	15
St John	14
St George	10
Trinity	9
St Christopher	8
St Nicholas	7
St Margaret	6
St Thomas	6
St James	5
Jesus	5

social function of the saints as a group was the same: they were testimony to the possibility of holiness for the laity. In this respect there was no consistent distinction between male and female saints, but the latter seemed more appropriate as emblems of the possibility of sanctification for the ordinary mortal. The humanisation of the saints occurred in the context of the developing affective Christocentric devotion, which stressed the relationship of the individual believer with Christ himself, and meant the end of devotional poetry exploring the mystical relationship of the reader with a particular saint. The demands of the *imitatio Christi* meant that the role of saints as humanising mediators between the christian and God gradually became redundant.

It was in line with this that by the fifteenth century narratives of martyrdom were not commonly depicted in the parish church. The martyrdom of a saint was no longer of intrinsic interest, but subsumed into Christ's passion and the tradition of empathetic devotion to his wounds. Parishioners were most likely to see images of saints on the lower tiers of the rood screen and in altarpieces, where they were clearly integrated into a Christocentric scheme of piety. The saints were a supporting cast for the Crucifixion, and the associated emphasis on salvation through Christ's passion was intensified by the fifteenth-century fashion for painting the Last Judgement over the chancel arch. The standing figures of saints on the rood screen, although often identified with reference to their martyrdom, were not there as martyrs emphasising their suffering and torment at the hands of non-christian tyrants, but as martyrs in the more precise sense of the word *martyrion*, those bearing witness. Even though their martyrdom could be seen as a re-enactment of Christ's passion, explicit details of the tortures inflicted paled in the visual and devotional shadow of the experience of Christ himself.

Such ideas, implicit in the iconography, were made explicit in devotional writings of the period. A good example is Nicholas Love's discussion of St Cecilia in his *Myrrour of the Blessed Lyf of Jesu Christ*, an early fifteenth-century translation of Pseudo-Bonaventura. Cecilia is said to have kept the gospel of Christ hidden in her breast, and it is clear that this is meant figuratively: she chooses certain parts of the life of Christ and keeps them close for meditation. The *Myrrour* goes on to explain that martyrs endure torments not through miraculous powers, but through contemplation: 'For what time the Martire stant with alle the body to rent, & never the lesse he is ioiful & gladde in alle his peyne, where trowest is then his soule and his herte? sothely in the wondes of Jesu.' By meditating on Christ's life and passion, not only martyrs but all christians will be able to bear tribulations with patience, and even joy.[36]

This new emphasis had a significant impact on the hagiography of virgin saints. According to Winstead the spirited lives of defiant virgin saints become decorous models of faith, courtesy and devotion. Thus Mirk's retelling of the story of St Margaret can omit her altercations with Olibrius.[37] The stories of virgin saints become interlarded with passages of Christocentric devotion and meditation from earlier Latin *passiones*. These had generally been omitted by Voragine and hagiographers of the period 1250–1400, in which virgin martyrs had been portrayed as confrontational and unruly. From the fifteenth century, readers were increasingly urged to follow the meditative example. Thus, the introduction to the early sixteenth-century prose adaptation of Voragine's life of St Katherine commends her for constantly meditating on Christ's passion:

This muste every creaturee remember as did this holy maiden and virgen; for she rememberde this daily and howrely and printid hit in hir mynde, and thoght on his passion and payne and rewardid hym with hir consiens and good herte to hir power.[38]

This curbing of the independent unruliness of female martyrs confined them to decorous, modest obedience, and therefore reduced the already limited extent they could claim the public theatre of martyrdom as their own. But at the same time, and perhaps more importantly, it significantly weakened the connection of female sanctity with virginity understood in a simply physical sense. The adaptation of the life of Margaret in the same collection praises her as a 'maiden...araide with instans of the drede of god, abiding in religion, presonable in honeste, singular in paciens' and says that she 'was faire in face and full of beute but she was fairer in bewte

[36] K. A. Winstead, *Virgin Martyrs: Legends of Sainthood in Late Medieval England* (Ithaca and London, 1997), p.118; M. G. Sargent (ed.), *Mirror of the Blessed Life of Jesus Christ* (New York, 1992), pp. 11–12.
[37] Winstead, *Virgin Martyrs*, p. 112.   [38] Ibid., pp. 116–17.

of ffaithe. She was not only a maiden of hir body but alsoo in mynde.'[39] In theory, of course, defence of mere physical virginity was always unimportant. As Aquinas pointed out, the true martyr died for faith, not for the defence of worldly concerns, whether virginity or geometry.[40] But such careful distinctions were often forgotten: the praise of heavenly virginity elided the dual qualifications of the virgin martyr and led to assertions of the equivalence of the preservation of chastity and the martyr's death. Thus, the author of the mid-twelfth-century *Heli Maidenhed* claimed that virginity could be equal to any martyr's death. In both life was exchanged for death and rewarded by a spiritual marriage with Christ.[41]

It is a paradox that the omission of narrative detail of the torments and tortures of saints made them more, rather than less, earthly and human. This can be seen most clearly in the transformation of ideas of the association of marriage and virginity with the saints. A striking illustration of the new possibilities is a prose legend of St Ursula written *c.*1450. After telling the story of the slaughter of Ursula, her bridegroom (the King of England) and her female companions, the author concludes 'And so she was wedded that day to the kyng of Englond full gloriously byfore the kyng of heven.' The story of the saint climaxes with her marriage to a fellow human in heaven instead of the expected, and standard, union of the martyr with Christ, the heavenly bridegroom.[42]

Among saints' lives, the story of St Ursula was one of the most obvious candidates for such a revision. After all, on the face of it Ursula accepted an earthly marriage and simply negotiated a postponement in order to go on pilgrimage. That the ceremony never took place was not due to her spirited resistance to marriage, but to meeting a martyr's death before her return. Her marriage to the King of England in heaven in the late medieval version was partly a legacy of the romance tradition, and reminds us that the two genres were often closely interconnected. Nevertheless, from a theological viewpoint this elaboration seems shocking, since human marriage should not take place in heaven. In pastoral terms though, this revised ending can be seen as reinforcing notions of the sanctity of earthly marriage, and the message may gain additional power from its occurrence in the unexpected context of the *vita* of a female virgin martyr. However, interpretation of this requires

---

[39] Ibid., pp. 116–17.

[40] M. Rubin, 'Choosing death? Experiences of martyrdom in late medieval Europe', in D. Wood (ed.), *Martyrs and Martyrologies*, Studies in Church History 30 (Oxford, 1993), pp. 171–2; Aquinas, *Summa Theologiae*, Blackfriars edition (London 1966), II. IIae. qu.124 art.3 ad 2; 42, p. 50.

[41] Rubin, 'Choosing death?', p. 156; B. Millet (ed.), *Hali Meidenhad*, EETS 284 (London, 1982), pp. 22–3.

[42] Winstead, *Virgin Martyrs*, p.113; text in G. N. Garmonsway and R. R. Raymo, 'A Middle English prose life of St Ursula', *Review of English Studies* new ser. 9 (1958), 355–61.

some caution: the marriage of the saint and king in heaven is spiritualised, and obviously modelled on the more usual idea of the mystical marriage of the female saint as the bride of Christ. A similar story occurs as a sermon exemplum in which an anonymous female saint is persuaded by her father to marry.[43] Although initially resistant to the idea, she promises out of filial love that she will marry if a suitable suitor presents himself, but when the suitors have assembled, she rejects them all, and is married there and then to Christ. Both this story and the revised life of St Ursula, although involving an acceptance of marriage, explore and define the contrast between earthly and spiritual marriage.

These reflections lead on to, and perhaps help to elucidate, Atkinson's observation that although late medieval saints are more likely to have a married history, this does not seem to coincide with an increased emphasis on the saint as bride of Christ in visual imagery and hagiography.[44] The narrative of Margery Kempe shows that such a connection was possible, but it remains true that visual depictions were rare in England. The image of St Agnes at Cawston (Norfolk) is the only wall painting depicting mystic marriage (Fig. 26).[45] The scene is notably absent from the much larger sample of images of St Katherine, despite being fairly common on the Continent in this period. Moreover, the Cawston St Agnes modifies the standard iconography by substituting the dove of Holy Spirit for Christ, suggesting that the lack of images is not simply due to the vagaries of survival, but is also linked to a distinctively English interpretation of the theme.

The standard iconography of the mystic marriage depicts the female saint being married to the Christ Child.[46] By rejecting this solution, the mystical and spiritual nature of the marriage was emphasised, but through a displacing of Christ which, given the Christocentric nature of English devotion, requires explanation. Late medieval Christocentric piety focussed on the humanity and passion of the adult Christ rather than the Christ Child. The absence of depictions of the mystic marriage with the infant Christ fits with the lack of images of the Nativity and of the Virgin Mary suckling the Christ Child. Instead, the Cawston artist chose to assimilate the idea of mystical marriage to the iconography of the Annunciation. The latter was a very malleable and transferable image, as shown by examples where the scene

[43] Ross (ed.), *Middle English Sermons*, pp. 79–82.
[44] C. W. Atkinson, 'Precious balsam in a fragile glass: the ideology of virginity in the later Middle Ages', *Journal of Family History* 8/2 (1983), 131–43.
[45] Rev. J. Bulwer, 'Notice of a mural painting discovered in the south transept of Cawston church', *Norfolk Archaeology* 3 (1852), 36–9.
[46] See, for example, the late fifteenth-century images reproduced in P. Philippot, *La peinture dans les anciens pays-bas xve – xvie siècles* (Paris, 1994), pp. 52, 86, 117.

Figure 26 Drawing of the wall painting of the mystic marriage of St Agnes,
Cawston (Norfolk)

included patrons, and by its extension as a form to depict St Bridget receiving
her revelations. The choice of the Annunciation as a model also had the
consequence of lessening the intimacy of ideas of mystic marriage. Patterned
on Mary, the bride of Christ becomes a humble recipient of grace.

This iconological interpretation gains further support from the texts of the two donors' scrolls. The recorded version is garbled, but the general sense is clear: the donors ask someone (presumably Agnes) to petition Mary, the queen of heaven and mother of Christ who died on the rood and saved us with his blood so bright, to pray to God that we may make a good end. The message of the scrolls shifts the meaning of the image to salvation and a good death. As a result Agnes's intimate relationship with Christ as a participant in mystic marriage is diminished. She is not to address Christ directly on behalf of the interceding mortal as a wife might petition her husband, but instead to direct the request through Mary, who is simultaneously queen of heaven and mother of Christ. This hierarchical approach by a member of Christ's 'family' echoes the forms of petition involving St Anne mentioned earlier. Even when the notion of the female saint as the bride of Christ is visualised, the intimacy of access implied is limited. The model being used is the Annunciation concept of the humble handmaid of the Lord to whom favour is granted, rather than that of a bride who is in an intimate relationship with Christ.

The idea that there was not a strong tradition of mystical marriage in late medieval England is reinforced by the treatment of St Katherine, who enjoyed a greater popularity than St Agnes. More lives of St Katherine survive, and narrative depictions of her life were more common. It is therefore particularly worthy of note that there are no depictions of her mystic marriage, and that not all the surviving late medieval English lives of St Katherine include this episode, whereas other aspects such as the taking of her body to Mount Sinai are standard. The English hagiographical tradition also modified the Continental version of the mystic marriage: in England Katherine is married to the adult Christ rather than to the infant.[47] Although this is a different solution from the one adopted at Cawston, both strategies testify to an unease about the Christ Child in English Christocentric devotion.

The rarity of mystic marriage iconography in the parish context, and the reluctance to link it with the incarnate figure of Christ, especially as an infant, was compatible with the meditative Christocentric focus of later hagiography. This development brought the adult Christ to the fore, and also stressed the humanity of the saints. Although saints could be models of faith and of Christocentric devotion, they were still closer to ordinary human experience than to the divine. As a result, the average christian could not aspire to be the bride of Christ, and even Mary was increasingly depicted at her coronation in a subordinate position to her son as part of the Trinity.

---

[47] K. J. Lewis, ' "Rule of lyf alle folk to serve": lay responses to the cult of St Katherine of Alexandria in late medieval England, 1300–1530', Ph.D. thesis, University of York (1996), pp. 241–3.

The implications of these developments for the laity are, however, less clear, particularly since the experience of Margery Kempe seems to run against the trend. Margery claims a spiritual relationship with both Christ and (more dauntingly) God. Should she be considered an exception to the general rule, and her ascent from Mary's handmaid to the daughter and spouse of Christ be seen as extraordinary? It is clear that the visual context of parish religion cannot have provided all the stimulus for such ideas, and that Margery's access to mystical devotional literature postdates the spiritual experiences she narrates, even if the narrative does not. Obviously, the precise content of sermons heard in Norwich and Lynn eludes us, and some indirect influence of Julian of Norwich is also possible. Nevertheless, it remains likely that such ideas were beyond the mainstream of religious culture as indicated by patronage decisions in a parish context. They were for those who took their religion more seriously than most, and who therefore transferred to the female saints the qualities of a spiritual élite. Saints became representatives of a higher spiritual state which was almost, but crucially not quite, beyond human reach in this world, rather than the earthbound footings of the heavenly structure. Of course, such a conception also had its limits. For Margery there was an important distinction between her relationship with Christ and with the Godhead. Christ's humanity meant that she could be comfortable with Christ, but she was more his daughter than his spouse, and she feared, and even attempted to resist, a closer knowledge of God.[48]

Distinctions in expected attainment, and the acceptance of the idea of a spiritual élite, centred most clearly on views of spiritual and physical chastity, which formed the basis of Margery's agonised concern that she was less acceptable to God than the virgin saints. Margery, in taking her preoccupation with religion beyond the norm, in effect placed herself at the cusp between the aspirations of the nun and the devout laywoman. Much of late medieval meditational piety did, of course, have the effect of blurring this distinction, and it was precisely this process which created tensions in the lives of the extra-devout.[49] Nevertheless, this same tendency could also serve to reduce the emphasis on the religious significance of physical chastity, and of the aspiration to become the bride of Christ. As a preacher put it, 'þer is doubull chastite, goostely and bodely'. Ghostly chastity may be kept by every married man or woman, but both ghostly and bodily chastity are necessary for a maiden to be Christ's spouse. Other people should seek the chastity of the

---

[48] See pp. 91–2.
[49] H. M. Carey, 'Devout literate laypeople and the pursuit of the mixed life in later medieval England', *Journal of Religious History* 14 (1987), 361–81.

soul undefiled by sin and thus hallow Christ in their hearts.[50] Such conclusions underpinned Margery's agony, but as importantly they also served to outline a respectable religious position for the average layperson for whom physical virginity was not an option. For most people, this dual sense of chastity encouraged the lack of emphasis on the religious value of maidenhood, which was seen as generally irrelevant for lay imitation of the saints. It was only for those like Margery, who took their religion more seriously than most, that becoming a bride of Christ was a serious aspiration, and this seemed to require the virginity of the cloister.[51]

Therefore, despite the general context of Christocentric devotion, and Margery's struggles to reconcile her spiritual life with her sexual history, the image of mystical marriage was not a dominant feature of late medieval lay religious culture, and the connection between marital status and sanctity was weaker in England than in other parts of Europe, such as Italy. The lack of emphasis on the idea of the bride of Christ meant that the barrier of the special qualification of virginity, which separated female saints from the majority of laywomen, was less significant. This development can be seen as a return to doctrinal purity, although this is unlikely to be the cause of the change. As Aquinas argued, although virgin saints died in defence of their chastity, they also, and more importantly, died in defence of their faith to avoid worshipping false gods.[52] The significant difference by the fifteenth century was that such ideas were being articulated in a context in which mystical bridal imagery had little place.

The reduced emphasis on saints as virgins and as brides of Christ affects our understanding of their association with earthly marriage and childbirth. Duffy, in discussing the imagery on the screen at Ranworth (Norfolk), points out that both virgin martyrs and fecund fertile saints (in this case St Anne and St Margaret) could be called upon for support in times of childbirth. Such a possibility challenges an oversimplistic application of role models (virgins apply to virgins; mothers to mothers). Duffy suggests that the ability of virgin saints to assist in childbirth was central to the resolution, in the religion of the laity, of the tension between family life and the value the Church placed on virginity. In his view it did so not by devaluing the status of virginity, but by using virginity to sanctify the female body:

The three Marys with their holy children were icons of the divine blessing on the earthiness of womanly things, of marriage and child-bearing, of fruitfulness and heaven's blessing on woman's labour. The figure of Margaret beside them also symbolized that

---

[50] Ross (ed.), *Middle English Sermons*, pp. 291–2.
[51] Early sixteenth-century printed editions of excerpts from Margery's *Booke* omitted all mention of these concerns. See above p. 93 n. 59.
[52] See p. 209.

blessing, but through a contradictory emphasis on the supernatural power of holy virginity, the untouched and inviolate female body as the meeting-place of earth and heaven, the spousals of human and divine.[53]

As has been argued, this interpretation starts from a view of the potency of supernatural virginity which overstates the general case. Nevertheless, the significance of the juxtaposition of particular virgin and fertile saints to bless childbirth requires further examination. The examples of both St Anne and St Margaret cast doubt on Duffy's assessment of the meaning of their role, and of the connections between sanctity, virginity and fertility.

The cult of St Anne was growing in popularity in the late Middle Ages, but its spread was quite regional. A comparison of rood screen paintings in Devon and East Anglia shows that Anne was a much less popular choice in Devon.[54] The abandonment in the fifteenth century of the imagery of St Anne teaching the Virgin to read did not result in the general introduction of devotion to the Holy Family, since the two devotions had quite different emphases (Fig. 27). First occurring in England in the early fourteenth century, the image of St Anne teaching the Virgin was more than a simple depiction of the maternal process of education. Rather, as shown by the frequent pairing of this image with the Annunciation, it seems to have had a more complex imitative function and served to show the place of devout education in the long sweep of incarnational history: the preparation of Mary's role begins as a child so that she is educated to respond appropriately to the Annunciation, and the same preparation is required of all christians.[55] In this depiction Anne is not presented as a nurturing, maternal figure. For this, appropriate images could be the Nativity of the Virgin Mary or a version of the intimate images of Mary suckling the Christ Child, but neither of these seemed appropriate. The portrayal of Anne and the Virgin in its fourteenth-century form did not place great emphasis on motherhood, and this can explain why there was no natural link between the two styles of devotion to her. Although the reading image was fairly widespread, devotion to the Holy Family (Anne, the three Marys and their children) took strongest hold in East Anglia, presumably assisted by the links between this region and the Continent.

The cult of Anne and the Holy Family could sanction motherhood, but it did so in a rather detached and not particularly intimate way. As important, if not more so, was the support the cult gave to ideas of lineage and fecundity. Gill's study of the paintings around the tomb of Peter Arderne at Latton (Essex) shows that childless couples could make Anne and the Holy Family

---

[53] Duffy, 'Holy maydens, holy wyfes', pp. 194–6.
[54] Ibid., pp. 178–9.
[55] Scase, 'St. Anne and the education of the Virgin'; Sheingorn, ' "The wise mother" '.

Figure 27 St. Anne teaching the Virgin to read, Beckley (Oxon.)

the focus of their devotions.[56] But such actions should be seen less as a sanctification of fecundity, and more as an expression of the belief that the divine rendering of the barren woman fruitful was a result of devout petition and the unfolding of God's plan. The offspring of the Marys was a means of providing Christ with kindred as much as, if not more than, a sanctification of fecundity. It was a livelier, and more intimate, version of the Tree of Jesse.

Anne, Mary and Margaret were all called upon by women for help during childbirth, but it is less clear that this was a result of the same, or arguably any, association with the sanctity of fecundity. The first two seemed quite simply appropriate in terms of the natural desire to reduce the pain of childbirth. A painless labour was appropriate for the Mother of God and for her mother, and was obviously an attractive idea for women who might otherwise expect to experience the curse laid upon Eve and her daughters. However, although the specialist functions of these saints involved mimesis, this did not necessarily involve the *sanctification* of childbirth and fruitfulness. In the case of the virgin saint Margaret mimesis obviously had to work in a different way: Margaret's safe delivery from the body of the devil underpins her ability to grant women safe delivery in childbirth. As such, it appears to make little reference to the 'supernatural power of holy virginity, the untouched and inviolate female body as the meeting place of earth and heaven, the spousals of human and divine'.

The interpretation of Margaret's reputation for assisting with childbirth is complicated by the fact that the scene of her supernatural delivery from the body of the tempting devil was viewed with increasing scepticism in the medieval period. Even Jacobus de Voragine was uncomfortable with this story, declaring that the episode of the dragon devouring her and then bursting open was clearly fabulous and preferring the version in which the demon appears in the form of a man.[57] Moreover, the identification of the demon with lust, as in a fourteenth-century Tuscan play of St Margaret, was not the principal focus in English narratives.[58] Mirk's list of what the demon represents is much more comprehensive: he caused the Jews to kill Christ, he makes men kill men and commit lechery and adultery, and he likes best of all to make men break their vow of baptism.[59]

We should therefore question whether Margaret's intervention was seen primarily in terms of the supernatural power of virginity, or of the power of faith against the earthly temptations of the devil. Holy virginity is not

---

[56] M. C. Gill, 'Late medieval wall painting in England: content and context (*c*.1350–*c*.1530)', Ph.D. thesis. Courtauld Institute of Art (2001), pp. 131–2. The Ardernes had two daughters, Ann and Elizabeth, whose name saints feature on the tomb, but wished for a son and heir.

[57] E. A. Petroff, *Body and Soul: Essays on Medieval Women and Mysticism* (Oxford, 1994), p. 98.

[58] Ibid., p. 103.   [59] Erbe (ed.), *Mirk's Festial*, p. 201.

simply the 'untouched and inviolate female body': what is important is the resistance of the virgin saint, and it is this that can imbue her with power. Virginity is significant as actively preserved virginity, which is a symbol of intact and steadfast faith. The meaning of virginity for the virgin saint is parallel to the martyrdom of Winifred, whom Mirk can call a martyr despite the fact that she was restored to life by intercession.[60] In this sense the virginity of Margaret did not prevent her being associated with help during childbirth, but neither did it in a physical sense enable her to do so. Similarly, St Katherine's refusal to accept an earthly husband did not prevent her being called upon for aid in finding a good husband or, more desperately, any husband at all. Later traditions associated with the fourteenth-century chapel of St Katherine at Abbotsbury (Dorset) clearly relate to the story, preserved in the fifteenth-century German life of St Katherine, that before her conversion Katherine was choosy about her future husband, demanding four husbandly qualities, which would ultimately be fulfilled in the person of Christ.[61] If Katherine's own demand could be met on such a scale, she was clearly the obvious figure to look to for assistance in the lesser task of finding a suitable human husband. It was the possibilities of mimetic intercession which were of prime importance. The cases of Katherine and Margaret were parallel to that of a saint like Apollonia, who was instantly linked to toothache. Virginity had its importance, and had led to the redescription of Apollonia as a nubile holy maiden rather than an elderly christian widow.[62] It was an expected, but, by the fifteenth century, a background feature, which was no more significant in helping with childbirth than it was in preventing the house being struck by lightning.

[60] Ibid., pp. 177–82.

[61] Lewis, ' "Rule of lyfe all folk to serve" ', p. 244; B. A. Beatie, 'Saint Katherine of Alexandria: traditional themes and the development of a medieval German hagiographic narrative', *Speculum* 52 (1977), 793; S. Dewar, 'St Catherine of Alexandria and her cult at Abbotsbury', *Proceedings of the Dorset Natural History and Archaeological Society* 90 (1969), 261, records two variants of rhymes used by women in search of husbands:

> A husband, St Catherine,
> A handsome one, St Catherine
> A rich one, St Catherine
> A nice one, St Catherine
> And soon, St Catherine

> Sweet St Catherine send me a husband
> A good one I pray
> But arn a one better than narn a one,
> Oh St Catherine
> Lend me thine aid
> And grant that I never may
> Die an old maid.

[62] Winstead, *Virgin Martyrs*, p. 9.

This interpretation, which foregrounds faith rather than virginity itself, explains not only why saints with seemingly incompatible characteristics could be called upon in childbirth, but also the respectability of the cult of the redeemed prostitute. When Isabel, Countess of Warwick, made her will in 1439 she specified amongst the instructions for her tomb, 'And my Image to be made all naked, and no thyng on my hede but myn here cast bak-wardys, and of the gretnes and of the fascyon lyke the mesure that Thomas Porchalyn hath yn a lyst, and at my hede Mary Mawdelen leyng my handes a-cross.' Isabel wanted herself to be portrayed as the repentant Magdalen, her hair grown long for modesty and shame, but she saw herself as a simple imitator of Mary Magdalen, who was to be depicted crossing Isabel's arms in a final gesture of peace and a good death.[63] That such a prominent, devout woman could wish to be intimately identified with the Magdalen suggests that devotion to the latter, as to the virgin saints, did not relate directly to her sexual history. A literal interpretation of the Magdalen as the redeemed prostitute did not account for the close identification of devout women with her. Rather, the narrative of redemption in sexual terms dramatised christian understandings of sin, faith and love. The language used to express this evidently reinforced the emphasis on female sexual reputation but fornication, whether spiritual or physical, could be viewed as emblematic. The use of such sexual language did not require a close identification of case histories.

The visually dominant aspect of the conflation of stories which constituted the figure of Mary Magdalen in late medieval devotion is of a saintly woman with a jar of ointment, and it is also this aspect which lingers in the saint's Reformation half-life. It is thus that Mary Magdalen is portrayed among the ranks of the saints on rood screens, and this was also the emphasis in the short prayers addressed to the saint in the printed primers. But for a medieval audience Mary Magdalen signified more than devotion to Christ regardless of expense. Her varied career could be used to justify female preaching, based on the tradition of her activities in Marseille, and to show the importance of faith and repentance.[64] As the only woman sharing the status of the apostles, and as the woman whom Christ loved most after his mother, Mary Magdalen was a powerful symbol of female potential in a framework which acknowledged the stereotypical female weaknesses, but also envisaged that they could be overcome through devotion to Christ.[65]

---

[63] McMurray Gibson, *Theater of Devotion*, pp. 11–12.

[64] A. Blamires, 'Women and preaching in medieval orthodoxy, heresy and saints' lives', *Viator* 26 (1995), 136–7; O. O'Sullivan, 'Women's place: gender, obedience and authority in the sixteenth century', *Reformation* 3 (1998), 225–58, discusses medieval evidence relating to Mary Magdalen (pp. 231–5).

[65] The Digby Mary Magdalen play refers to her as 'an holy apostylesse' (line 1381) who alone will teach God's laws to the people of Marseille.

Mary Magdalen was both the most sinful and the most redeemed. The author of Ms Royal 18 B xxiii asserted that no one was more sinful than Mary Magdalen, who had been filled with seven devils or seven deadly sins (Luke 11), and yet she was forgiven by God. That this was possible demonstrated the power of true devotion rather than conventional outward ritual observance:

'I preye þe who was or qwere was a more synne-fullere doere þan was Marie Magdalene?' and yet 'Many synnes were forʒeven hure, for she loved mekell." What loved she? Trewly to ask forʒeveness and mercy of God for hur ewill doyinge.[66]

And why I prey þe, founde she so gret grace be-forn God all myghtye? I rede of no fastyng þat she fasted be-forn þat tyme, ne of no barfote goynge, ne wulward. I rede of non suche penaunce þat she dud. How myght it þan be þat she was made so clene? Truly þe cause here-of telleþ Crist hym-selfe when þat he seid, 'Remittuntur [ei] peccata multa, quoniam dilexit multum – þer was forgeve to hur many synnes for hure love was grett.' Loo þan, þe good Lorde, how muche þat he charcheþ a man to love hym. And who-so ʒeves hym þe love of his herte, he shall have forʒeveness, have he never so grettly trespassed.[67]

According to its editor, the theology of this collection of sermons, which were produced in Oxford in the late fourteenth or perhaps early fifteenth century, is orthodox. This is probably true, but it is a pared-down orthodoxy. There are very few references to saints, and exempla which could be matched in saints' lives are given anonymous protagonists. The discussion of Mary Magdalen puts the accent on her love of Christ and true prayer and is dismissive of the value of pilgrimages and fasting. Mary Magdalen could therefore be a controversial figure whose message for the practice of ordinary christians could be hotly contested. Nicholas Love's *Myrrour* has to adopt ingenious arguments to counter the idea that the Magdalen's story supports the view that confession should be made direct to Christ or God rather than to a priest.

However, it is precisely this controversial relevance which accounts for the popularity of Mary Magdalen in the late medieval period. Her story addresses the issue of the relationship of the ordinary sinful christian with Christ, and contributes to the debates with lollards surrounding the significance of external forms of worship. The love and piety of Mary Magdalen intersected more readily with the experiences of the laity than that of the saintly virgin bride of Christ, and therefore devotion to her fitted naturally with the diminishing emphasis on mystical marriage. Not only was imitation of her a more plausible goal, but her life presented a relationship with Christ which seemed more appropriate: that of a humble devoted follower.

This was, of course, to a large extent inherent in the nature of the story of Mary Magdalen, but it is noticeable that her image was being shaped to fill

---

[66] Ross (ed.), *Middle English Sermons*, pp. 164–5.   [67] Ibid., pp. 199–200.

this role more clearly by the fifteenth century. In the thirteenth century wall paintings of the passion of Christ, such as the one at Winterbourne Dauntsey (Wiltshire), included Mary Magdalen anointing Christ and the Three Marys at the sepulchre. The *Noli me tangere* also occurred fairly frequently in the same period, as at West Harnham (Wiltshire) and Preston (Sussex). By the fifteenth century such themes were rare, and this cannot be simply explained away as part of the more general preference for standing figures of saints rather than narrative scenes. Narrative cycles of the passion of Christ continued, but the episodes involving Mary Magdalen were omitted.

The anointing and *Noli me tangere* were confusing episodes in the prevailing incarnational aesthetic of the fifteenth century. In the first, Mary Magdalen, a notorious sinner, touched Christ and anointed his feet; in the second the repentant Magdalen was forbidden by Christ to touch him before the Ascension. This acceptance and rebuff on the part of Christ meant that the tactile intimacy of the Magdalen and Christ was problematic. A Christocentric piety which stressed the physical humanity of Christ encouraged such contact as an image of the relationship between the christian and Christ, but was concerned that the limits of acceptability should be defined. As a result, the scene of Thomas's Doubt only became more frequent as it also became more acceptable by being transformed to make Christ, not Thomas, take the initiative in placing his hand in Christ's side.[68] Similarly, in a sermon exemplum a woman who will not confess to a grievous sin is encouraged by Christ to put her hand in his side. Having felt Christ's hidden parts, she is persuaded by Christ to confess her concealed sin.[69] In this context the problem with Mary Magdalen's anointing of Christ in the house of Simon the Pharisee is her boldness, a human sinner seizing the initiative in approaching Christ.

An ingenious, if ultimately rather clumsy, attempt to give the anointing episode the appropriate modesty can be seen in Mirk's sermon. In this version Mary goes to the house of Simon the Pharisee with her jar of ointment but is too ashamed to go before Christ. She therefore stands *behind him*, takes his feet in her hands, cries, wipes them with her hair, kisses his feet, and anoints him.[70] Mirk's imagining a physically very awkward position, and one not assumed in earlier iconography of this theme, shows the lengths to which he is prepared to go to reduce the boldness of Mary's humble approach to Christ. It is perhaps not surprising that fifteenth-century artists did not adopt this solution. Instead, implicitly recognising the difficulties with the standard

---

[68] McMurray Gibson, *Theater of Devotion*, pp. 16–18.
[69] Ross (ed.), *Middle English Sermons*, pp. 216–17. The story also appears in *Speculum Laicorum*, Bromyard's *Summa Predicantium* and Mirk's *Festial*.
[70] Erbe (ed.), *Mirk's Festial*, pp. 203–4.

iconography, they shied away from straightforward narrative renditions of the scene in favour of an emblematic approach which could conflate the anointing and the appearance of Christ in the garden in the context of the cult of the Five Wounds.

The emblematic solution was adopted in the painting at Drayton (Norfolk) in which Christ is crowned and shows his wounds, whilst Mary Magdalen kneels and holds up her vase of ointment.[71] The Magdalen's ointment is a complex symbol. In using such an expensive substance to anoint Christ's feet, Mary can be assumed to be expressing the depth of her devotion and penitence regardless of expense, but Christ while accepting this also links it to the preparation for his own death. The three Marys also take ointment to the tomb, and it is this ointment which Mary could be holding when she sees Christ in the garden. In fact, both jars of ointment express deep devotion in the context of the death of Christ, and for a late medieval audience the act of anointing could be equated with the act of prayer. It is perhaps not too far fetched to see Mary Magdalen's proffered ointment in the painting at Drayton taking on the symbolism it is given in MS Royal 18 B xxiii's sermon on the three Marys at the tomb: 'And þer-fore lett us folowe þe love of þise iii Maries and seche we Ihesus with swete oynttement; þat is to sey, with swete preyours, for þat is an oyntement of swete smell.'[72]

A painting at Bray (Berkshire) develops the implications of the Drayton iconography a stage further, closing the gap between the intimacy with Christ allowed to Thomas and to Mary Magdalen. As at Drayton, Christ appears showing his wounds and Mary holds her jar of ointment, but at Bray she touches the wound in Christ's foot with a finger of her right hand.[73] Mary Magdalen with her ointment jar symbolises human devotion and the promise of an eventual reward when she, and other devoted and penitent christians, may finally be permitted to touch Christ's wound.

On panels of rood screens Mary Magdalen is usually shown standing with her jar of ointment, rather than as the penitent Magdalen, covered with her long hair to hide her shame, who became especially popular in the iconography of the Counter Reformation. The late medieval choice deflects attention away from the Magdalen as repentant, but once fallen, prostitute to stress instead her role as a representative sinful human. But this is not a morbid emphasis on mankind's sinfulness. The Magdalen, whilst representing sinful

[71] Rev. F. C. Husenbeth, 'Mural paintings at Drayton', *Norfolk Archaeology* 3 (1852), 26–7.
[72] Ross (ed.), *Middle English Sermons*, p. 135.
[73] C. Kerry, *The History and Antiquities of the Hundred of Bray, in the County of Berks.* (London, 1861), p. 28 and illust. facing. Only part of the painting survives, making it impossible to know whether the figure of Christ was crowned.

humanity, is also abnormally sinful. More importantly, the accent is on her devotion to Christ and its reward, which is encapsulated in the symbol of the jar of ointment itself. Thus, despite their apparent similarities, Mary Magdalen and Thomas the Apostle carried very different meanings for a late medieval audience. The Magdalen in paintings like those at Drayton and Bray, or on a panel of the rood screen, was a cipher of human devotion and its anticipated heavenly reward, while Thomas, betwixt faith and doubt, was the recipient of divine guidance, whether concerning the Resurrection of Christ or the Assumption of the Virgin Mary.[74]

It is therefore understandable that there was uncertainty about whether it was appropriate to pray *to* Mary Magdalen. For Mirk her role was as a model to spur the believer to ask God for forgiveness, and he ends his sermon with the advice, 'Wherfor ye schul now knele downe and pray to God as he for ʒaf Mary Maudelen her synnys, soo he forgeve you your synnys, and grawnt you þe blys þat he boʒt you to. Amen.'[75] This conclusion is particularly striking since Mirk also includes an account of the Marseille phase of Mary Magdalen's life, in which, through her intervention, the barren wife of the Lord of Marseille conceives a child. Mirk has no such hesitations concerning Thomas. Instead, his conclusion, unusually in verse, calls on the saint for assistance:

> Wherfor pray we to hym to make us studfast yn our fay
> And helpe us yn oure long day,
> And bryng us þer as ys no nyght but ever day:
> That ys þe joy þat lestyth ay. Amen.[76]

In fact, the only parallel to Mirk's conclusion for Mary Magdalen occurs in his sermon for the feast of the Conversion of St Paul, in which the members of the congregation are instructed to follow Paul's example and amend their lives before it is too late.[77] Mirk's logic here seems slightly awry: Paul scarcely chose to amend his life, rather his conversion came by dramatic divine intervention and quite literally as a bolt from the blue. Mirk's pastoral purpose requires urging his parishioners to take the initiative in amending their lives, even if Paul did not. But where the Magdalen clearly did take the initiative, Mirk is concerned to stress (showing a concern which historians are perhaps readier to associate with protestant writers) that forgiveness was given by God. Gendered assumptions may have played a role here, but so too could

---

[74] Mirk makes this distinction explicit in his sermon for the feast of St Thomas: 'Moch more Thomas of Inde helpys me to þe fayth þat wold not byleve, tyll he had hondelet and groped þe wondes of Cryst, þen Mary Mawdelen þat bylevet anon at þe forme tyme and furst.' Erbe (ed.), *Mirk's Festial*, p. 18.
[75] Ibid., p. 208.   [76] Ibid., pp. 20–1.   [77] Ibid., p. 55.

a concern for pastoral and theological balance. As important was the need to police the limits of human contact with a human, and yet divine, Christ.

Mirk's concern to reduce the role of human initiative and to attribute developments to the direction of God or Christ is also a dominant feature of the Digby Mary Magdalen play.[78] The dramatist depicts Mary Magdalen's fall as sexual; she goes off with the gallant she encountered at a tavern, and waits for lovers in her bower for further delights. But she is also depicted as a naive sinner who does what she is told, and, perhaps sympathetically, wants some joy in her life rather than continued mourning for her deceased and respected father. She is assailed by powerful forces intent on corrupting her behaviour, but when God's angel intervenes she does not hesitate to reject her former life. In many ways the story of Mary Magdalen in this play is about the power of divine intervention. It is a play in which Mary Magdalen herself, despite her title of holy apostless, has very little independence of action. Instead, she is guided every step of the way by God's angel, who tells her what strategy to adopt. Her attempt to preach in Marseille (mainly recounting the days of Creation) is in itself of little effect: it is the earthquake, and the new ability of his queen to conceive a child and be preserved from death that is more impressive to the pagan king. Mary is directed by Christ, and this is the interpretation the dramatist chooses to emphasise. In the *Golden Legend*, upon which much of the second part of the play is based, it is the Jews' expulsion of Mary Magdalen which sends her to Marseille, but in Digby she follows Christ's instruction. Throughout the play not only Christ, but also Peter, are her masters. Thus, although the Digby dramatist seems to have given Mary greater prominence and independent agency by cutting back on much of the supporting cast in his source text, in fact he presents her even more strongly as the humble tool of Christ.

Yet Mary Magdalen, the humble tool of Christ, was also the patron of gilds and chantries and a saint whose intercession was sought in suffrages in Books of Hours. Despite Mirk's careful reservations, it was certainly thought that she could intercede on one's behalf. As a saint, Mary Magdalen could not in practice be limited to the role of exemplar, even if she may have fulfilled this role more clearly than many other saints in the later medieval period. Indeed, that the two roles co-existed illustrates the flexibility of orthodox late medieval devotional culture, in which the cult of saints could be maintained alongside critiques of its excesses, and could be inscribed in trends of devotion centred on Christ. The omission of the *Visitatio* from the English liturgies, but not Continental ones, reminds us that this was a comparatively

[78] F. J. Furnivall (ed.), *The Digby Plays with an Incomplete Morality*, EETS extra ser. 70 (London, 1896).

new emphasis, and one which developed as the cult of the Magdalen interacted with the evolving Christocentric piety.[79] Throughout, though, there
was a concern for distance, as shown by the omission of scenes involving
the Magdalen in fifteenth-century narrative depictions of the passion. The
Magdalen was more an emblematic christian sinner than a historical participant in the drama of the passion. As such, she belonged more to the
tradition of the cult of the Five Wounds than to meditational advice to envisage the scenes of the passion unfolding in one's home town. She was part
of the devotional culture assumed in the story, told by Foxe, of a martyr who
was asked to affirm his catholicism by saying words in honour of the Five
Wounds before the rood.[80] Even when the iconography of Five Wounds was
not abstracted, emblematisation could be recognised as the salient feature of
devotion.

The gradual separation of saints from their historical roles, and their increased humanisation, meant the loss both of the defiant female saint, and
also of the strong accent on virginity as an essential qualification for mystical
marriage with Christ. Instead, the relationship of the christian with Christ
was figured in ways that separated love from sexual relationships, and that
offered a greater immediacy of access rather than a total reliance on the
hierarchy of saintly intercession. At the same time, these developments did
not serve to accentuate the mystical aspects of the Christianity of the high
Middle Ages. The processes of humanisation brought saints more effectively
down to an earthly level; they specialised in dealing with problems of daily
life, and empathised mainly with the mundane. The nature of the evolving
Christocentric piety, which stressed the passion of the adult Christ but could
also disembody his sufferings in the cult of the Five Wounds, left little scope
for mystical devotion based on the Song of Songs. As a result, when the
majority of the laity looked to the saints for exemplars of conduct rather
than for daily assistance, it was a figure like the Magdalen, and not the virgin saints, who seemed to offer a pattern for emulation. Female saints, as
representatives of the weaker vessel, offered the clearest way of visualising
the possibility of the sanctification of ordinary mortals, as on the panels of
the rood screen. The history of the Magdalen showed the way forward even

[79] P. Sheingorn, *The Easter Sepulchre in England* (Kalamazoo, 1987), pp. 26–31, 48. On the
   Continent the *Visitatio* was more common than either the *Depositio* or the *Elevatio*. The only
   English text which includes the *Visitatio* is the fourteenth-century Barking ordinal which is
   closely related to texts from Rouen. The Uses of Sarum, York, Hereford, Exeter and Durham
   contain only the *Depositio* and/or *Elevatio*. The rarity of performances of the *Visitatio* in
   England probably accounts for the rarity of portrayals of the holy women on all but the
   most elaborate Easter sepulchres.
[80] Rev. J. Pratt (ed.), *The Acts and Monuments of John Foxe*, 8 vols. (London, 1877), vol. 8,
   p. 533 (examination of John Lithall, 1558).

more clearly. But that female figures seemed especially appropriate for this role was a consequence of the christian emphasis on the humble acknowledgement of weakness, rather than a message which could be read only by women. The whole slant of the trends in late medieval devotion was to reduce the extent of biological essentialism in defining the relationship of men and women with the saints.

5

Eve and the responsibility for sin

In Eileen Power's famous formulation, medieval women were continually oscillating between the pit and the pedestal.[1] At one extreme was the figure of the Virgin Mary, embodying female virtues, and at the other the figure of Eve, symbolising the disastrous consequences of female weakness and justifying women's inferiority and subordination. This tension in contemporary conceptions of women has been generally recognised by historians, but this often leads to oversimplified conclusions based on the mistaken view that the nature and importance of this polarity was unchanging. The fluctuating fortunes of the idea of Mary as the Second Eve redressing the consequences of the Fall demonstrate the interconnections between the two figures, and suggest that discussion in terms of a simple polarity will be misleading. Nevertheless, historians considering the Reformation attack on the medieval cult of Mary have generally taken the existence of a static polarised model for granted. They have paid little attention to the changing nature of the multifaceted figure of Mary and, even more surprisingly, have seen no need to examine attitudes towards Eve.

The central concern of this chapter is therefore to examine the image of Eve, the archetypal female sinner, which was presented to lay parishioners. In this discussion the Eve–Mary antithesis will not be central. This juxtaposition, like that of the vices and virtues, although acknowledged, was rarely stressed in the media of religious instruction (sermons, mystery plays, wall paintings and stained glass) which were encountered by most parishioners. Of greater importance in understanding the meaning of Eve for the laity is the relationship between her role and the gendered personifications of vices, such as the figure of Pride as a fashionably dressed woman. In both these cases, the appeal of strongly gendered stereotypes interacted with pastoral concerns which encouraged less gendered notions of morality. Furthermore, in dramatising these histories, gender stereotypes

---

[1] E. Power, 'The position of women', in C. G. Crump and E. F. Jacob (eds.), *The Legacy of the Middle Ages* (Oxford, 1926), p. 401.

could be deployed and subverted in favour of a more even distribution of responsibility.

The literary debate concerning the nature of women is also of less interest for this study. Not only is the extent to which these texts penetrated ordinary parishes uncertain, but they offered an essentially static model of the nature of the sexes, which was enlivened only by the ingenuity of the author in converting the limited reference texts to the argument in hand. In these rhetorical works there was little opportunity for the oscillation between pit and pedestal which was present in homiletic texts and gave attitudes towards women the potential for change. The lack of elasticity in the views of women's nature expressed in the *Querelle des femmes* was due to the fact that these arguments were conducted primarily in terms of the weaknesses and transgressions of Eve, and were based on a narrow range of sources. For these writers the nature of women was determined at the Creation and discussion of the relative merits of the sexes had to be based exclusively on the Genesis account and not on the apocryphal material, which would have permitted more latitude in interpretation. Even writers of works in praise of women felt obliged to start from the same position, which led them to adopt ingenious methods to subvert the obvious reading of the relation of the sexes at the Fall. Most commonly, as in the work of Agrippa, the fact that the woman was created last would be adduced as evidence for her superiority.[2]

The constraints apparent in this literary debate are scarcely surprising in the context of an Aristotelian intellectual tradition, which stressed the innate nature of living things at the creation of the species. By contrast, the religious culture of the Middle Ages propounded a much more flexible view of human nature. Christian teaching, despite forming the basis of the scholarly works, could not accept the proposition that human characteristics were both natural and immutable. Instead, it was concerned to stress both the need and the possibility of conquering the natural characteristics of the species. The lives of the saints were testimony to the extent of human potential, but as important was the discussion of those that fell, since this allowed the pastorally vital themes of vulnerability and responsibility to be explored.

Eve and Mary represent contrasting views of the capacity and nature of women. The former is weak and fatally subject to flattery, temptation and sin; the latter humble, meek, pious and virginal. But the same assumptions

---

[2] These works are discussed in L. Woodbridge, *Women and the English Renaissance: Literature and the Nature of Womankind, 1540–1620* (Brighton, 1984); C. Camden, *Elizabethan Women: A Panorama of English Womanhood, 1540–1640* (London, 1952). The response of female writers is considered in E. V. Beilin, *Redeeming Eve: Women Writers of the English Renaissance* (Princeton, 1987). Agrippa's text, *A Treatise of the Nobilitye and Excellencye of Womankynde* (transl. 1542), is discussed in Woodbridge, *Women and the English Renaissance*, pp. 38–42.

underlie the conception of both figures. The idealisation of Mary accepts many of the characterisations of the female sex inherent in the model of Eve and stresses the unique nature of Mary in comparison with other women. This continuity is scarcely surprising in a religious culture in which much scriptural exegesis had been concerned with demonstrating how the events of the Old Testament prefigured those of the New. However, whilst both figures propounded the same views of female weakness and the ideal of chaste, silent and obedient womanhood, the emphasis on female achievement or failure (even if both had been tested in extraordinary circumstances) still meant that the greater prominence of Mary or Eve could subtly shape gender expectations.

Liturgically the greater prominence of Mary was assured with five main feasts of the Church being in her honour. More importantly, as the mother of God she was attributed a particularly powerful role as an intercessor. In religious art, this aspect was predominant and the other parts of her life were seen as a prelude to her Assumption and Coronation. However, as discussed in Chapter 3, the significance of this role did not remain constant throughout the later Middle Ages. At the height of her popularity Mary's power greatly exceeded that of any other saint and rivalled that of even Christ himself, but the development of increasingly Christocentric parochial piety entailed modifications to Mary's position and her meaning for women. Nevertheless, her place in the church calendar, and her role as the most frequent patron of gilds, ensured her continuing prominence in parish religion.

The image of Eve and the story of her role in the Fall were presented to the laity in the parishes much less frequently than that of Mary. The pedestal was easily more visible than the pit. This was due to the obvious fact that Eve lacks feast days and an intercessory role and is therefore a less dominant figure in the cycle of the church year. However, the relative paucity of references to Eve need not mean that her story was unimportant in shaping the religious perception of the nature of women. In sermons, as well as in popular literature, many of the vituperative attacks on women take as their starting point the idea of women as daughters of Eve. Moreover, the history of the Fall did have a place in the cycle of the church year. Septuagesima Sunday, recalling the seventy years of the Babylonian Captivity, was set aside by the Church for penance and repentance and naturally became the occasion for sermons on the origin of man's sins, as for example in Caxton's additions to Voragine's *Golden Legend*.[3] The drama of the Fall was also

---

[3] The sermon for Septuagesima Sunday taken from Voragine's *Golden Legend* does not tell the story of the Fall, although it does, of course, allude to Adam in its explanation of Septuagesima as a time of penance symbolic of the deviation of the world from the time of Adam until Moses. The account of the Fall is found in Caxton's additional sermon for Septuagesima Sunday, entitled 'The life of Adam'. Ellis (ed.), *The Golden Legend*, vol. 1, pp. 52–6, 169–81.

important in the medieval mystery plays as the cause of the climax of man's redemption.

The moralising aims of preachers and the dramatic demands of the Corpus Christi plays, together with the amalgamation of Biblical and apocryphal sources, left room for considerable flexibility in the interpretation of the scene in the Garden of Eden. Even the principal question of the relative responsibilities of Adam and Eve for the Fall could be supplanted by a human interest in their subsequent lives together, drawing on details from the apocryphal *Life of Adam and Eve*, which circulated in a number of editions in the fifteenth century. For example, all that Robert Reynys, a churchwarden of the parish of Acle (Norfolk), recorded in his commonplace book was that 'Adam lyved ix c yeer and xxxti, and had xxxti sones and xxxti doghters. They dyed and were both beryed togedyr, Adam and Eve.'[4]

In accordance with the penitential theme of the time of Septuagesima, sermon literature concentrated more on the events of the Fall itself. The standard late medieval interpretation of the Fall is given by Caxton in his Old Testament additions to Voragine's *Golden Legend*. In this account Eve is seen as being more vulnerable to the temptations of the serpent than Adam, as she is less prudent and more likely to slip away from the correct path. She is led astray in particular by her pride in succumbing to the suggestion of the devil that by eating the fruit she will have the knowledge of God. Caxton is, however, clear that the blame for the Fall does not rest entirely with Eve, though it is she who has sinned most. Her sin consists both of pride and of eating the fruit, whereas Adam sinned only in eating the fruit. These differing degrees of sin are subsequently neatly related to the punishments and validated by them. The pride of Eve sentences her to subjection to man and her eating of the fruit to pain and sorrow in bringing forth her fruit, although this latter punishment is mitigated by the fact that to have children is also a blessing. Adam's punishment for eating the apple is the need for toil and struggle to produce food from the once fruitful earth.[5]

The story of Adam and Eve was also included in the service for Septuagesima Sunday in Mirk's *Festial*, but in this instance the story carries a more specific moral message. Mirk's chief concern is to warn his parishioners to 'labour busely', since it was Eve's idleness which made her vulnerable to the temptations of the serpent. In discussing the Fall, Mirk does not spell out as clearly as Caxton the degrees of blame attributable to Adam and Eve or the natural weaknesses of the female sex. However, his inclusion of an episode from the apocryphal *Life of Adam and Eve* of their lives after the Expulsion

[4] C. Louis (ed.), *The Commonplace Book of Robert Reynes of Acle: An edition of Tanner Ms 407*, Garland Medieval Texts (London, 1980), p. 225.
[5] Ellis (ed.), *The Golden Legend*, vol. 1, pp. 169–81.

shows that it is Eve, rather than Adam, who continues to be vulnerable to the temptation of the devil. The couple perform penance nightly for their sin by standing in cold water up to their chins. In the course of this, the devil tempts Eve three times that they should abandon this penance and she attempts to persuade her husband to do this. But this time Adam has learnt to resist the devil, and due to his new-found strength they both continue their penance until their deaths.[6]

Sermons on Septuagesima Sunday may have been only of limited effectiveness in transmitting the story of the Fall to the laity. In many places parishioners may only have heard a passing reference to Adam in an old-style sermon on the lines of Voragine's original text.[7] Furthermore, even if a detailed account of the Fall, as given in the sermons of Mirk and Caxton, was regularly given on this Sunday, it is probable that church attendance would have been lower than on the Marian feasts. However, the laity was also exposed to the story of Adam and Eve in paintings on the walls and rood screens of their parish churches, in woodcut illustrations and occasionally in mystery plays. The demands of these different media resulted in some variation in the treatment of the story of the Fall.

The number of surviving paintings depicting this subject forms a very small fraction of the corpus of medieval religious paintings in churches. This may be due in part to the vagaries of survival, but it seems more likely that it represents the late medieval situation.[8] Paintings of saints were much more likely to become the victims of Reformation and Civil War iconoclasm than portrayals of the Fall, which could not be held to give rise to superstition. The emphasis of the late medieval Church on intercession would also lead us to expect the majority of paintings to be associated with this purpose.

Of the eighteen known images of episodes of the story of Adam and Eve in English parish churches, just over half include the Temptation.

---

[6] *The Life of Adam and Eve*, in H. F. D. Sparks (ed.), *The Apocryphal Old Testament* (Oxford, 1984); Erbe (ed.), *Mirk's Festial*, pp. 66–8. This episode is also included in the fifteenth-century Wheatley manuscript: M. Day (ed.), *The Wheatley Manuscript from B.M. Add. Ms. 39574*, EETS orig. ser. 155 (London, 1917), pp. 76–99.

[7] The Septuagesima sermons in the *Speculum Sacerdotale* refer to the seventy-year Babylonian Captivity, but not to the Fall: Weatherly (ed.), *Speculum Sacerdotale*, pp. 48–51.

[8] Medieval depictions of Adam and Eve are known from the following churches: (S – screen painting; W – wall painting; G – stained glass; B – bench end)

early 16th cent. Fairford (G) (Glouc.), Bozeat (S) (Northants.)

15th cent. Kempston (S) (Beds.), Bradninch (S) (Devon), Broughton (W) (Hunts.), Osbournby (B) (Lincs.), Brooke (S), Martham (G), Poringland (S) (Norfolk), Great Malvern (G) (Worcs.).

14th cent. Bledlow (W), Chalfont St. Giles (W) (Bucks.), East Hanningfield (W) (Essex), Alveley (W) (Shropshire), Colton (W), Elford (W) (Staffs.).

13th cent. West Horsley (W) (Surrey), Easby (W) (Yorks.). 12th cent. Hardham (W) (Sussex).

Examples are also known from Brooke (Northants.), Little Easton (Essex), Newport (I. of Wight), Shenley Mansell (Bucks.), Swainsthorpe (Norf.).

These portrayals are iconographically very similar to the fifteenth-century Continental woodcuts of the *Biblia Pauperum*. Adam and Eve are shown standing on either side of the tree (with the exception of the twelfth-century painting at Hardham (Sussex), where Adam and Eve stand together on one side).[9] The serpent is depicted coiled round the trunk of the tree, and is frequently shown with a female head in accordance with Jewish tradition. The serpent's head is usually turned towards Eve and is sometimes portrayed in the act of offering the apple, despite the clear indications in Genesis that Eve took the apple directly from the tree.[10] The message of these illustrations is clearly consistent with the view of the Fall described by Caxton in his *Golden Legend*. Eve bears the greater blame for the Fall of mankind, and the portrayal of the serpent with a human female head further emphasises the association with the female sex. However, Adam's presence also ensures that he is implicated in the act even if he is not the first to succumb.

The same message is conveyed by the iconography of the surviving English woodcuts of the Fall. Once again the sample is small. For the period 1480–1535 Hodnett lists seven woodcuts treating the story of Adam and Eve, and since many of these were used to illustrate editions of the *Golden Legend* their similarity is unsurprising. These woodcuts do, however, display greater variety than is found in church decoration and include a curious group in which Adam and Eve are shown with St Katherine, presumably as a result of her role as protectress of the dying.[11]

Treatment of the story of the Fall in mystery plays was closely related to that in other media, although dramatic conventions and the stereotype of the woman, epitomised by the garrulous, domineering and foolish character of Noah's wife, meant that the tensions between the roles of male and female were more pronounced.[12] The lack of scriptural guidance for Adam's motives in accepting the fruit also opened up the possibility of different

[9] D. Park, 'The "Lewes group" of wall paintings in Sussex', in R. Allen Brown (ed.), *Anglo-Norman Studies 6*, Proceedings of the Battle Conference 1983 (Woodbridge, 1984), pp. 210–11, notes that the Hardham iconography of Eve's labour (depicted milking a cow rather than spinning) and of Adam and Eve covering their nakedness is also unusual.

[10] R. Woolf, *The English Mystery Plays* (London, 1972), p. 115, corrects the view of Bonnell that, in the depiction of the female-headed serpent, iconography was influenced by mystery plays. The idea of the female-headed serpent appears earlier in the writings of Bede on Genesis and in the *Historia Scholastica* of Peter Comestor. J. K. Bonnell, 'The serpent with the human head in art and mystery play', *American Journal of Archaeology* ns 21 (1917), 255–91.

[11] E. Hodnett, *English Woodcuts, 1480–1535* (Oxford, 1973).

[12] S. Sutherland, ' "Not or I see more neede": the wife of Noah in the Chester, York and Towneley cycles', in W. R. Elton and W. B. Long (eds.), *Shakespeare and Dramatic Tradition: Essays in honour of S. F. Johnson* (London and Toronto, 1989), pp. 181–93, recognises the dramatic potential of Noah's wife's scorn and haranguing of her husband, and argues (p. 191) that 'the essence of Uxor's character is far less wifely disobedience than the need to "see neede". Noah's wife enacts a pattern seen in Eve, Joseph, Mary's midwife, Thomas, and countless others unnamed and unconvinced.'

interpretations of this and of the relationship between the first couple. The story of the Fall survives in five different play cycles, not all of which are complete. Some are quite brief and deliver merely the bare essentials of the Biblical account. Others, especially the Cornish *Origo Mundi* and the York Cycle, treat the subject more extensively and explore ideas of responsibility and the relations between the sexes in a more complex way.[13]

Eve's motives are portrayed in accordance with the account in Genesis. In the 'Coventry', York and *Origo Mundi* plays she is persuaded by the serpent's argument that by eating the fruit she will become like God, whilst in the Norwich Grocers' play this argument is only clinched when the serpent assures her that he has been sent by God. In the Chester play the same argument of the power of the fruit is deployed, but it is also supplemented by the idea of Eve succumbing to the enticing beauty of the fruit. In the case of Adam the starkness of the Biblical text, 'and he ate', allowed greater dramatic licence. In the 'Coventry' play he is shown as reluctant to accept the proffered apple and refuses it twice for fear of God's threat, but he finally takes it having been persuaded by the thought of being like God. The treatment in the York play is similar, but the other dramatists see Adam behaving with less hesitation and make the ambition to be like God less central. In Norwich Adam accepts Eve's explanation that God's angel gave her the fruit without demur. In Chester Adam also shows no sign of reluctance in accepting the fruit, but this may be a sign of his naivety, rather than culpability, since Eve makes no mention of either the tree or of the serpent in presenting the fruit to Adam, who takes it unquestioningly because it is sweet and fair and he will do as she asks. The implications of the Chester interpretation are expanded and given an overtly sexual overtone in the Cornish *Origo Mundi*. Here

[13] O. Waterhouse (ed.), *The Non-Cycle Mystery Plays*, EETS extra ser. 104 (1909); K. S. Block (ed.), *Ludus Coventriae or The Plaie called Corpus Christi*, EETS extra ser. 120 (1922); S. Spector (ed.), *The N-town play: Cotton MS Vespasian D.8*, EETS supplementary ser., 2 vols. (London, 1991); H. Deimling (ed.), *The Chester Plays*, EETS extra ser. 62 (London, 1892); R. Beadle (ed.), *The York Plays* (London, 1982); E. Norris (ed.), *Ancient Cornish Drama*, vol. 1 (Oxford, 1859). The account of the Fall is missing from the Towneley play, which has the story up to Adam's warning to Eve not to eat the forbidden fruit. There is a break in the Norwich text after God summons Adam when the couple realise their fault and nakedness. Modern dating of these plays suggests that a chronological explanation of these differences is not appropriate even if it is possible that the Cornish text preserves an earlier form. All texts are known from presumably working copies of the middle to late fifteenth century and continued to be performed to the Reformation. Based on place name evidence and the lack of characteristically fifteenth-century English forms, the *Origo Mundi* has been dated to 1350–75. The surviving copy was made in the first half of the fifteenth century: D. C. Fowler, 'The date of the Cornish "Ordinalia"', *Medieval Studies* 23 (1961), 96–125. According to Woolf, the extant York text was written down *c.* 1450 and the Old Testament portion of the Chester cycle towards the end of the fifteenth century. The latter was closely modelled on the *Mystère du viel testament* which survives in a text of *c.* 1450. The 'Coventry', or N-town, cycle is also dated to the mid-fifteenth century: Woolf, *The English Mystery Plays*, pp. 305–10.

Adam's acceptance of the fruit is finally accomplished by Eve's threat of the withdrawal of her presence and of her love.[14]

The differences between these plays in their portrayal of the Fall and the nature of Adam's acceptance of the fruit show that there was no single attitude towards this before the Reformation. All the writers, following their scriptural model, are of course unanimous in the attribution to Eve of the initial responsibility, but they appear to be unaware of, or unconvinced by, Caxton's neat three levels of responsibility. In fact the views expressed in the mystery plays were even more complex and diverse than my summary of the accounts of the Fall itself suggests. In reflecting on blame and responsibility immediately after the Fall and after the expulsion from paradise, the writers of the more detailed plays of York and Chester cause their accounts of the Fall to intersect with stereotypes of female nature and marital relations. Thus in Chester, where Adam has fallen without being fully conscious that the apple came from the prohibited tree and Eve has been tempted by the beauty of the fruit more than by the serpent's promise, Adam after the expulsion launches into a speech warning men against the perils of 'womans intisement' and identifying the devil and Eve as brother and sister. This vivid speech probably had more impact than the earlier scene of God handing out the punishments after the Fall, in which he made it clear that Adam was also responsible because he followed his wife's bidding not God's command. In Chester Eve is not given the opportunity to respond to this attack, but the York dramatist develops the debate between the sexes. Eve accepts Adam's assumption that women are foolish, but then deftly turns this round to make the blame lie with Adam:

> Bot sethyn that woman witteles ware
> Mans maistrie shulde have bene more.
> (lines 136–7)

Siding with the patriarchal order, here envisaged as ideally prevailing before the post-lapsarian punishment of subjection, Eve claims that Adam should have prevented her. Adam's rejoinder, that Eve never took any notice of what he said, is left uncountered, and the exchange ends with Adam's appeal to God not to let men 'Triste woman tale' (line 150) as the couple look forward to a life without glee. In this account the dramatist manages to incorporate the gender stereotypes whilst still distributing the responsibility for the Fall between the sexes. The same end is achieved by a very different device by the

---

[14] J. A. Bakere, *The Cornish Ordinalia: A Critical Study* (Cardiff, 1980), pp. 51–2, argues that the playwright is 'sympathetic' to Eve, and that Adam has no right to blame her since, in a deviation from the scriptural text, it had been Adam who had asked God for a companion. It is, however, less clear why female use of sexual persuasion should be seen as less culpable in this episode than in the parallel story of David and Bathsheba (pp. 57–8).

'Coventry' author. After the expulsion Eve acknowledges that 'my husbond is lost be-cause of me' (line 385) and asks him to strangle her. Adam's refusal because he and Eve are one flesh also neatly serves to undermine arguments for gendered responsibility for the Fall itself without personalising it in York's terms of neglected duty.

The attempt to redistribute responsibility, whilst implicitly accepting prevailing gender stereotypes, can also be found in religious literature aimed at the clergy and pious laity. The audience of the text of *Dives and Pauper* is unclear, but as a cross between a devotional manual and a pastoral and homiletic guide for the clergy the work is clearly rooted in the parish rather than in the more rarefied rhetorical debates of the *querelle des femmes*. Nevertheless, like the York dramatist, the author adopts some of the strategies typical of that debate to secure his own end. He subverts the idea of the greater responsibility of Eve in order to make a pastoral point against male complacency.

For the author of *Dives and Pauper* Adam is more to blame for the Fall than Eve, and this case is buttressed by a range of supporting arguments.[15] Eve was deceived by an external (and therefore greater) tempter, whilst Adam was deceived by his own pride, which continued after the Fall, as he would not acknowledge his own guilt but accused others of it. St Paul's comment that mankind fell through the sin of only Adam is then used to confirm this conclusion as also, more ingeniously, is the fact that Christ was born a man, but took flesh from woman:

Crist becam nout woman but he becam man to savyn mankende þat as mankende was lost be man so mankende schulde be savyd be man, & þerfor in manhod he wolde deyyn for mankende for manhod hadde lost mankende. And also he becam man & nout woman to savyn þe ordre of kende and for þat womanys synne was lesse grevous þan Adamys synne & lesse deryd mankende, & woman was lesse infect in þe firste prevaricacioun þan was man þerfor God took his manhod only of woman withoutyn part of man.[16]

Here Mary is the counterpart of Eve, but the real actors, the blamed and the blameless, are Adam and Christ.

The intricacies of the author of *Dives and Pauper*'s argument may have escaped many, but perhaps the clearest indication of the extent to which the traditional views of Eve and Mary were not current in England on the eve of

---

[15] The author also strengthens his case by dismissing possible counter arguments. That Eve's punishment is greater does not prove her greater culpability: in this world God does not punish sins proportionately, and the more grievous sins are generally punished in the next world. That Eve sinned more than Adam because she put them both in sin is refuted by the observation that Adam was full of pride, which was understood as the root of sin, before Eve offered him the apple.

[16] Barnum (ed.), *Dives and Pauper*, p. 84.

the Reformation is the rarity of the idea of Mary as the second Eve redeeming the trespass in the Garden of Eden. The connection between the two women was a product of the tradition of scriptural exegesis exemplified in the block books of the *Biblia Pauperum*. The relationship of the image of Eve with the image of Mary in these works was more complex than the simple contrast of female weakness with female virtue because of the belief that the events of the New Testament were prefigured in the Old Testament. In this scheme the Temptation of Eve was frequently related to the Annunciation, as Eve was seen to have brought sin into the world whereas Mary brought man's redemption.

In the fifteenth and early sixteenth centuries the parallel between Eve and Mary was frequently included in the block books produced mainly in Germany and the Netherlands. The work of Guldan has also revealed many examples from France, Germany and Italy for this period in which scenes from the life of the Virgin Mary also incorporate illustrations of the Fall.[17] However, these portrayals cannot be easily paralleled with examples from England. The Old Testament types were, of course, portrayed in early sixteenth-century stained glass in the church of Fairford (Gloucestershire), which includes depictions of the Temptation of Eve and Moses and the burning bush as symbols of the virgin birth, Gideon's fleece as a type of the Incarnation and the Queen of Sheba bringing gifts to Solomon as the magi were to do to Christ at Bethlehem. Nevertheless, the Fairford example is only of limited significance since, even if the legend that the glass was captured at sea has to be discounted, the windows show strong Continental influence in both design and choice of subject matter.[18] Other examples, such as the glass in King's College chapel, Cambridge or Malvern Priory, are similarly the products of élite or ecclesiastical patronage and have little connection with the religion of the ordinary parish. Only the early sixteenth-century screen painting at Bozeat (Northamptonshire), in which the Expulsion is contrasted with the Annunciation, juxtaposes the stories of Eve and Mary, and here it may be significant that the principles of typological prefiguration are not followed closely: the penalty of the Expulsion, which fell upon Adam and Eve alike, begins to be removed with the Annunciation and Incarnation.

The general lack of interest in the typological relationship between Old and New Testament scenes in English late medieval art can be partly attributed to the fact that these schemes had never been very deeply rooted in the less élite forms of religious art, such as wall painting, and were almost entirely

---

[17] E. Guldan, *Eva und Maria: Eine Antithese als Bildmotiv* (Graz and Cologne, 1966).

[18] H. Wayment, *The Stained Glass of the Church of St Mary, Fairford, Gloucestershire* (London, 1984). The legend that the glass was captured at sea cannot be proven and Wayment concludes on the basis of iconography and style that the glass originated from the Low Countries.

confined to works in stained glass. More decisively, however, this was due to the development of the intensive devotional focus on the passion of Christ. As the New Law overshadowed the Old, the centrality of the Creation and the Fall in man's religious views of his history was undermined and the redeeming nature of Christ's passion supplanted the intercessory powers of the Virgin Mary.

The focus on the suffering Christ of the Crucifixion profoundly altered the view of the Fall. Although the Fall had necessitated the coming of Christ, it was now man's general weakness and tendency to sin rather than the details of this particular event that was adduced as its cause. The extent of Christ's suffering also meant that the idea of the Fall as the 'felix culpa' now seemed inappropriate. In the early fifteenth century the Fall could still be celebrated as the cause of Mary becoming Queen of Heaven, as in the poem 'Adam lay ibounden':

> Adam lay ibounden,
> Bounden in a bond:
> Foure thousand winter
> Thought he not to long.
> And all was for an apple,
> And apple that he tok,
> As clerkes finden
> Wreten in here book.
>
> Ne hadde the apple taken ben,
> The apple taken ben,
> Ne hadde never our Lady
> A ben Hevene Quen.
> Blissid be the time
> The apple taken was!
> Therefore we moun singen,
> 'Deo gracias!'[19]

However, at the end of the century it was inconceivable that these ideas could be transferred to a Christocentric context: the bondage of man for 4,000 years since the Fall could not be accounted a blessing for causing the Crucifixion.

Although Eve continued to form the basis of the negative stereotype of woman, pastoral concerns, and the development of an increasingly Christocentric piety, blurred gendered stereotypes of responsibility and weakness. The later medieval inclination was to associate Adam and Eve jointly in the responsibility for the Fall, whilst deploying and questioning narrower gendered assumptions. This presentation of the roles of Adam and Eve also interacted with the changing emphases within the cult of the Virgin Mary, even

[19] Davies (ed.), *Medieval English Lyrics*, pp. 160–1.

if (or perhaps more powerfully because) the antithesis was less frequently expounded. The image of Eve, and also of Mary, in late medieval parish religion differed significantly from modern assumptions. Mary, as we will see, was gradually stripped of her more human attributes and virtues, which relate directly to her position as virgin mother. Eve, whilst being portrayed as weak and vulnerable, was also shown in contexts which demonstrate either weakness or lack of thought on the part of Adam.

The influence of pastoral concerns on gendered stereotypes is even more marked in the treatment of the vices and virtues. From the Latin both virtues and vices were personified as women, making a gendered antithesis appear more difficult. Nevertheless, the Church's didactic agenda, based on its assumptions about human nature, encouraged more emphasis on the avoidance of sin, or at least the need for subsequent repentance, than on the virtues themselves. The female association with vices therefore had the potential to be more prominent. Visually on the walls of parish churches the Seven Deadly Sins were not routinely contrasted with the Virtues, or even with the Seven Works of Mercy. The latter, emphasising practical manifestations of the single virtue of mercy, seems to have been considered a more pastorally effective means of inculcating ideas of christian virtues. The Seven Deadly Sins show a similar, but less developed, tendency towards reduction: all seven sins were graphically portrayed, but the protagonist and the foundation of all the rest was thought to be Pride.

Although linguistics encouraged a female personification, the image of Pride could be male or female, or, as in Langland's *Piers Plowman*, change between the two in the course of the narrative, whilst the other six sins were personified male.[20] In imagery, the gender of Pride seems to have depended largely on whether the moralising emphasis concerned vanity in clothing and appearance, pride in worldly position and wealth, or (as in the case of Eve) the dangers of being beguiled by flattery. This connection, and the diversity of representation, can be seen in wall paintings of the theme of the Seven Deadly Sins and their association with the related iconography of the Wheel of Fortune and the Three Living and the Three Dead.

A group of paintings, mainly of the later fourteenth century, which adopt the iconographic formula of the Tree of the Deadly Sins envisage Pride as male. At Catfield (Norfolk) Pride is shown twice, once at the top of the tree, and once as a king falling headfirst into hell at its base (Fig. 28).[21] Situated immediately adjacent to a painting of a Wheel of Fortune, with its falling

---

[20] M. W. Bloomfield, *The Seven Deadly Sins: An Introduction to the History of a Religious Concept with Special Reference to Medieval English Literature* (Michigan, 1952), pp. 197–200, 213–14. In *Piers Plowman*, as well as in lollard and anti-lollard writings, Pride is female as a penitent and male as an assailant.

[21] D. Turner, 'Mural paintings in Catfield church', *Norfolk Archaeology* 1 (1847), 133–9.

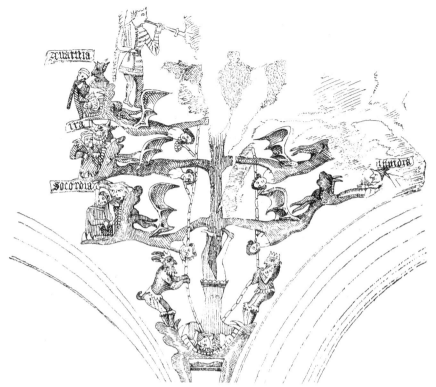

Figure 28 Wall painting of male Pride and the Seven Deadly Sins, Catfield
(Norfolk)

king captioned 'Regnavi' and the fallen one '[no]n regno', the connection
is clear. The loss of worldly position as the wheel turns is not simply the
result of the inexorable workings of fate or fortune, but linked closely to the
flourishing of the Seven Deadly Sins. That the victim is envisaged as a king
emphasises misplaced attachment to worldly wealth and status, and thus
carries the same meaning as the presence of kings in paintings of the Three
Living and the Three Dead. The theme of falling is also developed in the
Tree of the Deadly Sins at Hoxne (Suffolk), where devils are shown sawing
through the trunk of the tree to cause it to topple into the mouth of hell.

Paintings adopting the other possible iconographic convention, the portrayal of the Sins issuing from a human figure, are more likely to portray the
allegory in female terms. This is clearly the case at Raunds (Northamptonshire), where a fashionably dressed figure of Pride with sins issuing from her
is speared by a skeletal figure of Death (Fig. 29). The accent is now on the
vanity of dress, and the opponent is Death rather than the turns of fortune

Figure 29 Wall painting of Pride as a fashionably dressed woman, Raunds
(Northants.)

or the antics of devils luring the sinner as their prey. It is less clear whether
the protagonist in such images is always female. Nineteenth-century local
historians assumed that this was the case, but this seems to have been based
as much on their literary assumptions as on the detail of the visual evidence
itself. Many of the examples they discovered have deteriorated further since
that time making it more difficult to determine. Thus at Padbury (Buckinghamshire) Keyser in 1887 identified a painting of the Purging of the Seven
Deadly Sins with a richly dressed and crowned female figure in the centre
and a large figure of Death, but when the paintings were re-examined in
the 1960s little of the central figure was visible. Other descriptions seem
more confused: at Alveley (Shropshire) an image identified as the Triumph
of Woman, since there was a painting of the Fall elsewhere in the church,
appears to be a straightforward description of a female Pride with Death
shooting darts at her until we also learn that on her left was a knight in armour (presumably St George), piercing the head of the dragon under her feet.
Other examples at Little Hampden and Little Horwood (Buckinghamshire)
and Oddington (Gloucestershire) leave open the possibility that the central

figure may have been male. However, even if portrayals of the Sins in this form were more likely to show Pride as female, in gender terms the overall message of the image may have been more complex: at Padbury, although the central figure was a crowned woman, the figure of Gluttony was a man shown holding his head in his hand and being very sick.[22]

The personifications of Pride and the other vices in these two iconographic types seems to undermine apparently clear-cut gender boundaries whilst at the same time reinforcing them in a more specific manner, associating women with the frivolous vanity of fashionable costume, and men with false confidence in worldly status as the king loses his crown to Fortune or Death. This separation and balance was not the main concern, but rather an incidental consequence of overlapping trends: in the fifteenth century images of the Wheel of Fortune or of the Three Living and the Three Dead became less frequent, whilst images of Pride as a fashionably dressed woman predominated. The shift was not complete, as the all male Tree of the Deadly Sins at Hessett (Suffolk), and the less easily identifiable one at Ruislip (Middlesex) show, but it suggests a changing awareness of the nature of the root of all sins and its gender associations.[23] By the mid-sixteenth century a further possible shift can be identified as Pride was replaced by Covetousness and Avarice as the root of all evil in the writings of the so-called 'commonwealth men'. Avarice, as a sin most obvious in the public realm (especially in its close association with enclosures for pastoral farming), was most likely to be characterised as primarily a male fault, even if these men were also seen as being partly spurred on by their wives' vanity and their demands for costly fabrics and luxuries. Nevertheless, this still represents a significant shift in gender terms. Previously, although the miser could be male, avarice had found its most vivid expression in the social type of the dishonest alewife hauled off to hell still clutching her false measure, and at Bacton (Suffolk) offering a devil a drink.[24]

[22] J. G. Waller, 'On wall paintings discovered at Raunds and Slapton, Northamptonshire', *Arch. Jnl.* 34 (1877), 220–24; C. E. Keyser, 'On some mural paintings recently discovered in the churches of Little Horwood and Padbury, Buckinghamshire', *Records of Bucks.* 7 (1897), 219–20, 222–3; E. C. Rouse, 'Wall paintings in St. Mary's church, Padbury', *Records of Bucks.* 18 (1966–70), 28–9; Annual Excursion Report, *Shropshire Arch. & Nat. Hist. Soc.* 2nd ser. 5 (1893), xii. A drawing by Henry Marchant (1914) in the Alveley parish file in the Wall Paintings Archive, Courtauld Institute, redraws the knight in armour as a figure of death trampling the dragon and piercing the figure of Pride; C. E. Keyser, 'Notes on some recently-discovered wall paintings at Little Hampden church', *Records of Bucks,* 9 (1909), 415–24.
[23] Rev. Canon Cooke, 'Materials for a history of Hessett, part 2', *Proceedings of the Suffolk Institute of Archaeology and Natural History* 5 (1886), 29–35.
[24] Ashby, 'English medieval murals of the Doom', p. 237. At Chesterton (Cambs.) male figures of a miser and usurer are depicted in hell. An alewife with mug in hand appears in fifteenth- and sixteenth-century Dooms at Bacton (Suffolk); Barking (Essex); Brooke (Norfolk); Croughton, Mears Ashby (Northants.); St Michael's, St Albans (Herts.); St Thomas',

Moral concerns about the Seven Deadly Sins did not address all seven equally. Across the period as a whole, Lust occupied a prominent place alongside Pride and Avarice as a candidate for the root of all sins. Mirk, considering the phrase 'deliver us from evil' in the Lord's Prayer, explained 'þys evell þe may calle wele þe synne of lecherye' because lechery produces all other sins and leads to murder, envy, adultery and false suspicion.[25] Perhaps more than the other deadly sins, lechery, or lust, was most easily considered in a gendered manner, but the implications of this were complex and apparently contradictory. The prevailing late medieval assumption was that women were inherently more lustful than men, and that their sexual appetite, once aroused, was insatiable, as in the case of widows. But it was also possible to argue that their natural propensity made them less culpable in the sin of lust.

The standard image of lust was a couple embracing, but occasionally the painter went further and attempted to distinguish between the roles of the man and woman. In the portrayal of the Seven Deadly Sins at Padbury (Buckinghamshire) the artist added a sword piercing the woman's back, and a similar solution was adopted at Branscombe (Devon).[26] These images suggest a gendered view of responsibility, but it is less clear precisely what the sword signifies: the most culpable partner? a sentence of death for the adulteress? The problem clearly has two main aspects; the grading of responsibility for sin according to assumptions of natural propensity and weakness, and the relationship between lust and temptation. As such they are precisely the same problems which were addressed in all interpretations of the Fall, and not only in the *Origo Mundi* version in which the sexual relationship is explicitly foregrounded. This connection was recognised by contemporaries. It is no accident that the author of *Dives and Pauper*, who made Adam more responsible for the Fall than Eve also argued strongly against a sexual double standard.[27]

In *Dives and Pauper*, echoing the arguments in the York play of the Fall and the view of Augustine, adultery is considered a greater sin for a man than for a woman because 'þe heyere degre þe harder is þe fal & þe synne

Salisbury (Wilts.); Stoke by Clare (Suffolk) and Wymington (Beds.). She also figured in the Harrowing of Hell play in the Chester mystery cycle: Matthews (ed.), *The Chester Plays, Part 2*, pp. 329–30.

[25] Erbe (ed.), *Mirk's Festial*, p. 286.

[26] Rouse, 'Wall paintings in St. Mary's church, Padbury', 28–9; At Branscombe (Devon), the woman is speared by a skeletal figure of Death. Since the other scenes in this series no longer survive, it is unclear whether this convention was adopted in depictions of all the sins, or of lust only: Drawing by A. Hulbert, *Conservation News* 46 (Nov. 1991), 26, fig. 2.

[27] The anonymous *Dives and Pauper*, a treatise discussing the Ten Commandments, was written in English *c.* 1405–10. Printed editions of the text appeared in 1493 and 1496. The fullest discussion of this text and its treatment of the double standard is Karras, 'Two models, two standards'.

mor grevous', and because a man is supposed to be a model to his wife
and govern her. Following the same argument, lechery is more serious
in a cleric than a layman, for he too should set a higher example. It is
only man's social dominance and 'schrewidnesse' which has resulted in the
convention that men are less guilty, despite the fact that male adultery is more
common. From this social observation the pastoral concern of the author
becomes clear. He bewails the fact that in contemporary society the husband
who is chaste and true to his wife is scorned as not being a true man, and
suggests that men should be shamed into chastity by comparing their own
behaviour with the achievement of their less well-qualified wives. Placing
women on the pedestal of chastity and envisaging them always wedded to
Christ and thus able to remain chaste in the absence of their husbands, the
author then proceeds to the next logical step. He rejects the role of women
as temptresses and sees them instead as potential victims of malicious male
seducers. Women do not lead men astray: men go astray themselves first.
Thus Samson was already weakened by his lechery and misgovernment of
himself before the episode with Delilah; lust was in David's mind before he
saw Bathsheba, and in the minds of the elders who contrived to watch and
proposition Susanna.[28]

That such arguments were possible is significant, but their dominance is
less clear. The portrayal of the fate of the lecherous as mainly male souls burning in hell in texts like the *Ordinarye of Chrysten Men* (1506) or the *Kalendar
of the Shyppars* (1503) suggests that the author of *Dives and Pauper*
was not alone in recognising a pastoral urgency in such gendered terms
(Fig. 30). Even if religious authors were often happy to follow the lead of
scripture and focus on the chastity of the widow rather than the widower,
the poet Audelay could still describe the four abuses that God hates as a hard
priest, a proud friar, a lecherous old man and a cowardly knight.[29] Nevertheless, it was also more common (and perhaps easier) to depict the lustful
woman and wanton temptress than the male lecher in scenes of representative sinners being hauled off to hell in Doom paintings in the parish church.
Thus at Combe (Oxfordshire) a woman allows a devil to fondle her breast,
and at Chesterton (Cambridgeshire) 'luxuria' is shown as a temptress in a

[28] Barnum (ed.), *Dives and Pauper*, pp. 67, 110–11, 70–2, 80–1, 84–8.
[29] Rev. J. Ayre (ed.), *The Catechism of Thomas Becon with Other Pieces Written in the Reign
of Edward VI*, Parker Society 13 (1844), pp. 365–77, 520–1. Becon's *Principles of Christian
Religion* and *A New Catechism* include lengthy expositions of the duty of widows, shorter
comments on the duties of old men and old women, but no section on the duty of widowers:
Davis (ed.), *Medieval English Lyrics*, pp. 171–2, 'An old man shuld kepe him chast / And leve
the sinne of lechery; / All wedded men shuld be stedfast, / And foresake the sin of avowtry /
I say algate.'

Moze aſhamed wolde ye be/to be a coke foz wozmes. They that lyue
after deſyze of fleſſhe/lyueth after the rule of ſwyne/in etynge with=
out meaſure as vnreaſonable beeſtes. This is the hogge as it were
an abbot ouer glotonous people/of whom they holde theyz regule/
whereby they ben conſtrayned to kepe them in theyz clopſter/that is
in the tauerne and ale houſes. And lykewyſe as the hogge theyz ab=
bot lyeth in a rotten dongehyll/oz in the myzy puddle/ſo do they al=
wayes lye in the ſtynkynge affeccyon of Glotonye/tyll they be dzon=
ken and without wytte.

¶ The. vii peyne ſayde Lazarus/J haue ſene a felde ful of depe wel
  les/replenyſſhed with fyze and ſulphze wherout yſſued ſmoke
   thycke ⁊ contagyous/wherin al lecherous perſones were
      tourmented inceſſauntly with deuylles.

F all the. vii. deedly ſynnes/Lechery pleaſeth moſte vnto
the deuyll. Foz it fyleth and cozrupteth bothe ẙ body and
ſoule togyder/and by Lechery ẙ deuyll wynneth two ſou=
les at ones. And many Lecherous perſones wyll auaũte

Figure 30 The lecherous in hell, woodcut from the *Kalendar of Shyppars* (1511)

low-cut dress which she lifts with her right hand whilst placing her left hand on her breast.[30]

Lechery was the unmaking of a man. Mirk explained that when lechery fell on a man it led to the loss of his goods, reputation and friends. Even worse than this, his loss of grace meant that

his wytt schall apayre lytyll and lytyll, tyll he be a mopysche fole, and so suffyr hys lemon to be hys maystyr. And þen schall he go to noght, and schall never be delyverd þerof, but God sette wyth grete prayer hond to and delyver[d] hym.

Much of this, although stated less explicitly, could also describe contemporary assessments of the consequences of female lechery. The particularly male aspects are the transformation of the man into a 'mopysche fole' who will 'suffyr hys lemon to be hys mastyr'. The male lecher loses control of his wits, and of his ability to govern, which depends on the assumption of a natural male capacity for rational judgement. It is, however, less clear where the blame for this transformation was thought to lie. Men are clearly envisaged as vulnerable, as shown by Mirk's account of the answer to King Darius' question: which is strongest, a king, wine or a woman? The king has power to command, but can be overcome by wine. A woman is stronger than both because as his mother she brings up the king, or, as the king's mistress, can manipulate his moods.[31]

The answer to King Darius' question presents male vulnerability as unquestionably natural, and does not seek to explore the issue of male responsibility. But the latter was, of course, central to any concept of avoidable sin and hence to preachers' concerns, even if the precise relationship between male vulnerability and responsibility was often less than clear. Although the details of the stories vary, in exploring these issues sermon exempla rehearse the same gendered strategies and counter accusations as accounts of the Fall. Thus, another exemplum used by Mirk tells the tale of a woman who has been a man's mistress for many years and suddenly feels moved to mend her ways, having heard a sermon which graphically described the torments of the lecherous in hell. Meeting her lover on the way home, she refuses his advances and tells him of her resolution. His answer: 'Yf all þyng wer soþe þat ys preched, þer schuld no man ny woman be savet; and þerfor leve hyt not, for hit ys not soþe. But be we heraftyr of won assent, as we have ben befor, and I wyll plyght þe my trope þat I woll never leve, but hold þe allway,' persuades her to resume their relationship, and has a prophetic irony for the end of the tale. After their deaths a holy man prays to learn their fate. As he walks on, he hears their quarrelling voices coming from a black mist which

[30] Ashby, 'English medieval murals of the Doom', pp. 180, 237, 240.
[31] Erbe (ed.), *Mirk's Festial*, p. 287.

has risen over the water. The woman curses the man as the cause of her damnation, and in reply he places the blame on female lack of constancy rather than on his own lack of, even temporary, contrition:

Cursed be þou and þe tyme þat þou was borne, for þou hast made mee dampned for ever! For had I onys be contryte for my synnes as þu wer, I wold never have turned as þou duddyst; and yf þou hadyst holden good covenant wyth hym þat þou madyst, þou myghtyst have savid us bothe. But I behethe þe þat I wold never leve þe. Wherfor go we now boþe ynto þe payyne of hell þat ys ordeynt for us boþe![32]

Whilst enjoying the humour of the tale, the audience was clearly supposed to reject the man's attribution of responsibility, but this meant accepting individual responsibility rather than completely rejecting gender stereotypes. Female inconstancy, and the ease with which women can be misled by beguiling male arguments, are not questioned, but men should not use this as an excuse for their own conduct. To do so involves an abdication of responsibility, which runs counter to the innate (or stereotypical) male capacity for reasoned judgement.

Another exemplum told by Mirk, this time in the context of a wedding sermon, similarly accepts female stereotypes whilst retaining an idea of male responsibility. At night a charcoal burner sees a vision of a man on a black horse chasing a woman around his fire, cutting her to pieces with his sword and throwing her on to the fire. When called to account, the ghostly rider explains that in life he had enjoyed the woman 'undur hur husband; and þus uche nyght I schal slene hure and brenne hur in þis fyre, for scheo was cause of my synne'.[33] In this story the woman is claimed to be the cause of the man's sin, but his enforced participation in the nightly penitential task of pursuing, attacking and burning his lover suggests that he also shares in the responsibility for their adultery.

As in accounts of the Fall, the audience is assumed to realise that casting responsibility wholly on to the other, and especially the weaker, party is an inappropriate ploy, and one with which divine judgement will not concur. Tiers of responsibility are possible, and natural strengths and weaknesses must be taken into account, but it is generally uncertain how the prescribed penances reflect degrees of responsibility. Is it a lesser punishment to kill one's lover or to be killed by him? Similarly, it was unclear to contemporaries whether the punishments imposed by God at the Expulsion implied that Adam or Eve bore more blame for the Fall. A notion of sin, which stressed that the commission of an act can be mortal or venial, and also attempted to incorporate gendered ideas of responsibility for causation, was hard to square with a black and white view of the world. This did not, of

[32] Ibid., pp. 288–9.   [33] Ibid., p. 292.

Figure 31 Preface to the penitential psalms in a Book of Hours of the Sarum Use
(1502), depicting Bathsheba as Eve

course, mean that gendered stereotypes had to be jettisoned. They served a useful function as emblematic and powerful reminders of dangers which could beset the individual, but responsibility was measured according to how such dangers were confronted. Moreover, to the extent that such negative stereotypes defined female characteristics, they served to highlight women's achievements, and to make their falls less reprehensible.

This tempering of stereotypes with notions of contextualised responsibility was a feature of catholicism throughout the medieval period, but in the later Middle Ages the movement away from rigid gender stereotypes, and judgements based upon them, was given a further stimulus. The evolving Christocentric piety emphasised judgement by a compassionate, suffering Christ, and also weakened the idea of the Fall as the *felix culpa*. By rejecting its typological role, the human psychology, and the respective responsibilities, of Adam and Eve were highlighted. Both these developments meshed with enduring pastoral concerns which recognised the didactic value of associating vices with gendered personifications, but resisted linguistic determinism, and instead deployed such stereotypes flexibly in response to changing social concerns.

The outcome of these developments may be summed up by the changing iconography of the preface to the penitential psalms in Books of Hours of the Sarum Use. In the late fifteenth century the image of the Last Judgement was changed to one of David and Bathsheba (Fig. 31).[34] The new image clearly corresponded more closely to the content of the text, but also offered ambiguous readings of responsibility, lust and temptation, especially since the image of Bathsheba was also identified with that of Eve holding the fateful apple. If Bathsheba were to be exonerated like Susanna, this would also serve to implicate Adam more than Eve. Conversely, of course, salvaging the reputation of David would mean casting Bathsheba in the role of the more culpable Eve.[35] Viewed in conjunction with the penitential psalms, the first reading perhaps seems the more consistent and plausible, but the possibility of two interpretations was as important. The familiar stereotype of Eve, enshrined in the idea of pit and pedestal, was a long way from the complex views offered to the late medieval laity.

---

[34] Duffy, *The Stripping of the Altars*, p. 226.

[35] The late fourteenth-century Cornish play *Origo Mundi* demonstrates the extent to which the desire to develop this view could violate scripture. In this version it is Bathsheba who first suggests seeking Uriah's death, and David is portrayed as a victim of her female wiles as well as of his own lust. Unscripturally, the play also states that David repudiated Bathsheba after Uriah's death, whereas in fact he married her. It makes no reference to the fact that she was the mother of Solomon, who for finishing the temple (i.e. completing the preparations for Christ's coming) is the hero of the final section of the play: Bakere, *The Cornish Ordinalia*, pp. 57–8.

PART 2

6

Responses to Reformation change

In protestant as in catholic culture, women were considered 'to piety more prone', and, although each religion offered them different attractions, they could become tenacious adherents of either faith. That this was so does not make it redundant to interpret the impact of the Reformation in gender terms, but on the contrary more complex and significant. Following Joan Kelly's question, 'Did women have a Renaissance?', we might be tempted to ask, 'Did women, more than men, have a Reformation?'[1] Such a question addresses not only the association of women with piety, but also the extent to which the Reformation created a religious landscape that was much more overtly masculine, most obviously in displacing the Virgin Mary and the saints and also in changing the devotional relationship of the believer with Christ and God. Although the extent of these changes is often exaggerated, they were still significant, as too – given the female personification of Charity – was the redefinition of the value of ritual and the importance of good works.

The protestant Reformation exerted contradictory influences on the idea of the natural identification of piety with women. In denying the legitimacy of the practical acts of popular devotion, which had been most closely associated with the devotional sphere of the female, it undermined the female religious role. At the same time, the new doctrine of salvation by faith alone, and the associated belief in the spiritual equality of the sexes, theoretically made religion no longer the preserve of one sex more than the other. Yet, both in contemporary practice and in ideology, there was a continuing emphasis on the female as the model of piety and a considerable continuity in the particular appeal of religion to women.

This is apparent in the early years of the Reformation. Susan Brigden has drawn our attention to the attraction of the early revolutionary phase of protestantism to young people for whom it provided opportunities to rebel

[1] J. Kelly-Gadol. 'Did women have a Renaissance?' in R. Bridenthal and C. Koonz (eds.), *Becoming Visible: Women in European History* (New York, 1977), pp. 137–64.

154

against authority.[2] Similar considerations can explain the participation of women, whose position was also defined in terms of subordination, whether to husband or parents. Some of the descriptions cited by Brigden of crowds listening to preachers also draw attention to the presence of women. According to Henry Machyn, the sermon preached by Mary's chaplain, Dr Bourne, at Paul's Cross in 1553 was greeted with 'gret up-rore and showtyng at ys sermon, as yt [were] lyke mad pepull, watt yonge pepull and woman [as] ever was hard, as herle-berle, and castyng up of capes'.[3] Such descriptions may be misleading, and serve the polemicist more than the historian as a result of the general belief that both young people and women were endowed with less reason than men. In describing protestant adherents in such terms, catholic writers could aim to disparage their opponents' cause.[4] This was a frequently used rhetorical device, and was employed by writers like Sir Thomas More, who in selecting an example of the most foolish person chose to describe a woman, and by later protestant writers, such as Hooker, attempting to explain and denigrate the spread of puritanism.[5]

Female commitment to protestantism was not simply a handy myth in the service of polemic; it is also true that women could be the staunch defenders and supporters of either faith. This can be seen most clearly in cases of resistance to despoliation of churches or the prohibition of certain rituals. When the protestant Edward Underhill attempted to remove the pyx from the altar of the chapel of Stratford le Bow during Mary's reign, he was obstructed

---

[2] S. Brigden, 'Youth and the English Reformation', *P & P* 95 (1982), 37–67.

[3] Ibid., 62; J. G. Nichols (ed.), *Diary of Henry Machyn*, Camden Society orig. ser. 42 (1847–8), p. 41.

[4] Ibid., preface p. 5. The editor states that the diarist lacked 'any deep views either of religious doctrine or temporal policy'. However, his omission of any reference to the execution of Lady Jane Grey, his evident delight at Mary's accession and his keen interest in the ritual of catholic funerals all suggest committed catholicism.

[5] Campbell (ed.), *Thomas More's 'The Dialogue concerning Tyndale'* p. 164. See above pp. 40, 103–4. Rev. J. Keble (ed.), *The Works of Mr Richard Hooker*, 7th edn, 3 vols. (Oxford 1888), vol. 1, pp. 152–3, *Of the Laws of Ecclesiastical Polity*, Preface ch. 3.13:

it is also noted that most labour hath been bestowed to win and retain towards this cause them whose judgements are commonly weakest by reason of their sex . . . some occasion is hereby ministered for men to think, that if the cause which is thus furthered did gain by the soundness of proof whereupon it doth build itself, it would not most busily endeavour to prevail where least ability of judgement is: and therefore, that this so eminent industry in making proselytes more of that sex than of the other groweth, for that they are deemed apter to serve as instruments and helps in the cause. Apter they are through the eagerness of their affection, that maketh them, which way soever they take, diligent in drawing their husbands, children, servants, friends and allies the same way; apter through that natural inclination unto pity [sic], which breedeth in them a greater readiness than in men to be bountiful towards their preachers who suffer want; apter through a singular delight which they take in giving very large and particular intelligence, how all near about them stand affected as concerning the same cause.

by the wife of Justice Tawe and other women of Stepney.[6] In Exeter in
1536, the resistance to the dismantling of a rood loft at St Nicholas Priory
by two Breton carvers seems to have been carried out by women, despite
the reluctance of the authorities to believe so. In February the Mayor and
Sir Thomas Denys reported to the Marquis of Exeter that they had examined 'a greate numbre of wemen which were among other the chief doers
of the said unlawfull assemble and also dyverse of thaier husbonds', who
denied that 'there were any men disguysed or appareld in wemens appareill
amonge them' and that 'they were comaunded procured conceilled or abetted
by thaier husbondes or by any other men'. Examples of resistance to Reformation despoliation are sparse, but it is notable that the known instances
seem chiefly to have involved women.[7]

When the personal practice of either religion came under pressure, it was
similarly women who seem to have clung most tenaciously to their faith.
This is most evident for efforts to maintain catholic rites. As John Bossy has
argued, women, at least among the gentry, 'played an abnormally important
part' in the maintenance of catholicism. Women had a key role in sustaining
domestic catholic practices (especially fasting), were recusant whilst their
husbands conformed, and could be vital in sheltering and concealing missionary priests. For Bossy such roles were a consequence of a natural affinity
between women and catholicism, or, perhaps more precisely, of a female
antipathy towards a bibliocentric protestantism that required a standard of
literacy that few women could reach, and did not value their role as maintainers of ritual.[8] This may explain the continued attraction of catholicism
to some women, but the fact that women are seen primarily as the tenacious
defenders of catholicism rather than protestantism mainly reflects the fact
that officially supported anti-catholicism lasted longer. As it happens, the
clearest example of women being more committed adherents of their faith
than men comes from a protestant parish. Foxe tells us that in Stoke by
Nayland (Essex), although both men and women had initially refused to receive catholic mass, all the men took advantage of the sixteen-day amnesty
and conformed. The women were more steadfast in their resistance, and,
when the bishop's officers arrived, managed to escape punishment by going
into hiding.[9] Such edifying protestant stories are, of course, rare in Foxe, but
this need not indicate their actual frequency. In any protestant account of

---

[6] J. G. Nichols (ed.), *Narratives of the Days of the Reformation* (Autobiography of Edward
Underhill), Camden Society orig. ser. 77 (1859), p. 160.
[7] R. A. Houlbrooke, 'Women's social life and common action in England from the fifteenth
century to the eve of the Civil War', *Continuity and Change* 1/2 (1986), 171–89; *Letters and
Papers* x. 296, PRO sp 1/102.
[8] J. Bossy, *The English Catholic Community, 1570–1850* (London, 1975), p. 158.
[9] Houlbrooke, 'Women's social life', 174; Pratt (ed.), *Acts and Monuments*, vol. 8,
pp. 556–7.

the reign of Mary I, martyrdom would naturally loom large. Moreover, there may have been a fear that such women were not quite true protestants. A key to understanding the religious tenacity of the Stoke by Nayland women may be figures like Rose Hickman, who, although prepared to go into exile ostensibly for the sake of her faith, was more concerned to avoid pollution by catholic rituals than to listen to protestant sermons or discuss doctrine.[10] If such concerns were widespread amongst women, the strength of their adherence to protestantism may have had more in common with the response of their catholic sisters than is often assumed.

The public action of women at Stratford le Bow or Exeter, and the more private maintenance of catholic rituals, may have been inspired by the same catholic commitment, but they involved different ideas of gender roles. In the first, an assumed affinity with religion may have helped female activism in the public sphere to seem permissible. For the second, the definition of the role of women within the family may have encouraged a greater identification with ritual practices, going beyond such practical considerations as the importance of control over the kitchen in the maintenance of fasting. Although female involvement in riots, especially concerning grain, was a feature of early modern society, it still involved a problematic incursion of women into the public sphere, albeit one that was perhaps encouraged by the possibility of legal immunity.[11] On the other hand, adherence to, and maintenance of, ritual acts was an obvious outgrowth from areas of acknowledged female religious responsibility.

Although gender is not their main concern, the attempts of some anthropologists to explain changes in the social significance of ritual may also offer useful insights. Douglas, exploring the implications of Bernstein's work on language, has suggested that the contrast between the positional and personal family may explain adherence to ritual. In the positional family, where the role and status of each member is clearly defined within an unquestioned hierarchy, religion will be expressed through fixed rituals. The personal family treats all its members as individuals, and consequently religious experience is individualised and lays much less stress on particular actions. Douglas suggests that a movement between these two forms corresponds with the Reformation shift from catholicism to protestantism, a view that would be

[10] M. Dowling and J. Shakespeare (eds.), 'Religion and politics in mid Tudor England through the eyes of an English protestant woman: the recollections of Rose Hickman', *BIHR* 55 (1982), 97–102. For example, at the baptism of her child by a catholic priest, Rose ensured that sugar was used rather than salt (p. 100).

[11] See e.g. J. Walter, 'Grain riots and popular attitudes to the law: Maldon and the crisis of 1629', in J. Brewer and J. Styles (eds.), *An Ungovernable People: The English and their Law in the Seventeenth and Eighteenth Centuries* (London, 1984), pp. 47–84; K. Lindley, *Fenland Riots and the English Revolution* (London, 1982), pp. 40–1, 63, 72–3, 77, 176, 254.

accepted by few historians of the early modern family.[12] Nevertheless, these concepts may be helpful in understanding the respective roles of husband and wife in ritual. The role of the wife within the family was much more clearly positional than that of her husband. As Collinson has pointed out, the wife's responsibility of obedience to her husband was clearly spelled out, whereas the husband's duty to love his wife was vague and ill defined.[13] This discrepancy may mean that we should expect wives to cling more tenaciously to ritual than their husbands.

On its own, such a structural interpretation appears inadequate, even if it may help to explain why women assumed the role of maintainers of religion. Of greater importance was the strength of the stereotype of the woman as the pattern of piety, and as the individual primarily responsible for the religious well being of her household. This derived principally from the congruence between pious virtues and female ones, including domesticity, rather than from the strength of an identification of the female with gender-specific religious role models. Consequently, although a connection between religion, ritual practice and women might seem most appropriate in a catholic devotional context characterised by the cult of the saints and quasi-mechanistic observances performed in veneration, the continuing conception of the godly woman suggests that such associations were still appropriate in a protestant context. That only 48 women were included amongst the 358 Henrician and Marian martyrs who suffered for their protestant faith, and were glorified by Foxe, appears to suggest that claims for the greater appeal of the protestant religion to women seem ill advised.[14] However, such statistics may tell us more about the social structures of martyrdom, and have more in common with the factors inhibiting female participation in riot than they tell us about gendered patterns of religious commitment within the household.

The idea of a greater female attachment to catholicism once seemed to be the message of recusancy statistics, but historians are now more inclined to interpret them as an effect of the legal position of women.[15] The harshness of the recusancy laws, at least in theory, and the ambiguities of women's legal status may mean that such statistics reflect pragmatic family compromises. The Jacobean statute of 1610, issued in the climate of heightened concern following the Gunpowder Plot, showed awareness of such manoeuvres, and attempted to make families more responsible for the actions of their female members. At the same time, the statute attempted to counteract

---

[12] M. Douglas, *Natural Symbols: Explorations in Cosmology* (London, 1970), pp. 42–55.
[13] Collinson, *The Birthpangs of Protestant England*, pp. 89–90.
[14] Ibid., p. 75.
[15] M. B. Rowlands, 'Recusant women, 1560–1640', in M. Prior (ed.), *Women in English Society, 1500–1800* (London, 1985), pp. 147–80.

the pernicious influence exerted by catholic wives over their protestant husbands and to discourage such mixed marriages. The husband of a catholic wife was forbidden to exercise public office, and at her husband's death such a widow lost two thirds of her dower or jointure. Even if these stipulations were not always rigorously enforced, they clearly indicate contemporary perceptions that may not have been far from the truth. James, for example, has highlighted the key role of marriage to women from county recusant families in establishing catholic commitment amongst the mercantile elite of Newcastle.[16]

The analysis by Shiels of the 1615 visitation of Yorkshire permits a close investigation of the significance of recusancy statistics. These detailed returns echo the general pattern in including many more names of women than men. Overall, only a third of those presented were men. In some parishes, as at Drax (9) and Aughton (4), only women were listed. Even in parishes where recusants were numerous, women still predominated: at Easington, for example, 27 of the 32 recusants were female. Moreover, despite the emphasis on the role of the household in sustaining catholic recusancy, Shiels calculates that fewer than half of the names listed were members of a distinctly recusant family (i.e. of a household with more than one recusant). It is, however, less clear what this pattern indicates. Neighbourly solidarity, coupled with the need to present some recusants to meet the demands of outside authorities, may have meant that it often seemed sufficient to present only one member of the household. Such recusants could have been isolated individuals, or at the heart of a supportive network of catholic household piety.[17]

The possibility that the practical advantages of women's legal position were exploited means that recusancy statistics cannot confirm a greater female commitment to catholicism. This situation did, however, give women a dominant role in the maintenance of underground catholicism. The 'caretakers' of otherwise empty rest houses for missionary catholic priests were usually women, and women like Dorothy Lawson took advantage of their family's status, and of their own widowhood, to play a prominent part in sustaining regional catholic networks.[18] At a humbler social level, the importance of women as peddlers and hucksters meant that they could have a vital role in the distribution of catholic literature, whether concealed in

---

[16] M. James, *Family, Lineage and Civil Society: A Study of Society, Politics and Mentality in the Durham Region, 1500–1640* (Oxford, 1974), pp. 138–9.

[17] B. Shiels, 'Household, age and gender amongst Jacobean Yorkshire recusants', in M. B. Rowlands (ed.), *English Catholics of Parish and Town, 1558–1778*, Catholic Record Society Publications Monograph Series (London, 1999), pp. 131–52.

[18] James, *Family, Lineage and Civil Society*, pp. 143–6; W. Palmes (ed.), *Life of Mrs Dorothy Lawson of St Antonys near New Castle on Tyne* (Newcastle upon Tyne, 1851).

baskets of fish, as in the area around Newcastle, or on sale semi-openly as part of a broadsheet stock.[19] John Rhodes warned in 1602 that there were

> many such Pamphlets, together with other like Romish wares, that are sent abroad amongst the common people, both protestants and Papists in London and in the country, and that certaine women Brokers and Peddlers (as of late in Staffordshire there was) who with baskets on their arms, shall come and offer you other wares under a colour, and so sell you these.[20]

Anne Apicer, one of the recusants harboured by Frances Wentworth at Woolley, near Doncaster, who was described as a 'roamer to and fro', may have been such a peddler, but it is also likely that many sellers only had a vague idea of the content of the literature in their packs.[21]

Such observations, however, tell us little about the appeal of protestantism to men and women respectively. To go further, it is necessary to turn to a much-maligned source. Wills have become the staple tool for historians of lay piety, but the attractive image of them as 'mirrors of the soul' has been shattered by the critiques of numerous researchers. Scepticism was directed first at the idea that the religious preamble bequeathing the soul to God was a statement of the testator's personal faith: more recently, historians have questioned the relationship between pious provision during life and at death.[22] These arguments merit detailed consideration, but do not necessarily invalidate the use of testamentary material in the study of popular religion. Even if the image in the mirror is not crystal clear, we can still glimpse a partial reflection.

The greatest criticism of the use of will evidence as a testimony of religious belief has concerned the use of preambles. Widespread illiteracy, and the consequent recourse to a limited number of scribes, means that preambles

---

[19] H. Aveling, *Northern Catholics: The Catholic Recusants of the North Riding of Yorkshire, 1558–1790* (London, 1966), p. 159.

[20] M. Spufford, *Small Books and Pleasant Histories: Popular Fiction and its Readership in Seventeenth-Century England* (London, 1981), p. 11.

[21] Shiels, 'Household, age and gender', p. 140. In Spain, the Inquisition charged a shopkeeper with blasphemy for selling a broadsheet warning against gambling and prosecution as an *Ecce Homo*, even though the related iconography of the Christ of the Trades made such confusions possible: S. T. Nalle, *God in La Mancha: Religious Reform and the People of Cuenca, 1500–1650* (London, 1992), pp. 152–3. In England, it was even thought necessary to publish a pictorial guide to popish trinkets (B[ernard] G[arter], *A new yeares gifte*, 1579). This was ostensibly to aid good protestants in detecting catholic recusants, although it may have served as a disguise for catholic devotional use: Watt, *Cheap Print and Popular Piety*, pp. 178–80.

[22] Criticisms include M. L. Zell, 'The use of religious preambles as a measure of religious belief in the sixteenth century', *BIHR* 50 (1977), 246–9; J. D. Alsop, 'Religious preambles in early modern English wills as formulae', *JEH* 40 (1989), 19–27; Burgess, 'Late medieval wills and pious convention'.

are considered unreliable indicators of the testator's personal belief.[23] These problems can lead to a wholesale rejection of preambles, or to a modified belief in their value as revealing trends in religious ideas within a community rather than the views of particular individuals. Such conclusions do, however, seem unduly pessimistic. In a culture that is assumed to be highly religious, the bequest of one's soul cannot be a trivial matter. The awesome nature of the wording of the preamble was exploited by Bishop Hooper, who warned his clergy that use of the traditional catholic preamble bequeathing the soul to Christ, Mary and the saints was 'injurious to God, and perilous as well for the salvation of the dead, as dangerous unto the maker'.[24] Even many modern historians who are critical of the worth of religious preambles assume that catholics would be unlikely to accept a protestant preamble and vice versa, although people of diverse religious persuasions might shelter under the more neutral preamble dedicating the soul to Almighty God.

The attack on the presence of religious meaning in preambles rests on two charges: conventionality, and the poor correlation with other religious bequests in the will.[25] Of these, the first is clearly the weaker. Conventional formulae need not be devoid of meaning, and may even possess strength in terms of religious certainty through being orthodox and commonplace. The increasing range of formulae employed during the sixteenth century points to the continuing vitality of the preamble, not to its meaningless conventionality. The observed lack of correlation between the religious stances of the preamble and of the pious bequests appears a more serious challenge to the value of the preamble. But often the apparent discrepancy reflects not a testator hedging his bets by combining protestant preamble with catholic practice, but rather the historian's oversimplification of the religious character of preambles as catholic or protestant. The increasingly Christocentric focus of late medieval catholic devotion means that wills expressing a trust to be saved by the merits of Christ's passion, or of his blood-shedding, cannot be considered definitely protestant.[26] The catholic orthodoxy of such

---

[23] M. Spufford, 'The scribes of villagers' wills in the sixteenth and seventeenth centuries and their influence', *Local Population Studies* 7 (1971), 28–43.

[24] W. H. Frere and W. M. Kennedy (eds.), *Visitation Articles and Injunctions of the Period of the Reformation*, Alcuin Club Collection 15 (1910), Hooper's interrogatories for the dioceses of Gloucester and Worcester, 1551 2, p. 306. The vicar of Colley maintained that 'all those who went about to save souls departed by masses or diriges dyd wrong to chrysts blodde and ys thyss a robber or a soule murderer', Worcs. RO Visitation Act Book, depositions *c.* 1540, f. 129.

[25] Burgess, 'Late medieval wills and pious convention', pp. 14–30.

[26] Historians in practice apply different criteria to identify preambles as protestant. Zell, 'The use of religious preambles', 246, considers preambles to be protestant which mention the sole reliance of the testator on the mercy of Christ for his salvation. M. Spufford, *Contrasting Communities: English Villagers in the Sixteenth and Seventeenth Centuries* (Cambridge, 1974), p. 321, offers a more cautious approach. She views any will 'which stresses salvation

phrases is indicated by their similarity to the questions of faith put to the dying catholic, as elaborated in *ars moriendi* texts: 'Believe ye that ye may not be saved but by His passion and death? Yea. As long as the soul is in your body thank God for his death, and have a sure trust by it and by His passion to be saved.'[27] In catholic terms, such a preamble indicates a reduced belief in the importance of the intercession of Mary and the saints, but is still perfectly compatible with measures such as bequests for masses for the testator's soul.[28]

These considerations suggest that religious preambles may, after all, reveal patterns of male and female religious affiliation. Historians' attempts to uncover this have, however, come to the conclusion that little gender difference is observable. Litzenberger's study of the diocese of Gloucester divides the will preambles into three categories: traditional (references to association with the Virgin and/or the holy company of heaven which may include statements of trust to be saved through Christ's death); neutral (bequest of the soul to the Trinity, or Almighty God; references to God's mercy and/or to being saved through the merits of Christ's passion; references to being one of the elect); and protestant (reference to assurance of salvation by no other means than by God). She concludes that the difference in male and female behaviour was slight, even if slightly more pronounced than the differences between social groups. The one area in which the behaviour of male and female testators appeared to differ significantly was in the proportion preferring traditional preambles in the second decade of the reign of Elizabeth. For Litzenberger, this can be explained by women being more likely to conceal their catholic beliefs behind neutral statements. The lesser public self-confidence of women in the testamentary sphere lends this interpretation some plausibility, but it is notable that such considerations were unable to exert a detectable impact in the first decade. It was only as the Elizabethan church settlement became more established that women, and to a lesser extent men also, were less likely to opt for a traditional form of preamble. Consequently, if these figures show anything, they suggest the

---

through Christ's death and passion alone, or the company of the elect' as protestant, but also recognises that there are some wills in which the stress on salvation through Christ is so minimal that they cannot be classified.

[27] *Here begynneth a lytyll treatyse . . . called ars moriendi . . . the craft to deye for the helthe of mannes sowle* (1491), sigs. A.i.r. – A.iii.r. quoted in Brigden, *London and the Reformation* p. 22.

[28] Conversely, Alsop, 'Religious preambles in early modern English wills', 23–4, cites the London will of Richard Porye (1562), which begins with a 'typically protestant emphasis upon salvation through Christ's death and passion', with the preamble 'First I geve and bequeth my Soule to almightie God my only savior and redeemer, by the merits of Whose death and passion I am in full hope to be saved', and includes several requests for prayers for his soul, to support his view that in most cases the preamble is 'merely a formula, unrelated to the beliefs of the testators'.

Table 6.1. *Types of will preamble in the diocese of Worcester*

	Preamble	Male (EPK)*	Female (EPK)*	Female (All)**
Henrician	Traditional	60.0% (222)	66.6% (52)	83.1% (280)
	Ambiguous	40.0% (148)	33.3% (26)	16.9% (57)
	Protestant	–	–	–
Edwardian	Traditional	16.1% (24)	32.0% (8)	23.9% (27)
	Ambiguous	83.9% (125)	68.0% (17)	76.1% (86)
	Protestant	–	–	–
Marian	Traditional	39.0% (94)	54.1% (33)	55.0% (137)
	Ambiguous	61.0% (147)	45.9% (28)	44.6% (111)
	Protestant	–	–	0.4% (1)
Eliz. to 1570	Traditional	6.3% (16)	4.2% (2)	16.5% (41)
	Ambiguous	93.7% (237)	93.8% (45)	82.3% (205)
	Protestant	–	2.1% (1)	0.8% (2)

* All wills from the peculiar of Evesham and the deaneries of Powick and Kidderminster.
** All wills from the diocese of Worcester.

growing pressures of conformity rather than gendered patterns of religious affiliation: the percentage of protestant preambles increased by the same extent for both sexes.[29]

Adopting Litzenberger's categories for ease of comparison, the figures from the diocese of Worcester are shown in Table 6.1. Such categories are, however, problematic since they include a wide spectrum of religious positions in an attempt to delineate traditional catholic and protestant extremes. It can therefore be helpful to isolate and trace the popularity of particular forms of preambles as a proportion of the whole during the period. For this analysis two types of preamble have been chosen:

A: The completely neutral bequest of the soul to God
B: The 'traditional' bequest of the soul to God, Mary and the saints.

By looking at the popularity of these two, we may identify whether patterns of adherence to the most conservatively catholic form were gendered, and whether women were more likely than men to shelter behind the most neutral of all preamble forms (Table 6.2).

These figures suggest that there was a weaker commitment to the traditional B preamble in the three selected areas than was the case for the diocese

[29] Litzenberger, 'Local responses to changes in religious policy', and restated in C. Litzenberger, *The English Reformation and the Laity: Gloucestershire, 1540–80* (Cambridge, 1997), Table B.5, p. 182: 11.6% of female wills and 12.6% of male wills contain traditional preambles in Elizabeth's first decade; in the second, the percentages are 3.4 and 6.8 respectively.

Patterns of piety

Table 6.2. *Preambles of types A and B from the diocese of Worcester*

	Male (EPK)*	Female (EPK)*	Female (All)**
Henrician A	29.2% (108)	29.5% (23)	15.1% (51)
Henrician B	46.8% (173)	47.4% (37)	76.0% (256)
Edwardian A	63.1% (94)	52% (13)	61.9% (70)
Edwardian B	5.4% (8)	16% (4)	15.0% (17)
Marian A	46.1% (111)	39.3% (24)	37.3% (93)
Marian B	28.6% (69)	37.7% (23)	43.8% (109)
Eliz. to 1570 A	66.4% (168)	62.5% (30)	61.8% (154)
Eliz. to 1570 B	3.1% (8)	4.2% (2)	5.6% (14)

* All wills from the peculiar of Evesham and the deaneries of Powick and Kidderminster.
** All wills from the diocese of Worcester.

as a whole: just over three quarters of Henrician female testators in the diocese used this form, whilst in the male and female wills from the sample areas it occurred in just under half of the wills. Regional variations in preambles were significant, as was also the case in the diocese of Gloucester. This means that, despite the small numbers involved, matching male and female regional samples may give the clearest comparison of male and female behaviour. It is notable that during the reign of Edward the percentage of female testators employing B preambles was three times higher than of males, and the use of A preambles was correspondingly lower. Even in Mary's reign this discrepancy continued, as women showed a slightly greater preference for the B type and a lesser preference for the A type. During the first two decades of the reign of Elizabeth, the two sexes followed the same pattern, with almost two thirds of testators opting for the most neutral bequest of the soul to Almighty God. In the diocese as a whole, B preambles were now much rarer than they had been in the Edwardian Reformation. This evidence from the diocese of Worcester therefore contrasts with the conclusions drawn by Litzenberger from the neighbouring diocese of Gloucester. In Edwardian Worcester, it is women, rather than men, who appear bolder in their adherence to the traditional catholic formula, and their stronger commitment continued under the catholic regime of Mary. In this diocese it is the reign of Elizabeth that appears decisive, reducing male and female attachment to the traditional formula to a similarly low level.

Comparison of male and female reaction to the religious changes at parish level also suggests that some female testators clung more tenaciously to the old religion than did their male counterparts in the early years of the Reformation. Thus, at Ombersley (Worcestershire), where ten female wills survive, the preambles of wills of both sexes are broadly similar. A minority of the male wills employed the traditional catholic formula in the Henrician period, and there are no examples after 1540. All other testators, with one exception who trusted to be saved by the merits of Christ's passion, commended their souls to Almighty God, and it is this dedication that became standard in the Edwardian period. The reign of Mary saw no reversion to the dedication to God, Mary and the saints, but did witness the development of a focus on the person of Christ rather than of God. The female testators closely followed the male pattern in their choice of preamble, with the exception of two wills, written in 1545 and 1558, which retained the traditional catholic dedication of the soul to God, Mary and the saints.[30] The same pattern of a more enduring female attachment to catholic formulae is also found in Leverton (Lincolnshire): from 1547–1570 the only wills with the complete catholic preamble commending the soul to God, Mary and the saints were made by widows.[31]

However, not all parish samples tell the same story. At Powick (Worcestershire) B type preambles were favoured in the later Henrician period (1538–47) by the four female testators and 13 of the 15 men who made wills. No Edwardian female wills survive from the parish, but male testators masked their religious commitment by using the most neutral formula, bequeathing their soul to Almighty God. Mary's reign saw a wide diversity of preambles, suggesting the availability of many scribes and the possibility of more active selection. The five women's wills date from the years of high mortality at the end of the reign. Of these, two simply bequeathed their souls to God, two chose the formula of bequeathing their souls to God and the holy company of heaven (significantly omitting the standard commendation of the soul to the Virgin Mary), and one bequeathed her soul to God expressing trust to be saved by the merits of Christ's passion. All three types of preamble are present in the wills made by men, but it may be significant that two of the five male wills written in 1558 adopt the traditional preamble dedicating the soul to God, Mary and the saints.

The fragility of conclusions drawn from such small numbers of wills must be recognised. But the example of Powick might be thought to undermine the suggestion that women displayed a stronger commitment to catholicism. However, another interpretation is also possible. Powick differed from Ombersley and Leverton in its lukewarm adherence to protestantism. In both Edward's reign and in the early years of Elizabeth, all testators adopted neutral preambles bequeathing their souls to Almighty God (with the exception of one male B preamble in 1560). As notably, the Marian period saw a wide range of preambles compatible with catholic belief. In this parish there was no committed protestant majority with a dogged remnant of catholic women. Instead, the 'catholicism' of the parish allowed some testators to

---

[30] Worcs. RO CCW.   [31] Lincs. RO CCW (Leverton).

include the Virgin Mary in the traditional preamble whilst others omitted her, and other testators to concentrate on their hope to be saved by the merits of Christ's passion.

As at Powick, women in the diocese of Worcester seem more likely than men to favour modifying the traditional preamble to omit reference to the Virgin Mary whilst continuing to bequeath their souls to God and the holy company of heaven. Moreover, such preambles appear to have been more than a prudent strategy. In all reigns, 6–7 per cent of female wills proved in the diocese were of this type. Looking at the regional figures, the fact that three times as many women as men used this preamble in the Edwardian period may seem to support the prudential hypothesis, but this cannot explain its greater use in female wills written during Mary's reign. Since such preambles were always a minority choice, too much should not be made of these observations. Nevertheless, there are reasons why devotion to the Virgin Mary may have been more important for men than it was for women. Identification with, and devotion to, a saint of the opposite sex could fill an important psychological need, and other evidence suggests that women were not more likely to express devotion to female saints.[32] Thus, the initial paradox that women both displayed a stronger commitment to the traditional preamble bequeathing the soul to God, Mary and the saints, and were also more likely to omit Mary from this trio, can be resolved. A stronger female commitment to a traditional catholic position is part of the story. But when people were prepared to modify their position within an essentially catholic framework of belief in the saints, it was women, rather than men, who were more prepared to remove Mary from her pre-eminent position, and place her within the ranks of the holy company of heaven.

These observations also suggest that strongly Christocentric forms of preamble deserve closer examination. Litzenberger rightly points out that these belong in the ambiguous category, and can appear in wills that appear to be both catholic and protestant. However, this type of preamble is significant for two main reasons. First, since Christocentric piety provided the best bridge to protestant belief, such preambles must be fundamental to an understanding of gendered responses to Reformation.[33] Secondly, the corollary of the psychological arguments that diminish the significance of the Virgin Mary for women is that Christocentric devotion should appeal particularly to them.[34]

In the diocese of Worcester, Christocentric preambles grew in popularity during this period, and were most frequent in the Edwardian and early Elizabethan periods, being chosen in the latter by one fifth of testators of both sexes. The evidence presented in Table 6.3 does, however, give little basis for believing that such expressions of Christocentric piety appealed

[32] See pp. 47–8.   [33] See p. 4.   [34] See pp. 74–82.

Table 6.3. *Incidence of Christocentric preambles in the diocese of Worcester*

	Male (EPK)*	Female (EPK)*	Female (All)**
Henrician	61 (16.5%)	9 (11.5%)	33 (9.8%)
Edwardian	40 (26.8%)	4 (16%)	15 (13.3%)
Marian	48 (19.9%)	6 (9.8%)	25 (10.0%)
Eliz. to 1570	59 (23.3%)	10 (20.8%)	51 (20.5%)

* All wills from the peculiar of Evesham and the deaneries of Powick and Kidderminster.
** All wills from the diocese of Worcester.

especially to women. In both the diocesan and the regional samples, the female percentages lagged behind those of men until Elizabeth's reign, when the behaviour of both sexes was similar. However, such conclusions must be treated with caution. Christocentric piety, in particular, was highly regionalised. Even within the sample area, this type of preamble was much more frequent in the deanery of Kidderminster than in the deanery of Powick or the peculiar of Evesham. As in earlier parts of this discussion, the small number of female wills from the sample area presents problems, but it is notable, and unusual, that in this case the percentages follow those of the usually more conservative female diocesan sample.

More light may be shed on the pattern of these responses by considering the types of Christocentric preamble in greater detail (Table 6.4). Three distinct forms can be identified:

E: Bequest of the soul combining the idea of being saved by Christ's passion with a request for the intercession of the Virgin and saints
G: Bequest of the soul to God trusting, hoping and/or believing to be saved by the merits of Christ's passion
I: Bequest of the soul to Christ (and occasionally also to God) with a brief clarification, 'saviour', 'redeemer' etc.

Patterns of behaviour from these figures are not very clear, and any conclusions must be tentative. Perhaps the most interesting possibility is the apparent contrast between male and female preferences for G and I preambles. Comparing the male sample with the figures for the female wills from the whole diocese, it is noticeable that in all four periods a larger percentage of male Christocentric preambles expressed their trust in being saved by the merits of Christ's passion (G) than was the case for women, and that this pattern was reversed in the case of preambles bequeathing the soul to Christ (I). If such findings are sustainable from a wider range of case studies, it may be that the Christocentric piety of men and women had different emphases

Table 6.4. *Different types of Christocentric preambles in the diocese of Worcester*

	Preamble	Male (EPK)*	Female (EPK)*	Female (All)**
Henrician	E forms	27 (44.3%)	7 (77.8%)	16 (48.5%)
	G forms	26 (42.6%)	1	8 (24.2%)
	I forms	8 (13.1%)	–	3 (9.1%)
	Other	–	1	6 (18.2%)
Edwardian	E forms	10 (25.0%)	1	2 (13.3%)
	G forms	28 (70.0%)	2	6 (40.0%)
	I forms	1 (2.5%)	0	4 (26.7%)
	Other	1 (2.5%)	1	3 (20.0%)
Marian	E forms	18 (37.5%)	4	14 (56.0%)
	G forms	24 (50.0%)	2	6 (24.0%)
	I forms	6 (12.5%)	–	6 (24.0%)
	Other	–	–	4 (16%)
Eliz. to 1570	E forms	–	–	3 (5.9%)
	G forms	51 (86.4%)	8 (80.0%)	30 (58.8%)
	I forms	6 (10.2%)	1 (10.0%)	11 (21.5%)
	Other	2 (3.4%)	1 (10.0%)	7 (13.7%)

* All wills from the peculiar of Evesham and the deaneries of Powick and Kidderminster.
** All wills from the diocese of Worcester.

as well as much common ground. Men, by focussing on Christ's passion and the shedding of his precious blood, were drawing attention to the active, and the most male, role of Christ in securing their redemption, whilst the female emphasis on bequeathing the soul to Christ suggested ideas of union and devotion. It may indeed be that it was precisely because Christocentric piety could operate in both ways that gender patterns were not clear-cut. An important part of the appeal of Christocentric devotion may have been that it cut across gender boundaries. It provided overlapping, but distinct, ways in which men and women could journey from catholic to protestant belief.

In 1569, during the Northern Rising, the churchwarden of Sedgefield (Co. Durham), Rowland Hickson, organised a burning of protestant books, including the English Bible and the Book of Homilies. Not all the parishioners were in full agreement. According to the depositions taken after the defeat of the rebels, the parish clerk had burnt one old book of his own in order to save the Bible from the flames. Two witnesses also noted that a group of women had attempted to save some of the books, but Hickson would not let them and with threats prevented them 'stirring' any of the books on the fire. Nevertheless, as Margaret, the 66-year-old wife of the husbandman Thomas Snawsdon, testified, 'some of the leves of the said bookes the said wyffes toke away with them, to play their children withal'.[35] It is hard to be certain of the motivations of these women. It seems implausible that they challenged Hickson for twenty-four hours simply to obtain some drawing paper for their children, and yet this was the explanation that their neighbour Margaret Snawsdon was prepared to give the protestant regime.

As well as being a vivid vignette, this episode encapsulates many of the difficulties inherent in identifying reactions to the Reformation. The legal context is most obvious, whether shaping depositions in the aftermath of a rebellion, or influencing the names chosen in presentments for recusancy. But of even greater importance is the fact that there was no clear journey from catholicism to protestantism. Neither the point of departure nor that of arrival could be clearly mapped. If we assume, as is likely, that all the inhabitants of Sedgefield considered themselves catholic, then the parish clerk, the group of wives and the churchwarden had diverging opinions about the appropriate fate of the English Bible and the officially prescribed protestant texts. For Hickson, who was reported to have exclaimed as the fire burned, 'Lowe, wher the Homilies flees to the devyll', it was clear that such texts had no value, but the parish clerk, and perhaps also the wives, could not entirely concur.

Furthermore, although it is possible to argue that ritual, and hence also catholicism, exercised a greater appeal for women based on their role within the household and their responsibility for the religious well being of the family, it is also the case that protestantism provided similar opportunities, as illustrated by the history of Rose Hickman. An affinity with ritual was not, however, the only issue guiding the process of religious affiliation. The influence of different strands of Marian and Christocentric piety was vital, and provided various routes to catholic commitment and protestant understanding that appealed to parishioners of both sexes, but could also have gendered emphases. From all this, it is clear that the idea that women lost out in, and were largely alienated by, a move to a protestant bibliocentric religious culture that lacked the comforting presence of the Virgin Mary and the saints must be a gross oversimplification. Even if this view of the role of the Virgin and the saints in protestantism could be sustained, it does not do justice to the complexities of religious beliefs and preferences. Both women and men had a Reformation, and their experience of it could be shaped by their gender roles; but as important in determining receptivity were the local and personal contours of catholic piety.

---

[35] J. Raine (ed.), *Depositions and Other Ecclesiastical Proceedings from the Courts of Durham extending from 1311 to the Reign of Elizabeth*, Surtees Society 21 (1845), pp. 186–93.

7

Parish religion in the Reformation

For the laity, the Reformation made its most visible impact on the fabric and structures of parish life. The removal of saints, images and side altars, the dismantling of chantry and gild chapels and their replacement with white-washed walls, the voice of the preacher from the pulpit, and the attempt to enforce Sunday catechism classes can be seen as summing up the Reformation in the parishes. If, at the same time, the image of the godly is epitomised by the Baxter family reading scripture whilst their neighbours played on the village green, or by their practice of gadding to hear sermons by favoured preachers outside the parish bounds, then it might appear that there was little place for the parish church as the heart of the local protestant community. Nevertheless, as Maltby has argued, this picture is incomplete if it does not recognise the presence of deeply committed anglicans whose behaviour went beyond token conformity.[1] Indeed few, even those most dissatisfied with an official church that was 'but halfly reformed', saw separatism as an attractively easy option. Across the religious spectrum, ideas that the congregation was a mirror of the order of local society, that neighbours should be in charity with one another, and that a divinely ordained monarch could be head of the Church exerted a powerful force. This can be seen most evidently in the continuing concerns about social status and church seating, but it also induced an acceptance of the magisterial tone of the Reformation. Thus, although protestantism could accentuate individual relations with God, and the piety of the household rather than the parish, this trend, and the associated doctrine of spiritual equality, could be less corrosive of existing ideas than first appears. The latter doctrine, in particular, has been heralded as a significant opportunity for a reconstruction of gender relations on a religious basis. For women, it has seemed, there was a Reformation worth having. The validity of this assessment can be explored by focussing on patterns of church seating, the appointment of churchwardens, and the

---

[1] J. Maltby, *Prayer Book and People in Elizabethan and Early Stuart England* (Cambridge, 1998).

visual messages selected to replace the old images on the walls of the parish church.

The doctrine of spiritual equality opened up the possibility of the removal of gender distinctions in the religious sphere, but the maintenance of social hierarchy, whether in the relations of the patriarchal family or in the organisation of the congregation in the local church, was also considered essential. These priorities meant that the arrangement of the parishioners in the church was not a prime concern in the early years of the Reformation, although there were some significant changes. Old liturgical distinctions that had reinforced the notion of gender inequality were swept away in 1549. Most importantly, in the service for baptism the custom of saying different exorcisms and prayers over male and female children was abandoned. In matters of church seating the clergy offered less clear direction. The rubric of the 1549 Prayer Book encouraged the maintenance of segregation when it stated that 'So many as shall be partakers of the Holy Communion, shall tarry still in the quire, or in some convenient place nigh the quire, the men on the one side, and the women on the other side.'[2] Although the progress of reform led to the removal of this stipulation in the Prayer Books of 1552 and 1559, the absence of a replacement diminished the impact of this. Parishes were not obliged to break with past practice, and could continue to separate the sexes for the reception of communion and in arranging church seating.[3]

The removal of this communion rubric made gender segregation less practically necessary for the smooth ritual organisation of the congregation, but did not make the practice redundant. It was underpinned and sustained by the abiding concern for decency, and its usefulness in limiting opportunities for licentiousness was also recognised on the Continent. Where new reformed churches were built, as in Lyon, the design accommodated the separation of the sexes.[4] In less formal contexts this was also thought to be desirable. Many, but not all, contemporary woodcuts depicting reformed services and preachers separate the sexes, with the women typically occupying the position at the foot of the pulpit (Figs. 32 and 33).[5]

---

[2] E. Cardwell (ed.), *The Two Books of Common Prayer, Set Forth by the Authority of Parliament in the Reign of King Edward VI* (Oxford, 1841), pp. 280–1.

[3] Aston, 'Segregation in church', p. 281; K. B. Dillow, 'The social and ecclesiastical significance of church seating arrangements and pew disputes, 1500–1740', D.Phil. thesis, University of Oxford (1990), p. 129. Neither of these authors notes that this rubric was removed from the 1552 Prayer Book and did not appear in 1559.

[4] Aston, 'Segregation in church', p. 291, includes an illustration of the Calvinist temple at Lyon c. 1565.

[5] Aston, 'Segregation in church', p. 281, notes that the gender division is shown in Cranach's woodcut of the protestant communion and in the depictions of godly congregations in Foxe's *Book of Martyrs*. J. N. King, 'The godly woman in Elizabethan iconography', *Renaissance Quarterly* 38 (1985), 47, discusses the portrayal of women in the *Book of Martyrs*' images.

Figure 32 Thomas Bilney being pulled from the pulpit whilst preaching at Ipswich in 1527 before an audience divided by sex, from Foxe, *Acts and Monuments*

In reality, however, many English congregations were less disposed to continue the practice of gender segregation than the reformers hoped, but it is not clear that this always represented a rejection of their arguments. Taking a break from their labours, the carpenters of the village of West Bowden (Co. Durham), who were making new seats for their parish church, discussed whether the allocation of seats should be made according to gender. One member of the group, Robert Atchinson, argued forcibly against this on the grounds that it would give one Richard Clay a licence to make them all cuckolds.[6] In this view, the avoidance of promiscuity was best achieved

The frontispiece of the Great Bible includes a group seated on benches to hear a preacher amongst whom there seems to be no clear gender division.

[6] E. A. Foyster, *Manhood in Early Modern England: Honour, Sex and Marriage* (Longman, 1999), pp. 19–20, Durham University Library Archives, DDR/EJ/CCD/2 (formerly DDR Box 414). Only one deposition survives from this case. Thomas More's solution in his *Utopia* (1516) provided for oversight of junior members of the family, but not of wives: 'When they come thither the men go into the right side of the church and the women into the left side. There they place themselves in such order, that all they which be of the male kind in every household sit before the goodman of the house, and they of the female kind before the goodwife. Thus it is foreseen that all their gestures and behaviours be marked and observed abroad of them by whose authority and discipline they be governed at home.' R. Marius (ed.), *Thomas More: Utopia* (London, 1994), p. 128.

Figure 33 Godly congregation in the reign of Edward VI, detail from Foxe, *Acts and Monuments* (1641; illustration first used 1570)

by having all female members of the household closely under the eye of the male head of the family when they attended church services. Whether or not this opinion was commonly held, many parishes seem to have permitted the sexes to sit together in church, and the gradual evolution of the family pew may have been, in part, a response to the same demand. Although such developments are often linked with concerns to visualise social status within the congregation, this was usually compatible with the separation of the sexes: the seats of men, as well as of women, could be allocated to reflect gradations of social status.

The extent of gender segregation is hard to ascertain due to the necessary reliance on the evidence of individual parish conflicts that reached the attention of the authorities. Although the unusual vignette of discussions in West Bowden preserved in a church court deposition gives us a window on to lay attitudes, the outcome is unclear. It may be the case, as M. James argues, that a household and tenurially based arrangement of the congregation became the norm in northern society from the late sixteenth century, but the West Bowden carpenters were at least aware of other possibilities.[7] Moving southwards, Henry Dawrant, a cordwainer bearing witness in the archdeacon's court in Oxford in 1617, commented that 'he has heretofore lived in many several counties and towns...and he never knew but that the custom in all the said churches was always for men to sit there in seats by themselves apart from the women, and the women likewise by themselves'. This statement may have been a little disingenuous. Dawrant was, after all, aware that in the case in question the wardens of St. Ebbes, Oxford had adopted different principles, and he explained that 'he does much dislike' men and women sitting together 'for it is not decent and seemly'.[8]

Concerns about men and women sitting together 'promiscuously' in the congregation, and the insistence that there should be a return to the 'fashion of old' in which the sexes were separated, are often associated with the Laudian period, but they were not limited to the 1630s.[9] There seems to have been a continuing diversity of practice and expectations that centred not only on gendered notions of decency but also on social status and hierarchy, and contributions to the parish church. At Earls Colne (Essex) in 1617 the rearrangement of seating was based on three criteria: that it was more decent for men and women to sit by themselves on opposite sides of the church; that the aged who were hard of hearing had the right to sit nearer the pulpit than the young; and that there was an impropriety in 'aged women and church

[7] James, *Family, Lineage and Civil Society*, pp. 121–3.
[8] Dillow, 'The social and ecclesiastical significance of church seating', p. 131.
[9] The Laudians also tried to prevent women sitting in the chancel. Bishop Wren pronounced that at Fen Drayton (Cambridgeshire) 'ye women be not placed in ye chancell but removed into convenient seates in ye church': Aston, 'Segregation in church', p. 250.

elders' being placed lower than maids and young women 'who bore no charge about the mainteynance of the church'. Similarly, at Much Hadham (Hertfordshire) in 1603 it was reported that

ther is great disorder amongst the parishoners in their sittinge in the churche that boyes and younge men doe place themselves very disorderly amongst the aunscient sort of parishioners ther, and both women and men, maydens and mens wives promiscue sitt togither.

The churchwardens were ordered to ensure that the seats of men and women were separated and that the 'better and aunscienter' parishioners were seated according to their status.[10]

Such examples suggest that the Laudian 'campaign' did not set any radically new agenda, even if its views were not shared by all. As in so many areas, the novelty lay rather in giving such ideas the weight of episcopal sanction and intervention. But, even in these terms, it is notable that such attempts were not made in all dioceses, even when sets of injunctions borrowed heavily from each other. Some bishops, perhaps deliberately, left certain details of their expectations on church seating unclear: Bishop Williams's injunctions for Lincoln diocese in 1635 show a concern that order should be maintained and that the rank of householder be protected from assertive servants and young people, but fail to address gender issues directly. For Bishop Wren such concerns developed gradually, from an initial concern for obstructive private pews, to include men and women sitting 'promiscuously together' in his injunctions for Ely in 1638–9. It is only in this period (1638–9) that Laudians officially directed their attention to gender and church seating at diocesan level, but this effort was very limited.[11] Apart from Wren at Ely, Montagu at Norwich was the only other bishop to include the demand in his injunctions, although similar campaigns could be staged at different levels of ecclesiastical jurisdiction, such as Archdeacon Kingsley's instructions to the wardens at St Margaret's Canterbury in 1639, or the earlier attempt of Clement Corbett, vicar-general of the Bishop of Norwich, to order the male and female parishioners of West Walton (Norfolk) to sit on the north and south sides of the church respectively in 1633. Whether Corbett was actually able to enforce his will in West Walton remains in doubt.[12] The warning, given by Archbishop Neile to Bishop Bridgeman in 1635, against a scheme for segregating men and women completely in the diocese of Chester because it would 'beget more babbles, suits in law and prohibitions then either

---

[10] Ibid., p. 288.
[11] K. Fincham (ed.), *Visitation Articles and Injunctions of the Early Stuart Church*, vol. 2: *1625–1641* (Woodbridge, 1998).
[12] Fincham (ed.), *Visitation Articles*, vol. 2, p. 210; S. D. Amussen, *An Ordered Society: Gender and Class in Early Modern England* (Oxford, 1988), pp. 137–8; A. Fletcher, *Gender, Sex and Subordination in England, 1500–1800* (London, 1995), p. 267.

you or I would be contented to be trouble with' gave good practical reasons for a cautious approach from an impeccable 'Laudian' source.[13] Clearly a 'Laudian' concern for order in the congregation could cut both ways, leading to separation by sex being both advocated and rejected.

Ultimately, as in the evolution of seating practices in the pre-Reformation period, the priorities of individual parishes and of influential parishioners were decisive. This could produce acceptance of arrangements in which the principles applied seem inconsistent, but order was thought to be upheld. According to the pew plan for Holy Trinity, Dorchester, in 1617, men were seated in the main aisle in descending status from east to west, whilst their wives sat similarly in the side aisles and the daughters of respectable families sat at the back. This neat pattern was, however, broken in the south aisle where several wealthy parishioners shared seats with their wives.[14]

Such examples explain, and underpin, the difficulty of generalising about parish practice in the Reformation church. Separation of the sexes prevailed in some parishes in the late sixteenth and early seventeenth centuries. At St Michael's, Coventry women were sitting separately from their husbands in the late sixteenth century, and at Bampton (Oxfordshire) references in early seventeenth-century wills to the men's door and the women's door suggests the possibility of a longstanding tradition of segregation.[15] The rarity of such examples may be due more to the nature of the record than to the experience of most parishes. Imposition of change is, of course, more historically visible than continuity of separation, but it should be noted that gender segregation is often said to be supported by the inhabitants, or at least the principal ones. At Sherborne (Dorset) in 1628 the parishioners decided that no seat should be assigned without the consent of the churchwardens. They were concerned that men should 'be placed in seats fit for their rank and place as may be for decency and comeliness' and also expressed their 'dislike of the rude and disorderly standing and sitting of women upon the said forms amongst the men.'[16] The case of Stowe (Buckinghamshire) reveals that a period of disorderly seating could nevertheless coincide with respect for gender separation. In 1635 the dominant family in the parish, the Temples, asked for a commission for the vicar and churchwardens to enable them to place the inhabitants in the church 'according to their degree and quality'. The prevailing situation in Stowe church was described in

---

[13] Maltby, *Prayer Book and People*, p. 139 n. 27.
[14] D. Underdown, *Fire from Heaven: Life in an English Town in the Seventeenth Century* (London, 1993), p. 39.
[15] C. Phythian-Adams, 'Ceremony and the citizen: the communal year at Coventry', in P. Clark and P. Slack (eds.), *Crisis and Order in English Towns, 1500–1700: Essays in Urban History* (London, 1972), p. 59; VCH Oxfordshire, vol. 13, p. 55. It is, of course, possible that the names outlived the custom of segregation.
[16] K. Sharpe, *The Personal Rule of Charles I* (London, 1992), p. 395.

these terms: 'most of the parishioners do place themselves unreverently and without any order, some young men and servants taking place of married men and some maids sitting above married women, not having any respect unto the quality and condition of the person at all'.[17] Disorder here did not infringe gender boundaries of decency, but was in the terms familiar from a number of church court cases such as that of Ursula, the wife of Philip Cooke of Morston (Norfolk), who in 1615 refused to sit with married women and 'disorderly placeth herself among the maids'.[18] Women, especially perhaps newly-weds, could be happy to maintain gender bounds, but they did want to sit with their female friends in church. Despite the greater legal responsibilities placed upon churchwardens to report faults in their parish, the system of presentment at visitations continued to be inadequate, but it may be significant that parishes presented for permitting the sexes to sit 'promiscuously together' were always in a minority. Whether or not 'promiscuous' seating was the norm in the Reformation parish, it was only of sporadic concern.

As a recent study of surviving pewing plans has shown, there was wide local variation in the priorities determining the disposition of the congregation.[19] This situation, far from being disheartening to the historian, does in fact offer a valuable insight into the reaction of the laity to the Reformation and to the place of women within the religious life of the parish. As Margaret Aston realised, changes in seating practices responded more to pressures from the laity than to directives from the clergy.[20] For the laity in the late medieval as well as in the Reformation period, the arrangement of seating in the church ought to reflect the social order of the parish. The issue was not the ritual segregation of women, but the importance of the gender distinction in the reflection of the social order. The pressure for family pews was much more concerned with ensuring an accurate image of the social order than with any denial of the principle of gender segregation and sexual inequality. For some the concern was for social propriety in a moral sense, for others seating arrangements were a reflection of society itself.

Changes in the seating arrangements during the Reformation did not aim to counter the catholic belief in the spiritual inequality of the sexes. Rather, the continued emphasis on the reflection of secular society in the

---

[17] Fletcher, *Gender, Sex and Subordination*, p. 266.
[18] Amussen, *An Ordered Society*, p. 144 n. 22. She also discusses (p. 140) the case of Prudence Clark v. Susan Gyrney (1633), which shows that women in the same parish (in this case Earsham, Norfolk) could have different conceptions of what was appropriate. Susan, a servant, encouraged by some of the occupants of that seat, had sat in the lowest of the woman's seats rather than amongst the maids where she belonged because the maids' seat was too full, to the outrage of one occupant of that woman's seat, Prudence Clark.
[19] Dillow, 'The social and ecclesiastical significance of church seating', pp. 125–45.
[20] Aston, 'Segregation in church', p. 292.

congregation separated this issue from ideas of women's spiritual status. Puritan preachers provided intellectual confirmation of these priorities. Thus, William Gouge insisted upon both the subordination of the wife to her husband's authority and the equality of the sexes, but avoided contradiction by maintaining that this equality was only applicable in heaven.[21] This strategy denied the potentially revolutionary impact of the doctrine of spiritual equality in the interest of upholding the status quo, and the perceived need for hierarchy, in the secular sphere.

The same intellectual stance deadened the impact of the doctrine of spiritual equality on female participation in parish office holding. During the Reformation, the issues determining the selection of churchwardens were broadly similar to those in the later medieval period. Of central importance was the relationship between authority and representation that meant that women and children were thought to be represented by their husbands and fathers, who were deemed to exercise authority over them. In this scheme the position of widows as heads of households appeared anomalous, but this was increasingly resolved by their exclusion from positions of power. This process was encouraged by other developments. The changes of the Reformation period added to the legal responsibilities of churchwardens,[22] and this, as well as the loss of the accumulated expertise of women as wardens of lights and stores, helped to make female churchwardenship less acceptable. The development of a tighter vestry system may have made elections less democratic, making it more difficult for women to be chosen for office.[23]

As we saw in an earlier chapter, late medieval election procedures are uncertain, but we can be clearer about early Reformation practice.[24] The Bishop of Ely's description in 1564, which may also refer to pre-Reformation custom, envisaged a vestry that was 'of the whole parish, being a public assembly of all, young and old'. This probably included women, children and the unmarried, but it is likely that the group of thirteen people known as the 'assistance' would have been very influential in electing the churchwardens and, since this group consisted only of former churchwardens or constables,

[21] Gouge stated, 'If man and woman be compared together, we shall find a near equality.' However, his response to the question 'What then is the excellency of a husband?' revealed his view of the lack of any relationship between this doctrine and life on earth. He gave the answer, 'Only outward and momentary. Outward in the things of this world only... momentary, for the time of this life only': W. Gouge, *Of Domesticall Duties* (London, 1622), p. 423.
[22] Summarised in Kümin, *The Shaping of a Community*, pp. 241–9.
[23] Ibid., pp. 250–4, identifies the emergence of select vestries as 'perhaps the most dramatic change in parish government', and the period 1530–60 as 'crucial for the development of more oligarchical communal regimes', although he suggests that the impact of this may have been more delayed in rural parishes.
[24] See pp. 36–8.

women and members of other social groups were presumably less likely to be elected.[25]

The reality behind such elections is revealed by an unusually detailed entry in the accounts of Rotherfield (Sussex) listing those who chose the church-wardens 'for ye behove of ye parysh' in 1547. On this occasion the election was effected by a group of 21 men headed by the outgoing churchwarden.[26] Such a list is evidently too small to include even all the principal householders of the parish, and the fact that it does not include a single woman as a widow suggests that heading a household did not define participation. At another Sussex parish, Ashurst, in 1566 the election was even less representative. The clerk complained:

Neyther have they chosen churchwardyns accordyng to order yt is by ye voyse of the paryshe and the mynister together but ii or three pointed ii for churchwardyns before they came here and then put ye matter in questyon here and went ther waye therfore nothyng was done here accordyng to the trewe order yt hath byne used neyther in ther accountes makyng nor in choosyng ther churchwardyns.[27]

For the parish clerk, at least, the 'trewe order' of election was subverted when two or three took the power into their own hands. The participation of the clergy in the choice of churchwardens increased, at least in theory, during the Reformation. The joint election seen as the norm at Ashurst was included formally in the canons of 1571, and was elaborated in those of 1604 which specified that churchwardens 'shall be chosen by the joint consent of the minister and parishioners', and that if agreement was not forthcoming, 'then the minister shall choose one and the parishioners another'.[28]

These methods of selection suggest that those chosen will mainly rep-resent the views of the substantial male parishioners, and it comes as no real surprise to learn that, as in the late medieval period, those elected are

[25] J. Strype, *Annals of the Reformation and Establishment of Religion and Other Various Occurrences in the Church of England*, 4 vols. (Oxford, 1824), vol. 1/2, p. 132. The possi-bility of women participating in the election is also suggested by the practice of the medieval gild of St Mary at Beverley, which allowed its elder sisters a voice in the election of aldermen: J. and L. Toulmin Smith (eds.), *English Gilds*, EETS orig. ser. 40 (1870), pp. 149–50.
[26] E. Sussex RO CWA Rotherfield, PAR 465/10/3/1 p. 27.
[27] W. Sussex RO CWA Ashurst, PAR 11/9/1, MF978 p. 20.
[28] Rev. J. E. Farmiloe and R. Nixseaman (eds.), 'Elizabethan churchwardens' accounts', *Bedfordshire Historical Rec. Soc.* 33 (1953), xi. The election of separate wardens by the minister and his parishioners is not apparent in any of the surviving accounts before this date, and it contravened the principle of geographical representation found so frequently. It would seem to be a response to the new possibility of profound religious differences be-tween minister and congregation, although it could also serve to exacerbate it. In 1593 the vicar of Mansfield (Nottinghamshire) unsuccessfully claimed that the 'election of one of the churchwardens belonged by law or by virtue of a reasonable custom to the Vicar', whilst the parishioners maintained that they had elected both churchwardens from time immemo-rial: A. T. Hart, *The Man in the Pew, 1558–1660* (London, 1966), pp. 58–9.

normally drawn from precisely this group.[29] Explicit economic qualifications are hard to detect before the Reformation, but selection was probably linked to an informal assessment of probity and credit worthiness. The Reformation changes meant that many parish finances became more precarious and this development, coupled with the introduction of new structures of parish rates, seems to have encouraged attempts to establish a connection between residence, payment of rates or rent and liability to parish office. Such obligations were, however, contested in a number of parishes, suggesting their innovatory character. In a dispute in the Berkshire parish of Compton Beauchamp in 1570 it was stated that the office of churchwarden 'by ther custome' rotated amongst households paying for the holy loaf.[30] This seems to have been a local custom, and it seems unlikely that it was typical. Similarly, a dispute concerning the refusal of a parishioner of Mytton (Yorkshire) to serve as churchwarden in 1571 makes it clear that the rent qualification was a particular parish ordinance. It was not attributed customary status, despite the fact that the defendant was claiming exemption because his rent was below the threshold of one mark.[31]

The development of rotation arrangements in the Reformation period might be thought to have increased the chances of women, at least as widows of more substantial householders, serving as churchwardens.[32] In fact, this does not seem to have been the case, as women who were nominated in this way either chose, or were encouraged to choose, deputies to stand in their stead. The methods of selection, and the association of experience as a churchwarden with eligibility for the potentially powerful offices of the manorial or borough administration, suggest that the election

[29] See pp. 37–8. In the parishes of Chester there was a hierarchy of parish offices, and the churchwarden was almost always a freeman: N. Alldridge, 'Loyalty and identity in Chester parishes, 1540–1640', in S. Wright (ed.), *Parish, Church and People* (London, 1988), pp. 106–7. In rural parishes the situation is less clear. On the manors of Halesowen (Worcs.) and Worfield (Shropshire) the office of churchwarden frequently preceded the holding of manorial office: C. Peters, 'Women and the Reformation: social relations and attitudes in rural England, c.1470–1570', D.Phil. thesis, University of Oxford (1992), p. 220. But Nair's study of the Shropshire parish of Highley reveals many churchwardens of low social status, especially in the late Elizabethan and early Jacobean periods. Thus in 1582 one servant and two cottagers are identified as wardens: G. Nair, *Highley: The Development of a Community, 1550–1880* (Oxford, 1988), p. 29.

[30] J. Martin, 'The people of Reading and the Reformation 1520–1570: leadership and priorities in borough and parishes', Ph.D. thesis, University of Reading (1987), p. 200n.

[31] Purvis (ed.), *Tudor Parish Documents of the Diocese of York*, p. 188. Two cases from Nottinghamshire (Elston, 1577 and Lowdham, 1584) show that particular houses were liable to parish office: Hart, *The Man in the Pew*, pp. 60–1.

[32] The evidence of rotation disputes contrasts with the occasional references in other pre-Reformation accounts to individuals refusing the office of churchwarden and paying a fine to secure their exemption. In these instances the wardens appear to have been chosen rather than being obliged to serve their turn according to a rota based on the occupation of property. For example, Stratton (Cornwall) in 1518, CWA Stratton, BL Addl. MS 32, 244.

of churchwardens was seen as part of the male sphere of the exercise of public authority. Thus, although at Bramley (Hampshire) Joanne Terry, the executrix of Richard Terry, was listed as one of the wardens in 1563–4, the practice of allowing the widow to complete her husband's two-year term as warden was soon abandoned: in 1579–80 Maryan Redyng, the widow of John Redyng, was represented as warden by John Philippes.[33]

The same assumptions operated in secular office holding. Even on manors in which there was a direct link with tenure of a particular property, the holding of manorial office by a female tenant could not be contemplated. At Worfield (Shropshire) in 1566 Alice Wartor was forced to nominate John Walker as her deputy to serve in the office of bailiff, and shortly afterwards surrendered the land which carried this office-holding responsibility. On this manor, as elsewhere, women, who might be substantial tenants in their widowhood, never held office as manorial jurors.[34] It is consequently scarcely surprising that female churchwardens were exceptional. In the vast majority of parishes with surviving accounts in this period there were never any female churchwardens. Nevertheless, that women did occasionally serve as churchwardens suggests that the association of the office with religion was able to blur the boundaries between the male and female spheres to create situations that simply were not possible in secular offices. The widow of a churchwarden may have had a choice that was not open to her as the widow of a manorial juror.

But such openings were rare, and it is possible that they were seen more as burdens than opportunities. The upheavals of religious change in the mid-Tudor period did not result in very large numbers of female wardens. In the visitation returns for the diocese of Worcester in *c.* 1540, for example, there are no female churchwardens. The returns of the commissioners for church goods during the reign of Edward VI produce a similar picture, although this may be distorted by the difficult circumstances of religious change. Returns for Dorset, Devon and Worcestershire do not list any female churchwardens, whilst those for Surrey contain only one example in the parish of Gatton.[35]

---

[33] Williams (ed.), *Hampshire Churchwardens' Accounts*, pp. 46, 62. The wardenship of Henry Rychebell's widow at Shere (Surrey) in 1560 also seems to have been a case of a widow completing her husband's term of office. Surrey RO (Guildford) CWA Shere P S H/S H E R/10/1 f. 37v.

[34] Shropshire RO Worfield manor court rolls 1374/1/763 and 765. In the customary of the manor of Tettenhall Regis, which dates before 1604, the widow was responsible for the rent of her third of the holding, but it was the heir who owed suit of court: J. and L. Toulmin Smith (eds.), *English Gilds*, p. 433.

[35] Worcs. RO Visitation of the diocese of Worcester, *c.* 1540, 802.0; PRO E 117 2/17, E 117 8/22 Dorset, Devon and Worcestershire; 'Inventories of the goods and ornaments of the churches of the county of Surrey in the reign of King Edward VI', *Surrey Arch. Coll.* 4 (1899), pp. 1–189. At Gatton Dame Elizabeth Copley, widow, was lady of the manor that was coterminous with the tiny parish: VCH Surrey Reigate Hundred, pp. 196–200.

Nevertheless, the fact that a majority of female churchwardens from the earliest surviving accounts to 1570 held office in the 1540s and 1550s means that some connection between Reformation changes and the ability of women to become churchwardens in the short term appears possible.[36]

If this was the case, it may have been due less to the content of the new doctrines than to the office itself becoming less desirable in a period of religious change. Many accounts reveal evidence of dislocation in the Edwardian and Marian periods, although this may have resulted more from a desire to protect church goods and revenues than from problems in procuring wardens. The only parish in which the accounts show Reformation tensions causing substantial difficulties is Mere (Wiltshire), where the parishioners were thrown into turmoil by the death of Queen Mary and the subsequent re-establishment of protestantism:

By occacon of some varyannce and Contencon amonge certeyn of the parysheners of Mere Aforesayd There were no newe Churche wardeyns Chosen nor appoynted for the year ffolowyng but the eleccon of them at this day for sondry Consideracons was deferred. And afterward as well by occacon of the Contynuannce of the sayd varyannce and Contencyon As also by occacon of the deathe of or soveraigne lady Quene Marye (who dyed the viith day of Novembre in the sayd yere of or lord 1558) And by occacon of the Alteracon of some p'te of Relygyon and of the servyce and Ceremonies of the Churche which then ensewyd There were no newe churchewardenys Chosen at any time in thies yere. Neyther was there eny Ale made nor eny other profytte or Revenue comyng or growyng to the use of the Churche thies yere. Neyther was there eny money or other Charges thies yere imployed or bestowed apon the Reparacon of the sayde Churche nor eny other wayes concernyng the same Churche.[37]

That the situation at Mere was too contentious for the appointment of new churchwardens did not result in the subsequent election of women to this post. The weak tradition of women serving as churchwardens probably made it hard to pressurise them into filling an unpopular post. Instead, it may be that it was in parishes where the Reformation changes were less divisive

[36] The surviving churchwardens' accounts for the period until 1570 provide references to twenty one female churchwardens, making a total of twenty two, including Gatton. Of these, only three held office in the period when Reformation influence can clearly be ruled out: Yatton (Somerset, 1496), Nettlecombe (Somerset, 1524?) and Morebath (Devon, 1528). The last two parishes also produced female churchwardens in the 1540s. But a connection with Reformation change is hard to substantiate. At Coldridge (Devon) a tradition of female churchwardens began in the final years of Mary's reign and continued into the reign of Elizabeth (female churchwardens appointed in 1556, 1558, 1559, 1561, 1562, 1565 and 1566). No other parish matches this pattern, but Woodbury, also in Devon, had a female churchwarden in the reigns of both Edward and Mary (1550–1, 1557–8). Churchwardens in parishes in large urban centres have not been studied systematically. However, Margery Mathew, widow, was warden at St Ewen's, Bristol in 1528: B. R. Masters and E. Ralph (eds.), *The Church Book of St. Ewen's, Bristol, 1454–1584*, Bristol and Gloucestershire Archaeological Society – Records Section 6 (1967), p. 167, f. 143r.

[37] Baker (ed.), 'Churchwardens' accounts of Mere', 29.

and/or where the male population was somewhat apathetic towards religion that opportunities for female churchwardens could be created. Whatever the case, it is hard to make a strong argument for the emergence of female churchwardens in this period as indicative of the new belief in the spiritual equality of the sexes encouraging women to exercise public authority in the parish.

The gendered pattern of parish office holding seems to have been largely independent of religious change, whether in terms of doctrine or dislocation. Instead, it remained subject to the same pressures that had caused the pre-Reformation parish gilds at Woodland and Broadhempston (Devon) to change from female to male wardens.[38] These attitudes persisted in the nineteenth century: an influential guide for churchwardens explained that a woman was not exempt from the duty of churchwarden 'although the courts would, in all probability relieve her from the burden of serving, unless the necessity of the case required that she should do so'.[39] Although the incidence of female churchwardens in the later sixteenth and early seventeenth centuries has not been studied systematically, it is clear that they do occur in some parishes that did not produce female churchwardens in the earlier period. For example, in Badsey (Worcestershire) Margaret Pegyn the elder served as a churchwarden in 1622.[40] At St Budeaux (Devon), where unfortunately the earlier churchwardens are unknown, one man and one woman were regularly chosen to serve in the early seventeenth century.[41] However, parishes such as Bishops Stortford (Hertfordshire), in which no woman was elected as churchwarden in the period 1482–1875, were probably more typical.[42]

In the choice of churchwarden, and more obviously in the practices of the church below this level of leadership, local traditions could nevertheless be important. In some areas there may have been some continuity of the more informal groups of maidens, young men and wives, as well as obvious reasons not to include their presence routinely in the official record. These groups may have been particularly significant for women: at Norton Fitzwarren (Somerset) in the early seventeenth century many of the young men's wardens were female.[43] Even if such women considered themselves to be protestant, their commitment to such activities may not have been

[38] See pp. 35–6.
[39] C. G. Prideaux, *A Practical Guide to the Duties of Churchwardens* (London, 1841), p. 4.
[40] Worcs. RO CWA Badsey, 850 Badsey B A 5013/2.
[41] D. M. Palliser, 'The parish in perspective', in S. Wright (ed.), *Parish, Church and People* (London, 1988), p. 23.
[42] J. L. Glasscock (ed.), *The Records of St. Michael's Parish Church, Bishops Stortford* (London, 1882), pp. 111–17.
[43] Somerset RO Norton Fitzwarren Vestry Book, D/P n.fitz 9/1/1. From 1581–1613 all the young men's wardens were male. From 1614 to 1643 14 of the wardens were female.

dissimilar to that of Katherine Lacy of Sherburn (Yorkshire) who during the revolt of 1569 encouraged a group of her neighbours to perform the old dances and mummeries inside the parish church.[44]

It was not only because the protestant impact was limited that office holding and the organisation of church seating were not the main concerns of people like Katherine Lacy. For most people, the Reformation in the parishes was signalled primarily by the use of the vernacular for the liturgy, and by the removal of images and the whitewashing of church walls. The latter process is often assumed to have been particularly detrimental to women. As Claire Shen comments, in the late medieval period 'representations of female saints about the church... served both male and female piety, in contrast to the post-Reformation church, in which male parish officers and male preachers were not offset by female examples of holiness.'[45] However, such statements oversimplify. Not only is it clear that gendered devotion to male and female saints respectively was less evident than such assumptions expect, but the lavish use of whitewash did not create a complete vacuum. It has long been appreciated that image destruction was less than total, and in stained glass lagged behind the cheaper and easier obliteration of paintings because of, or on the pretext of, the greater cost of reglazing. Dowsing's catalogue of destruction in East Anglia during the Civil War, and the expenses of the parish of Lowick (Northamptonshire) 'for glasing the windowes when the Crucifixis and scandalus pictures was taken down' in 1644, may partly represent attacks on images added as part of the 'Laudian' emphasis on the 'beauty of holiness', but it seems unlikely that this accounts for the whole.[46] The relationship of protestants to images was, as Patrick Collinson and Tessa Watt have reminded us, more complex.[47] A straightforward move from iconoclasm to iconophobia breaks down when the range of media including visual representations is considered. Even in terms of religious content, the reuse of wood blocks perpetuated the ambiguity of the boundaries between catholic and protestant positions.

Curiously, the emphasis on restoring images to our understanding of protestant culture has led to the neglect of text. Although polemicists in the 1560s and 1570s could summarise the conflict between catholic priest and protestant minister in terms of the power of the cross and the Bible over

---

[44] J. C. H. Aveling, *The Handle and the Axe: The Catholic Recusants in England from Reformation to Emancipation* (London, 1976), p. 39.

[45] C. S. Shen, 'Women and the London parishes, 1500–1620', in K. L. French, G. G. Gibbs and B. A. Kümin (eds.), *The Parish in English Life, 1400–1600* (Manchester, 1997), p. 256.

[46] Aston, *England's Iconoclasts*, pp. 74–84; J. C. Cox, *Churchwardens' Accounts from the Close of the Fourteenth Century to the Close of the Seventeenth Century* (London, 1913), p. 89.

[47] Collinson, *From Iconoclasm to Iconophobia*, and an edited version in Collinson, *The Birthpangs of Protestant England*, pp. 115–21; Watt, *Cheap Print and Popular Piety*.

demons,[48] the concern of historians to make parish protestantism popular, and the widespread assumption of our largely non-religious age that sermons and catechising must have been generally seen as tedious and boring, have discouraged enquiry into the message conveyed to parishioners on the walls of their parish church and given preference to that in their homes or in the alehouse. Of course, this partly seems justified. Broadsheets pasted on walls with woodcuts and words that could be memorised to well-known ballad tunes probably made more impact in a semi-literate age. Within the parish church, parishioners could rely on the minister's exposition rather than the texts painted on the walls. Edward Ward, a husbandman of Langton, near Gainford, who appeared before the Durham church court for marrying his uncle's wife within the prohibited degrees, may have been simply trying to evade responsibility, but his explanation also rings true. The court official recorded:

He saith that ther is dyvers writing [presumably the tables of kindred and affinity] hanginge upon the pillers of ther church of Gainford, but what they ar, or to what effect he cannott deposse; saying that he and other parishioners doith gyve ther dewties to be taught such matters as he is examined upon, and is not instruct of any such.[49]

Nevertheless, of all the texts in the Reformation parish church, the officially prescribed tables of kindred and affinity were perhaps the least inspiring, and the ones least likely to cause the minister to wax lyrical in his sermons. However, since, with the exception of the Creed, Lord's Prayer and Ten Commandments, the Reformation Church made no attempt to define precisely which were the suitable texts of scripture that it was advisable to paint on the freshly whitewashed walls, the eventual choice corresponded to the religious interests of at least a section of the parish.[50] Even if the conflict provoked

---

[48] For example, in 1609 a group of catholic players performed at Gouthwaite Hall, near Ramsgill, Yorkshire. According to a visiting anti-catholic witness, Sir Stephen Proctor, at the end of the disputation between a catholic priest and a protestant minister, 'one of the players [had] in his armes a great yellowe coloured crosse from whence the divells still fled, and the English minister had under his arme or in his hand a booke like a Bible, and being asked what he could say or how he could defend his religion, he answered, "By this book", and then offering to s[h]ew it foorth it was rejected and that after some flasheinges of fire the said English minister was carried away by the divell or divells.': A. Fox, 'Religious satire in English towns, 1570–1640', in P. Collinson and J. Craig (eds.), *The Reformation in English Towns, 1500–1640* (Basingstoke, 1998), pp. 230–1.

[49] J. Raine (ed.), *Depositions and other Ecclesiastical Proceedings from the Courts of Durham Extending from 1311 to the Reign of Elizabeth I*, Surtees Society (1845), p. 59.

[50] That the Elizabethan Church failed to prescribe or suggest texts is perhaps less surprising than that the more zealously protestant leadership of the Edwardian Reformation did not attempt this. Indeed, that some Edwardian parishes took the initiative to paint more than the standard Creed, Lord's Prayer and Ten Commandments is only known from Marian reaction. In 1554 Bishop Bonner instructed that 'certain scriptures wrongly applied to be painted on the church-walls' by protestant heretics in the reign of Edward VI should be

at Bury St Edmunds (Suffolk) was on a scale not normally matched elsewhere, it illustrates the sectional advocacy and topicality of such issues. In
this parish, the more zealous protestants wanted to emphasise their hard-
line position by having the text of Revelation 3.16 painted in the parish
church: 'because thou art lukewarme, and neither cold nor hot, I wil spew
thee out of my mouth'.[51] Other leading parishioners or ministers may have
been less provocative in their choices, but it seems likely that when texts were
painted over images their content was a matter of topical interest. Indeed, at
times, the texts chosen could conduct a dialogue with the obliterated images
themselves. At Radnage (Buckinghamshire) the text of Habakkuk 2.18–20,
which questions the value of man-made idols that are covered in gold and
are lifeless, was selected.[52]

The texts chosen fall into a number of categories, and not all were directed
at the whole parish audience. Several were designed to keep the minister
himself up to the mark, or, failing that, to give his congregation the scriptural weapon with which to admonish him. At Bowness (now St Martin's,
Windermere) the text of 2 Timothy 4.2 in the Coverdale Bible version was
painted on the third pillar on the north, presumably adjacent to the pulpit.
The preacher was instructed: 'preach thou the worde, be fervent, be it in
season or out of season: Improve, rebuke, exhorte with all longe sufferynge
and doctryne', a text which may also have helped backsliders to stomach
their minister's verbal chastisement of them.[53]

Other texts addressed the parishioners as a whole. Bowness was unusual
in choosing to transcribe extensive extracts from its favoured catechism,
Thomas Dawson's *Short Questions and Answeares* (1590), on the walls of

---

removed: Pratt (ed.), *Acts and Monuments*, vol. 6, p. 565. Some evidence can also be found
in the churchwardens' accounts of Mary's reign. Thus, at St Mary's, Devizes (Wilts.) in
1555, in addition to expenses on the rood loft, in making the altar, and 'for defacing the x
commandments', the wardens recorded that they had paid out a further 2s 4d 'for defacing
the scriptures on the walls': Cox, *Churchwardens' Accounts*, p. 185. The 1547 inventory
of church goods for Dovercourt (Essex) includes a payment of £7 'for tylyng, whiting and
writyng of the churche': Rev. G. H. Benton, 'Wall paintings formerly in the churches of
Dovercourt and Hazeleigh', *Trans. Essex Arch. Soc.* 20 (1933), 244.
[51] D. MacCulloch, *Suffolk and the Tudors: Politics and Religion in an English County,
1500–1600* (Oxford, 1986), p. 204.
[52] E. C. Rouse, 'Wall paintings in Radnage church, Buckinghamshire', *Records of Bucks.* 15
(1947–52), 138. Rouse considers that this text, and an accompanying one from 1 Timothy
2. 1–5, could date from the middle of the sixteenth century.
[53] *An Inventory of the Historical Monuments in Westmorland* (RCHME, London, 1936),
p. 146. In the early seventeenth century at Witnesham (Suffolk) on the north wall next to
the pulpit was painted the following texts: 'We are ambassadors for Christ, God making
his appeal through us' and 'Woe to me if I do not preach the Gospel'. The same message
was repeated at Yaxley (Suffolk): 'Necessity is laid upon me, ye woe is me if I preach not
the Gospel'. G. Yule, 'James VI and I: furnishing the churches in his two kingdoms', in A.
Fletcher and P. Roberts (eds.), *Religion, Culture and Society in Early Modern Britain: Essays
in Honour of Patrick Collinson* (Cambridge, 1994), pp. 190–1.

the parish church, but this was only really an extension of the normal practice of depicting the Creed and the Lord's Prayer. Other parishes adopted different solutions in an attempt to instruct the laity in the doctrines of protestantism. At Puddletown (Dorset) a sixteenth-century depiction of a Bible held in two hands was accompanied with explanatory texts, including one from Timothy that summarised the protestant position, 'The holy scriptures are able to make thee wise unto salvation through faith which is in Christ Jesus', whilst the words from Revelation on its open pages stressed the threat of plagues that would be visited upon those who tampered with the true words of scripture.[54] In the seventeenth century at Bradford on Avon (Wiltshire) the Creed was supplemented with two black-letter inscriptions relating to baptism and the Lord's Supper, the latter consisting of a central depiction of a loaf of bread flanked by tables listing the 'Works of God's Ministers' and the 'Works of God Himself'.[55]

Less theologically complex, and in closer continuity with pre-Reformation trends, a significant number of texts focussed on the transience of life and impending mortality, a concern that would gradually take on pictorial form with depictions of Death and Time in many parish churches. At Bedale (Yorkshire) a text in an elaborate strapwork frame warned, 'The voice said Cry. And he said what shall I cry. All flesh is grasse and all the goodliness thereof is as the flower of the field.'[56] Such warnings could be counterbalanced with a reminder, based on Hosea 13.14, of Christ's victory over death. The west wall of the church at Checkley (Staffordshire) was filled with emblems of mortality, time and eternity, but the accompanying text from Hosea made these images much less gloomy.[57] Those texts exhorting parishioners to remain in charity with one another also built on a significant pre-Reformation theme. At St Mary Bourne (Hampshire) the inscription in a cartouche dating from the second half of the sixteenth century takes its text from Ephesians 4. 31–2: 'Let all bitterness and wrath, and anger, and clamour, and evil speaking be put away from you, with all malice. And be yee kinde one to another and tender harted, forgiving one another, even as God for Christ's sake, hath forgiven you.'[58] At Bratton Clovelly (Devon) a seventeenth-century exhortation to hospitality was perhaps more powerful.

---

[54] J. Newman and N. Pevsner, *Dorset* (London, 1972), p. 350 and pl. 45.

[55] Rev. W. H. Jones, 'Bradford-on-Avon, part 2', *Wilts. Arch. & Nat. Hist. Soc. Mag.* 5 (1859), 212, 231–2. On the basis of the lettering and the ornamental style, Jones considers that these texts cannot be earlier than the reign of James I.

[56] Tobit Curtis Associates, 'Analytical survey and proposals for the conservation of wall paintings, St Gregory's church, Bedale, Yorks.', Nov. 1997. A copy of this report is deposited in the Wall Painting Archive, The Courtauld Institute, London.

[57] R. Garner, *Natural History of the County of Staffordshire, Supplement* (London, 1860), pp. 9–10.

[58] Illustrated in E. L. Lillie (ed.), *Danske Kalkmalereier, 1536–1700* (Copenhagen, 1992), p. 43.

The text (Hebrews 13.2) reminded that in receiving guests some entertained angels unawares, a clear reference to Abraham and Sarah and the Lord's promise to them that Sarah, despite her age, would conceive a child.[59]

General exhortations to charity towards one's neighbours, like the reminders of mortality, were not socially or gender specific, but some parishes also chose texts that aimed more precisely at the vices or failings of particular social groups. Perhaps the best sequence survives at Holdenby (Northamptonshire) where the texts from the Bishops' Bible have been dated to *c.* 1575. These included instructions, taken from Colossians, to servants to be obedient to their earthly masters, and to their masters that they should treat them appropriately. Parishioners were also warned, on the authority of Proverbs 23, not to remove ancient boundary markers or to trespass upon the fields of the fatherless. The congregation at Ashby St Legers in the same county were warned to leave the gleanings of the fields for their poor neighbours (Leviticus 19.9–10). At Bratton Clovelly the catalogue of vices was quite comprehensive and uncompromising. Taking verses from 1 Corinthians, the text warned: 'Be not deceived: neither fornicators, nor idolaters nor adulterers, nor effeminate, nor abusers of themselves with mankind. Nor thieves, nor covetous, nor drunkards, nor revilers, nor extortioners shall inherit the Kingdom of God.'[60]

Relations within the family could also be a topic for concern. In the 'Laudian' sequence of inscriptions painted on the walls of the church at Sherrington (Wiltshire) in 1630, a text over the south door of the nave reminded parishioners to 'Honour thy father and thy mother that thy days may be long in the land which the Lord thy God giveth thee.'[61] Evidence of similar concerns, though more focussed, survives at Holdenby where the texts were drawn from Ephesians 6 (Fig. 34). The obedience of children towards their parents was extended with the instruction to fathers not to 'provoke their children to wrath: but bring them up in instruction and information of the Lord' (Ephesians 6.4). Such reminders were perhaps unexceptionable, but it is also clear that in some parishes it was considered appropriate to set out the respective duties of husbands and wives, in line with the predominant concerns of a flourishing genre of godly advice literature. The chapel of St Thomas the Martyr at Brentwood (Essex) was demolished in the late nineteenth century, but the report of the paintings discovered at this time

---

[59] S. R. Blaylock and P. J. F. Bishop, 'St Mary's church, Bratton Clovelly, Devon: recording of wall paintings, 1993', *Exeter Museums Archaeological Field Unit Report* no. 93.31 (Exeter, 1993).

[60] Parish files at the Wall Paintings Archive, The Courtauld Institute, London; Blaylock and Bishop, 'St Mary's church, Bratton Clovelly'.

[61] W. H. Yeatman-Biggs, 'Wall paintings in Sherrington church', *Wilts. Arch. & Nat. Hist. Mag.* 50 (1942–44), 63–5. The 'Laudian' character of this scheme is betrayed by the inclusion of 1 Chronicles 16.29 (Worship the Lord in the beauty of holiness).

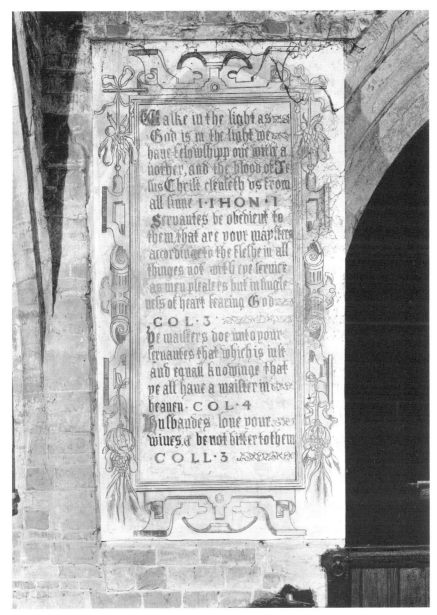

Figure 34 Reformation period inscription, including the instruction that husbands should love their wives and be not bitter to them, at Holdenby (Northants.)

records that on the west face of the chancel arch a fragment of an inscription survived: 'The dutie of Husbandes to the[ir]. . . . . . Gathered out of the hol[y]. . . .'.[62] It seems likely that this was balanced by a similar text detailing the duties of wives to their husbands, and it is notable that such prescriptions were given pride of place.

The chancel arch, the home of the Doom in the immediate pre-Reformation centuries, was adopted as the site for paintings of the royal arms in the Reformation period.[63] These depictions set forth a visually dominant expression of royal supremacy and the importance of authority. As such, it may be no coincidence that at Brentwood the chancel arch was seen as the suitable place for the exposition of authority and obligations within the family. As Susan Amussen has reminded us, it was a commonplace of early modern thought that the family was the microcosm of the state, and the context in which subjects were trained in their duties of obedience.[64] The text underneath the royal arms of James I at Winsford (Somerset), although not making the family context explicit, recognised the broader social implications, and, following the Geneva Bible translation, commanded, 'Curse not the king, noe not in thy thought; neither curse the rich in thie bed chamber for the fowle of the heaven shal carry the voice and that which hath wings shall declare the matter.'[65]

Imagery was most easily permitted in the Reformation parish church when it bolstered the authority of the state and the nation. In addition to the mandatory royal arms, some parishes thought it appropriate to depict those favoured scenes of God's special providence towards the English nation. At Bratoft (Lincolnshire) the destruction of the Spanish Armada was painted over the chancel arch in the early seventeenth century. The depiction of the military encampments of David and Goliath at Bratton Clovelly, with an extract from Hebrews 11 in a roundel above ('who through faith subdued kingdoms and put to flight armies of aliens'), can be seen as developing the same theme in a, perhaps more acceptable, scriptural form.

It is similarly the importance of magistracy, and in this case also ministry, that explains the presence of images of Moses and Aaron flanking the tables

---

[62] *Essex Archaeology* 5 (1873), 99. Those who observed the work dated this inscription to the reign of Edward VI, but the lack of any visual record means that this remains uncertain.

[63] The painting of royal arms began in the Henrician period, and was continued thereafter. An early record of this practice occurs in the churchwardens' accounts of Yatton (Somerset), where in 1541–2 the wardens recorded the expenditure of 13s 7d 'to a gylter of Brystow for gyltyng ye kings arms'. Cited in Cox, *Churchwardens' Accounts*, p. 233. See also H. M. Cautley, *Royal Arms and Commandments in our Churches* (Ipswich, 1934).

[64] S. D. Amussen, 'Gender, family and the social order, 1560–1725', in A. Fletcher and J. Stevenson (eds.), *Order and Disorder in Early Modern England* (Cambridge, 1985), pp. 196–217.

[65] Yule, 'James VI and I: Furnishing the churches', p. 192. Illustrated in Cautley, *Royal Arms and Commandments*, pp. 50–1. The arms were painted in 1609, and the text is Ecclesiastes 10.20.

of the Ten Commandments.[66] These depictions cannot have failed to make a striking impact, especially when, as was the case at Combe (Oxfordshire), their towering figures occupied the position opposite the entrance door that had been reserved for the similarly gigantic figure of St. Christopher. Whereas previously parishioners might have cast a quick glance towards St Christopher in the belief that if they did so they would not perish without the last rites that day, now they were confronted by the stricter, and apparently uncompromising, demands of the Ten Commandments. John Bossy has argued that the later medieval centuries had already witnessed a shift in theological discussions from the Seven Deadly Sins to the Ten Commandments.[67] Whatever the strengths of this case in the English parish context, it is clear that the Commandments were more insistently emphasised during the Reformation, even if their uncompromising nature could be on occasion softened by the continuation of a Christocentric framework. At Ludlow (Shropshire) the Ten Commandments date from 1561 and are surrounded by two IHC monograms and two crucifixes, as well as two Tudor roses.[68] The consolidation of the emphasis on the Ten Commandments was, however, less significant in the Reformation context in terms of its implications for the discussion of vice than it was for its clearer articulation of ideas of the authority of God, the magistracy and the clergy, and the duty of obedience. The sins of avarice, lust etc. were, after all, clearly catered for in the second table of the Commandments, and the need to avoid them did not fade from view with the disappearance of purgatory. Obedience to authority was, however, as Rex has argued, a dominant feature of the Henrician Reformation, especially as Tyndalian ideas of obedience broadened the demand to honour thy father and mother from one's natural parents and the Church to include a strong emphasis on obedience to the authority of the magistrate.[69] In the reign of Elizabeth, this could be graphically depicted. At Tivetshall (Norfolk) the queen's arms over the chancel arch were part of an elaborate tiered structure. The lowest plinth carried the Commandments, and the upper one the words from Romans enjoining everyone to be obedient to the higher powers.[70]

[66] Known examples include Hurley (Berks.), Weston Turville (Bucks.), Edmondthorpe (Leics.) and Combe (Oxon.).

[67] J. Bossy, *Christianity in the West, 1400–1700* (Oxford, 1985), p. 38.

[68] For a discussion of the importance of the Commandments see Aston, *England's Iconoclasts*, pp. 344–70. The illustration of the Ludlow table of Commandments in this volume (p. 332) has been cropped, and does not show the crucifixes and IHC monograms. A full illustration can be found in Cautley, *Royal Arms and Commandments*, p. 117. Other parishes could choose to accentuate the judgmental aspect of the Commandments: at Great Snoring (Norfolk) they were depicted with elements of the Doom.

[69] R. Rex, 'The crisis of obedience: God's Word and Henry's Reformation', *Historical Journal* 39/4 (1996).

[70] J. Phillips, *The Reformation of Images: Destruction of Art in England, 1535–1660* (Berkeley and London, 1973), fig. 28.

In such structures the subtleties of gender had no real place. The tables of the Law were upheld by magistracy and ministry; ideas of family could be represented by depictions of the Tribes of Israel, or lists of the respective duties of wives and husbands. The parish church had no place for female imagery. At Passenham (Northamptonshire) the Pietà was given a male cast as Joseph of Arimathea, rather than Mary, was depicted holding the body of Christ that had been taken down from the cross (Fig. 35).[71] Protestant sensitivity to the Marian cult, and the desire to follow scriptural reference, may explain this particular development. But it was also symptomatic of a more general concern. It is notable that many religious scenes figure in the domestic context that did not find a place on the walls of the Reformation parish church.[72] For some, such as the stories of Susanna or Tobit, this may simply have been due to their somewhat ambiguous position in the penumbra of acceptable apocryphal texts.[73] Nevertheless, this consideration cannot apply to the portrayal of Adam and Eve. The apparent absence of this theme in parish churches suggests that its content was seen as inappropriate. The ambiguities of the relationship between gender and responsibility explored in domestic imagery of the Fall did not fit with the clarity of authority and message that characterised the selection of texts and images in the Reformation parish.[74] From this perspective, it may also have been the unsettling questions about the probity of those in authority in the story of Susanna that were as significant as its apocryphal status in excluding it from the parish church.

The Reformation parish church was therefore an island within the wider religious and cultural experience of the laity. It was here that the social order was most clearly delineated and given religious sanction. Hierarchies of order and obedience to male authority were proclaimed as divinely ordained and

[71] The paintings were executed 1626–8 under the patronage of Sir Robert Banastre, lord of the manor of Passenham. The role of Joseph of Arimathea in begging Pilate for the body of Christ and placing it in his own tomb is, unlike the Marian Pietà, supported by scripture: Matthew 27.58–60. Joseph of Arimathea may have had further significance for those influenced by Bale's and Foxe's accounts of the history of Christianity in England. Claiming to follow Gildas, both authors attributed the initial conversion of England to Joseph, and associated the arrival of Augustine in 597 with the beginnings of the corrupt influence of the Church of Rome: H. L. Parish, *Clerical Marriage and the English Reformation: Precedent, Policy and Practice* (Aldershot, 2000), p. 105.

[72] Domestic wall paintings are more comprehensively surveyed for some counties more than others. See for example, M. Carrick, 'Sixteenth and seventeenth century wall painting in the county of Essex', M.Phil. thesis, University of Essex, 3 vols. (1989); F. W. Reader, 'Tudor mural paintings in the lesser houses in Buckinghamshire', *Arch. Jnl.* 89 (1932), 368–98; F. W. Reader, 'Tudor domestic wall paintings', *Arch. Jnl.* 92 (1935), 243–86 and 93 (1935), 220–62.

[73] E. Rouse, 'Elizabethan wall paintings at Little Moreton Hall', in G. Jackson Stops (ed.), *National Trust Studies 1980* (1979), pp. 112–18.

[74] See pp. 301–10.

Figure 35 Joseph of Arimathea holding the body of Christ, Passenham (Northants.)

unproblematic, as were the duties of individuals to family members and neighbours. Seating patterns, despite their diversity, shared this aim of imposing a visible order, and the more thorough exclusion of women from key office holding positions in the parish, such as churchwarden, in the later Reformation period can be seen as part of the same process. However, although these considerations created an environment characterised by male authority, this was very far from encapsulating the total religious experience of the average protestant parishioner. The world of cheap print and paintings in the alehouse and home was not more real than that of the parish church, but each was understood through the message of the other. Seating disputes provide the most obvious illustration of this. The ambiguities of social status were translated into closely fought contests between different interpretations, all of which shared the concern that order should be upheld. A similar yearning for social order, fused with personal interest, could give exhortations to maintain customs like gleaning a powerful force, and instructions to masters and servants could similarly strike a receptive chord. However, whilst such prescriptions, like the Commandments themselves, provided a yardstick against which behaviour could be judged, they offered no guidance in sorting out the complexities of human behaviour and responsibility such as could be found in broadside ballad or apocryphal story. This did not make the parish church a cold, irrelevant monument to prescription: its messages did have an appeal for all social groups, men and women alike. But it did mean that on its own it had very little to say about how religion should guide the individual in negotiating the messy complexities of gender and social position in the world.

8

The godly woman

The idea that women were 'to piety more prone' was a commonplace of early modern comment and was translated into the stereotype of the godly woman. This idea was present in the pre-Reformation period, but it was stressed less, being revealed more by omission than by advocacy: in anti-female literature this was the one female virtue which was not thought to be subverted in actual practice. This low-key approach suggests the need to explain the prominence in the Reformation period of the idea of the naturally religious woman who became emblematic of godliness, and all the more so since it is far from clear that this was a universal consequence of the introduction of Reformation ideas.

Most obviously, in the German Lutheran Reformation the first stereotype of the sincere follower of the true religion was male, the figure of Karsthans or the common man.[1] In this context it is tempting to see this as the product of a fusion of religious reform and social protest, which was to be realised in the Peasant War (1525), and which built upon a tradition of protest with a strong peasant identity, the Bundschuh revolts. In such a framework the lack of an equivalent to Karsthans in the English Reformation appears to need little further explanation, the influences of the Peasant War upon Kett's rebellion (1549) notwithstanding. However, such links, although valid, do not reveal the whole story: in the cause of reform the Karsthans figure was more than a manifestation of the link between divine law and social justice, it was an appeal for the application of plain commonsense to the interpretation of the scriptures and the practice of religion untrammelled by the corruption and self-interest of the clerical hierarchy and the social elites. Fundamentally, in early modern terms it was an appeal to disinterested rationality, a quality that was by definition thought to be male. In contrast, the godly woman of the English stereotype was emblematic of dedicated piety and devotion. At

---

[1] R. W. Scribner, 'Images of the peasant, 1514–25', in J. Bak (ed.), *The German Peasant War of 1525* (London, 1976), pp. 29–48; K. Uhrig, 'Der Bauer in der Publizistik der Reformation bis zum Ausgang des Bauernkrieges', *Archiv für Reformationsgeschichte* 33 (1936).

the foot of the pulpit she was a naturally receptive vessel for the words of the preacher (Figs. 32 and 33).[2] Despite lamenting the evident change in policy, many reformers would have recognised the reasoning behind Henry VIII's withdrawal of individual access to the Bible from most women.

The contrast between the situation in England and Germany was not simply the well-worn theme of official versus spontaneous Reformation. The core ideas which produced the Karsthans image were common in reform movements in England both before and during the 'official Reformation'. As Shannon McSheffrey has shown in her study of gender and later lollardy, women focussed on pious recitation whilst men were entrusted with the roles of scriptural interpretation.[3] The startling possibility of women priests within lollardy did not in fact suggest a radically different position.[4] lollards could entertain the idea of women priests, but this was only within a framework of disregard for religious ceremony. In doing so they did not elevate or transform women's status, but used female inferiority to disparage the value of the liturgy.

The difference lay in the failure of lollardy to produce a rallying stereotype equivalent to Karsthans. In comparison to Germany in the 1520s, lollardy was a less self-confident religious movement operating in a context of a much less well-developed polemical culture of cheap print. English Reformation stereotypes, when they appeared, derived from official establishment inspiration. This impulse characterised the godly as pious recipients rather than down-to-earth Biblical commentators. The frontispiece of Henry VIII's Bible, in which the Word is handed down to the people, epitomised this tendency. Although the common people, both men and women, were being given the scriptures, they were characterised as recipients rather than interpreters. The scrolls 'Vivat rex' and 'Long live the king' and the hierarchical organisation of the page emphasised the benevolence of the political order rather than social subversion.

As loyal subjects the recipients of the Word of God in the Bible frontispiece were men and women, but the pious response demanded by official conformity suited conventional feminine attributes: believers as grateful, humble

---

[2] King, 'The godly woman in Elizabethan iconography', discusses (p. 47) the images of women at the foot of the pulpit in Foxe's *Acts and Monuments*. The title page of the Matthew Bible (1537) (Fig. 41) provides an exception to the portrayal of the representative christian as female in the English Reformation. Of all English Bible title pages, this one follows Lutheran iconography most closely. The figure at the base of the tree being guided from the Old Testament to the New is male, but he is not an independent Karsthans figure, or a naturally receptive vessel: he has to be pointed in the right direction. Colin Clout and Martin Marprelate cannot be considered as equivalent to the German Karsthans. Their popularity was more limited and lacked visual form, and they focussed on exposing clerical hypocrisy and pretension.

[3] McSheffrey, *Gender and Heresy*, pp. 55–61.

[4] The evidence is discussed in M. Aston, 'Lollard women priests?', pp. 49–70.

and submissive vessels rather than male reasoners and interpreters. Despite the polemical value of denigrating an opposing religious viewpoint in terms of the number of foolish women amongst its adherents, the female virtues of submissiveness and piety made the image of the godly woman powerfully attractive. But it was not a simple image. On the contrary, it was an image which thrived and drew its strength from its conquest of the inherent contradictions in early modern notions of women. The very idea of women as vessels, or natural recipients of the Word of God, could not be divorced from the adjective normally qualifying that notion: women were weaker vessels. The naturally pious were also those naturally lacking in virtue and the ability to control and govern their own conduct. One simple consequence of this was that exemplary godly women became even more worthy of praise and emulation; a model for other women to aspire to and a potential cause of shame for men if they could not even match up to the achievements of a woman. As Thomas Gataker preached in the funeral sermon of Rebecca Crisp (1620),

Examples of this Sex are in some respect of the twaine the more needfull... Now as there is a necessitie of knowledge, faith, feare of God and other spiritual graces and some good measure of them, unto either. Examples of the weaker Sex apparently proving this, are in that regard more effectuall; for that, as they shame men, if they come short of such, so they give women incouragement to contend and good hope to attaine unto, what they see other of their Sex have before them by like contending attained.[5]

However, in gender terms such a position was far from straightforward. There was no single model of pious conduct to which both men and women could aspire. Even Gataker, who saw the exemplary life of Rebecca Crisp as an encouragement to both sexes, acknowledged that imitation of it was especially relevant to women. Similar views were expressed by Lancelot Langhorne in his sermon on Mrs Mary Swaine in 1611: 'Let us all for our application learne of a woman of the weaker sex: especially women, imitate her.'[6] The female pattern of piety, as exemplified in these funeral sermons, was not irrelevant to male religious conduct, but neither was it identical with it. To complicate matters further, the achievement of these exemplary women consisted to a large extent in transcending the natural frailties of their sex, and could even involve the acquisition of male qualities of strength, wisdom and understanding. Thus Gataker praised Rebecca Crisp for 'such graces as are not so ordinarily incident to that sex, sharpness of apprehension, and soundnes of judgement'. Another subject, Joyce Featley, earned similar

---

[5] J. L. McIntosh, 'English funeral sermons, 1560–1640: the relationship between gender and death, dying and the afterlife', M.Litt. thesis, University of Oxford (1990), pp. 64–5.
[6] Ibid., p. 65.

commendation from the same preacher: God 'had endowed her with a greater measure than ordinarie, in that Sex especially, of wisdome, of discretion, of understanding, of knowledge'.[7]

Nevertheless despite these overlaps, as Jeri McIntosh has noted, there was also a distinctive model of male godly conduct. For men the emphasis was not on dedication to private prayer and devotion, but rather on the honest pursuit of a public career as magistrate or governor of a household and public conformity to the established religion.[8] To modern eyes there may seem to be little equation between such activities and the godly woman spending hours kneeling in prayer in her closet. But both could be seen as the performance of a divinely ordained calling. All positions of authority were divinely ordained, and the protestant idea of vocation incorporated the assumption of the natural female propensity to ritualised acts of devotion. It seems no accident that the division of religious activity in such sermons mirrors the ideal roles in the poems 'How the good wife taught her daughter' and 'How the wise man taught her son'. But this apparent continuity suggests some significant inconsistencies in the protestant position. Private devotion and the examined conscience could not be advocated by protestants as particularly female, and the idea of spiritual equality could not be interpreted in terms of radically different relationships of man and woman with the divine. Nevertheless, the omission of anecdotes of private devotion from the eulogies of pious men, and the concentration on public roles, implies that even in the world of godly exemplars this was the case. The model of conduct is not that of a representative christian, but of a representative man or woman. Preachers' appeals to their audiences to learn from the godly life slightly blurred this inconsistency, but they could not see godliness as completely divorced from gendered attributes.

This insistence on gendered patterns of godliness is curious, appearing to bear little relationship to the lives of the godly (Nehemiah Wallington's voluminous jottings serving as a unique, but not insignificant example)[9] or to a consistent protestant theology. Both these discrepancies seem surprising. Even if the funeral sermon bears but slight resemblance to the life of the individual commemorated, we would expect the process of edification and eulogy to remove the wrinkles, rather than the testimonies of personal piety. Even to preachers the private devotion of a layman appears to have been an embarrassment, and best overlooked. The modesty of individuals expressing a desire not to be commemorated in a funeral sermon could be disregarded and transformed into evidence of godliness, but male acts of private devotion could not even be introduced by a parallel disclaimer of modesty. The doctrinal inconsistency is perhaps even more surprising. At the heart of the

---

[7] Ibid., p. 16.   [8] Ibid., pp. 108–24.   [9] P. S. Seaver, *Wallington's World* (London, 1985).

Reformation divide was the conflict over the role of works and free will in obtaining individual salvation, with the reformers stressing the inadequacy of man's efforts and the importance of God's grace. And yet in these funeral sermons we are presented with a very different picture of the lives of the godly. Here, as Collinson has observed, theology is conspicuously absent, and its place is taken by a description of individual godly achievement and innate virtue.[10]

This contrast between the content of funeral sermons and the protestant doctrine of salvation led Collinson to see the funeral sermon as 'a cuckoo in the protestant nest', and to explain its awkward presence he noted that the sermons follow the models of Classical panegyric due to a continuing Erasmian tradition and to a more radical protestant unease with the idea that the life of a godly individual could be treated in sermon form. In his view it was therefore the conventions of the genre which accounted for the stress on achievement rather than on the action of God's grace.[11] Observation of the similarities in emphasis on virtue, moderation and individual achievement, however, does little to explain why such a treatment continued to be seen as appropriate in a changing religious climate. After all, the split between Erasmus and the reformed tradition was precisely over the question of free will. It is also difficult to see the conventions of funeral sermons, which were written by authors from across the protestant spectrum, being shaped by the concerns of more isolated radical individuals. Certainly, the division of the funeral sermon into two parts – a sermon proper on a scriptural text, and the 'lean-to' devoted to the exemplary life of the deceased – can be seen as a concession in this direction (if not more prosaically as a handy device enabling a busy preacher to recycle at least half of a funeral sermon), but a real concession would have had to reinforce the doctrinal concern under-pinning this objection. Only the insertion of reminders of the inadequacy of individual effort could counter the view that the funeral sermon propagated misleading and dangerous doctrine.

The protestant orthodoxy of the preachers of such sermons is, however, not open to question. How then can we reconcile the claims of the critics and the content of the sermons themselves? An answer can be found in Lake's characterisation of the puritan spiritual dynamic and his view of the role of the preacher as navigating the laity between the objective truth of doctrine and the subjective world of experiential piety.[12] In their roles as pastors the hard doctrines of predestination fade into the background and

---

[10] P. Collinson, 'A magazine of religious patterns': an Erasmian topic transposed in English protestantism', in D. Baker (ed.), *Renaissance and Renewal in Christian History*, Studies in Church History 14 (Oxford, 1977), p. 242.

[11] Ibid., pp. 234, 243.

[12] P. Lake, *Moderate Puritans and the Elizabethan Church* (Cambridge, 1982), p. 155.

are replaced by a concern with the spiritual struggle of living in the world, and the continual oscillation between faith and doubt. Individual inadequacy and reliance on the grace of God underpin such pastoral care, but the focus is the search for assurance, which can only be realised by continuous vigilance against false assurance, continuous efforts to resist temptation, and true repentance for inevitable lapses. In this view the search for assurance and the process of sanctification require individual achievement, even if they are not its products.[13]

Such an interpretation helps to explain the persistence of gender difference in the religious models offered by these protestant sources. The possibility of individual achievement is circumscribed by gender. Even if godly women can attain a degree of discretion more usually associated with the opposite sex, this does not negate the significance of the gender divide. This gender distinction evidently derives from assessments of the innate characteristics of each sex, assessments that remained fundamentally unchanged from the fifteenth to seventeenth centuries, but it also relies on the context in which men and women are assumed to operate. Consequently, the extent to which protestant authors reiterated and reinforced notions of the public and private spheres as male and female respectively strengthened the tendency for godliness to be perceived in gender terms, the theoretical claims of spiritual equality notwithstanding. The separation of spheres, like gender distinctions in the importance of private devotion, was of course more significant in theory than in practice, but the combination of such models did not lack power. Even if they did not always shape behaviour, they could shape public commendation and a somewhat shamefaced embarrassment.

The spiritual dynamic of protestantism was rooted in a struggle in the world and with the world. As such there was, of course, a continuity with the preceding christian tradition, but with the significant difference that in this life escape from the world was no longer a possibility. One consequence of this focus on the world was manifested in the zeal of the godly for further reformation, both of the Church and of society. More generally, this viewpoint was expressed in the doctrine of the calling, a doctrine which enshrined acceptance of the social order, and more particularly of the gender order. The doctrine of the calling fitted neatly with the doctrine of separate spheres, attributing primarily domestic responsibilities to women. As a result men and women's encounter with the world was conceived in radically different ways. Women, shielded to some extent from pride and attachment to worldly affairs (if not from the temptations of desiring a new dress),[14]

---

[13] Ibid., pp. 147–9.

[14] P. Lake, 'Feminine piety and personal potency: the 'emancipation' of Mrs Jane Ratcliffe', *The Seventeenth Century* 2/2 (1987), 151.

had a much narrower arena of struggle with the world, the household itself. Moreover, within the household the demands of wifely subjection entailed a recognition of inferiority, and were a preparation for the relationship of the individual with the divine.

These considerations mean that the persistence, and perhaps even strengthening, of the association of women with a propensity to piety (as distinguished from a more overarching concept of godliness) in the protestant tradition should come as no surprise. The polemical value of the image of the godly woman was fully realised. As McIntosh observed, the fact that funeral sermons on women were more likely to be reprinted has to be explained in terms of the congruence between feminine virtues and piety.[15] But at the same time we must be careful not to confuse a particular style of piety with the larger concept of godliness. In certain contexts in protestant rhetoric feminine virtues had their uses (as did feminine vices in portrayals of Mistress Missa and the Whore of Babylon). Thus, although only about ten per cent of Foxe's martyrs were women, female martyrs were overrepresented in ballads.[16] As models of faith and humility, female martyrs, like the virgin saints before them, provided apposite and powerful material.

Recognition of the strength of the traditional connection between piety and gender roles and its continuation in a protestant context means that we need a more subtle investigation of the significance of religious change. It seems that the association between women and piety was more strongly articulated during this period. By the middle of the seventeenth century élite epitaphs suggest that religiosity had developed to an unprecedented extent as the defining feature of a virtuous and praiseworthy female life. A good example of this is the following lines on the monument of Richard Lybbe and his wife Anne of Hardwick (Oxfordshire) in 1651:

> He whose renowne for what compleateth man
> Speakes lowder, better things than marble can,
> Shee, whose religious deeds makes Hardwick's fame.
> Breathe as the balme of Lybbe's immortal name.

But, even if this trend could be proven, the developments during this period are likely to have been more complex as styles of piety, and their gender implications, evolved during the process of religious change. It is not simply a question of the contrast between catholic and protestant (and even that question is less clear-cut than might first appear), but also of the evolution

---

[15] McIntosh, 'English funeral sermons', p. 10. McIntosh also notes that when funeral sermons of both husband and wife were printed, only that of the wife was reprinted. For example, there were three editions of the funeral sermon of Elizabeth Juxon, but only one printing of the sermon for her husband, despite the fact that both sermons were by the same preacher, Stephen Denison.

[16] Watt, *Cheap Print and Popular Piety*, p. 90.

within protestant experience itself. A distinctively female religious experience was conventionally thought to be based on a mixture of humility and emotion. Such attributes had lain at the heart of the empathetic mysticism of the later medieval period, but the transfer to protestantism involved an element of discontinuity. Much of later medieval devotion had involved empathy with the all too human sufferings of Christ and, to a lesser extent, of his mother Mary. Such minute devotional identification had little place in the protestant scheme, at least in the earlier decades of reform. The combined emphasis on the gulf between God and man, and the sweeping away of human representations – first (and for a wider variety of reasons) of the saints, and soon afterwards the replacement of the figure of God as an old man with the Hebrew tetragrammaton – advocated an impersonal spiritual relationship whilst at the same time accentuating its individual nature. In the long run such coldness and distance were unsustainable. The bridge between cold doctrinal purity and the comfort of practical piety can be seen as emerging in the 1580s, fostered by the works of divines like William Perkins.

Such a chronology leaves the experience of committed protestants of the first half century of the Reformation rather vague and undefined. Sustained primarily by the example of martyrdom (as canonised in 1563 in the work of Foxe), and by the avoidance of the taint of catholic practice, protestant experience may have been gendered in a very different way from the later period of experiential religion already described. In this earlier period the association of women with ritual observance may have been more significant. Just as women could play a key role in sustaining catholic rituals of feast and fast, so they could also be crucial in subverting it.[17] More generally, in a period in which popish ceremonies were the focus of contention and of fears of pollution, women's role as the guardians of ritual for the health of the household may have taken on new importance. The strategies of Rose Hickman to avoid contamination with popish rituals, such as her substitution of sugar for salt when her child was baptised by a catholic priest, can be seen as protestant superstition rather than belief, but to assess Rose's actions in these terms is to misunderstand their significance. Instead they betray the need for ritualised support and validation of religious choice. In the same way Rose's comments about the hardships that befell her sister-in-law fit with a belief in God's providence, but also provide a validation for the choice of exile.[18]

In the second period (roughly from the middle of Elizabeth's reign) the need for religious support could be internalised. Paradoxically, as the campaign

---

[17] This argument is made with reference to the appeal of catholicism in Bossy, *The English Catholic Community*, p. 158.

[18] Dowling and Shakespeare (eds.), 'Religion and politics in mid Tudor England', 97–102.

to dehumanise the image of God the Father increased, the need to humanise the spirituality of the godly was recognised. A means of balancing these conflicting demands was a renewed emphasis on the role of Christ, who could be seen as the merciful aspect of God. Consequently, a Christocentric piety was possible, but it differed from the later medieval tradition in being more wary of its carnal aspects. This distancing increased during the course of the Reformation, as can be seen in the development of ideas of the christian as the bride of Christ, and of a protestant interpretation of the imitation of Christ.

In the early Elizabethan years popular love songs could be transformed to make Christ the object. For example, the song 'Dainty come thou to me', was rendered as 'Jesu come thou to me'. But, despite this model, there was a clear reluctance to develop the romantic theme in relation to Christ. After the address in the first verse, the idea of the singer as the spouse of Christ was not very fully developed.[19] Instead, the content of the ballad was more accurately summarised in its longer title: 'The sinner, dispisinge the world and all earthly vanities, reposeth his whole confidence in his beloved Saviour, Jesus Christ.' As Watt has described, protestant unease with the mixture of sacred and profane led to a phasing out of popular tunes and a change in ballad content. By the early decades of the seventeenth century modelling the relationship of the sinner and Christ on a popular love song was no longer possible.[20] Nevertheless, it was precisely in this period that the idea of the bride of Christ emerged in funeral sermons. In the context of protestant fears of ecstatic physical union, a negative view of the fleshly man, and debates over whether the erotic language of the Song of Songs indicated that it was not really part of scripture, the idea of the christian as the bride of Christ could only continue when the union took place after death and could be safely divorced from the lusts of the flesh. It was not part of the language, even in terms of expressing yearning, for the godly individual during life. The more protestants saw man's nature as wretched and sinful, the less they were able to envisage a union with the divine in this world.

[19] The first verse is as follows:

> Jesus my loving spouse,
> eternall veritie
> Perfect guide of my soule,
> way to eternitie, –
> Strengthen me with thy grace,
> from thee Ile never flee,
> Let them say what they will,
> Jesu, come thou to me.

'The sinner despising the world and all earthly vanities...' was entered in the Stationers' Register, 1568–9: Rollins, *Old English Ballads*, p. 198.

[20] Watt, *Cheap Print and Popular Piety*, pp. 39–73, 104–5.

The theme of the mystic marriage with Christ, whether of an individual believer or of a saint like St Katherine, had been conspicuously absent in late medieval popular devotion in England. Its return recalled the world of fourteenth-century mysticism, and, as in that period, it was a development of particular importance for women. McIntosh notes that funeral sermons of both men and women could contain references to the theory of the soul as the bride of Christ, but it was only sermons on women which could envisage the union of the soul of the commemorated individual with Christ.[21] Conversely, and significantly, in ballads before 1640 the repentant sinner was always male.[22] In part, the greater readiness to envisage a woman as the bride of Christ simply reflected Christ's masculinity, but it was also the result of the idea that the humility and obedience of the wife in her earthly life had trained her to be an especially fitting bride of Christ. Indeed, much of puritan conduct literature in explaining the duty of obedience saw the wife as simultaneously the bride of her husband and of Christ. Although the husband was also subordinate to divine authority, the parallel here was usually drawn in terms of the secular hierarchy in the world, rather than of a marital relationship. Some leeway was offered by the possibility of defining the soul of any christian in female terms, but this was largely limited to private male devotion, and was easily outweighed by the strength of texts like Ephesians 5.22–33 in modelling the role of the husband in terms of the care of Christ for his Church.[23] Even at death the possibility of viewing Christ as spouse was clearly gendered, drawing attention to the fact that for contemporaries 'head' and 'spouse' were awkwardly overlapping terms.

But in Christocentric piety in the Reformation, as in the late medieval period, union (Christ as spouse) was less significant than ideas of imitation (Christ as exemplar). In the latter we might expect gender distinctions to be more muted, even if both are, by definition, unequal relationships. The imitation of Christ in the Reformation drew inspiration from earlier catholic sources.[24] John Rogers's translation of Thomas à Kempis gained protestant respectability due to its copious scriptural references in the margins. Although it omitted some passages inconsistent with protestant doctrine, it retained the essence of the original catholic devotional text, and kept its distance from the carnal aspects of the later medieval focus on the sufferings of Christ and the cult of his wounds. Protestant reformers were, however,

---

[21] McIntosh, 'English funeral sermons', pp. 181–6

[22] Watt, *Cheap Print and Popular Piety*, p. 108.

[23] S. H. Moore, 'Sexing the soul: gender and the rhetoric of puritan piety', in R. N. Swanson (ed.), *Gender and Christian Religion*, Studies in Church History 34 (Oxford, 1998), pp. 175–86.

[24] E. K. Hudson, 'English protestants and the *Imitatio Christi*, 1580–1620', *Sixteenth Century Journal* 19/4 (1988), 541–58.

suspicious of catholic-style meditation on the detailed events of Christ's life and passion, even if performed with the stimulus of text rather than image. Calvin defined the *imitatio Christi* in very different terms: the aim was to imitate not the particular actions of Christ, but the general direction of his spirituality through 'denial of ourselves and willing acceptance of the cross'.[25] For many godly protestants the medieval balance had shifted. The emphasis was not on realising the extent of Christ's sacrifice for mankind, but on the individual's recognition of their own unworthiness. As a result, protestant meditation could focus on the Ten Commandments rather than the passion of Christ.[26] In doing so, gendered notions of participation could become correspondingly weaker.

Reference to à Kempis and Calvin, as well as the continuing Lutheran strands in the Reformation, reminds us that the place of Christ could differ significantly across the spectrum of protestant piety. A Christocentric focus could be seen by some protestants as a dangerous course, a regression from Calvinism towards Catholicism, Lutheranism or Laudian Arminianism. Despite this variation, it is clear that in the Christocentric aspects of devotion there was a certain continuity through the late medieval and Reformation periods which fostered a particularly female experience of spirituality. To the extent that the Reformation encouraged a view of the godly woman as a potential bride of Christ and weakened more inclusive later medieval ideas of *imitatio Christi*, it reinforced the image of the woman as the subordinate, pious vessel.

It was this context which underpinned the development in protestant culture of models of godly conduct from amongst the ranks of saints, biblical and apocryphal characters, and martyrs. The godly woman could be the bride of Christ and a receptive vessel, but her identity and her conduct were patterned much more on human godly exemplars. For many indeed Christ was seen as too high to be a possible model. Edward Bunny, in the preface to his protestant adaptation of Robert Persons's *First Booke of the Christian Exercise* (1584), encourages readers to overcome their fear of tribulation by remembering the sufferings of those before them, especially Christ, 'But if this great example of Christ seem unto thee too high for to imitate: look uppon some of thy brethren before thee, made of flesh and blood as thou art.'[27]

The range of human and divine exemplars invoked by reformers to guide the conduct of the laity is the subject of the following chapters. In examining interpretations of individual exemplars we will see the extent to which their

---

[25] W. J. Bouwsma, *John Calvin: A Sixteenth Century Portrait* (Oxford, 1988), p. 92.
[26] Hudson, 'English protestants and the *Imitatio Christi*', 557n.
[27] Cited ibid., p. 555.

histories reshaped gender ideals. The Reformation introduced a new cast of martyrs and favoured Biblical figures, but these acted alongside reinterpretations of figures from the catholic past, including such controversial figures as the Virgin Mary. As Anthony Stafford realised, this diverse cast played greater or lesser parts in the same script. In his manuscript defence of his published work advocating emulation of the virtues of the Virgin Mary he reminded his adversary Henry Burton that

> I have publish't no more in praise of this glorious Virgin, then one of his owne profession hath printed in commendation of his owne wife, to whom he gives the Epithite of Excellent, and avoucheth her to bee as perfect a Creature, as Mortality can boast of, deriving her by a long Pedegree from Foxes martyrs yet doe not I averre that hee hath Deified her, for I confesse she would have made a very sorry Goddesse, I should have said a shrewish for I thinke shee excells Juno herselfe in wrath and jealousie. I see no reason why Burton should bee angry that I should find out as many perfections in Gods own Mother, as hee or any of his sottish Brethren can espy in any of their purest wives, when the eggs of their eies are at the highest elevation.[28]

This was clearly a polemical defence, but Stafford had identified a crucial aspect of the protestant search for models of virtue which could encompass the human and the divine. If at one extreme Burton would not admit the Virgin Mary alongside the godly wife, for most protestants the spectrum was wider: the stories of saints, martyrs and Old Testament figures offered interlocking patterns of godly life, and a shared understanding of the godly woman.

---

[28] A. Stafford, 'A iust Apology or a vindication of a booke entituled The Femall Glory from the false, and malevolent aspersions cast uppon it by Henry Burton of late deservedly censured in the Star Chamber', Queen's College, Oxford, Barlow MS 227 (unpaginated).

9

The Virgin Mary and the saints

The appropriate role of the saints in the true religion was fiercely contested in the Reformation, as it had been in lollardy, and was an important touchstone of belief. The testing of images to see if they would retaliate, and when they did not respond using them, as a group of lollards did, as firewood to cook one's dinner was an attack which was not limited to the cult of saints, but struck at the heart of the catholic system of access to sacred power. Protestant image destruction was more far-reaching and, alongside the dissolution of monasteries and chantries, was arguably the most important part of the attack on catholic practice and belief. But, in gender terms, it is significant that this hostility to the cult of saints mainly took the form of opposition to idolatry and superstition, and was not conducted in terms of the role of the saints as models for the laity. Even when critical of the use of images, Henrician and Edwardian royal injunctions acknowledged this positive role: 'images serve for no other purpose but to be a remembrance whereby men may be admonished of the holy lives and conversation of them that the said images do represent.'[1] The idea that christians could benefit from the example of the lives of the saints continued to be maintained publicly in Elizabethan protestantism. *The Second Book of Homilies* (1563) clearly rejected the idea of saints as mediators, and asserted that saints know no more of what we do on earth and in our hearts than we do of them in heaven. Nevertheless, the homily 'Agaynst parell of idolatry' still instructed preachers to exhort their congregations 'to the folowyng of the vertues of the sainctes, as contempt of this world, povertie, sobernesse, chastitie, and such like vertues, which undoubtedly were in the saints'.[2] But, despite this advocacy, there was a growing opinion which doubted, and questioned, the definition of the 'holy lives and conversation' of the saints.

Within this debate the place of the Virgin Mary raised further problems. Aspects of her role were clearly validated by scripture, but from the

---

[1] Bray (ed.), *Documents of the English Reformation*, pp. 181 (1538), 249 (1547).
[2] *The Second Book of Homilies* (1563), p. 166.

perspective of reformers many of the worst excesses of catholic superstition seemed to crystallise around her cult. It was lollards, rather than protestants, who allegedly dubbed the pilgrimage image of Our Lady 'the witch of Walsingham', but the same idea of the image as a powerful instrument of delusion and bewitchment made sense to their successors. It is, however, too simplistic to see the Reformation as involving the 'loss' of the Virgin Mary. It was much harder to totally remove the mother of Christ than it was to ridicule a saint specialising in curing toothache. Consequently, the process of adaptation needs closer examination. Did Mary continue to have a significant role in protestantism, or was the exemplar swept away with the idol? Roston's description of Reformation culture in terms of 'a descent down the ladder of sanctity' has suggested to many that this question does not need asking.[3] In drama and popular literature New Testament subjects were abandoned in favour of a move towards 'safer' apocryphal and Old Testament figures. Finally, the logical outcome of this draining of the sacred was the development of the funeral sermon eulogising the godly christian. The late medieval stereotype of the 'witch of Walsingham' was clearly incompatible with this kind of agenda, but she was also largely a figment of the imagination. Roston's 'descent' was a process of reducing exemplars to a more human level, and, as such, was one in which the Virgin Mary as a human mother was potentially able to participate. The fate of Mary, therefore, may be said to hang in the balance in the Reformation. Clearly inappropriate as an intercessor, how well she could survive as a prominent exemplar depended on the extent to which she was identified as an emblem of catholicism, and the extent to which hostility to catholicism was thorough and uncompromising. Obviously, neither of these aspects was self-evident: the strengthening of late medieval Christocentric devotion had made Mary appear less central to catholicism, and the desire for a national Church encouraged the possibility that anglicanism could offer a broad religious umbrella. It was far from clear how well Mary would survive the challenge of the Reformation.

For these reasons alone it seems too simplistic, when drawing up a balance sheet of the effects of the Reformation, to assume the 'loss' of the Virgin Mary. For her, as well as for many of the saints, a role of exemplar could be created which overlapped with, but was thought to differ from, late medieval assumptions. Alongside the ridicule of saints specialising in curing toothache, finding lost keys or getting rid of unwanted husbands, the reformers' attack on the qualifications of the saints for sanctity operated on two fronts. On the one hand, the lauded virtues of the saints were seen to be incompatible with protestant ideals of human conduct. On the other, there were doubts concerning the historical authenticity of the saints and their miracles.

[3] Roston, *Biblical Drama in England*, pp. 118, 120.

Of these, the former point was the more significant, and was taken up vigorously by protestant polemicists like John Bale. His *The Actes of Englysh Votaryes* (1560) aimed to expose the abuses of the saints of the popish religion, and much of the work's force was directed against the false association of virginity with sanctity. For Bale such claims were in direct contravention of the word of God and his elevation of the holy state of matrimony:

Marke the lives of theyr Englyshe saints, almost from the beginning, & ye shal not find one of them canonised for prechyng Christes verity a right, nether yet for leading a life after the perfitt rules of the Gospell. Not one comend they for worshipping of God without mens traditions, nor yet for executing the works of mercy, unless it were to theyr advauntage. Never reckoned they wedlocke any godly estate of living, though it wer an onlye ordre instituted of God in the beginning, yea, for his Priestes also. Commonly they have diswaded both men and women from it, as from a most pernicious evill, or from a myschief of all mischiefes, calling it folishnesse, filthinesse, beastlinesse, a walking in darckenesse, a maintenaunce of lechery, a fulfilling of fleshly desires, a ground of all vice, an entraunce of death, a corrupting of maidenhode, a lake of miserye, a clay pit of unclennesse, a thraldome of Egipte, a net of Sathan, a snare of the Devill, and a ponde of perdition, looke John Capgrave in Catalogo Sanctorum Angliae ... In the history of Sainte Ursula have they named them aungels of darkenesse, which hathe perswaded marriage lawful.[4]

The reaction of Bale, and many of his protestant contemporaries, was not to deny the possibility of sanctity, but to transfer it to martyrdom for the faith rather than the defence of the unnatural state of virginity. Thus, as catholic observers scoffed, protestants could countenance the Marian martyrs being treated as saints and their relics being collected, as those of the lollards had been before them. In this case catholic ridicule was stronger than protestant logic: the outcome of the protestant position should have been the inclusion of those saints who met their deaths through refusal to worship pagan idols. In practice, the protestant attempt to filter out unacceptable saints in 1549 resulted in the acceptance of only those saints for whom there was a clear scriptural basis, principally the apostles and evangelists.

But we are dealing here with powerful polemic rather than logic, and this was driven as much, if not more, by a concern to advocate clerical marriage as by an objective assessment of the cult of saints. As we have seen, virginity was not so central to the image of saints in late medieval devotion as the writings of Bale would lead us to assume, and medieval theologians knew that dying for the faith made a saint.[5] It was not the virginity of the saints that made them lay exemplars. Moreover, in vernacular devotional literature Bale's final example of St Ursula was far from calling those in favour of Ursula's marriage 'aungels of darcknesse', but rather transposed

[4] J. Bale, *The Actes of Englysh Votaryes* (London, 1560) f. 2v–f. 3r.   [5] See p. 117.

her marriage to the King of England to a heavenly context.[6] Protestants themselves also had a more complex view of the value of celibacy than Bale's attack on virgin saints suggests. Whilst, of course, rejecting the idea that there was any value in vows of chastity, they acknowledged that for those who had the gift a celibate life, free from the cares of marriage and household, could be beneficial in allowing the individual to devote more time to spiritual concerns.[7] Household advice literature, for obvious reasons, was not so explicit, but it was commonly noted that the number of hours to be spent in devotion above the recommended minimum, which was usually achieved by extra early rising, would depend on the burden of household tasks. Nevertheless, these were practical concerns, rather than suggestions for exemplary conduct. The option of celibacy was seen as an extraordinary divine gift of no value in itself, and 'true virginity' was an uncorrupt faith.[8]

Such considerations mean that more care is needed in assessing the significance of the 'loss' of the saints. It was evidently a different climate. The attack on the intercessory role of the saints was thorough, but this had already been largely detached in the late medieval period from their role as exemplars: virginity itself was not seen as the source of their sacred power. But even for those saints that survived the Reformation winnowing, the importance of their personal histories was subtly undermined. The readings for saints' days in the new Prayer Books broke with the tradition, popularised in pre-Reformation works like Mirk's *Festial*, of recounting the life of the saint. Instead, the feast was an occasion for the expounding of a particular text of doctrine or urging a particular aspect of christian conduct. It is a moot point whether this exhortatory approach was better suited to conveying the preacher's message, but it is clear that it reduced the sense of human identification with the saints.

Popular art and literature both responded to and reinforced this change. Art, drama and popular literature eschewed the stories of the saints and focussed on Old Testament characters and the apocryphal stories of figures

---

[6] See above pp. 112–13.

[7] A sermon of Archbishop Sandys, published in his sermon collection in London in 1585, on the text, 'Marriage is honourable in all' (Heb. 13.4.) provides a good example. He reminded his audience that 'There be, no doubt, that have the gift of chastity by birth; and there be those that have made themselves chaste by endeavour: but of this all men are not capable. As it is the gift of God, so it seemeth to be a rare and not a common gift. Such as have it and so live sole, they are more fit to labour in God's church, it must needs be granted, for they are cumbered with fewer cares. But be these cares never so many and great, better it is to marry than to burn, and to be burdened with ordinary and honest cares, than with unordinary and dishonest carelessness to be destroyed': Rev. John Ayre (ed.), *Sermons and Miscellaneous Pieces by Archbishop Sandys*, Parker Society (Cambridge, 1842), p. 316.

[8] Bale, *The Actes of Englysh Votaryes* , f. 2v–f. 3r. According to Bale, 'true virginity is a faith uncorrupted, or a beleve governed by thonly word of God without all superstitions of men', and this is the only sense in which Mary was a virgin.

like Susanna.[9] Popular treatment gave these christian models a human identity, but provided no model of human sanctity, whilst the recognised saints risked becoming rather colourless individuals. This was, of course, largely what was intended, and was a solution that could seem even more justified as the idea of the awesome nature of the Almighty became more pronounced during the Reformation.[10] The refusal to portray God in human form, and the consequent recourse to the device of the tetragrammaton to represent the divine presence, encapsulate this greater emphasis on the distance of the omnipotent divine being.[11] These developments did much to seal the fate of the saints in protestantism, stressing, even more than their earlier placing on the lower panels of the rood screen had done, the gulf between their humanity and the divine.

They also prompted a re-evaluation of the relationship of the christian to Christ and his passion. The affective devotion of the later medieval period had advocated an empathetic approach to the sufferings of the human Christ. In protestant thought Christ's passion was increasingly viewed as part of the pre-ordained divine plan. Consequently, Christ's human attributes were not stressed and his role as mediator was denied. In John Daye's officially sponsored *Booke of Christian Prayers* (1578) the new Reformation prayers, influenced by the ideas of Calvin, were less likely to see the Crucifixion as

---

[9] Watt, *Cheap Print and Popular Piety*; R. H. Blackburn, *Biblical Drama under the Tudors* (The Hague, 1971); H. C. White, *Tudor Books of Saints and Martyrs* (Wisconsin, 1963).

[10] This was recognised by Weber, who saw it as characteristic of Calvinism and the natural corollary of a belief in predestination: 'The Father in heaven of the New Testament, so human and understanding, who rejoices over the repentance of a sinner as a woman over the lost piece of silver she has found, is gone. His place has been taken by a transcendental being, beyond the reach of human understanding, who with his quite incomprehensible decrees has decided the fate of every soul and regulated the tiniest details of the cosmos from eternity': M. Weber, *The Protestant Ethic and the Spirit of Capitalism* (London, 1930), pp. 103–4.

[11] Collinson, *The Birthpangs of Protestant England*, pp. 115–21; M. Aston, 'The *Bishops' Bible* illustrations', in D. Wood (ed.), *The Church and the Arts*, Studies in Church History 28 (Oxford, 1992), pp. 267–285, shows how Continental woodblocks were altered for the first 1568 edition of the Bishops' Bible to remove the figure of God and replace it with the tetragrammaton. Phillips, *The Reformation of Images*, pp. 173–5, 160–7, describes how the question of images also underpinned the Laudian–Puritan divide. Puritans founded their arguments on the ideas put forward by the influential Elizabethan author William Perkins, who maintained that christian images and pictures consisted essentially in sermons and the right administration of the sacraments, 'For in them Christ is described and painted out unto us.' For Perkins the Incarnation also should not be seen as a licence to image God in human form since, like the communion, Christ Incarnate was a temporary sign of Christ's presence. Laud, whilst welcoming images for their didactic value, was careful not to imply that it was possible to represent God the Father. In his defence of images in response to the Sherfield case, he commented, 'I do not think it lawful to make the picture of God the Father; but 'tis lawful to make the picture of Christ, and Christ is called the express image of His Father. I don't mean to say that the picture of Christ as God the Son may be made; for the Deity cannot be portrayed or pictured, though the humanity may' (Laud, *Works* VI.i, pp. 16–17).

an 'imagined reality'.[12] Such habits of mind were, though, hard to break. Alongside the new prayers, the collection also included translations of pre-Reformation affective prayers. This serves as a useful reminder that within protestantism there was an ill-defined space for those saints whom the reformers found most difficult to categorise, especially the Virgin Mary and Mary Magdalen who were witnesses to Christ's passion. That the Virgin should have been problematic is self-evident, but the position of the Magdalen is more curious. Included in the list of saints in 1549, she was omitted in 1552 and, even more strikingly, from the longer list in 1559, despite her symbolic importance as testimony to the saving power of faith. But the ability of both figures to find a niche in the interstices of protestant condemnation of the cult of the saints makes them figures of even greater importance for an understanding of the gender impact of the Reformation changes.

Attacks on the role of the Virgin Mary and the saints were a feature not only of the protestant Reformation, but also of the lollard movement that preceded it, interacted with it, and shaped lay experience. Lollardy also demonstrates the possibility of two distinct responses that were also available as options in the Reformation, and so provides a useful starting point. Although it has been easy to assume that total rejection characterised lollard views of the Virgin Mary, we need to distinguish between hostility to image worship and to the Virgin Mary per se. The 'witch of Walsingham' can be a deluding evil image, but there may still be a place for Mary in lollard belief, especially as much of lollard critique revolves around asserting the distinction between sign and signified. There is also a danger that lollard views of Mary can be easily lost: if orthodox they may pass without notice by their catholic interrogators, while protestant chroniclers of lollard activity, such as Foxe, may be happier passing over Marian emphases. It is therefore significant that references to Mary do come through in these sources, and that those that are hostile focus mainly on the use of Marian images or the invocation of the Virgin Mary, especially in childbirth.[13] Moreover, describing the cult of images of the Virgin in terms of witchcraft was not without its own gender significance in a culture in which the stereotypical witch was female.

Perhaps the most striking evidence for the continuing place of Mary in what can be broadly defined as lollard belief is the choice of texts translated into English for lollard use. The wife of Robert Pope, persecuted by Bishop Longland of Lincoln, possessed a number of English books against

[12] E. Duffy, 'Devotion to the crucifix and related images in England on the eve of the Reformation', in R. Scribner (ed.), *Bilder und Bildersturm im Spätmittelalter und in der frühen Neuzeit* (Wiesbaden, 1990), p. 32.
[13] For an example of lollard criticism of the practice of invoking the Virgin Mary to help in childbirth, see Pratt (ed.), *Acts and Monuments*, vol. 4, p. 206.

the Romish religion and 'another book of the service of the Virgin Mary in English'. Similarly, Richard Colins of Ginge had 'a book of our lady's matins' in English.[14] Such references are usually seen as inexplicable,[15] but they could be part of a coherent viewpoint which gave Mary a greater role in popular lollardy than is often assumed, linking her more with God than with the disparaged cult of the saints. For Robert Rave of Dorney 'folks were ill occupied that worshipped any things graven with man's hand; for that which is graven with man's hand is neither God nor our Lady, but made for a remembrance of saints. Nor ought we to worship any thing but God and our Lady; and not images of saints which are but stocks and stones.' Compatible with this was the exchange recorded between William Dorset and his wife. When he discovered that she was planning to go on pilgrimage to our Lady of Willesdon, he did not tell her that she should not worship Mary, but that Mary was in heaven.[16]

Variations of this theme can be found in other depositions. Thus John Blomstone was persecuted at Coventry in 1509 for a variety of beliefs including the assertions 'That there was as much virtue in a herb, as in the image of the Virgin Mary' and 'That it was foolishness to go on pilgrimage to the image of our Lady of Doncaster, Walsingham, or of the Tower of the city of Coventry: for a man might as well worship the blessed virgin by the fire-side in the kitchen, as in the aforesaid places, and as well might a man worship the blessed Virgin, when he seeth his mother or sister, as in visiting the images; because they be no more but dead stocks and stones.'[17] Such statements were critiques of the cult of images, which, as Pecock realised, was the centre of the lollard position.[18] They did not deny the role of Mary, but ridiculed the means of access through specified stocks and stones.

The reaction of Joan, the wife of Lewis John, of the diocese of London can be understood in the same way. Joan maintained that there were no holy days but the sabbath and she despised the pope and his pardons and pilgrimages, 'insomuch as when any poor body asked an alms of her in the worship of the Lady of Walsingham, she would strait answer in contempt of the pilgrimage, "The Lady of Walsingham help thee:" and if she gave anything

---

[14] Wife of Robert Pope, ibid., p. 230; Richard Colins of Ginge, ibid., p. 236.

[15] McSheffrey, *Gender and Heresy*, p. 70.

[16] Robert Rave of Dorney, Pratt (ed.), *Acts and Monuments*, vol. 4, p. 233; William Dorset, ibid., p. 238.

[17] John Blomstone, ibid., p. 133.

[18] Lollard opposition to sacraments and images was based on the same premise and was countered by Pecock by appealing for the necessity of 'seeable rememoratijf signs' which Christ had provided in addition to scripture: A. E. Nichols, *Seeable Signs: The Iconography of the Seven Sacraments, 1350–1544* (Woodbridge, 1994), p. 102; C. Babington (ed.), *The Repressor of Over Much Blaming of the Clergy by Reginald Pecock, DD. sometime Lord Bishop of Chichester*, Rolls Series, vol. 19/1 (1860), pp. 208–16.

unto him she would then say, "Take this in worship of our Lady in heaven, and let the other go." ' Alms in worship of the Virgin are acceptable, but not of the localised, earthbound image at Walsingham. Interestingly, it seems likely that Joan's position only just survived Foxe's doctrinal censorship. Instead of deletion, he added his own commentary upon Joan's words, which shows his unease with this stance as part of the genuine protestant tradition. These words 'declareth, that for lack of better instruction and knowledge, she yet ignorantly attributed too much honour to the true saints of God departed, though otherwise she did abhor the idolatrous worshipping of dead images'.[19]

It was therefore perfectly possible in later lollardy for lollards to describe Mary as 'our blessed lady', as Richard Grace did,[20] whilst also to disparage the cult of saints in ways ranging from the relatively sophisticated remarks of Joan John to cruder attacks. A good example of the latter can be found in the presentment of John Burne from Holburn in Belford (Northumberland) before the Court of Audience at York because the vicar overheard his conversation in the churchyard on the eve of St Mary Magdalen's day. Having been told by Robert Peres's wife that tomorrow would be Mary Magdalen's day, Burne replied, 'Nay it is Mary hoore Day. There is no moo Maries but oon', an answer which clearly combined a coarse rejection of the cult of saints with devotion to the Virgin Mary.[21]

In this context lollard possession of English versions of Our Lady's matins is explicable, as is also the continuing importance of the Ave Maria. Robert Hilman of Coventry had 'the salutation of the angel' in English and other lollards were accused of learning the Ave in English, often alongside the Pater Noster and Creed. For some though, the content of the Ave Maria was more problematic: Margaret Bowgas was asked in 1532 whether she said her Ave Maria and replied that she said 'Hail Mary' but 'will say no further'. In 1541 John Sempe and John Goffe were presented for 'dispraising a certain anthem of our Lady ginning "Te matrem" etc.; saying that there is heresy in the same.'[22] Although Mary could have a significant place in the beliefs of many labelled as lollards for their disparagement of the cult of saints, this was an inclusion which always had carefully defined limits, and some responded with outright rejection. The fuller Bennet Ward, for example, clearly ruled out Marian worship along with that of the saints, and was investigated in 1521 for saying 'That it booteth no man to pray to our

[19] Joan John, Pratt (ed)., *Acts and Monuments*, vol. 4, p. 176.
[20] Richard Grace, ibid., p. 240.
[21] A. G. Dickens, *Lollards and Protestants in the Diocese of York, 1509–1558* (Oxford, 1959), pp. 36–7.
[22] Robert Hilman, Pratt (ed)., *Acts and Monuments*, vol. 4, p. 135; Marian Morden, ibid., p. 227; William Littlepage, ibid., p. 228; a group, ibid., p. 584; Alice Atkins, ibid., p. 225; Margaret Bowgas, ibid., vol. 5, p. 39; John Sempe and John Goffe, ibid., p. 447.

Lady, nor to any saint or angel in heaven, but to God only, for they have no power over man's soul.'[23]

Despite the problem of distinguishing early protestants from lollards, it is clear that veneration of Mary, rather than her image, could have a place in the beliefs of some people labelled as lollards. It was possible for some, whilst rejecting all idolatry, to distinguish between Mary and the rest of the saints, but for others such distinctions made no sense at all. For protestants veneration of Mary became even more closely associated with her rejected powers of intercession. This might seem to signal a victory for the second interpretation, but it is less clear whether this lasted beyond the period of iconoclasm and the dismantling of catholic structures of devotion.

In this respect, as in many others, the Henrician Reformation was less of a watershed than that of Edward or Elizabeth, even if it set the agenda for the longer process of official reformation in parish practice. As Duffy notes, the adoption and continuation of the primer tradition in the Henrician Reformation resulted in the possibility of continuing Marian devotion, even if one of the most important prayers in honour of the Virgin Mary, the Salve Regina, was rewritten as Salve Rex and transferred to Christ.[24] The compromise that was reached was closer to the lollard position which distinguished between Mary and the other saints, and it was also concerned to establish the boundaries between Christ and his mother.

The 'Admonition to the Reader' in the 1535 primer by John Byddell, which was printed with the royal arms of Henry VIII and Anne Boleyn, provides a good example. The author argues that much of the Marian content in previous primers amounts to blasphemy. Prayers to Mary deflect from Christ and words of scripture are perverted by being falsely attributed to Mary. Such primers maintain the erroneous assumption that a prayer addressed to Mary will be sweeter to her than one addressed to Christ, and claim that images are not abused, and yet offer special benefits for prayers when said in front of Our Lady of Pity. Yet this was not a complete and straightforward attack on Mary. In calling upon Convocation to forbid 'such blasphemous slanders both against God and also our blessed lady', the author suggests the need for appropriate respect to be shown to the Virgin. At the same time he makes a clear differentiation between Christ and the saints, including the Virgin Mary: 'It is not meet, comely, nor fitting that in our prayers we should make a God and Saviour of any Saint in heaven, no not of our blessed lady. Neither is it meet to make them check with our Saviour Christ, much less than to make them checkmate.' Such actions defile Christ's precious blood and the inspiration of the Holy Spirit.[25]

[23] Bennet Ward, ibid., vol. 4, p. 226.
[24] Duffy, *The Stripping of the Altars*, pp. 444–7, 537–43.
[25] E. Hoskins (ed.), *Horae Beatae Mariae Virginis or Sarum and York Primers with Kindred Books and Primers of the Reformed Roman Use* (London, 1901), pp. 201–3. The complete

It might seem contradictory that this primer restored the litany that had
been omitted from its first edition in 1534, but it still only gave it half-hearted
support. The earlier omission was justified not because saints are not to be
prayed to at all, but because many people worship them in a superstitious
manner and think that Christ will only hear their prayers via Mary and the
saints. Whilst it is true that we need a mediator, that mediator to God is
Christ alone. The change of policy in deciding to print the litany is not an
abandonment of this position, but rather, as Luther advocated, to satisfy the
weak. The author then goes on to express the hope that they will not abuse
it, and casts doubt on the validity of prayer to all those saints named, many
of whom are of dubious sanctity and canonised by the bishops of Rome.
Quite clearly, for those who read the preface, the primer was not a ringing
endorsement of prayer to Mary and the saints, but as a whole the preface did
allow the possibility of prayer and the placing of Mary in a distinct category
worthy of respect.[26]

Similar ideas occur in the prologue to John Mayler's 1539 primer for John
Wayland. Since in previous primers many scriptures were 'distorted unto
our Lady, which in their own native sense are nothing meant of her, but of
Christ, the Wisdom of the Father', the author states that he

thought it my bounden duty towards God's true and sincere honour, to set forth such
a manner of Primer; wherein might be no such distorted Scripture or false honour
of that most immaculate Mother of God, lest the youth should learn to take such
Scriptures to be of our Lady which are of God, and to give such praise to her as
should only be given to God, but to know first the true honour of God, and to know
the honour that belongeth to that blessed Virgin Mary, and to the Holy Saints.[27]

The continuing inclusion of the Hail Mary in reformed Henrician primers
was also contained within clearly defined limits.[28] As part of a general concern to make sure Lauds is understood as praise, the texts clarify that this
is praise not intercession, and remind their audience that Mary herself acknowledged that she was not worthy. The Pater Noster is similarly to be seen
not as a petition but as praise. However, in this interpretation the idea of mediation should not be completely abandoned, but transformed in the sense
of remembrance and directed towards an earthly rather than a heavenly audience. The salutation of the angel at the Annunciation has a mediatory role
insomuch as it reminds us of the grace God gave Mary, and it is therefore appropriate that 'we may desire also that she may be known and exalted above
all men. For she was full of grace, whereby it is known that she had no sin

text of the Admonition is printed in E. Burton (ed.), *Three Primers Put Forth in the Reign
of Henry VIII* (Oxford, 1834).
[26] Hoskins (ed.), *Horae Beatae Mariae Virginis*, pp. 203–4.   [27] Ibid., p. 226.
[28] An extensive discussion of the Hail Mary as summarised in these two paragraphs was included in Byddell's 1535 primer: Burton (ed.), *Three Primers*, pp. 66–8.

imputed to her. And this was a special favour of God, to be full of goodness, and void of all evil.' Primarily, though, the focus of praise in saying the Hail Mary was not supposed to be Mary herself. Although it was possible for the prayer to be said carnally, it was truly and spiritually said with the heart,

> when we do praise her Son Jesu Christ, in all his works, words, and passion, and say well by him. When we are gladly content to suffer persecution for his truth's sake, rather than to forsake it. When for his sake we are content to love our neighbour as ourself. But this can no man do, except he be inspired with pure and true faith, knit and joined unto charity. For without this faith can no heart be good, but rather of nature full of curses and rebukes towards God and his saints.

In the same way as shortly afterwards the collects of the reformed Prayer Book of 1549 shifted the accent of the retained feast of the Purification to the Presentation of Christ in the Temple commemorated on the same day, so an understanding of the Hail Mary should displace Mary from the centre.[29]

Despite these modifications, the Henrician Reformation of the 1530s, like the strand of lollardy it unconsciously followed, retained a significant place for the Virgin Mary even in works designed to push forward a reformed interpretation of the cult of the saints. Iconoclasm, although affecting a number of prominent Marian pilgrimage images, did not remove the visual presence of the Virgin Mary. In many cases, such as Worcester and Rewe (Devon), the offerings and rich mantles adorning the images could be removed, but the images themselves remained and could still attract devotion.[30] That such compromises were possible was largely due to the fact that catholicism and protestantism were on converging paths due to shared Christocentric emphases. Significantly, the catholic restoration in the reign of Mary I did not strongly assert the place of the Virgin: in the new primers 'Salve Rex' was not changed back to 'Salve Regina'.[31] By the middle of the century, catholics and protestants could agree about the problem of inappropriate veneration and the need to preserve the importance of Christ in the scheme of salvation, even if there was room for disagreement on whether a satisfactory solution

---

[29] Cardwell (ed.), *The Two Books of Common Prayer*, p. 228: 'Almighty and everlasting God, we humbly beseech thy Majesty, that as thy only begotten Son was this day presented in the temple in the substance of our flesh; so grant that we may be presented unto thee with pure and clear minds, by Jesus Christ our Lord.'

[30] Duffy, *Stripping of the Altars*, p. 403, Whiting, *The Blind Devotion of the People*, pp. 67–8. In their defence the four men (presumably churchwardens) appealed to the royal injunctions proscribing offerings to abused images as a licence for their action, and maintained that the objects removed had been converted to the use of the parish of Rewe.

[31] Duffy, *Stripping of the Altars*, pp. 541–2. Even catholic writers in the reign of Mary I seem to have been reluctant to push the Virgin forward: L. Wooding, 'From humanists to heretics: English catholic theology and ideology, *c.* 1530–*c.* 1570', D.Phil. thesis, University of Oxford (1994), p. 75, maintains that 'there was a remarkable absence of references to the Blessed Virgin; few of the Marian works make even a passing reference to any of the saints, confirming the assimilation of reformist emphases within English Catholicism.'

had been achieved. Foxe's commentary on the Primer and Our Lady's matins, which was published in Mary's reign, focused on the criticism that Mary is wrongly considered as a mediator and usurps the office of Christ.[32]

Edwardian image destruction was in most areas more far-reaching than during the reign of Henry VIII, but the possibility of Marian devotion was not completely obliterated. The primer was not revised until 1553 and, although it removed all mention of the Virgin Mary, its publication so close to the end of the reign meant that it had little immediate impact. Separate from these developments, the Edwardian period is also the one in which the limits of the displacement of Mary in protestantism were most thoroughly clarified and explored as a result of the need to counter lollard and anabaptist views which, in reducing the role of Mary, could also be seen as diminishing the humanity of Christ.

These issues came most notoriously to the fore in the case of Joan Bocher, who was eventually burnt for heresy in May 1550. As Edward VI's *Chronicle* records it, Joan was burnt 'for holding that Christ was not incarnate of the Virgin Mary'.[33] Since this is unlikely to have been the only unorthodox view she held, the choice of this charge suggests that this opinion struck a raw nerve.[34] Joan's argument was in fact a more sophisticated version of the vivid image associated with lollards and early protestants which compared Our Lady to 'a bag of saffron or pepper when the spice was out', or in a more homely, but perhaps less apt, comparison 'lykenede our ladie to a poding when the meate was ought'.[35] Such similes deprived Mary of any contribution to the flesh/humanity of Christ (the bag clearly does not alter the saffron), and were meant to mean that after the birth of Christ his sanctity in no way inhered in her (despite the actual staining qualities of saffron). The implications of Joan Bocher's view were similar, but she believed that although Christ took no flesh of the Virgin, nevertheless he was her spiritual seed. In this view the birth of Christ could be seen as the supreme product of faith, but the consequence was that it seemed to endanger Christ's humanity, which reformers saw as absolutely necessary if Christ was to be the new Adam.

For many early reformers the correct attitude towards the Virgin Mary was clear: devotion to her could be argued away with the same arguments as were deployed against all the saints – that they usurped the veneration due to God

---

[32] Pratt (ed.), *Acts and Monuments*, vol. 7, p. 129–38.

[33] W. K. Jordan (ed.), *The Chronicle and Political Papers of Edward VI* (1966), p. 28.

[34] In Cranmer's Register similarly a single article of belief was recorded, 'that you beleve that the worde was made flesshe in the virgins Belly But that Christ toke flesh of the Virgin you beleve not because the flesshe of the Virgin being the outwarde man was sinfully gotton, and borne in Synne But the worde by the consent of the inwarde man of the virgin was made flesshe': Lambeth Palace Lib. Reg. Cranmer f. 75r. Cited in J. Davis, 'Joan of Kent, Lollardy and the English Reformation', *JEH* 33/2 (1982), 232.

[35] Dickens, *Lollards and Protestants in the Diocese of York*, p. 75.

alone. In this sense an attack on their cults was a liberation of God–Christ, and a restoration of their true position. But Mary's intimate connection with the incarnate and redeeming Christ presented more problems. Latimer, under the guise of discussing preachers' use of similes, felt the need to defend himself in his 'Sermon of the Plough' from the accusation that he had used the saffron bag analogy. He went on to argue that, even if he had, this did not have to be to the dishonour of the Virgin Mary:

> For I might have said thus: as the saffron-bag that hath been full of saffron, or hath had the saffron in it, doth ever after savour and smell of the sweet saffron that it contained; so our blessed lady, which conceived and bare Christ in her womb did ever after resemble the manners and virtues of that precious babe that she bare. And what had our blessed lady been the worse for this? Or what dishonour was this to our blessed lady?[36]

The main concern of these early reformers was not, however, the honour of the Virgin Mary. Latimer himself was critical of some of Mary's actions and concerned to cut her down to human size.[37] What these remarks reveal is a realisation that disparaging Mary could have adverse consequences for the reformers' understanding of the status of Christ. To say, as a reforming preacher did in Kent in 1536, that the Virgin was only the mother of Christ and could do no more than other women was less problematic to reformers than was the claim made by William Thorneton of Sawston (Cambridgeshire) in 1540 that Christ had no mother but the Holy Spirit, or the beliefs of Joan Bocher.[38]

Why the idea that Christ took no flesh from the Virgin Mary was more difficult can be seen clearly in Roger Hutchinson's attempt to refute Joan's position in his *Image of God or Layman's Book* (1550). Hutchinson's concern in this work is to refocus religious attention on God *and* Christ, whilst criticising catholicism for its adherence not to one master but to a multiplicity of saints. In this discussion it is notable that the status of Mary receives very little attention. In the section of the work against praying to saints she is simply listed amongst other saints for her role in assisting in childbirth. More

---

[36] Rev. G. E. Corrie (ed.), *Sermons by Hugh Latimer, Sometime Bishop of Worcester, Martyr, 1555*, Parker Society (Cambridge, 1844), p. 60. Robert Barnes also had to disassociate himself from the use of the saffron bag analogy in 1540. 'I have been sclaundered to preach that our lady was but a saffron bag, whiche I utterly protest before God that I never ment it, nor preached it: but all my study and diligence heath ben utterly to confounde and confute all men of that doctrine as are the Anabaptistes whiche denye that our savioure Christ dyd take any fleshe of the blessed vyrgyn Mary: which sects I detest & abhore': M. Coverdale, *A confutacion of that treatise, which one John Standish made agaynst the protestacion of D. Barnes* (Zurich, 1541?), sig. C5r, cited in I. B. Horst, *The Radical Brethren: Anabaptism and the English Reformation to 1558* (Nieuwkoop, 1972), pp. 63–4.

[37] See p. 225.

[38] Davis, 'Joan of Kent, Lollardy and the English Reformation', 230–1; J. Davis, *Heresy and the Reformation in the South East of England, 1520–1559* (London, 1983), pp. 37, 83.

significantly, Hutchinson's attempted refutation of Bocher's views deals entirely with arguments for the necessity in the scheme of redemption that Christ was made flesh, and sees the idea of the spiritual seed as insufficient for Christ's humanity.[39]

The uneasiness here seems palpable, if perhaps somewhat surprising. After all, the reformers' aim of humanising the false goddess Mary and their concern for the humanity of Christ could be seen as easily compatible. That things were not quite so straightforward stemmed from the problem of where in practice to lay the stress amongst the competing elements of the Trinity. Too great an emphasis on the Holy Spirit had to be checked as leading to the uncontrollable excesses of anabaptism. As Hutchinson realised, the relationship with the other two persons of the Trinity was also problematic and more complex. His resolution followed patriarchal assumptions in asserting that God the Father had to be in control, although in practice God and Christ were as one mind.[40] Given the Christocentric emphasis of later medieval religion, Hutchinson's difficulty here, and the need for such an elaborate setting out of his case, is more explicable than it seems in interpretations of the Reformation agenda that focus simply on the need to rid the Church of the abuses of the cult of Mary and the saints. Christocentric devotion could be a bridge to a Lutheran-style Reformation typical of Henrician evangelicals, but dominant reformers would increasingly (especially in the reign of Elizabeth) see it as detracting from the majesty of God, in the same way as Marian devotion had been criticised for deflecting the believer from God and from Christ.

Hutchinson's text was not the only response to this problem, and some reformers clearly feared that versions of the celestial flesh doctrine were widespread. Hooper asserted that 'thys ungodlye opynyon is gotten into the hartes of manye' in his 1549 text designed to counter such views, *A lesson of the Incarnation of Christe that he toke his humanitie in and of the Blessyd Virgine*. The topicality of this work is suggested by the unusual appearance of three editions in the year of its publication. The inclusion in Hooper's visitation of the dioceses of Gloucester and Worcester in 1552 of an article affirming that Christ 'in the substance of our nature took flesh of the substance of the Virgin Mary' may simply reflect Hooper's zeal, but it is also possible that the contrary ideas were to be found in parts of England not normally associated strongly with lollardy or with Dutch anabaptist influences.[41] The need to respond directly to the Bocher case prompted

[39] J. Bruce (ed.), *The Works of Roger Hutchinson*, Parker Society (Cambridge, 1842), pp. 171–2, 143–50.
[40] Ibid., p. 164.
[41] Horst, *The Radical Brethren*, pp. 140, 173. Less surprisingly, Ridley's visitation articles for the diocese of London in 1550 included the question 'Whether any teacheth and sayeth

Edmund Becke's *A brefe confutacion of this most detestable & anabaptistical opinion that Christ did not take flesh of the blessed Vyrgyn Mary . . .* (1550), and his use of popular verse form in a short pamphlet may have meant that this more effectively reached a wider audience. Recalling God's promise to Eve that the seed of woman would tread down the serpent's head, he asked,

> How can it be called the sede of a woman truly
> Which taketh no substaunce, nor part of her bodye?

For Becke it is self-evident that to conceive and bear a child means that the child took flesh from its mother. To claim anything else is 'as true as an oringe springes of an oke'.[42]

The works of Hutchinson, Hooper and Becke may have had a limited appeal, but they also responded to a demand that was strongly felt in some quarters. However, merely asserting that Christ took flesh from the Virgin was a weak defence, and one that became increasingly vulnerable as the changing religious tide aimed to sweep away not only Mary, but Christ as well. This development did not, of course, amount to a complete denial of the incarnation; rather it reflected a tendency to interpret the first commandment as focussed on God alone. In the short term the weakness of the defence was the main issue. As the quotation from Becke illustrates, the defenders of orthodoxy had no real response to Joan Bocher's final observation,

It is a goodly matter to consider your ignorance. It was not long ago since you burned Anne Ascue for a piece of bread, and yet came yourselves soon after to believe and profess the same doctrine for which you burned her. And now forsooth you will needs burn me for a piece of flesh, and in the end you will come to believe this also, when you have read the scriptures and understood them.[43]

The fact that spiritual interpretations of the eucharist could become more widely acceptable than a spiritual understanding of the incarnation is significant. It suggests the enduring importance of the connection of sinful humanity with the flesh, and the tension this created with the exaltation of the divine. In many ways this discussion of Christ's incarnation was a re-run of debates about the Immaculate Conception of Mary; if Mary was to undo the work of Eve, she needed to take on Eve's humanity, frailty and sinfulness, but increasing veneration of Mary promoted a desire to honour perfection.

---

that Christ took no Flesh & Blood of the Blessed Virgin Mary?': Frere and Kennedy (eds.), *Visitation Articles and Injunctions of the Period of the Reformation*, pp. 272 (Hooper), 233 (Ridley).

[42] E. Becke, *A brefe confutacion of this most detestable & anabaptistical opinion that Christ did not take flesh of the blessed Vyrgyn Mary nor any corporal substaunce of her body* (London, 1550), unpaginated.

[43] Cited in Davis, 'Joan of Kent, Lollardy and the English Reformation', 233.

Thus, it was perfectly compatible that Latimer should oppose Joan Bocher's views whilst maintaining the sinfulness of Mary. His arguments for the latter were most effectively summarised in his defence of his preaching in Bristol in 1533.[44] Criticised for declaring Mary a sinner, Latimer maintained that to say so did not dishonour Mary any more than the Bible dishonoured Peter and Paul, David and Mary Magdalen by calling them sinners. Moreover, he argued, those who saw Mary as sinless were in danger of seeing her as not saved by Christ, since 'It hath been said in times past, without sin, that our lady was a sinner; but it was never said, without sin, that our lady was not saved but a Saviour. I go not about to make our lady a sinner, but to have Christ her Saviour.'[45]

Revealingly, although such views ruled out veneration, Latimer encouraged emulation. It was precisely because these figures were sinners who had received the offer of salvation that they were valid models for emulation. Disparaging remarks about Mary of the saffron-bag type did not do this, despite their usefulness in corroding Marian veneration or idolatry. In this respect Joan Bocher's 'seed of faith' might seem to have more potential for christian emulation in a protestant context, but in a reform framework in which the humanity of Christ was envisaged only in post-lapsarian terms it could have no place. Despite the difficulties, the middle course had to be charted.

This course could be hard to maintain, and made it necessary to police surviving catholic imagery that now took on a new and more dangerous aspect. Concerns about depictions of the Annunciation showing Christ descending in the form of a child on a ray of light were, of course, most obviously part of a campaign to finish the incomplete task of Reformation iconoclasm. Such images were probably most popular in stained glass, and this was a medium which had largely escaped in the first phase of destruction, due to the fact that it was less likely to attract an idolatrous response and also to the costs of re-glazing. But by this period this iconography carried new dangers of misinterpretation. Contrary to the original medieval intention, such images could be thought to represent the view that Christ did not take flesh from the Virgin Mary, whether in terms of a saffron-bag or a two-seed view of the incarnation.

The call in visitation articles for the removal of such images of the Annunciation was not the only concern about surviving Marian imagery. Unsurprisingly, images of the Assumption came in for similar censure.[46]

---

[44] For details of the local context of this dispute see M. C. Skeeters, *Community and Clergy: Bristol and the Reformation, c. 1530–c. 1570* (Oxford, 1993), pp. 38–46.

[45] Corrie (ed.), *Sermons and Remains of Hugh Latimer*, p. 228.

[46] Strype, *Annals of the Reformation* (1824), vol. 1/2, p. 497: 'Whether all aulters, images, holy water stones, pictures, paintings, as of th'assumption of the blessyd virgin, of the descending

These observations remind us that in visual terms the changes of the Reformation did not blot out the image of Mary as effectively as is often supposed. The same was also true of the liturgy, especially during the Henrician Reformation. The 'loss' of the devotional focus on Mary was a long-drawn-out process of reshaping. But in gender terms, although both the lollard and the protestant positions drastically affected the visual presence of Mary, they may have been less significant for the use of Mary for emulation. It is oversimplistic to see an attack on Marian veneration as getting rid of the Virgin Mary to the detriment of women and their access to a female role model.

Most obviously, the Mary of the Magnificat continued to occupy a prominent place in the religious consciousness of both sexes. When in 1545 Roger Clarke of Mendlesham was burnt at Bury, his last words before being tied to the stake drew a strong parallel between the christian martyr and the Virgin Mary: 'he came, and kneeled down, and said "Magnificat" in the English tongue, making as it were a paraphrase on the same, wherein he declared how that the blessed Virgin Mary, who might as well rejoice in pureness, as any others, yet humbled herself to her Saviour'. Cicely Ormes, the wife of a worsted weaver of St Laurence's, Norwich, martyred in September 1557, similarly identified herself with Mary. As the fire was kindled she said, 'My soul doth magnify the Lord, and my spirit rejoiceth in God my saviour.'[47]

Letters of consolation and support written by protestant martyrs and teachers also drew upon the Magnificat and other Marian references as models for godly conduct, and to describe godly women. Thus John Careless, writing to Lady Anne Knevet, clearly drew upon the Magnificat in his gratitude and praise of her. Henry Bull's edition modified the phrasing but kept the central idea: 'O happy are you that ever you were borne, that God wil so mightely bee magnified in you. O blessed woman that so surely belevest and hast so plentifully tasted of Gods holy spirit, that out of thy wombe doe flow the ryvers of the waters of life.'[48]

Luther's commentary on the Magnificat validated this text as suitable for protestants, but he was careful to distance it from catholic emphases.

---

of Christ into the virgin in the forme of a lyttel boy at th'annunciation of the aungel, and all other superstitious and daungerous monuments; especially paintings and images in waul, boke, cope, banner, or elsewhere, of the blessed Trinitye, or of the Father, (of whom there can be no image made) be defacide and removyd out of the churche, and other places, and are destroied.'

[47] Roger Clarke, Pratt (ed.), *Acts and Monuments*, vol. 5, p. 532; Cicely Ormes, ibid., vol. 8, p. 428.

[48] T. Freeman, ' "The good ministry of godlye and vertuouse women": the Elizabethan martyrologists and the female supporters of the Marian martyrs', *Journal of British Studies* 39/1 (2000), 29. John Philpot's detailed application of each verse of the Magnificat to Elizabeth Vane in a letter to her did not survive Foxe's censorship (ibid., pp. 25–6).

He focussed on Mary's lowliness and humility and advised people to 'not make too much of calling her "Queen of Heaven" '. As he explained, 'For in proportion as we ascribe merit and worthiness to her, we lower the grace of God and diminish the truth of the Magnificat.'[49] The expressions of the martyrs given above conform to Luther's guidance, as does the treatment of Mary in Erasmus' *Paraphrases*, a copy of which was to be purchased by every parish according to the injunctions of 1547 and 1559. His description of the visit of the Magi emphasises the low-key, prosaic nature of the scene:

they espye the palace of the new kyng: a filthy and a vile cotage or stable. Sincere Godlynes is nothyng troubled with these thynges. They enter in; they fynde the infante not differyng in appaurance from others; they fynde the mother nothyng gaye or gorgious to loke to. All theyr stuffe shewed and testified povertie and simplicitie.[50]

The emphasis of Erasmus on the poverty of the Holy Family is, of course, not new, but his insistence on Mary's plainness is a significant development. Mediaeval hagiography clearly associated beauty with sanctity, to the extent of transforming aged martyrs such as Apollonia into beautiful young maidens, and the cult of the Virgin Mary in particular had produced fulsome praise of her beauty.

Perhaps paradoxically, the effect of deflecting attention from Mary as Queen of Heaven was to make the model of Mary more accessible, and more powerful, for godly men and women. The image of a humble, modest, and even plain Mary filled with divine grace bestowed upon her by God could be the image of the godly layperson. In such an image the role of merit was conveniently glossed over: she was 'the blessed Virgin Mary, who might as well rejoice in pureness, as any others',[51] and the Virgin Mary at her prayer desk in portrayals of the Annunciation was also the godly protestant reading in the closet.

The Annunciation was not the only Marian moment to find favour with the reformers. The circumstances of persecution highlighted other Marian scriptural passages, giving a new resonance. The words of Simeon to Mary, 'The sword shall pierce thy soul, that the thoughts of many hearts may be opened' (Luke 2.35), which had inspired elaborate catholic imagery of the Sorrows of the Virgin shown with a sword piercing her breast, were adopted as the appropriate metaphor for the godly compassionately beholding the sufferings of protestant martyrs. John Philpot, writing to Lady Vane, assures her that 'the swords which pierced Mary's heart in the passion of our Saviour, which daily also go through your faithful heart, be more glorious and to be

[49] L. Roper, 'Luther: sex, marriage and motherhood', *History Today* 33 (Dec. 1983), 35.
[50] D. Erasmus, *The First Tome or Volume of the Paraphrases of Erasmus upon the Newe Testament* (London, 1548), f. 26.
[51] Pratt (ed.), *Acts and Monuments*, vol. 5, p. 232.

desired than the golden sceptres of this world'. Lady Vane here is clearly assimilated to the model of Mary, but it is also clear that Philpot does not see this as an appropriate description of his own state (although he feels that it ought to be); whilst wishing that he could mourn more, he is joyful at the thought of the reward prepared for him in heaven.[52] The same image is used in a more impersonal way by the martyr Thomas Whittle writing 'to all the true professors and lovers of God's holy gospel within the city of London' in 1556. The 'sword' is understood here explicitly as the 'cross of persecution', and is said to be necessary to cleanse and scour faithful hearts that, like iron, are in danger of becoming rusty if not frequently scoured.[53] Here the reference to Mary is still maintained, but she is simply the recipient, as the reader also is, of Simeon's words. The letters of Philpot and Whittle demonstrate the continuing currency of a Marian image, and suggest that for many readers, especially those influenced by a catholic heritage, such verbal imagery had strong resonances and encouraged the conception of a godly life patterned on the Virgin Mary. For protestants Mary was no longer the saintly woman par excellence, but she was a model for the saints. The words of 'good' Elizabeth to her 'dear cousin' Mary, 'Happy are you, and happy shall you be for ever more, because you have believed', were, as in the letter written by John Careless to his brother T.V., words of consolation for all christians cast in the role of Mary.[54]

The identification of the christian with Mary embraced Mary's humanity as well as her special spiritual status. This formed a powerful combination in which criticism of Mary, designed to prevent superstitious veneration, could also produce a more effective and realistic model for the godly christian. Thus Latimer several times in his sermons criticises the pride and arrogance of Mary, who interrupts Christ's sermon in the Temple because she wants to be recognised as the mother of Christ by the assembled crowd.[55] Ostensibly, this is mentioned to highlight the incongruity of the papists' worshipping a sinless Virgin Mary. Additionally, and a point which can hardly have been

---

[52] John Philpot, Pratt (ed.), *Acts and Monuments*, vol. 7, p. 705.
[53] Thomas Whittle, ibid., p. 726.   [54] John Careless, ibid., vol. 8, p. 189.
[55] Latimer, following the interpretation of St Augustine and St John Chrysostom, explains Mary's interruption of Christ's sermon as follows: 'she was pricked a little with vain-glory; she would have been known to be his mother, else she would not have been so hasty to speak with him. And here you may perceive that we gave her too much, thinking her to be without any sparkle of sin; which was too much: for no man born into this world is without sin, save Christ only ... We must hear his word and do it: for truly if Mary his mother had not heard his word and believed it, she should never have been saved. For she was not saved because she was his natural mother, but because she believed in him; because she was his spiritual mother. Remember therefore that all who do his will are his kinsfolk' (The fourth sermon on the Lord's Prayer 1552). The same point is made in the sermon 'On the epistle for the twenty-third Sunday after Epiphany' preached in the same year: Corrie (ed.), *Sermons by Hugh Latimer*, pp. 383–4, 515.

lost on an audience imbued with the idea of Mary as exemplar, such lapses rendered Mary a more approachable model for humanity. At the same time, in accounts of martyrdom and letters of godly comfort, a positive Marian role for the godly woman emerged, a woman who can be a chaste and godly partner for the godly minister or martyr, the woman as the vessel of spiritual grace and understanding partnered with the educated male.

The theological reluctance to cast any human completely in the role of Christ meant that this human relationship fell somewhat short of the Mary–Christ model. The male godly martyr portrayed himself less like Christ than like Paul. Letters of comfort sent from prison were based on the Pauline epistles.[56] The godly male martyr took on an apostolic role as the companion and follower of Christ who carries on spreading his work, and thus carries on that part of Christ's work from which women are most excluded. Moreover, although godly women wrote letters of comfort, the authors in collections of letters of martyrs are male, despite the importance of the epistolary spiritual comfort that they received, and sometimes acknowledged, from godly women.[57] This suggests that, at least in the mid-late sixteenth century, there was still some reluctance to give even godly women a prominent sustaining and teaching role. Within this form praise of the godly woman could be appropriate in public, as it was later to be in the development of the funeral sermon and godly life, but female articulation of godly counsel was more problematic. Anne Askew's account of her trial is remarkable, but also perhaps possible because it does not presume to counsel. Thus, although the male godly martyr or minister was more comfortable with the role of an apostle than that of Christ, the ideal female model was still compatible with Mary, defined as a spiritual vessel rather than an active counsellor. Even the relationship described by Peter Lake between Mrs Jane Ratcliffe and her godly minister can be fitted into this model, despite the arguments for puritanism empowering women.[58]

It was, in fact, the inability of the Marian model to provide a positive example of female advice-giving to counteract the precedent of Eve that accounts for its continuing appeal. It offered the possibility of asserting the mutually supportive relationship of the godly couple whilst preserving the hierarchy implicit in the domesticated image of the male head of household as bishop. Authors of godly advice literature stress the importance of a wife's spiritual counsel, but maintain that this should be correctly given with due

[56] J. R. Knott, *Discourses of Martyrdom in English Literature, 1563–1694* (Cambridge, 1993), pp. 84–93.
[57] Freeman, ' "The good ministrye of godlye and vertuuose women" ', 8–33, stresses the importance of female sustainers for the survival of Marian protestantism, and notes that Foxe and Bull were reluctant to acknowledge this: the latter, in publishing two letters from John Careless to Margery Cooke, systematically omitted her name and changed the gender of the pronouns to make it appear that Careless was dependent on male spiritual support (29–30).
[58] Lake, 'Feminine piety and personal potency'.

humility, modesty and a true sense of her subjection to her husband. In the ideal case, the wife would look to her husband for knowledge and be guided by him. But religion was more than knowledge, and for the godly the spiritual relationship between husband and wife was not envisaged as one-sided, even if it was hierarchical. Consequently, in such discussions the model of Mary was inadequate on its own to describe the ideal female image. A range of models had to be drawn upon to fill out the composite list of positive female attributes, creating a somewhat chameleon-like existence for the godly woman. Nevertheless, in the eyes of heaven, and consequently for the individual christian woman, the Marian model, albeit conjoined with the earthly domestic diligence of Martha, occupied pride of place. The epitaph of Dame Dorothy Selby at Ightham (Kent) in 1641, although of an unusual woman perhaps best known for her part in the discovery of the Gunpowder Plot, makes this point more eloquently than most. After comparing her to Dorcas and commenting on the needlework that adorned her tomb, her qualities are further described:

> She was
> In heart a *Lydia*, & in tongue a *Hannah*,
> In zeale a *Ruth*, in wedlock a *Susanna*,
> Prudently simple, providently wary,
> To the world a *Martha*, and to Heaven a *Mary*.[59]

All this suggests the possibility of a greater presence of Mary in Elizabethan protestantism than is usually assumed. As an emblem of virtue and spiritual humility, Mary had a role that was not matched by any other godly figure. As a potential inspiration, we need to think of Marian influence across the presumed Reformation divide. Such continuity was not without its problems, and there were factors that could exert an influence in the opposite direction. Most obviously, a thoroughgoing fear of catholicism could drive Mary out. Yet this does not seem to have happened. Despite arguments that the nature of the Elizabethan Settlement of 1559, and the concessions to catholics it contained, was a response to a fear of catholicism, Elizabeth's unshaken adherence to this position in the years that followed lends credence to the view that what was achieved corresponded in general to her own religious preference.[60] It is also notable, and somewhat surprising, that even

---

[59] T. F. Ravenshaw, *Antiente Epitaphes, from AD 1250 to AD 1800, collected by T. F. Ravenshaw* (London, 1878), p. 92.

[60] The 'fear of catholicism' argument is presented most strongly by Haigh: C. Haigh, *Elizabeth I* (Longman, 1988), pp. 28–33, and restated in C. Haigh, *English Reformations: Religion, Politics and Society under the Tudors* (Oxford, 1993), pp. 237–42. Recent discussions of Elizabeth's religious preferences include P. Collinson, 'Windows in a woman's soul: questions about the religion of Queen Elizabeth I', in his *Elizabethan Essays* (London, 1994), pp. 87–118; S. Doran, 'Elizabeth I's religion: the evidence of her letters', *JEH* 51/4 (2000), 699–720.

in the heightened atmosphere of the last quarter of the sixteenth century the theory of catholics as traitors, rather than heretics, was sustained not only in the trials of priests but also in book censorship.[61] Moreover, Mariolatry did not feature strongly in anti-catholic polemic. The desire for a national Church under a broad anglican umbrella encouraged the possibility of continued Marian influence in the form that had most gender significance, as an influential female exemplar. This can be illustrated by the case of Elizabeth herself. Despite Hackett's sage reminders of the interchangeability of the attributes of Mary and of classical female goddesses, it is still significant that it was possible to use Mary for Elizabeth without fear that risk was being incurred.[62]

Nevertheless, the place of Mary in English protestantism from the reign of Elizabeth to the early decades of the seventeenth century is much less well charted, with the obvious exception of the Marian attributes accorded to the Queen herself. The relatively unexamined assumptions of 'loss' in the Henrician and Edwardian Reformations are assumed to have become entrenched in the Elizabethan period and after, especially as the debate moved on to the place of Christ and God and their depiction in human form. However, although in visual terms the 'loss' may have been fairly complete and Marian veneration outlawed in consciously protestant practice, the image of Mary as a focus for emulation continued, and was reinforced as Foxe's *Acts and Monuments*, which was ordered to be placed in every parish church, became staple reading for conscientious protestants.

It should, therefore, not come as a great surprise that when Dorothy Leigh recommends the selection of biblical names for children in her *Mother's Blessing* (1616), she comments that some of her audience will wonder, 'since I set down names for the imitation of their virtues that bore them, why I placed not Mary in the first place, a woman virtuous above all other women'. Her explanation is telling and strong testimony of the continued significance of Mary as a positive, and enabling, symbol for women:

I presumed that there was no woman so senseless as not to look what a blessing God hath sent to us women through that gracious Virgin, by whom it pleased God to take away the shame which Eve, our grandmother, had brought to us. For before, men might say, 'The woman beguiled me, and I did eat the poisoned fruit of disobedience, and I die.' But now man may say, if he say truly, 'The woman brought me a Saviour, and I feed on him by faith, and live.' Here is the great and woeful shame taken from women by God working in a woman: man can claim no part in it; the shame is taken from us and from our posterity for ever ... Will not therefore all women seek out this great grace of God, that Mary hath taken away the shame which before was due unto us ever since the fall of man?

[61] C. S. Clegg, *Press Censorship in Elizabethan England* (Cambridge, 1997).
[62] H. Hackett, *Virgin Mother, Maiden Queen: Elizabeth I and the Cult of the Virgin Mary* (Basingstoke, 1995).

Leigh is, of course, careful to state that making a god of Mary and praying to her is wrong. Mary's importance lies in the comfort she gives to women by reversing the curse of Eve, and in her admirable chastity. The latter, conceived in more than the narrow sexual sense, is Leigh's main theme, and she urges that 'especially above all moral virtues, let women be persuaded by this discourse to embrace chastity, without which we are mere beasts and no women'. As an exemplar, rather than as a result of her role in christian history, Mary in this view appears to be similar to Susanna, a quasi-apocryphal model of female christian virtue, but she also remains 'a woman virtuous above all other women'.[63]

Mary, therefore, did not disappear from the religious landscape of the later Reformation, although few published texts took her as their main theme.[64] Even strongly catholic authors writing in the more favourable environment of the 1630s assumed that many, or perhaps most, protestants respected Mary. Thus, the catholic author of *Maria Triumphans* (1635), a fictional debate in defence of the Virgin between an imprisoned catholic priest and a precise, or puritan, preacher at Paul's Cross, was at pains to point out that respect for Mary did not divide neatly along protestant and catholic lines. He aimed to vindicate the Virgin and save her from the indignities 'which she suffereth from the envenomed Tongues, & Pens of our *Precisians*; for the more temperate and learned *protestant* is far from such Exorbitancyes'.[65]

There are, of course, dangers in allowing a tract of the 1630s to represent dividing lines in early seventeenth-century religion, but it is possible to identify texts and stratagems which illustrate the way in which it was possible and desirable to include and limit the presence of Mary in a protestant religious framework in this period. As has been noted by White, the *Song of Mary, the Mother of Christ* (1601) focusses more on the life and passion of Christ than on Mary herself.[66] This is perhaps unsurprising, but the text deserves more comment than it has attracted. Given protestant sensitivities, we need to wonder why the poet did not set himself the easier task of presenting his topic without the problematic voice of Mary. To avoid misunderstandings,

---

[63] D. Leigh, *The Mother's Blessing: or, The Godly Counsel of a Gentlewoman not long since deceased, left behind her for her children* .. (London, 1616), Ch. 9, reprinted in S. Brown (ed.), *Women's Writing in Stuart England: The Mother's Legacies of Dorothy Leigh, Elizabeth Joscelin and Elizabeth Richardson* (Stroud, 1999), pp. 27–30.

[64] An s t c title search revealed only the English works mentioned in this chapter. In print Mary was perhaps most visible in Christmas carol broadsheets.

[65] *Maria Triumphans being a Discourse, wherin (by way of Dialogue) the B. Virgin Mary Mother of God, is defended, and vindicated from all such Dishonours and Indignities, with which the Precisians of these our dayes, are accustomed uniustly to charge her* (1635), sig. A2v.

[66] White, *Tudor Books of Saints and Martyrs*, pp. 293–4; anon., *The Song of Mary the Mother of Christ: Containing the Story of his Life and Passion* (London, 1601).

the poet is concerned to show her as subordinate in the heavenly hierarchy. It is Christ who chooses Mary to sing from amongst the heavenly choir of angels, and she only begins to tell her story when she has prostrated herself on the ground and kissed the Saviour's feet.[67] But, although marginalised as a humble figure at the feet of Christ whose story this is, Mary has a significant role to play as witness and guide. Having asserted her unworthiness, and her spiritual joy at the presence of Christ within her womb, her description of her delight in the infancy of Christ conveys every mother's affection in an intimate and appealing way. Through Mary's testimony, we too can experience the divine infancy, which is conveyed in language reminiscent of pre-Reformation devotional poems:

> My cross was always mixed with sweet,
> Who alwaies might adore my Saviours feete,
> Imbrace my God, my loving infant kisse.
> And give him sucke, who gives the Angels foode,
> And turn my milke into my Saviours bloud.
>
> Sometimes he cast his hand about my necke,
> And smylyng lookt his mother in the face:
> Some ioy or skill, I found in every becke,
> Each day discovered wisdom, love and grace,
> I cannot utter what I did espye,
> When I beheld his little glorious eye.[68]

However, unlike the late medieval examples, the *Song of Mary* does not go on to contrast this delight with the sorrow of Mary at the Crucifixion. The hints are there of course (my cross, the sweet and sour, Simeon's prophecy), but Mary's role as a witness in the poem ends with Christ's youth, and the poet tells us that he will pass over this quickly, though it is important and potentially enough for a volume, and move on to the most significant episode: the passion of Christ.[69] Contrary to our expectations, this does not mean that the poem climaxes with the Crucifixion. Rather, after a long description of the Agony in the Garden, it concludes with the *Ecce Homo*.[70] As a result, the final emphasis is on Christ and the relationship between his wounds and our sins. Mary has no place, not even as eyewitness, although this is still theoretically her song. This stress is clearly deliberate. The other texts printed and bound in the same small volume develop the same argument. There is another poem which focusses entirely on Christ's Agony in the Garden, and the collection ends with 'A Sinners supplication' in which the sinner asks for Christ's mercy for having made Christ's 'wounds so wide'.

In the *Song of Mary* the message of the Pietà has been transferred to male figures, and has been transformed from uncontrolled grief to a more rational

---

[67] Song of Mary, pp. 3–7.   [68] Ibid., p. 10.   [69] Ibid., p. 11.   [70] Ibid., pp. 19–21.

compassion.[71] In the late medieval context the cult of the Five Wounds and devotion to the Pietà could co-exist in a climate of affective devotion. Both periods emphasised the unworthiness of the sinner, but with the Reformation emotive empathy became less acceptable. In asking his readers to 'behold the man', the *Song of Mary* poet wished to stir their emotions, but not primarily to empathise. His aim was that we should transform our behaviour and take comfort from our deductions of God's response. The injunction 'behold the man' is meant to provoke us to cease sinning and intensifying Christ's wounds, and to follow the example of Pilate, a heathen with a hard heart who was nevertheless softened by seeing Christ. As importantly, we are to learn from the example of Pilate to imagine the even greater compassion of God. The image of the Pietà in which the Virgin Mary held her son Christ has been replaced by the compassionate God the Father:

> Doubt not at all, if *Pilates* heathen heart
> Did waxe more soft by such a pittious view;
> The loving father will regard the smart
> Of his deare Sonne, in such a ruefull hew.
> And grace and mercy will thereof ensue:
> To them which humbly doe demand the same,
> In Christ his Sonne, our crowned captaines name.
>
> He doth behold his Sonne with tender eyes,
> His sores and woundes be alwaies in his fight;
> And he again to christians dayly cryes,
> Beholde my Sonne your Saviour, in this plight,
> Retaine this patterne with you day and night.
> Be like your King, reioyce in paine and scorne,
> You being his members, who was prickt with thorne.[72]

In the process, of course, God is given feminine maternal attributes, but at the price of a compassionate, grieving role for the real mother. The christian is not asked to model him or herself on Mary, or even on God, but to be at least as compassionate as Pilate and not as hard-hearted as the Jews. God's compassion is beyond human measure, whilst the maternal response which Mary is allowed is a childlike delight in the toddler. The conclusion reminds us of another maternal comparison favoured by reformers in their description of God: God's love for mankind is compared to the strong love of a mother for her child, but whilst contemporary mothers can be so unnatural as to commit infanticide, God never abandons his children.[73] Once again,

---

[71] A similar concern underpinned the seventeenth-century choice of iconography in the church of Passenham (Northants.), where the body of Christ is depicted supported by Joseph of Arimathea, rather than Mary, following the scriptural text (Fig. 35).

[72] *Song of Mary*, p. 21.

[73] See for example Latimer's 'First sermon on the Lord's Prayer' (1552) in Corrie (ed.), *Sermons by Hugh Latimer*, p. 334.

although conceptualised in terms of human response, this serves only to reinforce human inferiority.

A gap between human capacity and the divine was not of course a Reformation invention, but the changed metaphors seem significant. The virginity and chastity of the saints appeared to place them beyond the reach of the aspiring devout layperson in the world, but empathetic affective devotion could narrow the gap. The Reformation validated the super-maternal as a way of envisioning the reaction of God, but it advocated for the christian a development from the dependent frailty of the child to the strength of the christian warrior. In the *Song of Mary*, the humility, modesty, love, compassion and industry of Christ are envisaged as indispensable armour for the christian:

> Thus must they arme themselves, that meanes to war
> With flesh, the world, the devill or suttle foe
> Our sword and target, speciall weapons are
> These thirty yeares our Lord did arme him so
> Not for because himselfe had any need
> But leaving us a rule in every deed.[74]

The same idea is expressed even more fully in the writings of George Gifford, an Essex clergyman. The process of religious conversion can be understood in terms of a parallel between spiritual and natural birth. As the weak child covets the mother's breast, so the convert seeks, and is nourished by, the sincere milk of the Word of God. As the christian grows to man's estate he becomes a valiant soldier in the battle with Satan.[75]

In this development the maternal side of God does not disappear. Even more than the natural adult, the spiritual adult remains a dependent and beloved child. Moreover, it is oversimplistic to divide, as some psychologists of religion have done, the loving and punishing attributes of God as maternal and paternal respectively.[76] As the *Song of Mary* poet reminds us, God can be, like the stereotypical mother, a refuge in our fear and feebleness, but, at the same time, we can feel buffeted by God's maternal/paternal discipline. God treats his own children

> With comforts crosse, with sweet to mixe the sour,
> 'Twixt weale and woe, to weild them unto blisse.
> The one doth shew his goodness and his love,
> The other doth our gratefull patience prove.

---

[74] *Song of Mary*, p. 12.
[75] G. Gifford, *Foure Sermons* (London, 1598) sig. F–F₂, cited in D. Willis, *Malevolent Nurture: Witch-Hunting and Maternal Power in Early Modern England* (Cornell, 1995), pp. 104–5.
[76] Beit-Hallahmi and Argyle, *The Psychology of Religious Behaviour, Belief and Experience*, esp. Ch. 6, summarises relevant research findings; R. H. Potvin, 'Adolescent God images', *Review of Religious Research* 19/1 (1977), 43–53, corrects the view that loving and punishing God images are bipolar.

> If comfort cleane did want we were dismaide,
> If all were joy, our tryall were the lesse:
> When danger comes, we run to him for ayde,
> We try his grace, and feele our feebleness.[77]

God is a composite parent, but at the same time a composite mother, and a classic attachment figure. The change is not a draining of the feminine and maternal, even if God is clearly Our Father, but a model of the divine which is parental. For both laymen and laywomen there are points of identification. The metaphor is literally a homely one which is rooted in the everyday life of the family. But behind this deceptive familiarity lies an insistence on distance, and a sense that ultimately, given man's inherent sinfulness, the fear of God and the threat of discipline should guide christian behaviour. Presuming upon the mercy and love of God, despite its unimaginable extent, is a licence to sin, as Robert Greene explained in his discussion of Susanna's response to the elders.[78]

The gender implications of this position are complex and hard to resolve. Willis, whilst acknowledging that the protestant God has maternal attributes, argues that the impact of this virtually pales into insignificance in the context of the 'banishing of female presences from the supernatural realm', but also suggests that 'draining the maternal from the supernatural realm might have positive as well as negative consequences for women, opening up possibilities for cross-gender identifications with the Father and for the construction of roles for women that move them beyond the narrow confines of their maternal function'.[79] Such an interpretation is problematic, not only because it identifies maternal in terms only of reproduction and nurture, but also because the basis for cross-gender identifications is left unclear. To adopt a broader understanding of maternal, embracing in Klein's terms the good and the bad mother who offers both love and discipline, clearly creates difficulties of gender clarity, but may be more realistic. The attachment figure has no necessarily gendered qualities, even if feminist influences in psychoanalysis claim the virtues of the 'good enough mother'.[80] But, perhaps paradoxically, this is the point. Medieval devotion to the Virgin Mary could interact with gendered understanding, but, as we have seen, it clearly was not gender specific. The apparently hostile male supernatural realm of the Reformation Church provided a reference point of *parental* guidance for both sexes. Moreover, it is possible that we should attempt, more than is often done, to separate devotion to divine figures, who are recognised as sources of authority, from devotion to figures who are inspirations for more attainable emulation. For

---

[77] *Song of Mary*, p. 9.   [78] See p. 264.
[79] Willis, *Malevolent Nurture*, pp. 105 n. 24, 109.
[80] E. Young-Bruehl, *Subject to Biography: Psychoanalysis, Feminism and Writing Women's Lives* (Cambridge Mass. 1998), pp. 226–46.

the latter, it is hard to see the Reformation depriving the laity of female models, as the redefined role of Mary and the popularity of figures like Susanna
testify. The limitation of the numinous, even when it was as far-reaching as
in the later Reformation, need not be seen in such gender-unbalanced terms.
Viewing the possibility of cross-gender identifications as transformative is
misleading in this context. Gender roles overlapped, and each individual os-
cillated between identifying with the authoritative, supportive *parent* and
the dependent christian child.

This notwithstanding, gender clearly does have a role, but its influence
is likely to be greater with those lesser models for emulation, the pool of
characters after whom Dorothy Leigh thought it advisable to name a child.
Here gender has a role because cultural assumptions of male and female behaviour are reinforced by didactic iteration of stories of fellow mortals. The
daughter learns the approved virtues of Mary or Susanna, or, if she does not,
risks loss of her reputation. In this framework the descent down the ladder
of sanctity makes sense, and in general terms the trio of virtuous female
qualities – chastity, silence and obedience – continues unchanged despite
the Reformation. Indeed, one is even tempted to suggest that the approved
cultural wisdom of proverbs such as 'maidens should be seen and not heard'
may be more influential. The descent down the ladder of sanctity may simply
be a means to provide appropriate stories to replace the old. This though, as
we shall see, would be to oversimplify the case. Whilst the stories of a virgin
martyr and of Susanna can both be seen as a defence of chastity according
to the dictates of faith, the second was not simply a replacement of the first.

That such replacements involved more far-reaching change can also be
seen by comparing the roles of the Virgin Mary and Mary Magdalen. Both
women were compassionate witnesses of Christ's passion, but, despite being considered a saint by catholics, the Magdalen was less problematic than
the Virgin for protestants. Mary Magdalen could not rival Christ or claim
extraordinary purity and grace, and was thus better suited to represent the
desired response of the ordinary sinful christian who can be saved through
faith. The idea that the Magdalen replaced the Virgin does though involve
a paradox that needs to be explained. The only change in saints' days honoured in the revision of the Prayer Book in 1552 was the omission of Mary
Magdalen, and the Elizabethan Prayer Book kept to this decision. This
change of policy seems surprising, since her story epitomises salvation by
faith and the role of repentance, as was stressed by the words of the collect:

Merciful Father, give us grace, that we never presume to sin through the example of
any creature; but if it shall chance us at any time to offend thy divine majesty, that then
we may truly repent, and lament the same, after the example of Mary Magdalene,
and by lively faith obtain remission of all our sins; through the only merits of thy
Son our Saviour Christ.[81]

[81] Cardwell (ed.), *The Two Books of Common Prayer*, p. 248.

The omission of Mary Magdalen in 1552 is also significant because in 1549 she had been the only female follower of Christ to remain visible in the calendar of the Church. The chosen Epistle for the day, Proverbs 31 (Whosoever findeth an honest faithful woman, she is much more worth than pearls…), developed the idea of the Magdalen being representative of women, rather than of everyone. This double-edged scriptural passage can be seen as the charter of recognition for the industrious, godly housewife, but also carried with it the assumption that women worthy of such high praise would be quite rare. Alongside the general message from Proverbs, the protestant service offered a pared-down version of Mary Magdalen's story, including only the ointment episode and glossing over the nature of Mary's sin in quoting direct from scripture (Luke 7). There was also no identification of Mary Magdalen with the woman in the garden who first sees the risen Christ.[82] In view of this, it seems surprising that such a restrained version of Mary Magdalen did not survive in the liturgy, buttressed by the chance to clarify the proper protestant understanding of the relationship between repentance and faith, and the use of Proverbs 31 to underline the proper role of a godly woman in the patriarchal system. These parts are all impeccably scriptural and compatible with a protestant outlook.

It is clear that the advantages of the Magdalen's story were recognised in the early years of the Reformation, and also in works that could be seen as transitional like Latimer's Sermon on the Card (*c*. 1529). Latimer appealed to his audience to take Mary as a pattern:

I would to God we would follow this example, and be like unto Magdalene. I doubt not but we all be Magdalenes in falling into sin and in offending: but we be not again Magdalenes in knowing ourselves and in rising from sin. If we be the true Magdalenes, we should be as willing to forsake our sin and rise from sin, as we were to commit sin and to continue in it.[83]

And Latimer was not alone. In Cranmer's unpublished Thirteen Articles (1538), the Magdalen is linked with David and Peter as a saint whose penitence made her worthy of emulation. Lewis Wager's *An interlude of the Repentaunce of Mary Magdalen* was entered in the Stationers' Register in 1566, four years after the death of the author, but was probably written in the reign of Edward. Its publication in the reign of Elizabeth, and its impeccable theological basis which drew heavily on Calvin's *Institutes*,[84] suggests that the problem was not so much with the story of the Magdalen as with her

---

[82] This scene is, of course, mentioned in the gospel for Easter Day, but the version chosen (Mark 16.1–8) describes the appearance of Christ to the three Marys. John 20.1–18 describes Mary's weeping at the tomb, the appearance of Christ as a gardener to her, and the *Noli me tangere*: Cardwell (ed.), *The Two Books of Common Prayer*, pp. 141–2.

[83] Corrie (ed.), *Sermons by Hugh Latimer*, p. 16.

[84] P. Whitfield White (ed.), *Reformation Biblical Drama in England: The Life and Repentance of Mary Magdalene – The History of Esau and Jacob* (London, 1992), p. xxii, xxxii–xxxiii.

inclusion in a calendar of saints' days. The verdict appears to have been that she belonged rather in the company of figures like Susanna, useful conveyors of edifying doctrine existing on the margins of the scripturally sanctioned canon.

A concern for scriptural purity underpinned both the 1549 and 1552 Books of Common Prayer. Devereux's analysis of the new collects notes that the degree of scriptural quotation is striking. In 1549 the only non-scriptural attribute of a saint mentioned is the crucifixion of St Andrew, and it seems significant that this was replaced in 1552 with a reference to Andrew's first following of Christ (John 1.35–42).[85] In this context the demotion of Mary Magdalen seems less surprising, perhaps especially since the Conversion of St Paul could seem a safer vehicle for a similar message. Paul's transformation by the overwhelming influence of God was summarised in the collect:

God, which hast taught all the world, through the preaching of thy blessed apostle Saint Paul; Grant we beseech thee, that we which have his wonderful conversion in remembrance, may follow and fulfil the holy doctrine that he taught [*1552* thy holy doctrine]; through Jesus Christ our Lord.[86]

Nevertheless, it remains puzzling that the Magdalen's fall from grace also extended to the omission of her name from the lesser category of black-letter saints. Whilst the intended purpose of this group of saints remains unclear, the inclusion of saints like Anne suggests that concerns about perpetuating extra-scriptural accretions did not guide the choice.[87] Indeed, although the composite identity of the Magdalen was impossible to prove from the Bible, one might have thought that the increasingly broad protestant conception of the body of the saints would have reduced the force of such difficulties. After all, the collect for All Saints, reinforced by the text of Matthew 5 and the omission of direct references to saints in the litany, seemed to celebrate the entire christian community rather than selected saints:

Almighty God, which hast knit together thy elect in one communion and fellowship, in the mystical body of thy Son Christ our Lord; grant us grace so to follow thy holy saints in all virtues and godly living, that we may come to those unspeakable

---

[85] J. A. Devereux, 'Reformed doctrine in the collects of the First Book of Common Prayer', *Harvard Theological Review* 58 (1965), 49–68.

[86] Cardwell (ed.), *The Two Books of Common Prayer*, p. 226.

[87] D. Nussbaum, 'Reviling the saints or reforming the calendar? John Foxe and his 'Kalendar' of martyrs', in S. Wabuda and C. Litzenberger (eds.), *Belief and Practice in Reformation England: A Tribute to Patrick Collinson from his Students* (Aldershot, 1998), pp. 125–7, notes that the selection criteria of the *c.* 60 black-letter saints restored to the Prayer Book in 1561 are obscure, although there is a tendency to emphasise the Anglo-Saxon heritage of the English Church and its links with the primitive Church. The rubric stated that there should be no communal veneration of black-letter saints. The list of saints can be found in Rev. W. Keatinge Clay (ed.), *Liturgical Services: Liturgies and Occasional Forms of Prayer Set Forth in the Reign of Queen Elizabeth*, Parker Society 27 (Cambridge, 1847), pp. 444–55.

joys, which thou hast prepared for all them that unfeignedly love thee; through Jesus Christ.[88]

Such views, though, were hard to assimilate fully, given the difficulty of recognising the elect and of jettisoning assumptions of hierarchy.

But, in many ways the 'liberation' of Mary Magdalen from the ranks of the saints allowed her to emerge as a more useful and powerful model. In descriptions of sorrow at the death of Christ, the compassion of the Virgin Mary had to be distanced from ideas of maternal intercession with her Son, whilst that of the Magdalen posed no such difficulty. The Virgin's grief was also less useful as a model due to her presumed, and unshaken, confidence in the Resurrection. Mary Magdalen's persistence in grief matched that of the believer who has lost the assurance of Christ's presence and promise. It therefore reflected the experience of the ordinary christian more closely, and provided hope and comfort for spiritual troubles on a personal level. It is these problems and contrasts which explain why Mary Magdalen is not a simple substitute for the Virgin Mary. Texts like *Marie Magdalens Funerall Teares* (1594) and *Marie Magdalens Lamentations for her master Christ* (1601) differ from *The Song of Mary, the Mother of Christ* (1601) not merely in changing the protagonist who grieves for Christ's death. The theme in the Magdalen texts is bewilderment at the sudden loss of the object of faith and love, and the painful search for its cause in the worth of the individual seeker of Christ.

Robert Southwell's *Funerall Teares*, and the *Lamentations*, which have been attributed to G. Markham, are two closely connected texts. The similarities are striking and Markham, in turning the topic into verse, may well have been working from Southwell's earlier prose text. At first sight it seems surprising that a work by a Jesuit priest who was shortly to suffer martyrdom at the hands of the Elizabethan regime should be taken over so readily by the protestant cause.[89] But it is clear that there was much more overlap in devotional styles than the prevailing climate of anti-popery suggests. The story of Mary Magdalen's mourning and search for Christ could be part of Ignatian Counter-Reformation devotion, and also seem particularly pertinent to the psychology of protestantism and the godly examined conscience in the later sixteenth and early seventeenth centuries. It may even be that, despite the apparent polarisation due to persecution, this possibility was more evident in this later period of the Reformation: Lewis Wager's Edwardian dramatisation

---

[88] Cardwell (ed.), *The Two Books of Common Prayer*, p. 265.

[89] F. W. Brownlow, *Robert Southwell* (New York, 1996) gives an account of Southwell's life (pp. 1–17) and a discussion of the text and its relationship to a popular medieval homily ascribed to Origen, printed in London in Latin in *c.* 1504 and in English translation in 1565 (pp. 34–43). *Marie Magdalens Funerall Teares* was licensed by the Archbishop of Canterbury, and by 1630 ten editions of had been published: Clegg, *Press Censorship*, p. 80 n. 5.

of Mary Magdalen had focussed on her rejection of her sinful life and had omitted her grief at Christ's death.[90]

The two works do have some differences in emphasis. Of the two, Southwell's work seems much more straightforward: its prime concern is to describe the difficulty Mary Magdalen experiences in transferring the focus of her love from the mortal, fleshly Christ to the risen, living God. Thus, he puts more stress on Mary's refusal to address the two angels who ask the seemingly inappropriate question 'Why do you weep?' To Mary their lack of mourning and compassion only serves to intensify her grief, as does the risen Christ's initial refusal of her request to be allowed to kiss his feet. Mary is shown here as unable to read the signs which would give her the comfort of the Resurrection, a promise which in her grief she has overlooked. She cannot see the angels other than as insensitive human bystanders, and cannot take in the implications of the fact that the shroud in the tomb is unstained despite Christ's lacerated body and the sticky qualities of myrrh. Her perspective is too earthly to grasp the scope of the miracle, and it is this weakness which explains Christ's refusal to let her kiss his feet. Mary needs to be weaned of her desire for his external presence, but this is a painful and confusing process and Christ's final permission is his compassionate response to her grief and her faith. Mary is thus portrayed as the representative christian, too earthly to grasp the spiritual world fully, but one whom Christ understands and meets halfway. Southwell concludes by advising the christian soul to take Mary for its mirror and to follow her affection so that similar results may follow.

Markham's work follows the same narrative and spiritual development, but is a little more optimistic in tone; his Magdalen seems to have a slightly easier journey towards the realisation of the meaning of the Crucifixion, and her tears, which are both instruments of her blindness and the cause of her revelation, are seen in a more positive light. It is in Markham's work too that issues of gender are more directly addressed. Those tears whose value is so ambiguous can be womanish, but whilst the apostles have fled, Mary has the manly strength to remain by the tomb despite the risks. The angels note her 'manly courage' in coming to the tomb, but maintain that she is 'too much woman now' if she cannot stop her tears.[91] Nevertheless Mary persists and her tears seem to evoke Christ's response. It is these same tears that are also advocated for the contemporary christian living in a world of hardened unrepentant hearts which have forgotten Mary's example.

---

[90] L. Wager, *The Life and Repentance of Marie Magdalene* (1566); Blackburn, *Biblical Drama under the Tudors*, pp. 131–6, discusses the play briefly. A more extensive consideration can be found in the introduction of Whitfield White (ed.), *Reformation Biblical Drama in England*, pp. xx–xxxiii.

[91] Markham, *Marie Magdalens Lamentations*, sig. D–Dv.

Womanish tears and seeking of Christ are, it seems, the only possible godly response and, although in the preface maids and matrons are the presumed imitators of Mary, Markham concludes like Southwell with a general appeal to the christian soul to take Mary as its mirror in seeking Christ.[92]

Thus both works offer a very different perspective on dealing with female grief at Christ's death from that presented in the *Song of Mary*. The absence of issues of intercession and maternal influence allowed Mary Magdalen to emerge as the representative and uncertain christian who is trying to understand her relationship with Christ. In her sorrow she rejects the desire to die and be buried in Christ's tomb as a presumptuous desire, but one in which she would find solace if it could happen without her seeking. Similarly, she imagines the 'sweet divine felicitie' of being nailed to the same cross upon which Christ was crucified, pierced with the same spear and the same crown of thorns, but then recognises her unworthiness for such a 'glorious death'.[93] Ultimately, although love wishes most to be united with the thing that it loves, Christ's spiritual presence is a greater joy and gift, even if the christian child can only be weaned gradually from his external presence. The Virgin Mary, although similarly having to come to terms with the death of Christ, could not represent such a clear path of spiritual development.

Mary Magdalen did not, of course, completely overshadow the Virgin in this period. There was always some unease about taking such a sinner as a model for women to aspire to, which was partly met by figures such as the pure, chaste and godly Susanna. Moreover, if the Magdalen was effective it was less as a gendered model of social virtues, and more as a seeking christian soul. Other developments in this period also encouraged a greater emphasis on the Virgin Mary herself, and advocated emulation as due honouring of her. Chief amongst these was the changing nature and importance of anti-popery. In the early decades of the Reformation anti-popery existed in a polarised relationship and validated the godly, but by the second quarter

---

[92] Markham explains in the preface,

> And Marie shewes to maids and matrones both,
> How they should weepe and deck their rose-like cheekes
> With showers of greefe, whereto hard hearts are loth,
> And who it is her matchlesse mourning seekes.

The first verse of the concluding appeal is as follows

> Oh christian soule take Marie to thy mirrour,
> And if thou wilt the like effects obtaine,
> Then follow her in like affections fervour,
> And so with her, like mercie shalt thou gaine:
> Learn sinfull man of this once sinfull woman,
> That sinners may find Christ, which sin abandon.

(Markham, *Marie Magdalens Lamentations*, Aiv.v, Hv).

[93] Ibid., Biii.v.

of the seventeenth century it was possible to see anti-popery as counterproductive, as a hindrance to the aim of reunion, and as a creator of recusancy.[94] Those who held such views can be broadly defined as Laudians, and thus they clearly were not shared by all. Even amongst this group there were different responses to the appropriate role of the Virgin and the saints.

The 'Laudian revival' gave no public place to Mary and the saints in the Church. From a puritan perspective the most evident innovation here was the respect for the name of Jesus. That Mary and the saints were not given a greater role may have been partly due to pragmatic concerns, given English anti-catholic sensitivities. But 'Laudian' views were more clearly thought out than this suggests. Several authors felt the need to adopt a more forgiving attitude to the idea of idolatry, one that was prepared to declare more openly the case for honouring the saints and to judge the risk of blasphemous idolatry as the lesser evil. The view that in the protestant attitude towards the saints the baby had been thrown out with the bathwater was also encouraged by the stance adopted by the more puritan wing. A puritan defensive strategy, which disregarded well-known scriptural supports for Mary's status, such as the Hail Mary, could alienate not only Laudians but also more moderate protestants. It is notable that both catholic and protestant authors promoting Mary as a figure to be honoured identified their readership as consisting of both catholics and of more moderate protestants.[95]

In all this debate the idea of the invocation of the saints was treated very circumspectly. Most were doubtful whether Rome's claim that saints were merely 'mediators of intercession' was understood in practice, but some were prepared to minimise the gravity of this offence. Sidestepping the argument a little, Montagu in his *New Gagg* objected to prayers to saints largely because of the 'unaptnes of the Agent'. Saints could not hear prayers, but if they could Montagu would be prepared to ask Holy Saint Mary to pray for him. In an earlier work, *Immediate Addresse unto God Alone*, Montagu had explained, 'I will not, I dare not be so harsh and rigorous, as to condemne them of Impietie for so Calling unto them [saints]', and although more is addressed to them than ought to be the case, 'yet nothing is detracted there from the Creator, in giving them that they are not capable of'.[96] Clearly, few of Montagu's contemporaries were likely to be convinced by this line of reasoning, which, by mere assertion, left no basis for any idea of blasphemy.

---

[94] A. Milton, *Catholic and Reformed: The Roman and Protestant Churches in English Protestant Thought, 1600–1640* (Cambridge, 1995), Ch.1.

[95] *Maria Triumphans* (1635), A2v. cited above (p. 229); A. Stafford, *The Femall Glory: or the Life and Death of our blessed Lady, the holy Virgin Mary, God's own immaculate mother* (London, 1635).

[96] Cited in Milton, *Catholic and Reformed*, pp. 206–7.

The concept of blasphemy was central to those authors who, whilst asserting (whether truthfully or otherwise) their opposition to praying to the Virgin Mary, defended the idea that she should be honoured. Both John Taylor's *The Life and Death of the most blessed among women, the Virgin Mary Mother of our Lord Jesus* (1620) and Anthony Stafford's *The Femall Glory or the Life and Death of our blessed lady, the holy virgin Mary, God's own immaculate mother* (1635) argue that disparagement of the Virgin Mary is odious to God.[97] A comparison between the two texts suggests that in the mid-1630s there was, as we might expect, a greater possibility of elaborating the role and qualities of Mary than in 1620, even if neither author escaped disapproval for his work. This can be illustrated most clearly by the treatment of such episodes as the death of Mary. Taylor concludes his work stating that Mary was buried at Gethsemane, whilst Stafford subscribes to the idea of the Assumption, despite expressing some caution in accepting this doctrine. He concedes that the apostles did not write details of Mary's later life and death, but this, he explains, was not because it lacked worth, but simply because they were too busy converting the Gentiles. Whilst it is impossible to say that the traditions surrounding Mary are true, Stafford will not condemn them as erroneous: 'for ought I know they may have passed by unwritten Tradition from man to man'. This uncertainty does not cause Stafford to hold back: in the engraving accompanying the text a nimbed figure of Mary rises heavenwards in a cloud supported by angels.[98]

---

[97] For Stafford the instruction to 'honour thy father and mother' also applies to Christ, and ingratitude is odious. Consequently, puritans who disparage Mary and reject the testimony of the Hail Mary are informed: 'Of one thing I will assure them, till they are good *Marians* they shall never be good *christians*; while they derogate from the dignity of the *Mother*, they cannot truely honour the *Sonne*' (Stafford, *Femall Glory*, p. 223). Taylor saw both catholics and some protestants as disparagers of Mary: 'As amongst women she was blest above all, being above all full of Grace, so amongst Saints I beleeve she is Supreme in Glory: and it is an infallible truth, that as the Romanists doe dishonour her much by their superstitious honourable seeming attributes; so on the other part, it is hellish and odious to God and good men, either to forget her, or (which is worse) to remember her with impure thoughts, or unbeseeming speech for the excellency of so devine a Creature' (J. Taylor, *The Life and Death of the most blessed among women, the Virgin Mary Mother of our Lord Jesus* (London, 1620), sig. A3). In contrast, John Shaw's *The Blessednes of Marie the mother of Jesus* (London, 1618) although beginning with three lines from St Luke's gospel in support of Mary's blessedness (Blessed art thou among women / Blessed is she that believed / All generations shall call me blessed, Luke 1.28, 45, 48), is not concerned with the honour given to her. Mary is blessed because she bore Christ and believed instantly, and is therefore an example for christians who should also put on Christ and believe. Most of the text explains why Christ's passion was necessary, and the protestant theology of salvation.

[98] Taylor, *The Life and Death of the most blessed amongst women*, c6v; Stafford, *The Femall Glory*, pp. 205–11. Stafford is able to enlist some protestant authors in support of his position on the Assumption, notably Bullinger and Brentius. The engraving faces p. 208 and carries the verse, 'What honor could to this greate Queene be done, / More then to be taken up, to heaven high / And there have G O D for Father, Spouse & Sonne, / The Angells wayte, the World stand wondring by.'

In many ways the mid-1630s was, of course, an unusual period, one in which it was possible for a catholic author to address the Queen, another Mary, as the advocate and patron who will support the author's desire to vindicate the Virgin Mary.[99] Thus, Taylor's strategies and difficulties in 1620 may be more helpful in representing the limits of Mary's position in the early seventeenth century. Taylor's starting point, as he tells us, was a book in prose of the life, death and burial of Mary that he found in Antwerp and has now turned into verse, having duly drained it of the 'poyson of Antichristianisme'.[100]

Taylor sticks scrupulously to the scriptural account. The one exception, Mary's Temple education, probably seems admissible because it emphasises learned godliness and pious dedication. There is no room in Taylor's text for speculation about the veracity of later, and perhaps orally transmitted, traditions. His caution is most pronounced concerning invocation and adoration of the Virgin. The opening verses assure the reader that only invocations of the Trinity are appropriate and not of Mary:

> I will no prayers not invocations frame
> For intercession to this heavenly Dame:
> Nor to her name one fruitlesse word shall run
> To be my Mediatresse to her Sonne.[101]

Moreover, and much more surprisingly, Taylor, whilst providing a detailed account of Christ's Nativity and life, omits all reference to the Adoration of the Shepherds and of the Magi. Since these were, of course, events clearly attested in scripture, the only explanation seems to be that he feared lest these events might imply adoration of the Virgin as well as of the Christ Child.

Rejection of adoration and intercession leaves Mary pre-eminently with the role of exemplar, and it is in this way that God wishes her to be honoured. Taylor desires 'all hearts to give the holy Virgin such honour as may be pleasing to God; which is that all should patterne their lives to her lifes example, in lowlinesse and humility, and then shall they be exalted where shee is in Glory, with eternity.'[102] Of these virtues humility was central: when Taylor imagines Mary in heaven it is in terms, paradoxical in an earthly context, of the exaltation of humility.[103] But it is also hard for the reader not to assume that Mary was an exemplar who was relevant primarily to

---

[99] For example, *Maria Triumphans* (A 3–A 3v) contains a dedication to the Queen, which plays on the role of Queen Mary as advocate and patroness as the Virgin Mary is to her.
[100] Taylor, *The Life and Death of the most blessed amongst women*, A 3.
[101] Ibid., A 8.   [102] Ibid., A 8.
[103] 'There mounted (meeke) she sits in Maiestie, / Exalted there is her humility': ibid., C 6.

the female sex. This is particularly clear in his account of Mary's response to the Crucifixion:

> These seas of care (with zealous fortitude)
> This Virgin pas'd amongst the multitude.
> (Oh gracious patterne of a sex so bad)
> Oh the supernall patience that she had,
> Her zeale, her constancy, her truth, her love,
> The very best of women her doth prove.
> Maids, wives & mothers, all conforme your lives
> To hers, the best of women, maids, or wives.[104]

Of course, in some ways this impression was hard to avoid. Exaltation of Mary as the best of all women provided a natural connection, and for many it would have seemed obvious to see her as the 'gracious patterne of a sex so bad'. But for male authors like Taylor who wrote out of a professed regard for Mary's sacred memory, and esteemed her above all angels, prophets, apostles, evangelists and saints, true honour of the Virgin Mary through emulation could not be confined to the female sex. Stafford was also faced with the same problem, and, having titled his work *The Femall Glory*, felt the need to preface it with separate addresses to the feminine and masculine reader respectively. Of these, the first is much as we might expect, but the address to the masculine reader is more interesting. Although touching only briefly on the idea of emulation, Stafford reminds the reader that Mary brought the same eternal benefit to men as to her own kind, and that consequently she, 'whose meanest perfection farre excels all your so long vanted masculine merits',[105] requires not only gratitude but imitation. Moreover, this is more than mere preliminary dressing, since the demands of Marian imitation and the ways of the male world are contrasted later in the text. In discussing humility, a key Marian virtue for Stafford as well as for Taylor, Stafford's definitions of types of humility which fall short of the desired true christian humility all draw their examples from the male world of public office holding.[106] If true honour of the Virgin was emulation, acceptance of her exceptional status required that such a demand should not be gender specific.

In the Reformation of the sixteenth and early seventeenth centuries, as in the lollard movement of the late medieval period, attacks on the Virgin Mary led to a redefinition of her significance rather than to her disappearance. Increasingly important was her role as a model for emulation primarily, but far from exclusively, for women. Her survival, though, depended on denying her powers of intercession and on reducing her to a more human level, whether

---

[104] Ibid., c4–c4v.   [105] Stafford, *The Femall Glory*, b6–b6v.   [106] Ibid., pp. 64–70.

by insisting upon her physical plainness or by denying her bodily Assumption into heaven. Strikingly, such modifications were adopted even by the most ardent of Mary's supporters. Stafford, who, as we have seen, went furthest as a protestant author to glorify the Virgin, added a detail to his discussion of the Annunciation which goes further than usual in humanising Mary's response to the arrival of the angel. The Virgin, like the Magdalen in *Funerall Teares*, initially can only see the angel in earthly terms. Like Rosetti's Mary, Stafford's sees the startling male presence of the angel as a threat of sexual violation.[107] The idea that the Virgin was on the verge of falling is probably less central here than it was in the nineteenth century, even if Mary's caution in perceived danger is presented by Stafford as exemplary to his readers. Of greater importance is the fact that both Mary and Mary Magdalen, despite their closeness to God, can be bereft and uncomprehending of his presence. Even when glorified the most in a protestant context, they share human bewilderment and lack of understanding in the face of the works of God.

In this the Magdalen, and to a lesser extent the Virgin Mary, differ from other female models who became more prominent with the Reformation, such as Susanna. The latter, as we shall see, has no doubts or uncertainties. Unquestioning obedience to God's law guides her conduct. Although women in both groups could be called upon as exemplars of female conduct and virtues, this was much more clearly the case with figures like Susanna, who could embody the good woman of Proverbs without complication. How effective such stories were in influencing behaviour it is, of course, impossible to say. But it is significant that contemporaries felt the need to offer both types as a comfort and an ideal, and that the representative christian struggling with her faith in the world was a woman persisting in 'womanish tears' rather than St Paul receiving illumination on the road to Damascus. The portrayal of scriptural and apocryphal figures to a lay audience largely foreshadowed the preoccupations and popularity of the edifying lives of the godly in funeral sermons.

The Reformation therefore did make a difference. The stress on the omnipotence of God and the removal of the narratives of saints from the celebration of the church calendar redefined the female religious figure. Even if these figures are to be viewed in a positive light for women, as assertions of the power of faith to overcome female sexuality and of the integrity of female conduct, it is clear that their status was inferior to the claims of pre-Reformation saints as testimony to the human capacity for sanctity. But in a world in which the human soul was seen as quintessentially human, rather

---

[107] L. Nochlin, *Women, Art and Power and Other Essays* (London, 1989), pp. 78–9; Stafford, *The Femall Glory*, pp. 36–8: 'She trembled at his salutation, thinking him to be a man subject to abhorred Lust, and therefore feared violence...'

than divine, such a development cannot be considered particularly detrimental to women. Moreover, insofar as the christian soul was envisaged in terms of feminine behaviour or personified as the Magdalen, the model of spiritual ascent was one in which 'womanish tears' and female example showed the way. The Reformation attempted to redefine due honouring of the saints as emulation. The extent to which it succeeded in this, and also in perceiving God's power as parental rather than paternal, meant that the Reformation did not create a masculine religious landscape in which it was hard for women, in following the 'holy lives and conversation of the saints', to find a comfortable place.

10

The return to the Old Testament

> At vacant times it was her chiefe delight,
> To reade the stories of God's glorious might,
> Where all the choisest precepts she could find,
> She stor'd as heav'nly *Manna* for her mind:
> The Lives of choicest *Dames* of Iewish nation,
> To her as patternes are for imitation
> Which oft with needle, lest she should forget
> She in most curious colours neately set.[1]

Aylett's description of the godly Susanna propounded the ideal of the contemporary godly woman receiving heavenly nourishment from Biblical exemplars, and fixing their example firmly in her mind in the chaste labour of sewing. His embellishment of the apocryphal life of Susanna in this way to illustrate her godliness demonstrates the importance of such models of behaviour. Even accounts of Judith, a figure perhaps less readily associated with quiet domestic industry, were recast in the same mould: early seventeenth-century poems similarly added references to Judith embroidering to indicate her youthful education in virtue and her pious industry as a wife.[2] This view was not simply the preserve of male authors. Whether or not successful internalisation was achieved by the act of sewing, Dorothy Leigh could advocate the same principle in her *Mother's Blessing* (1616). In discussing the naming of children she recommended the selection of Biblical names, 'to make them reade in the Bible the things which are written of those saints and learne to imitate their vertues'.[3]

The increasing popularity of Old Testament stories in the Reformation period has been often noted. This descent down the ladder of sanctity, to use Roston's apt image, offered the possibility of models of conduct without the

---

[1] R. Aylett, *Susanna; or the arraignment of the two uniust elders* (London, 1622), pp. 27–8.
[2] V. R. Geuter, 'Women and embroidery in seventeenth century Britain: The social, religious and political meanings of domestic needlework', Ph.D. thesis, University of Wales (Aberystwyth) (1996), p. 99.
[3] Leigh, *The Mother's Blessing*, (London, 1616), Ch. 10 reprinted in Brown (ed.), *Women's Writing in Stuart England*, p. 30.

fear that they would be tainted with past traditions of catholic veneration and worship.[4] Such ideas also underpinned Dorothy Leigh's explanation of why she did not put Mary forward as the most appropriate name to give one's daughter, and Calvin's more general prohibition of giving children saints' names.[5] The extent to which these Old Testament figures became visible has been emphasised by Watt and Geuter.[6] Their images appeared in ballads pasted on alehouse walls, on painted cloths and wall paintings, and were the subject of embroideries, but (with the exception of Moses and Aaron, the prophets and the apostles) they did not appear on the walls of the parish church. This pattern fits with the cautious attitude towards the possibility of image veneration, but also had the effect of removing female figures from the public religious sphere.

Nevertheless, many of the Old Testament images which were popular in secular contexts at this time stressed female protagonists, and explored the conflict between gendered assumptions of behaviour and the demands of faith and obedience to God. Donald Lupton in 1632 listed the typical imagery within a well-established rural alehouse: 'In these houses you shall see the History of Iudeth, Susanna, Daniel in the Lyons Den, or Dives & Lazarus painted upon the Wall.'[7] In Geuter's sample of seventeenth-century embroideries 40 per cent depicted Biblical scenes, among which Old Testament subjects were predominant, including Esther, Rebecca and Susanna as well as scenes like the Sacrifice of Isaac and the story of David and Bathsheba.[8] Foister's study of references to art in probate inventories presents a similar picture. In this source the middle of the sixteenth century sees the emergence of the Biblical narrative subject, either drawn from the Old Testament and apocrypha or using a parable from the life of Christ. In particular, Foister singles out seven significant subjects dating from this period: Absalom, Judith, Solomon, Bathsheba, Christ and the Woman at the Well, and the Good Samaritan.[9]

The placing of such imagery in the home and in the alehouse did not mark a distinct break with pre-Reformation practice: the popular devotional image of the head of St John the Baptist, for example, had been confined to domestic

---

[4] Roston, *Biblical Drama in England*, p. 120.
[5] See pp. 228–9; P. Benedict, *Rouen during the Wars of Religion* (Cambridge, 1981), p. 105, notes that Calvin's prohibition was followed with varying degrees of strictness in France and Geneva.
[6] Watt, *Cheap Print and Popular Piety*; Geuter, 'Women and embroidery'.
[7] Watt, *Cheap Print and Popular Piety*, p. 194.
[8] Detailed evidence for figural embroidery dates from the 1620s, but the development of pattern books, and literary comments such as the text in Aylett's *Susanna* quoted above, suggest that the fashion was already well developed by this date. Unfortunately Geuter does not provide a full chronological analysis of her sample: 'Women and embroidery', pp. 276–7, 285.
[9] S. Foister, 'Paintings and other works of art in sixteenth-century English inventories', *Burlington Magazine* CXXIII no. 938 (May 1981), 273–82.

religion. Adherence to protestantism accentuated, but did not initiate, the use of religious images for emulation rather than devotion in the secular sphere. As Foister's study suggests, from around the middle of the sixteenth century in catholic as well as protestant contexts, religious pictures with slightly more worldly overtones, such as images of Mary Magdalen or of St Jerome in his study, were more likely to be found in parlours than in private chapels. For Foister, referring to images of St Jerome, this can be explained by the fact that they were 'pictures for enjoyment not devotion', but this seems to oversimplify the response to such images and to make the (surely unwarranted) assumption that the sacred connection of these images could be ignored.[10] Whilst a catholic, and even more a protestant, who acquired this kind of image would be unlikely to engage in the kinds of meditative devotions which would have been stimulated, say, by an image of the Crucifixion in late medieval piety, this does not simply replace devotion with enjoyment. An image of St Jerome in his study is not simply an excuse to admire and enjoy the virtuosity of the painter in depicting the objects surrounding the scholar at work. It also makes explicit the connection between the scholar's vocation and the advance of religious understanding, whether envisaged within the framework of christian humanism or of protestantism. In validating such endeavour it is a devotional object in the sense that it promotes, prompts and sanctifies behaviour, but not of course in the sense that devotion is offered to it.

The assumption behind such imagery therefore corresponds to the well-known advice of the Italian Renaissance, according to which children especially should be surrounded by appropriate religious imagery to inculcate the desired virtues as they grow up.[11] The extent to which this was a feature of pre-Reformation practice in England is, however, more doubtful. Foister notes that most images mentioned in inventories occur in private chapels in the early sixteenth century, but reminds us that this does not rule out the presence of cheaper unrecorded imagery, whether of paper or painted cloth, in other rooms. Occasionally, more detailed inventories hint at this kind of educational programme. The inventory of Alexander Plymley, a mercer and citizen of London (1533), lists only two images outside the chapel and the chapel chamber: a wooden gilt and painted image of Mary Magdalen, and (perhaps significantly) an image of Our Lady in the maidens' chamber.[12]

In the later sixteenth and early seventeenth centuries the idea that moulding behaviour was the primary purpose of such imagery was more clearly

---

[10] Ibid., 276.
[11] P. Burke, *The Italian Renaissance: Culture and Society in Italy* (Oxford, 1986), p. 127.
[12] Foister, 'Paintings and other works of art', pp. 278, 276, 282.

propounded, especially for women. As the quotation from Aylett's *Susanna* above suggests, the development of figural embroidery formed a key part of this educative strategy. This built on the idea that industrious attention to needlework kept girls out of mischief, and added the possibility that hours spent embroidering godly models would encourage emulation of their virtues.[13] Consequently, the subjects chosen, and found in pattern books, concentrate on the virtuous, despite Calvin's belief that focussing on examples of God's punishment of the wicked would be a more effective didactic strategy.[14]

As we have seen, the range of such models was wide, and it is consequently difficult to assess which figures were most formative in refashioning gender roles in the later sixteenth and seventeenth centuries. Three considerations seem relevant in making a case for the dominant influence of a particular model. Despite the probable bias towards higher social groups, the popularity of various embroidery subjects must be indicative, as too must be conclusions drawn from the more socially inclusive analysis of the names given by parents to their children. More subjectively, we need to make a distinction between those figures whose stories served to reiterate well-worn themes, and those that offered more scope for the exploration of the ambiguities of gender roles and responsibilities.

Geuter's list of the most popular Biblical subjects in seventeenth-century embroideries includes four female names that also became reasonably frequent choices as baptismal names: Hester, Rebecca, Susanna and Judith.[15] The other two, Bathsheba and Abigail, seem to have had a significance that did not fit so easily into the process of emulative name-giving. Of the four, Hester was probably the least influential, despite numerically topping Geuter's list. The frequency of this subject can be explained to a large extent by the political use of it during the Civil War. The identification of Henrietta Maria with Hester meant that the standard portrayal of Hester petitioning her husband Ahasuerus and giving him good advice could be used as a royalist image to counter the idea that she exercised undue and nefarious

---

[13] Geuter, 'Women and embroidery', Chs. 2–3. For some Puritan commentators the type of sewing could also be important in forming character and avoiding indulgent frivolity. Thus, Thomas Milles could advise in 1613, 'Fear God and learn woman's housewifery, / not idle samplery or silken folly': cited in R. Parker, *The Subversive Stitch: Embroidery and the Making of the Feminine* (London, 1984), p. 90.

[14] Bouwsma, *John Calvin*, pp. 91–2.

[15] Geuter, 'Women and embroidery', pp. 276, 285. The catalogue comprises 770 embroideries with a total of 950 subjects of which 919 are figurative. Biblical subjects account for 395 (43%) of the whole. The numbers of embroideries featuring women were Hester (45), Rebecca (31), David and Bathsheba (18), Susanna (16) Judith (13), David and Abigail (10): S. Smith-Bannister, *Names and Naming Patterns in England, 1538–1700* (Oxford, 1997), p. 144, Appendix C and D.

influence over Charles I.[16] It is unclear how many embroideries in the sample date from this period, and it would clearly be unwarranted to suggest that the theme had no wider significance. Two plays on the subject, one of which is now lost, are known to have been written and performed in the sixteenth century. 'A newe interlude drawen oute of the holy scripture of godly Queene hester' was staged in 1525, and was opportunistically turned into print shortly after Elizabeth's accession in 1561. However, as the following lines from the introductory verse on the title page suggest, it had little to offer in reshaping gender roles:

> Come nere vertuous matrons and women kind
> Here may ye learne of Hesters Duty
> In all comliness of vertue you shal finde
> How to behave yourself in humility.[17]

For embroiderers, as well as dramatists, Hester symbolised the modest wife who knew how to assist her husband by offering sage advice with due humility. For some, even this view of Hester's role may have seemed too assertive: for Elizabeth Joscelin Hester's exemplarity could be summarised with a reference to her teaching her maids to fast and pray.[18] Those girls who were given the name of Hester were offered an uncomplicated model of female duty, and the self-evident nature of this message perhaps explains why from 1538 to 1700 it could only rank between 20 and 50 in the list of most popular baptismal names.

Similar concerns about female assertiveness may have underpinned the less than impressive fortunes of Judith as a girl's name in England. In contrast, Judith was a much more popular choice in drama in Germanic areas and as a baptismal name amongst French Huguenots. For such embattled communities, whose faith was threatened by Muslim Turks or French catholics, the example of Judith as a divine instrument preserving the godly people from being overwhelmed by their foes had obvious appeal.[19] The increasing popularity of Judith as a female name in the last decades of the sixteenth century in England suggests that the English response, although more muted, had similar causes. As a consequence, the gender implications of

---

[16] Ibid., pp. 299–313.

[17] W. W. Greg (ed.), *A new enterlude of Godly Queene Hester edited from the quarto of 1561*, Materialen zur Kunde des älteren englischen Dramas (Louvain, 1904).

[18] 'but if you will desire prays follow the example of those religious women whoos virtuous fames time hath not powr to race out, as devout Anna whoo served the L: wth fastinge and prayr. Luke 2 iust Elizabet whoo served god w^{th}out reproof, religious Ester whoo taught her mayds to fast and pray Est.4.15 and the chast Susanna whoos story I hope the strictest will allow for a worthy example': Brown (ed.), *Women's Writing in Stuart England*, p. 116.

[19] E. Purdie, *The Story of Judith in German and English Literature* (Paris, 1927); Benedict, *Rouen during the Wars of Religion*, pp. 105–6.

Judith were less significant. Judith's assertiveness was translated as an extra-ordinary example of God making the naturally weak strong by faith to fulfil his design, and thus did more to reinforce assumptions of female weakness than anything else. This, coupled with the unease about the use of female seductive charm in the service of God, rendered Judith more acceptable as an emblem of divine providence than as a model for female conduct. The logical outcome was the puppet shows of Judith and Holofernes, the precursors of Punch and Judy, in which characters were black and white, and good triumphed over evil in an act of dramatic and decisive violence.[20]

The female Biblical name that experienced the most dramatic rise during this period was that of Susanna, closely followed, but with a more delayed chronology, by Sarah. Both Rebecca and Judith made much slower progress, reaching a position in the early to mid twenties by the middle of the seventeenth century, by which date Sarah and Susanna occupied seventh and eighth place respectively. The popularity of Sarah as a name for daughters, which continued to develop at the Restoration, differed from that of other female Biblical names. Relatively insignificant until entering the 'top twenty' in the 1570s, this choice was not backed up by visual depictions or dramatisations of her life. Rather, it reflected the growing impact of godly advice literature in which Sarah was frequently typified as the model wife.[21]

Susanna, like Sarah, was a model wife, but her story had much more dramatic and emulatory potential. Moreover, her narrative focussed on the question of chastity, which is usually seen as central to notions of female honour in the early modern period. At the same time it allowed for the exploration of notions of male and female responsibility for chastity that went beyond familiar bland stereotypes and related more closely to the dilemmas of real life. It is this potential that explains why Dorothy Leigh singled out Susanna as a particularly suitable name to give one's daughter in her *Mother's Blessing* (1616), a popular work that secured a wide audience.[22] As she explained, this was partly because the virtues of the other Biblical names given to her children were thought to be self-evident (an indication perhaps of the relative modernity of Susanna as a model), but more importantly because Susanna's history seemed to encapsulate all the necessary virtues which fell under the general heading of chastity.

---

[20] J. Wiltenburg, *Disorderly Women and Female Power in the Street Literature of Early Modern England and Germany* (Charlottesville and London, 1992), pp. 161–2; Purdie, *The Story of Judith*, p. 76.

[21] See pp. 326–7.

[22] Seven editions of the work were printed within the first five years of its publication, and by 1674 there had been 23 editions published. Printed as a duodecimo, its purchase was within reach of most pockets: the price noted on the title page of a copy of the 1633 edition was 10d. Brown (ed.), *Women's Writing in Stuart England*, pp. 3, 12.

Chastity in Dorothy Leigh's discussion of Susanna is defined in broad terms. It is the avoidance of idleness and of all 'vain delights', including pride and vanity in dress, and their replacement with humility and christian virtues outwardly manifested in reading, meditating and acting upon the scriptures. Thus far Leigh's argument is unsurprising, but it becomes more interesting when she places the need for chastity in the context of contemporary gender relations. The point of the story of Susanna is that it reverses the assumptions inherent in the story of Eve: although Adam was beguiled by Eve, nowadays men are more likely to deceive women as the elders did Susanna. The moral is that the only way to avoid this outcome is for women to be chaste like Susanna:

> Man sayd once, *The woman which thou gavest mee, beguiled me, and I did eate.* But wee women may now say, that men lye in waite every where to deceive us, as the Elders did to deceive *Susanna.* Wherefore let us bee, as she was, chaest, watchfull, and wary, keeping company with maides. Once *Iudas* betrayed his Master with a kisse, & repented it: but now men, like *Iudas*, betray their Mistresses with a kisse &, repent it not: but laugh and reioice, that they have brought sinne and shame to her that trusted them. The only way to avoid al which, is to be chaste with *Susanna*, and being women, to imbrace that vertue, which being placed in a woman, is most commendable.

Leigh's argument is however more complex than it first appears. She is not simply turning the tables by identifying every man as a potential seducer rather than every woman as a potential temptress. The chapter concludes with the hope that 'women be perswaded by this discourse, to imbrace chastity, without which we are meere beasts, and no women'. Pursuit of chastity is not merely a defensive strategy, but one that simultaneously humanises and feminises women. More than this, it is the only means to preserve and nurture the conjugal relationship: a woman's failure to keep chaste entails destroying 'both the body and the soule of him, shee seemeth most to love'. Ultimately, the model of Susanna, in Leigh's interpretation, shows that in a dangerous world the onus lies upon women to assert their femininity and to preserve their chastity.[23]

All this, it could be argued, is only tangentially linked to the story of Susanna. Although Susanna was chaste, her drama actually depends on her being insufficiently (but still reasonably?) 'watchfull and wary'. Moreover, what might seem to be the salient feature of the story, Susanna's fortitude and obedience to the law of God despite its worldly consequences, is omitted in Leigh's account. This possibility of developing aspects of the godly model in order to make didactic points makes it much more difficult to understand

---

[23] D. Leigh, *The Mother's Blessing*, Ch. 9 reprinted in Brown (ed.), *Women's Writing in Stuart England*, pp. 27–30.

the contemporary response to these figures, especially in visual depictions which may trigger other associations, and do not always clearly spell out the intended message, even when such depictions are accompanied with explanatory text. At Little Moreton Hall (Cheshire) part of a painted paper frieze depicting the history of Susanna still survives with each image separated by a short text, but this does little more than concisely summarise the apocryphal account.[24] Nevertheless, it may be precisely the ability of stories like that of Susanna to sustain problematic and unsettling readings that accounted for their popularity and gave them an educative capacity beyond figures like Hester, who functioned primarily as an emblem of a deferential pose.

In embroidery a narrative sequence was rarely attempted. By far the most frequent individual scene is that of Susanna being surprised by the elders while taking her bath (Fig. 36). The significance of this choice is hard to determine. Since figurative subjects developed out of a tradition of embroidering a random collection of flora and fauna, the garden setting of this part of the history of Susanna had an obvious attraction. Additionally, the Ovidian impulse may have helped to make the fountain scene standard, and it is certainly the case that from a distance scenes of Susanna, Bathsheba and the classical Diana and Actaeon are virtually indistinguishable. In all these themes there may also be a certain attraction in a sanctioned portrayal of a beautiful female nude (as is also argued for depictions of Mary Magdalen and of Lucretia). But whilst this voyeuristic element is often thought to devalue such depictions as religious images, it may actually be that it was precisely this that gave the image moral power. The male viewer, who is aware of these stories, is caught admiring the female nude in the manner of the elders and is reminded that he, like the elders (or like Actaeon and David), needs to control such desires. Conversely, the woman who embroiders the cushion may, as Aylett wished, be reminded that vulnerability is no excuse for abandoning the defence of her chastity.[25]

The attractions of the bathing scene cannot, however, entirely account for the popularity of the history of Susanna. Woodcuts illustrating surviving ballads do not show Susanna bathing. This may in part be due to the comparatively small stock of woodblocks, and the associated lack of concern by printers to ensure a good match between ballad content and image. However, the fact that a bathing image could have been used to illustrate a range of ballad texts suggests that it was not thought to significantly increase ballad sales. Instead, the ballad 'The Constancy of Susanna' was illustrated by two woodcuts; the first an all-purpose image of a woman standing between two

[24] Rouse, 'Elizabethan wall paintings at Little Moreton Hall'.
[25] Aylett, *Susanna*, pp. 21–2.

Figure 36 Susanna and the Elders, mid-seventeenth-century embroidery

men, and the second a court scene, whilst the 'Story of David and Berseba' carried an image of a king and a chaste courtship scene (Figs. 37 and 38).[26]

The ballad treatment of Susanna and Bathsheba differed from that in other literary forms, perhaps partly because the length gave less scope for elaboration. It was more closely scriptural, even to the extent of detailing Bathsheba's beauty but not Susanna's. There was no direct scriptural reference to Susanna's beauty, but attributing this to her was not a very daring presumption since beauty was generally seen to provoke lust. This contrasts sharply with more erotic treatment of Susanna in Ovidian mode in plays such as Garter's *Godlye Susanna* (written *c.* 1568, publ. 1578):

> Her brestes that are so round and fayre, her armes that are so long,
> Her fyngers straight with vaynes beset, of blew and white among.
> Her middle small, her body long, her buttockes broad and round,
> Her legges so straight, her foote so small, the like treads not on ground.[27]

Aylett adopts a similar approach, but then holds back, stopping in mid description of the beauty of different parts of Susanna's body. Having titillated the reader, he remarks that the grave muse cannot tell more, and catches the reader in the pose of the elders.

On first reading, the ballad 'The Constancy of Susanna' seems, like the Little Moreton Hall texts, to do little more than present the Biblical story. There is little characterisation and Susanna is not shown doubting her decision. As a result it seems easy to dismiss this text as being an unrealistic, and therefore an ineffective, model to a lay audience. Of course, this was not what contemporaries, or at least the author, thought. As the refrain of the first verse asks, 'Why should wee not of her learne thus to live godly?'[28] And there is a possibility that the surprising omission of a reference to Susanna's beauty was a subtle device to increase the lack of sympathy with the elders: David was beguiled by beauty, whilst the elders were more thoroughly corrupt and aimed to seduce chaste godliness.

These interpretations may be taking us too far, but it is clear, as Wiltenburg has pointed out in her comparison of street literature in England and Germany, that the possibilities of the Susanna theme in ballad literature were more flexible than we might think by examining the English evidence alone. The German version emphasises that women should imitate Susanna as a model of a virtuous and submissive wife, whilst the English ballad presents her as a model for all. In England it is not Susanna's faithfulness to her husband, but her faithfulness to God that makes her worthy of emulation. This

---

[26] C. Hindley (ed.), *The Roxburghe Ballads* (London, 1871), vol. 1, pp. 190–6, 270–6.
[27] T. Garter, *The Commody of the moste vertuous and Godlye Susanna, never before this tyme Printed (London, 1578)* (Malone Society Reprints, 1936), lines 416–19.
[28] Hindley (ed.), *Roxburghe Ballads*, vol. 1, p. 190.

Figure 37 Woodcuts from the ballad of the Constancy of Susanna

difference, according to Wiltenburg, was part of a larger contrast between the literatures of the two areas. English popular literature is more likely than the German to explore the distinction between submissiveness and obedience, and even to suggest advantages for young women and widows in being free of the burdens of the married state.[29] This contrast is hard to explain, but it serves to remind us that when religious stories were translated into popular forms they assimilated the gender assumptions of popular literature without abandoning their edifying purpose.

[29] Wiltenburg, *Disorderly Women and Female Power*, pp. 50–66, 86–7.

Figure 38 Woodcuts from the ballad of David and Bathsheba

Wiltenburg's study does not include drama, but the work of Paul Casey allows us to see that here also there were significant contrasts between English and German treatments of the theme. Most notably, as in Italy, from the mid-1530s onwards the German tradition felt the need to elaborate the corruptness of the elders as judges by including subplots of the fate of widows and peasants seeking justice at their hands. This had the obvious effect of making the attempt on Susanna's chastity and reputation less central. More interestingly, this development changed Susanna's role in relation to her husband, Joachim. In the earlier German dramas Susanna had been subordinate to her husband to the extent that in the *Susanna* of Sixt Birck (1532) the impassioned plea to God for justice was placed in Joachim's mouth rather than Susanna's. The later diversification of plots allowed Susanna more of a role as an unmistakable emblem of good confronted by the elders, who were now more clearly defined as thoroughly evil. But the dramatist could allow Susanna to regain her voice only by avoiding the issue of the relationship between husband and wife; Joachim was now conveniently removed by being away on business when the elders seized their opportunity.[30]

The German dramas, like the German ballads, bear little close resemblance to their English counterparts, and essentially for the same reason. Although the religious concern was the same, the delineation of gender and marital relations followed separate paths. Perhaps the most effective of all the English Susanna texts, Thomas Garter's *The Commody of the moste vertuous and Godlye Susanna* (1578), explores these themes with a subtlety unimaginable in the German tradition with its concern for clear, unquestioned hierarchy. The absence of courtroom subplots in the English tradition is more surprising, given the general popularity of legal dramas. Even Aylett's legal background resulted simply in a concern to clarify guidelines for correct legal procedure, and an attempt to cast Susanna in the role of Justice. It is hard to escape the conclusion that English writers felt the need to keep the Susanna story central: although depth of characterisation remained minimal, the protagonist was a model for all, demonstrating the correct balance of a godly concern for honour, reputation and obedience.

The portrayal of these ideals has often seemed unconvincing to modern commentators. In particular, since Susanna is not shown doubting her decision these texts have been seen as offering an unrealistic, and therefore not very useful, model to a lay audience. Such comments need more careful consideration. Susanna's emblematic clarity may have a power in advocating

---

[30] P. F. Casey, *The Susanna Theme in German Literature: Variations of the Biblical Drama*, Abhandlungen zur Kunst-, Musik-, und Literaturwissenschaft 214 (Bonn, 1976); C. L. Baskins, ' "La festa di Susanna": virtue on trial in Renaissance sacred drama and painted wedding chests,' *Art History* 14/3 (1991), 329–344.

codes of conduct, which does not depend on the text offering a convincing portrait of human frailty confronted with a dilemma. Furthermore, the later sixteenth- and early seventeenth-century English treatments of the theme show that, although the central decision of Susanna is portrayed as unproblematic, writers were able to offer more complex reflections within the story, whether concerning the motivations of the elders or the relationship between Susanna's notions of obedience to God and to her husband. Within all this Susanna still emerged as an untainted ideal figure, but one whose behaviour is refracted through the circumstances of everyday life.

The Susanna story presented any dramatist with problems. Not only did the requirement of Susanna's certainty obstruct the development of plausible psychology, but her story also raised difficult theological questions. Susanna's perfection made God's testing of her hard to understand. As a punishment it was clearly more likely to be admonitory than castigatory, but this implied that part of the point of Susanna's story was a warning against complacency. The need to explain God's motives in putting Susanna to the test and coming to her rescue, even if underexplored by the writers themselves, formed part of any godly response which sought to understand and take Susanna as a model of the relationship between human and divine, rather than simply as an emblem of chastity. For such people the model became a little more real and spoke more urgently to their attempts to negotiate a way between the demands of the world and the demands of God, even if Susanna's certainty meant there was no 'test' in terms of being tempted to act differently.

To see these points more clearly, it will be helpful to look in detail at Garter's *The Commody of the moste vertuous and Godlye Susanna*, since drama, as we saw in the earlier discussion of Adam and Eve, offered more scope for development of broader religious themes. At the end of the play the main good characters spell out its message for a christian audience. They conclude with speeches praising and thanking God for his intervention and promise that they will strive even more to live according to God's will. Susanna's final words are in a similar vein:

> No, no good Lord above the rest to prayse thee I am bound,
> That me doest help myraculously, and eake my foes confound.
> I was but dead, and thou to lyfe, restoredst me silly wight,
> What is she then that beareth breth, that more can shew thy might,
> And this thyne act shall so increase, within me evermore,
> And from thy lawes I will not slyde, although I dye therefore.
>
> (lines 1427–32)

However, within the context of the play this conclusion lacks conviction: Susanna has shown no signs of sliding. She is not tempted by the elder's

proposition and reminds him immediately that adultery is punishable by
death by both the law of God and earthly law. When the elders continue
to insist, Susanna responds with an appeal to God outlining her position,
but, although this speech sets out the consequences of both courses of action
open to her, there is still no sense that Susanna is in a real quandary:

> Oh Lord, oh God, oh king of blisse, what stormes doe stop my breth,
> If I fulfill your fylthy lust, I know it breedes my death,
> And if I doe not, then ah, alas, you trap me in your bandes,
> And thus can I pore Innocent, by no meanes scape your handes.
> Well better it is without the act, your daunger to fall in,
> Then to attempt my Lord my God with this so vyle a sinne.
>
> (lines 767–72)

Garter's treatment of Susanna is not a living portrait of a frail human being
subject to temptation and indecision, but rather a faithful exposition of the
agenda set out in the prologue:

> Of Susan's lyfe the story is, what trouble she was in,
> How narrowly she scaped death because she would not sinne,
> How wonderously she was provokte, how vertuously she fled,
> The strong assaultes of wicked men, that lecherous lusts hadled [sic],
> To ravish her, and to pollute, her chaste and wyfely view,
> This is the somme of all that shall be shewed unto you.
>
> (lines 10–15)

It seems, in fact, that the audience is to take the devil's assessment of Susanna
at the beginning of the play at face value. Susanna's remarkable godliness
has been demonstrated by the devil's failure in the past to corrupt her by
all the usual weaknesses to which women were assumed to be susceptible: pride, gluttony, envy, sloth and covetousness. Only lust, aided by ill
repute, is left, and the play goes on to show the devil failing in this last
attempt. There are, however, two other places in the play where Susanna's
status as a paragon might be thought to slip slightly: the scene of Susanna
as a shrewish wife calling Joachim home to dinner, and the scene in which
Susanna declares herself to merit God's praise above all other contemporary
women.

The scene of Susanna as a shrewish wife in fact serves to demonstrate how
far Susanna is from that stock stereotype of a woman. Although Joachim
can assert that all women are shrews, and that the unfortunate condition of
a married man is to obey his wife's desires, it is clear that this is light banter
possible only because it is so far from the reality of their relationship. Joachim
has been portrayed as a man engrossed in the burdens of his responsibility
for justice as a magistrate, and Susanna's reminder of the meal time can be
seen as care for her husband, not inappropriate nagging. The exchange of
words shows Susanna undeserving of the label of shrew or chiding wife.

She does not mention Joachim's lateness directly, and, in a response totally uncharacteristic of a shrew, she accepts that title to avoid argument:

SUSANNA I will not say unto you now, what you did cause me thinke,
　　　In deede I will conceale it now, and at the matter winke.
IOACHIM What Susan doest thou chyde me now, I will tell thee my mynde,
　　　That women there be none at all, but shrewes they are by kynde,
SUSANNA Well, well, to avoyde this controversye, I will confesse that cryme,
　　　And I pray you hartily to aryse, and let us home to dyne.
　　　　　　　　　　　　　　　　　　　　　　　　(lines 353–58)

Later, the dialogue widens into a discussion of the obedience appropriate in a marital relationship. Joachim expresses his willingness to obey Susanna's request that he comes home to dinner, and suggests that both husband and wife should be obedient at different times ('As I doe you, so shall you me, obay another tyme', line 377). This departure from the standard idea of obedience as the wife's duty is further clarified by Susanna's response that she will only obey her husband's commands where they coincide with reason:

And reason good in fayth my Lorde, both now and always to,
That I should follow your behestes, as reason wils me do.
　　　　　　　　　　　　　　　　　　　　(lines 378–9)

For Susanna, judgement rather than unconsidered obedience to the demands of men is not only the key to the success of her relationship with Joachim, but also a training ground for her response to the elders. This link is indicated by the similarity of Susanna's response to the elders in this conversation and in the later proposition scene. Her discernment means that she questions the integrity of the elders' words from the beginning:

Ye speake it well in very deede, but it were harde to fynde
If both your wordes and hart did gree in uttering this your mynde,
　　　　　　　　　　　　　　　　　　　　(lines 370–1)

and she is of the same opinion in the proposition scene,

Alas me thinkes your thoughtes and wordes together do not gree
　　　　　　　　　　　　　　　　　　　　(line 767)

In the opening scene the Devil had blessed his son Ill Repute for his enterprise against Susanna with the same blessing he had given to the serpent who had seduced Eve, but such deceptions and temptations have no effect on the godly Susanna.

But if Susanna can see through the deception of others, is she perhaps in danger of deceiving herself? Susanna's speech on entering the orchard to bathe suggests that this might be the case, as she expresses a very high opinion of her worth in the eyes of God:

> If any woman in this world, my God may iustly prayse.
> It is I good Lorde above the rest, that liveth in these days.
>   (lines 674–5)

But the 'if' here is significant, and Susanna recognises that, although her worldly prosperity is a result of God's blessings towards her and her husband, their faith has not been tested in adversity:

> Thou blessest me my lord my God, and eake my loving Spouse,
> My cattayle in the field abroade, my servauntes in the house.
> My Corne both in the Barne and field, doth yeeld full great increase,
> And thus O Lord thy benifytes, towardes us doth never seace.
> O Lorde doe graunt that these thy giftes doe not our harts so fyll,
> That if thou lay thy hand on us, we take that part for ill.
> But as by this thy providence, we live and take our rest,
> We may if any storme doe fall, account it for the best.
>   (lines 676–83)

Far from vaunting a false godliness, Susanna as a true protestant is aware of God's favour and her dependence on his assistance.

Nowhere in the play does Susanna wonder why the 'storm' has befallen her at God's command. Like Patient Griselda, whose story still enjoyed some popularity in the later sixteenth century, Susanna accepts unquestioningly the misfortune that occurs. Both heroines are subject to immutable commands to which they have to submit, but here the parallel ends. Griselda's commands are those of her husband, but Susanna has already stated her case against obedience to a husband's will where it conflicts with reason.[31] The episode with the elders makes it clear that reason is to be equated with divine providence and divine law: it is to the will of God that Susanna knows she must submit unquestioningly. The examined conscience which was an important feature of this strain of protestant piety is absent from Garter's depiction of Susanna. Susanna is not perfect, and indeed it is part of human nature that she cannot be (as her father says, 'all flesh is frayle', line 876), but the point of Susanna's story in Garter's rendition is not to show that God sends misfortune to chastise the reprobate or as a warning to the complacent godly. Instead it demonstrates the correct godly response when the storm sent by God seems out of all proportion to the life of the individual, and the difficulty in such circumstances without God's assistance of accepting God's providence 'for the best'. The test that Susanna passes with

---

[31] It is notable that early modern retellings of the Griselda story brought the protagonist closer to the figure of Susanna: J. Bronfmann, 'Griselda, Renaissance Woman', in A. M. Haselkorn and B. S. Travitsky (eds.), *The Renaissance Englishwoman in Print: Counterbalancing the Canon* (Amherst, Mass. 1990), pp. 211–23; L. Bliss, 'The Renaissance Griselda: a woman for all seasons', *Viator* 23 (1992), 301–43; V. Comensoli, *Household Business: Domestic Plays of Early Modern England* (Toronto and London, 1996), pp. 49–64.

God's aid is not simply to adhere to God's law by withstanding temptation and the loss of earthly reputation, but her uncomplaining acceptance of the whole ordeal. She offers a model to all protestants trying to retain their faith when misfortune seems out of scale, such as with the loss of a child or a loved one.

But if this is the message of Garter's *Susanna*, we may question its gendered significance. In detaching misfortune from being a consequence of particular sin, it is able to be a less clearly gendered play, whilst still reinforcing the idea that obedience to God requires chastity. It may also be, as Calvin would have wished, that to understand the story of Susanna we should concentrate on the elders as much as on Susanna herself. Just as in the classic medieval virgin martyr story, Susanna is able to resist the lustful desires of ungodly men in positions of authority. Quite clearly, in a christian world the need for chastity applies to men as well as women, and the elders who are weak enough to be the tools of the devil and to maintain their story under Daniel's questioning with a brazen lack of remorse will receive divine punishment without mercy.

These two sides of the story of Susanna are emphasised in the lengthy explanatory title of Robert Greene's prose work, *The Myrrour of Modestie* (1584). He explained to his readers that in this mirror 'appeareth as in a perfect Glasse howe the Lorde delivereth the innocent from all imminent perils, and plagueth the bloodthirstie hypocrites with deserved punishments shewing that the graie heades of dooting adulterers shall not go with peace into the grave, neither shall the righteous be forsaken in time of trouble'. Foregrounding these two examples means that Greene, more than Garter, dwells on the dehumanising nature of the elders' lust for Susanna. He describes the elders as 'Dronken sodenlie with the dregs of filthie desire' and not 'remembring the counsell of the wise, who wisheth a man not to gaze upon the glittering beautie of a woman, least he fall through that which is precious in hir, nor to yield to the alarums of inordinate lust. that he both destroie not himself, and his heritage. This wholesome doctrine nothing cooling their desires, they stil walowed with the Sow in their wickedness.'[32] But, despite the vividness of this writing, Greene's main concern is not to paint the elders as hopelessly evil and lustful, but rather to show how being seduced by the wrong religious arguments can lead to downfall for the ungodly.

This case is built up from small details, such as one of the elders' observations that 'Susanna is the saint whom I do serve', as well as more sustained reflections on the paradoxes produced by belief in a God who is both merciful and judgemental, and the difficulty of keeping God's law.[33] Thus, balancing

---

[32] R. Greene, *The Myrrour of Modestie* (London, 1584), Aiii, Aivr–v.
[33] Ibid., Avi.v.

his fear of God against his passion for Susanna, the elder concludes, 'but he yt is so scrupulous for the observing of the law, shall both passe his daies without pleasure, and yet at last be found a sinner. I meane therefore whatever the lawe wishes at this time to have mine own will.'[34] Such religious reflection is rare in portrayals of the elders, who are more often represented by the arguments Greene makes them use in their conversation with Susanna: 'your beautie shall beare the blame, as the onlie cause of this enterprise', a device which implies that responsibility rests with the Creator rather than with his creatures.[35] Unusually, but in keeping with the promise in his title, Greene also devotes more space to Susanna's balancing of her options. Although she is easily aware that the all-seeing God and her own conscience invalidate the elders' claims that a secretly committed sin is of lesser importance, Susanna is more tempted by the idea that God's mercy will countenance her infringement of his law. Not wishing to bring shame and dishonour on her family through the elders' unjust accusations, she toys with the idea of agreeing to their demands and sinning in the hope of mercy, before finally dismissing this tempting strategy as blasphemy and reminding herself that it is better to fear God rather than man, since God has the power to kill body and soul, and man the body alone.

Obedience to the law was, of course, central to all accounts of Susanna. Knowledge of God's law, and in particular his sentence of death for the adulterer, provided an incontrovertible guide for the christian in negotiating the temptations of the world and the flesh, even if the Old Testament setting of Susanna's story gave little clear guidance how this was to be fitted with the more compassionate view of the New Testament. A further obvious contrast was between the practice of earthly and divine justice. This theme was evident in Susanna's surprise that the elders who should be maintainers and guardians of the law were enticing her to break it, and in the contrast between their actions in judging and accusing Susanna and the legal procedures adopted by Daniel that ensured the vindication of the innocent.

It is therefore unsurprising that Robert Aylett, a lawyer specialising in religious verse on the side, should choose to use the story of Susanna to develop the legal theme further and to explore the theme of justice and the perversions of justice in the legal system. In his *Susanna; or the arraignment of the two uniust elders* (1622) his concern is less with the characters themselves than with the triumph through God of Justice. In doing so, he accentuates the tendencies already present in earlier treatments of the story to see Susanna's response as unproblematic, that of a heroine who suffers no agonies of temptation, and loses much of the moral subtlety of Garter and Greene. Since Susanna, as we are told in the opening summary of the argument

[34] Ibid., Avi.   [35] Ibid., Avii.v.

and moral of the history, is Justice and Astraea, such uncertainties become unthinkable.

Justice was conventionally portrayed as a woman, but in the story itself true justice, and the valuable procedural principles that witnesses should be separately examined, and that accuser, witness and judge should not be the same person, are administered and determined by the spirit working in Daniel, not Susanna. Susanna's case is righteous, but she does not personify justice as an active determining force. Instead, Susanna is portrayed as the ideal female litigant in Stretton's terms.[36] Far from being the importunate suitor, she submits herself to the verdict of the court. Although she formally pleads not guilty, in Aylett's description of the trial as a funeral complete with mourning friends and family (the only difference according to the poet being that 'A Coarse is dead, and *Susan* is to dye'),[37] her submission to the court and to the ways of the world is complete. At the same time such a depiction underlines Susanna's rejection of the flesh both in terms of sexual pleasure and of life itself in accordance with the dictates of a higher obedience to God.

An explicit contrast is drawn between Susanna's obedience and the response of Eve. This point is introduced early in the poem, when we learn of a cap or band that Susanna made for her husband with the embroidered image of Eve and the serpent, but also with its antidote: Abraham's knife stayed by the angel which praises his faith and firm obedience.[38] The parallels with the story of Susanna are clear, and reinforced later in the poem as the elders hiding in the garden aiming to seduce Susanna by fair promises are equated with the subtle serpent's persuasion of Eve.[39] In rejecting their arguments Susanna too has the model of Eve in mind, and desires to avoid like punishment. Through the example of Eve, the poet seems to say, women are able to avoid the same trap. Nevertheless, as history shows, not all women have the perspicacity, fortitude and good luck of Susanna: Lucretia yielded through fear of shame, and Thamar was forced against her will. These examples notwithstanding, and rather idealistically, Aylett wishes to criticise the contemporary response of the 'femalesmasculine' who put their trust in the carrying of weapons to defend their honour whilst naked Susanna

---

[36] T. Stretton, *Women Waging Law in Elizabethan England* (Cambridge, 1998), pp. 51–5.
[37] Aylett, *Susanna*, p. 30.   [38] Ibid., p. 13.
[39]
> As subtile Serpent close himselfe did hide
> In *Eden*, till a fit time he espide,
> When *Adam* to some other corner gone,
> He there might take *Eve* naked all alone;
> So these two Elders of the Serpents breede,
> Who beare like enmity to all her seede,
> This naked Dame alone, watch to assaile,
> And first with promises seeke to prevaile

Aylett, *Susanna*, p. 18.

overcame her tempters two to one.[40] The model for chaste women should be Susanna:

> Henceforth let all the ladies that live chast,
> Be with the title of *Susannas* grac't.[41]

Bathsheba is missing from Aylett's list of examples here, but his arguments remind us that Susanna and Bathsheba, although both models of female beauty and innocence, offered very different answers to the question of female response and responsibility. Greene's elders in their attempt to seduce Susanna used the example of Bathsheba to persuade her into compliance with their will.[42] Thus, any understanding of the model of Susanna in this period will be incomplete without consideration of the complementary figure of Bathsheba, whose image rivalled that of Susanna in popularity, but who was a much less common choice as a christian name for daughters.

The story of Bathsheba shifts the emphasis to David, and takes further the tendencies within the story of Susanna to focus on the elders. Although images of David and Bathsheba focus on fair Bathsheba bathing in the spring, in the accounts themselves Bathsheba is not the focus of the story, but is reduced to a figure of beauty who provokes David's fall. In the ballad 'The Story of David and Bathsheba' her extraordinary beauty is clear:

> Her beauty was more excellent
> and brighter than the morning Sunne
> Her body like a Lilly flower,
> was covered with her golden haire.[43]

and it is this beauty, rather than her behaviour, which provokes uncontrolled desire for her in the King. Despite consenting to a sexual liaison with David, Bathsheba is portrayed throughout as a pure innocent. The 'silly little sheep' of Nathan's parable is more than just a figure for the theft of valued possessions, it represents the nature of Bathsheba herself. This interpretation, which avoids such popular notions as woman as temptress and draws no hard comparisons between the resistance of Susanna and the compliance of Bathsheba, can largely be explained by the fidelity of the ballad to the scriptural account. However, it sits rather uneasily with early modern ideas of adultery, and the ballad's aim of warning that God punishes murder and adultery. Perhaps as a result of this, the author extends the Biblical account, elaborating on Bathsheba's beauty and introducing the adjective 'silly' into Nathan's description of the sheep (Bathsheba). Throughout Bathsheba is

---

[40] Ibid., pp. 21–2.   [41] Ibid., p. 43.
[42] R. Greene, *Myrrour of Modestie*, in A. B. Grosart (ed.), *The Life and Complete Works in Prose and Verse of Robert Greene*, Huth Library, 15 vols. (1881–6), vol. 3, p. 24.
[43] *Roxburghe Ballads*, vol. 1, p. 272.

given few human qualities and no personalised voice. Her speech to the King informing him that she is with child is reported, not enacted, and the author misses the opportunity of her showing some remorse for her sin. Her mourning for the death of her husband Uriah, for which there is clear scriptural warrant, is omitted from the ballad. Bathsheba is portrayed as a pretty parcel passed between men and with no control over, or responsibility for, her own fate.

As was the case in similar interpretations of Susanna and the elders, to make this interpretation more acceptable for an early modern audience the ballad author felt the need to paint David's iniquities more darkly than the scriptural text. The greater innocence of the heroine required representing the seducers as more steeped in wickedness. Thus, David's desire for Bathsheba, Nathan reveals, is not his first fall on that long slippery slope familiar to readers of penitent criminal ballads. Nathan accuses David:

> Thy Lord's wives thou thine own hast made,
> and many more of faire beauty.

But what has attracted the wrath of God, it appears, is not so much these earlier seductions or David's liaison with Bathsheba but his treatment of Uriah:

> Why hast thou so defilde thy life,
> and slaine Uriah with the sword,
> And taken home his wedded Wife,
> regarding not God's holy Word?[44]

In fact, the focus of the ballad becomes the contrast between Uriah and David. It is Uriah, not David, who puts duty above pleasure to the extent of disregarding his sovereign's instructions that he should sleep that night with his wife because of his duty as a soldier for the defence of Israel. As he says with unconscious prophecy,

> "The Arke of God," (Uriah said)
> with Judah's Host and Israel,
> Keepe in the Field, and not a man
> within the house where they doe dwell.
>
> Then should I take my ease," quoth he,
> "in beds of Downe with my faire wife?
> O King," he said, "that must not be
> so long as I enjoy my life."[45]

Casting the story in terms of the conflict between pleasure and the duty of public office allows Bathsheba's response to events to be marginalised. Rather

---

[44] Ibid., p. 275.   [45] Ibid., p. 273.

than being a problematic female figure, she can be reduced to a cipher of beauty. The blame attaches to David, as it did to Actaeon for gazing upon Diana, despite Bathsheba's complicity in the liaison.

Such an interpretation carried a valuable moral message for a male audience and identified male fornication as part of a wider metaphor for abuse of office and public status. The consequence, though, was an interpretation at odds with the standard message for women. For Bathsheba her beauty can be seen as an excuse, which exonerates her from blame, whereas when the elders try to put the same argument to Susanna it is condemned as morally invalid. The significance of the interpretation of Bathsheba offered by the ballad becomes clearer when we contrast it with Calvin's own view. Calvin, partly as a partisan for David and also driven by a concern to maintain moral order, sees Bathsheba at fault not only for bathing, 'but she ought to have been more discreet; she should have thought how not to be seen'.[46] In the words of Dorothy Leigh's discussion of Susanna, she should be 'watchful and wary'. Maintenance and defence of chastity were the female duty, and one that Bathsheba signally failed to consider.

In this context, it is unsurprising that the story of Susanna seems to have been more popular than that of Bathsheba as a model for women. But it is more surprising that the morally problematic element of Bathsheba's story was not addressed more directly in England. On the Continent two contrasting strategies were adopted. In the images of Lucas Cranach the elder, Bathsheba is depicted clothed, with her maids carefully washing her foot in a stream. Such chaste action clearly was not intended to arouse an onlooker's desire. The other strategy shifted the focus from the moment of bathing to the receipt of King David's summons, and hence to the turning point for Bathsheba when she holds her fate in her own hands.[47]

The apparent absence of such solutions in England suggests that different issues were seen to be important, and that Bathsheba, as the ballad treatment suggests, was not the centre of her story. In fact, the combined effect of the stories of Bathsheba and Susanna carried very different gender messages than is often assumed. Both stories emphasised male culpability and lust and saw the female protagonist as the unwitting temptress due to her natural, rather than painted, beauty. They did, of course, differ sharply in their view of female responsibility, but this was not the main issue: the unconscious temptress who submitted to adultery could retain her innocence, even if Susanna's was the nobler course. Instead, allocation of moral responsibility was shifting towards the greater culpability of the man and the conception

---

[46] Bouwsma, *John Calvin*, p. 53.
[47] E. Kunoth-Leifels, *Über die Darstellung der "Bathsheba im Bade": Studien zur Geschichte des Bildthemas 4. bis 17. Jahrhundert* (Essen, 1962).

of a world in which, as Leigh noted, the vulnerable woman who did not consciously seek to tempt men was surrounded by male seducers. Whilst seeming
to maintain the gender order in stressing God's disapproval of adultery, the
stories of both Susanna and Bathsheba questioned male ability to control
their lusts and to exercise true authority. Susanna, rather than Bathsheba,
was the ideal of female conduct, but women in the seventeenth century were
embroidering both these stories in about equal numbers.[48] Even if the subjects of women's embroidery were limited to godly women who adhered to
the values of patriarchy,[49] such images could still convey notions which were
subversive of the gender order.

[48] Geuter, 'Women and embroidery', p. 285, lists 18 examples of the story of David and
Bathsheba and 16 of the story of Susanna.
[49] Parker, *The Subversive Stitch*, p. 98.

11

Martyrs

The woodcut illustrating Bale's account of the interrogation and martyrdom of Anne Askew casts her in the role of a protestant saint. She stands nimbed, and carries a large Bible and a martyr's palm; the papal dragon lies at her feet (Fig. 39). In such representations, as well as in the examples of crowds seeking a martyr's relics, protestant martyrs can be seen as a replacement for the saints. But the gap they filled was more than simply an emotional one: the martyr validated religious truth and as a human recipient of divine favour qualified as a model for godly emulation. As such, the role of martyrs in protestantism has much in common with all the categories of godly exemplars we have considered so far: they are the weak made strong by faith, and this enables them to be obedient to divine command rather than to the demands of family and the world. In view of this it is unsurprising that accounts of female martyrs are predominant. The assumed weakness of women meant that their martyrdoms stressed more clearly and impressively that God was working through them. As John Bale wrote, describing the martyrdom of Anne Askew:

it may well be said that Paul verifieth, 2 Cor. xii. "The strength of God is here made perfect by weakness." When she seemed most feeble, then was she most strong. And gladly she rejoiced in that weakness, that Christ's power might strongly dwell in her. Thus chooseth the Lord the foolish of this world to confound the wise, and the weak to deface the mighty; yea, things despised, and thought very vile, to bring things unto nought, which the world hath in most high reputation.[1]

Such ideas and arguments were paralleled in funeral sermons and accounts of godly lives, as has been noted, but there was also a parallel with the ungodly: witch trial pamphlets were more likely to focus on women rather than men. The devil, like God, could choose the weaker sex as agents to demonstrate his power of harm. In this case, unlike the martyrs, the majority of

---

[1] Rev. H. Christmas (ed.), *Select Works of John Bale D.D., Bishop of Ossory Containing the Examinations of Lord Cobham, William Thorpe and Ann Askewe and The Image of Both Churches*, Parker Society (Cambridge, 1849), pp. 143–4.

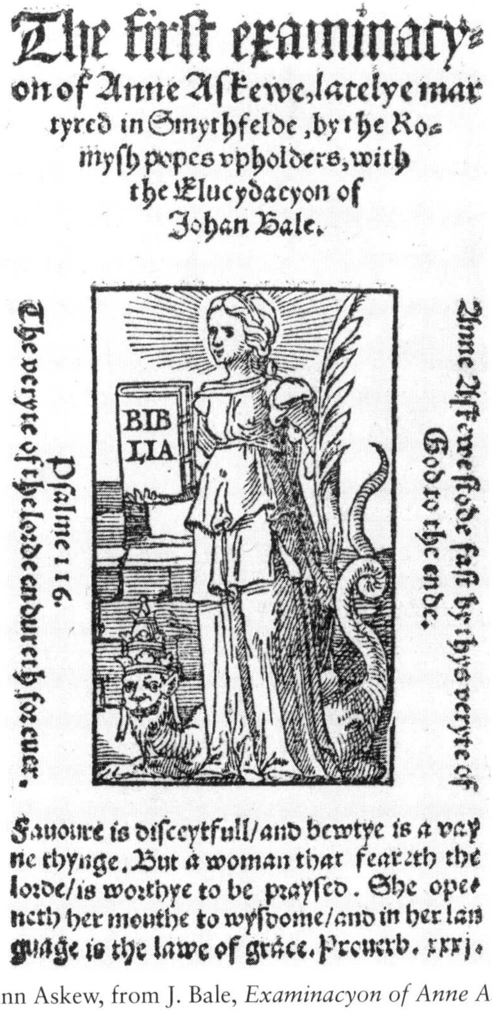
The first examinacyon of Anne Askewe, latelye martyred in Smythfelde, by the Romysh popes vpholders, with the Elucydacyon of Johan Bale.

The verytie of the lorde endureth for euer. Psalme 116.

Anne Askewe stode fast by thys verytie of God to the ende.

Fauoure is disceytfull/and bewtye is a vayne thynge. But a woman that feareth the lorde/is worthye to be praysed. She openeth her mouthe to wysdome/and in her language is the lawe of grace. Prouerb. xxxj.

Figure 39 Ann Askew, from J. Bale, *Examinacyon of Anne Askew* (1546)

those accused as witches were also women, but there were still important discrepancies between actual accusations and sensationalised pamphlet reports. For example, the pamphlet account of the Maidstone trials of 1652 concentrated on the six Cranbrook widows who were considered the 'most notorious' rather than discussing the five married women and six men also arraigned.[2] As with the martyrs, different stereotypes could operate

2 M. Gaskill, 'Witchcraft in early modern Kent: stereotypes and the background to accusations', in J. Barry *et al.* (eds.), *Witchcraft in Early Modern Europe: Studies in Culture and Belief* (Cambridge, 1996), p. 261.

in accusation and in literature. This prompts reflection on the similarities in public response to both forms of behaviour. If female weakness is as stirring when it is transcended as when it leads to a fall, the issue is not so much the distance of action from gendered assumptions of nature as a fascination with the weaker sex as protagonists, or as transgressors of normal boundaries. Representations of male behaviour may need to be contained within narrow limits, whilst female behaviour allows the imagination to explore possibilities which can then be reined in by ensuring that all this clearly occurs under male guidance whether for good or ill. Thus, murder pamphlets before 1640 focus almost exclusively on wives killing their husbands, despite the fact that crime statistics suggest that husbands' murdering their wives occurred at least twice as often as the reverse. But, lest this be seen as an example of women acting independently and assuming power, we need to remember that murderesses were shown as acting with a male partner. Although such women attacked the patriarchal order of their own families, their actions and choice became comprehensible in terms of their submission to other men.[3]

This brief consideration of the darker side of women assuming a dominance contrary to their ideal roles within the patriarchal gender system might seem to be a digression from the theme of martyrdom, but it highlights important similarities and can explain the fascination with female protagonists whatever their actual numerical strength. Just as importantly, it suggests the strength of a conceptual framework in which extraordinary female action needs to be subsumed within an understanding of male capability. Thus, the female martyr is imagined either as becoming male, or as a passive conduit of divine power emanating from a male deity. In the former case, the achievement of martyrdom is arrogated to the male sphere, whilst in the latter, although the divine source of the transformation may be the same, the process of martyrdom is viewed as a transition in which notions of gender seem to have little significance. Strength is not required, but rather the acceptance of divine assistance. However, although it is tempting, it would be mistaken to describe this process as gender neutral. The passive recipient was, once again, most easily envisaged as the weaker vessel, and this association with women was further strengthened by the image of the martyr as the bride of Christ. In both situations the ideal martyr is a woman, but also one who clearly acts within the dominant male framework of values.

In late Antiquity the idea of the female martyr becoming male predominated, and vestiges of this tradition remained in the early modern period, not least because martyrologists took early christian martyrs as their models.

---

[3] F. E. Dolan, *Dangerous Familiars: Representations of Domestic Crime in England, 1550–1700* (Ithaca and London, 1994), pp. 14, 25.

Thus, as is well known, Bale used Blandina as a model in his presentation of Ann Askew. Nevertheless, the second interpretation of the nature of martyrdom also struck a deep chord in protestant mentality: the martyr, like the ordinary protestant, as ultimately the passive recipient and vessel of grace. Both these strategies had co-existed in the medieval hagiographical tradition, even if they had varied in importance at different times. A further complicating factor in Reformation accounts of contemporary martyrdoms was the shift of emphasis from the experience of martyrdom itself to the experience of imprisonment and interrogation. Explicable in terms of the need to assert the tenets of a disputed faith and to vilify one's opponents, this shift raised the problem that the female disputant transgressed gendered assumptions of decorum. If the female accused was to demonstrate the truth of protestant doctrine by outwitting her interrogators in religious debate, she would need to become male. The alternative solution was to cast the martyr in the role of Susanna, passively awaiting the intervention of God. Vindication or martyrdom testified to the justice of the position in the eyes of God, but in choosing this option the author was not able to convey doctrinal arguments as effectively as when the martyr engaged in spirited religious debate with her persecutors. These conflicting strategies were malleable and could be creatively combined. Consequently, Reformation accounts of martyrs offered their readers a range of gendered interpretations without ever losing sight of the overarching framework of male authority. The martyr could be used both as a confrontational weapon in religious debate, and in a more quietistic vein.

This can be seen most easily in the case of Anne Askew, for whom the accounts of Bale and Foxe and the two ballads allow us to see the different ways in which the same martyr can be presented in the protestant tradition, and to speculate on the way in which the image of the martyr could be transformed in the seventeenth century as she became more closely associated with the emerging tradition of the funeral sermon and accounts of the lives of the godly. The presentation of Ann Askew in these sources also has a lot in common with the treatment of other martyrs by Foxe, and significant affinities with the catholic hagiographical tradition as exemplified by Mush's life of Margaret Clitherow. These similarities are, of course, the result of a shared hagiographical heritage and gender assumptions. Although martyrdom can be seen as empowering, only the martyr's experience of this is purely spiritual. Contemporary onlookers, whether catholic or protestant, have to view it through their inappropriate social frames of reference. Thus, in gender terms catholic and protestant martyrs fight the same battles and act within broadly shared patriarchal assumptions, but this does not mean that individuals like Askew and Clitherow become interchangeable models.

I

Anne Askew, a protestant gentlewoman from Lincolnshire with friends and contacts among the evangelical ladies at Court, was burnt for her eucharistic beliefs, and probably her courtly connections, on 16 July 1546. Her case became a cause célèbre, especially with the publication in Wesel of the *First Examinacyon of Anne Askew* in November 1546 and of the *Latter Examinacyon* in the following January. The texts, which consisted of Anne's account of her trials interlarded with Bale's edifying commentary, were immediately popular and went through four further editions in the Edwardian period. Later, Anne's words, without Bale's additions, were also incorporated into Foxe's *Acts and Monuments*. This publishing history alone suggests Anne's importance in the protestant tradition, and it is also borne out by the comments of the godly themselves, especially during the Marian persecutions. When William Tyms of Hockley (Essex) wrote to the godly women of his parish in 1556 he provided them with a list of scriptural models, and also instructed them to remember the blessed martyr Anne Askew and follow her example of constancy. Similarly, Robert Glover wrote to his wife reminding her of Anne Askew's example.[4]

Anne can be assumed to be the author of the text attributed to her by Bale. Early modern prison regimes were certainly lax enough for the smuggling of Anne's writings to be plausible, and, as Fairfield has commented, the style of 'patient simplicity' is unmatched in the rest of Bale's writings.[5] Beilin goes further, arguing for Anne's 'self conceptualisation', and sees Anne as assimilating the experience of martyrdom differently from Bale's interpretation in his commentary.[6] However, it is unclear why we should see Anne's presentation of herself 'in public as fully participant in the "gifts of the Lord"' as at odds with Bale's interpretation. Rather, both narrators seem to share common assumptions of the meaning and process of martyrdom. Bale does not create Anne's conceptualisation, but it is unclear that he radically dissents from it. In his view, true martyrdom consists not in miracles, but in persevering faithfully to the end, and he sees Anne as an example of the way

---

[4] L. P. Fairfield, *John Bale: Mythmaker for the English Reformation* (Indiana, 1976), p. 135, describes the story of Ann Askew as 'something of an early best-seller'. In the 'Second Lamp' of Thomas Bentley's *The Monument of Matrones: conteining seven severall lampes of virginitie* (London, 1582), pp. 214–15, three prayers of female martyrs are included: Agnes, Eulalia and Anne Askew, as well as the prayer of the mother of the martyr John Bradford. William Tyms in Pratt (ed.), *Acts and Monuments*, vol. 8, p. 114; Robert Glover, ibid., vol. 7, p. 388.

[5] Fairfield, *John Bale*, pp. 133–4. Fairfield also argues that Bale may have modified some of Askew's phrases, such as the use of the words 'mutuall partycypacyon' in defining the eucharist.

[6] E. V. Beilin, 'Anne Askew's self portrait in the *Examinations*', in M. P. Hannay (ed.), *Silent but for the Word: Tudor women as Patrons, Translators and Writers of Religious Works* (Kent, Ohio, 1985), p. 79.

in which God chooses the foolish and weak of the world to confound the oppressors of true belief. For Bale it is polemically appropriate that his protagonist should be 'a gentlewoman very young, dainty and tender', a 'blessed woman', who can be compared with Lydia, Cecilia and especially Blandina who 'was young and tender; so was Anne Askewe also: but that which was frail of nature in them both, Christ made most strong by his grace'.[7] Similarly, the self-possessed Anne, 'participant in the gifts of the Lord', sees herself as an example of the weak made strong.

In her text the fact that she is a woman is also used by Askew to play with her interrogators and avoid answering them. Thus, when she refers a question (about whether a mouse who eats the host receives God) back to her questioner and is told that such a tactic is against the order of the schools, her reply, 'I told him I was but a woman and knew not the order of the schools', shelters behind her sex. But this sheltering is itself provocative and disruptive. Whilst ostensibly claiming the place in debate assigned to her by the patriarchal system, Anne refuses to adopt the submissive and obedient role expected of women. Later exchanges illustrate the same process: 'Then he asked me why I had so few words. And I answered God hath given me the gift of knowledge, but not of utterance. And Solomon saith that a "woman of few words is a gift of God." Prov. xix.' Even more strikingly, Anne is prepared to use the Pauline text constraining women to support her stance under interrogation: 'I answered that it was against St Paul's learning, that I, being a woman, should interpret the scriptures, specially where so many wise learned men were.'[8]

Anne's answers, if they are taken at face value rather than being seen as witty rhetorical power games, suggest that her committed protestantism co-existed with an acceptance of women's role in a patriarchal framework. In social terms Anne's religion is not empowering in a form that a feminist could recognise, but the strength of her belief empowers her to the extent that she is able to face a martyr's death. This involves a sense of superiority or, perhaps more accurately, a sense of distance from those who lack faith. Her use of the instruction not to throw pearls before swine – acorns are enough for them – creates a situation in which ultimately persecutors cannot touch the martyr who has faith; but she is also powerless to touch them in terms of conversion to true doctrine by her words.[9] Moreover, she is not given the sanction to try, even though she can appeal to God to do it

[7] Christmas (ed.), *Select Works of John Bale*, pp.140–2. Blandina, like Anne Askew, was burned with three companions, and this also encouraged Bale to develop the comparison.
[8] Ibid., pp. 158, 170, 172. In the *Latter Examinacyon* (p. 155) Anne also defines Paul's prohibition of women teaching in congregation as limited to women preaching from the pulpit.
[9] Christmas (ed.), *Select Works of John Bale*, p. 149.

at the time of her death.[10] This seems to suggest that protestant martyrs have to forsake not only the miraculous achievements of earlier saints,[11] but also their ability to speak effectively to the unregenerate as mouthpieces of God. Despite her learning, and despite her witty responses which frequently wrongfoot her interrogators, Askew cannot be a St Katherine. At the same time her steadfast belief in scripture means that her responses cannot simply be rhetorical devices. Far from being an emblem of female empowerment, Anne appears to accept Solomon's view that a 'woman of few words is a gift of God' and Paul's prohibition of women interpreting the scriptures.

Bale makes little direct comment on Askew's use of such texts which defined women's subordinate role. To him they were presumably unexceptional. Where he does take up the reference, it is to develop it in a way which diminishes its gendered message. Perhaps surprisingly, he uses Solomon's text to draw a parallel between Anne and Christ, both of whom were of few words at their trial and wrongly convicted.[12] This reminds us that, despite the attractions of a female subject as the most effective exemplar of the weak made strong by faith, the task of the martyrologist is to create a model for the representative christian. In this process the martyr can be conceived as being like Christ, but the more important message is that no woman or man can be a martyr without Christ's aid. Ultimately, the reader needs to remember that the martyr is always more a frail human than male or female.

It is only the intervention of Christ which gives Anne the possibility of acting and embracing martyrdom in the way that she does. This applies both to her physical endurance of torture and to her mental state of being able to be 'merry' in the face of death. Although the initial Blandina comparison suggests that there is something distinctive about female frailty being made strong by grace, Bale's comments on Anne's ability to withstand torture make it clear that this frailty is common to mankind. Confronted with the challenge of potential martyrdom, gendered differences in strength become insignificant:

Right far doth it pass the strength of a young, tender, weak, and sick woman (as she was at that time to your more confusion) to abide so violent handling, yea, or yet of the strongest man that liveth. Think not, therefore but that Christ hath suffered in her, and so mightily shewed his power, that in her weakness he hath laughed your mad enterprises to scorn. Ps. ii.

---

[10] Cf. Gouge, *Of Domesticall Duties* (1622), p. 194, who warns that prospective marriage partners should not presume that a godly spouse will be able to convert an unbeliever, since conversion is beyond human power. Conversely, Gouge thought it essential that a husband and wife of the same religious faith should support each other spiritually. See below p. 318.

[11] Christmas (ed.), *Select Works of John Bale*, p. 139.   [12] Ibid., p. 170.

The insignificance of gender in martyrdom is directly related to the idea of Anne as a member of Christ who suffers like a lamb. As Bale goes on to explain,

> as concerning the innocent woman, whom you so cruelly tormented, where could be seen a more clear and open experiment of Christ's dear member, than in her mighty sufferings? Like a lamb she lay still without noise of crying and suffered your utmost violence, till the sinews of her arms were broken, and the strings of her eyes perished in her head.[13]

The analogy between Anne and the Lamb of God reinforces the sense in which the martyr and Christ are inseparable. In the words of Bale's concluding description of Anne, she is a martyr 'canonised in Christ's blood'.[14] The force of this image is not simply the explicit contrast with false canonisation by pope, priests and bishops, it is also meant more literally: according to Psalm 2, which is much quoted in Bale's text, 'Christ hath suffered in her, and so mightily shewed his power.' This represents a transformation of the medieval idea of Christ's continued suffering, which is now principally reserved for the context of martyrdom: persecutors 'make' Christ suffer in order to shield his own from otherwise unbearable torments 'in response' to their faith, and to demonstrate God's power in the world.

The idea that the protagonist is Christ, and not the martyr, is picked up in Anne's ballad, made and sung by her whilst in Newgate, which concludes the *Latter Examinacyon* and may also have circulated separately: Christ is Anne's shield, Faith the strong weapon which will not fail in need, and Christ will fight in her stead.[15] In such an understanding a narrowly gendered interpretation of the concluding quotation that 'God hath chosen the weak things of this world to confound things which are mighty' (1 Cor. 1.27) could have been problematic. This was obviously the case in pastoral terms, but perhaps as importantly it also exposed the same unease as there was with the idea that the devil chose to demonstrate his power through weak, female witches: is the power of God, or of the devil, really so significant if he can work only through weak women? These considerations meant that, although it was attractive to the religious propagandist to concentrate on female martyrs (Bale, it will be remembered, never followed up his accounts of Anne Askew with the promised accounts of the martyrdoms of the three men who died with her), their status as the most powerful testimony to the power of God and of the protestant cause could be double-edged. As a result, it made sense to do as Bale did and try to play down the gender implications whilst using

[13] Ibid., p. 225. [14] Ibid., p. 238.
[15] D. Watt, *Secretaries of God: Women Prophets in Late Medieval and Early Modern England* (Woodbridge, 1997), p. 95, reviews the arguments for the indebtedness of Anne Askew to Surrey's poem 'Ecclesiastes, Chapter Three'.

the daintiness and tenderness of a young gentlewoman to capitalise on the
reader's sympathy.

II

The same issues of balance confronted the other influential martyrologist of
this period, John Foxe, although in many ways the sheer juxtaposition of accounts of male and female martyrs in his *Acts and Monuments* rendered this
problem less difficult. Foxe also uses Askew's text for the two examinations,
but presents this straight, not interspersed with commentary as Bale did.[16]
There are however some modifications. Towards the end of the *First Examinacyon*, Foxe adds the confession of belief signed by Ann Askew from
Bonner's episcopal register, with the comment that the fact that date and
content differ from Anne's testimony shows how little trust is to be placed
in such bishops and their registers. More significantly, Foxe omits Bale's
'The voice of Anne Askewe out of the 54th Psalm of David, called Deus in
nomine tuo', the accompanying scriptural texts, and the ballad which Anne
Askew made and sang in Newgate. The result of these omissions is to tone
down claims for Anne's special status. As Betteridge has noted, the claim
that Anne's voice is 'out of' a psalm gives her authority as a mouthpiece of
God.[17] Also, although the ballad gives the greater role to Christ supported
by Faith, it presents Anne as more of an active christian warrior than is the
case in the preceding prayers which Foxe preserves. His conclusion, having
described her martyrdom, presents an image of Askew as a passive exemplar: 'as a blessed sacrifice unto God, she slept in the Lord A.D. 1546 leaving
behind her a singular example of christian constancy for all men to follow'.

These subtle changes in the presentation of Anne Askew mean that Foxe
is more likely to use notions of gender transformation than Bale. Foxe's
emphasis on the passivity of female martyrs encourages him, as Macek
has noted, to interpret their experience of martyrdom like the accounts of
early christian martyrs. Women's participation in martyrdom is associated
with the assumption of active male strength: their 'womanyshe and wyvishe
hartes' gain 'a bolde and manlye stomache' through divine aid.[18] In descriptions of martyrdom, and of struggles to avoid recantations, positive
manliness (i.e. strength not brutality) can be attributed to women, but such
strength is not innate, it is given by God or Christ. Even when strength and

---

[16] Foxe omits Paget's questioning of Anne in the *Latter Examinacyon*, presumably to preserve
the latter's reputation. *Latter Examinacyon*, pp. 203, 205.

[17] T. Betteridge, *Tudor Histories of the English Reformations, 1530–83* (Aldershot, 1999),
p. 80.

[18] E. Macek, 'The emergence of feminine spirituality in the *Book of Martyrs*', *Sixteenth Century
Journal* 19 (1988), 65, 79.

manliness are not directly equated, this is assumed. A good example is the description of Anne Potten and Joan Trunchfield. Foxe first tells us that,

as they were both by sex and nature somewhat tender, so were they at first less able to endure the straitness of the prison; and especially the brewer's wife was cast into marvellous great agonies and troubles of mind thereby. But Christ, beholding the weak infirmity of his servant, did not fail to help her when she was in this necessity,[19]

and when they are mentioned again:

In whose suffering their constancy worthily was to be wondered at, who being so simple women, so manfully stood to the confession and testimony of God's word and verity.[20]

Commenting on this material, Macek argues that 'Foxe's powerful imagery ambiguously associated women's participation in the passive action of martyrdom with the active strength of man in general, and Jesus Christ in particular.'[21] However, we need to clarify the use of 'passive' and 'active' here, especially in view of the focus in these narratives on struggling against the temptation to recant, and also to distinguish between the active strength of men and of Christ. A more accurate interpretation may be Ong's view that 'the masculine in Jesus' redemptive action is complemented by this feminine strength-in-quietness – which is not passivity at all but a free and active choice'. This can be combined with Petroff's observation that 'in the crucifixion women saw a powerful male figure saving the world by suffering passively, as women suffer. The opposites of passive and active, female and male were reconciled in this single act.'[22] In the person of Christ, assumed gender characteristics disintegrate and recombine in a manner that fuses male and female attributes. To the extent that the martyr became Christ, it made little sense to see the martyr as conventionally male or female.

A different, but still compatible, approach was developed by John Bradford, who went further than was usual for sixteenth-century protestants

---

[19] Pratt (ed.), *Acts and Monuments*, vol. 7, p. 373.
[20] Ibid., vol. 8, p. 102. The case of the seven martyrs burnt at Canterbury, of whom four were women, develops the same theme, and also illustrates the way in which the fact that their victims were women could be used to blacken their persecutors further: 'What heart will not lament the murdering mischief of these men, who for want of work do so wreak their tine on silly poor women, whose weak imbecility the more strength it lacketh by natural imperfection, the more it ought to be helped, or at least pitied; and not oppressed of men that be stronger, and especially of priests that should be charitable.

But blessed be the Lord Omnipotent, who supernaturally hath endued from above such weak creatures with such manly stomach and fortitude, so constantly to withstand the uttermost extremity of these pitiless persecutors: as he did before strengthen the mother of the seven sons in the Maccabees, and as he hath done since with divers and sundry other godly women in these our latter days (ibid., vol. 8, p. 326).
[21] Macek, 'The emergence of feminine spirituality', 79.
[22] The views of Ong and Petroff are cited ibid., 78.

in eroding gendered interpretations of the process of martyrdom. Writing to a gentlewoman, he recommended to her Basil the Great's account of the virtuous widow Julitta, who refused to worship false gods for the sake of her life and her lands. At the place of execution Julitta 'exhorted all women to be strong and constant: "for", saith she, "ye were redeemed with as dear price as men. For although you were made with the rib of man, yet be you all of his flesh, so that also in the case and the trial of your faith before God, ye ought to be as strong." '[23] Bradford's account of Julitta seems to be working with different assumptions from those of Foxe's accounts of the Marian martyrs, denying the comparative weakness of the female sex and suggesting that there is no gender deficit which should be made up by Christ. In doing so, he echoed his source. Foxe's account of Julitta in the 1570 edition of *Acts and Monuments* gives the same interpretation, supported by a more conventional understanding of the properties of flesh and bone. Julitta urges that people should

> cease to accuse the fragilitye of feminine nature. What? are not we created of the same matter, that men are? Yea, after God's image and similitude are we made, as lyvely as they. Not flesh onelye God used in the creation of woman, in signe and token of her infirmity and weakenes, but bone of bones is she, in token that she must be strong in the true and living God, al false Gods forsaken.[24]

For contemporaries, the fact that Eve was created from Adam's rib was used more often as a justification for a wife's role as a subordinate, but not entirely subject, helpmeet to her husband than to undermine gendered conceptions of strength. Indeed, the core of the case for wifely subjection was precisely the weakness of the woman and her consequent need for guidance and protection. This may suggest that Julitta's argument, although available to the assiduous reader of *Acts and Monuments* and to Bradford's correspondents, stood much less chance of becoming commonly accepted. The other option, which preserved innate gender characteristics but recognised the divine role in supplementing deficiencies to create a more androgynous model, could be assimilated more easily. It preserved the hierarchy of the household, whilst also fulfilling the pastoral demand that capability for martyrdom should not be seen in too starkly gendered terms.

Whatever the interpretation chosen, both views primarily relate to mustering sufficient strength to face martyrdom, and not succumbing to the temptation to recant. In gender terms the experience of the martyr's death itself may be understood in a different way. In essence martyrdom involves a conceptualisation of the union with the divine, whether as the object of God's

---

[23] Pratt (ed.), *Acts and Monuments*, vol. 7, p. 191.
[24] Ibid. (1570 edition), pp. 132–3, cited in Macek, 'The emergence of feminine spirituality', 78.

will, or more personally in terms of a relationship with Christ. The latter was probably more common, but the former was not insignificant, especially as it could be used to strengthen less gendered interpretations of martyrdom. A further variation, the identification of the martyr with the Virgin of the Magnificat, placed less emphasis on the idea of union, but clearly saw the martyr as an instrument in relation to God.[25]

The idea of martyrdom as a fulfilment of the prophecy in Malachi 3.2–4 of the Lord's sudden coming 'like a refiner's fire' to purge his people 'as gold and silver' saw the martyr as an object of God's will.[26] It also viewed the process of burning in a way that seems to detach the body from gendered connotations. Martyrdom, although envisaged in the sixteenth century as a distinctively 'embodied' experience,[27] had the potential to be imagined in ways that could circumvent gender, whilst retaining a conception of the frail and unrefined human body as inferior. However, despite the frequency of this imagery and its prophetic scriptural power, such ideas could not entirely shape the understanding of the process of martyrdom. Foxe's accounts of sixteenth-century protestant martyrs combine such scriptural quotation with references to the martyr's need for male strength and women's greater fear. The process leading to refinement, if not refinement itself, was clearly gendered. Furthermore, the Malachi prophecy was not the only scriptural source to be used to interpret the process of martyrdom. The idea of the martyr as a spouse of Christ, or as being robed in a wedding garment for admission as a *guest* to the heavenly wedding feast, could facilitate the maintenance of gender distinctions. The account of a female martyr can easily exploit the erotic potential of, or at least adopt, bride-of-Christ imagery, whilst the male martyr was more easily envisaged as the guest at the wedding feast.

In practice, the gender associations of bride-of-Christ imagery in accounts of martyrdom were less clearly defined. The conventional view of the human soul as feminine offered the possibility of blurring these associations, but in itself this is an insufficient explanation. This view was present in funeral

---

[25] See pp. 223–4.

[26] J. M. Mueller, 'Pain, persecution and the construction of selfhood in Foxe's *Acts and Monuments*', in C. McEachern and D. Shuger (eds.), *Religion and Culture in Renaissance England* (Cambridge, 1997), pp. 169–70.

[27] Ibid., pp. 169–72: 'A consistently remarkable feature of the Marian protestants' figurations of their deaths at the stake is how frankly they address the embodiedness of the experience, even when . . . the vocabulary is filtered through biblical typology . . . In place of images of embrace or coition, the body is conceived as raw stuff for processing into an entity of qualitatively different kind. In such figurations, moreover, the experiential factor – what it is like to undergo burning – registers itself decisively. Out of a rich array of possible Biblical types for the fitting of a human being for union with the divine, choice goes to the wedding guest's garment and the purified gold and silver. These have immediately recognisable correlates in the shift or shirt worn at the stake and the residue of bones and calcined powder left after a fire put to a body has burned itself out' (p. 170).

sermons, but in this context, as we have seen, it was women, rather than men, who could be seen as marrying Christ at their deaths.[28] This was partly because such sermons accented the parallel between the relationship of the godly woman with her earthly husband and that with her heavenly spouse. As importantly, martyrdom created a situation in which the gender attributes of both Christ and the martyr were perceived as overlapping, and less rigidly defined. The female martyr's need to acquire manliness for martyrdom influenced the use of Bridegroom imagery: the 'manly' martyr was also the bride of the Bridegroom. At the same time, the manliness of Christ, and of a few male martyrs, was understood in a feminised way. This can be seen clearly in Foxe's praise of Bartlet Green for his 'maidenly modesty', 'mercy and piti- ful compassion', which leads to the conclusion 'that there is no other thing wrought in nature, wherein man resembleth more truly the image of the high majesty of almighty God, than this'.[29] Nevertheless, in general Foxe's male martyrs are godly and steadfast in their faith, and often able disputants in their interrogations, and they lack the Christ-like, feminine qualities ascribed to Bartlet Green. Gender assumptions were maintained, but could be flexible enough to allow the bride of Christ to be of either sex.

This was encouraged by the tone of the Bridegroom imagery used. The equation of martyrdom with meeting the Bridegroom is clearly expressed by the words and actions of the martyrs. Elizabeth Folkes, one of the Colchester martyrs in 1557, embraced the stake and said, 'Welcome love!' At the mar- tyrdom of Christopher Wade of Dartford (Kent) in 1555 one Margery Polley called out to him these words of comfort: 'You may rejoice, Wade, to see such a company gathered to celebrate your marriage this day', and when Wade came to the stake he embraced it and kissed it.[30] Such references envisage the encounter with the Bridegroom in sober, and not particularly erotically charged, terms. The Bridegroom of the martyrs does not draw its inspira- tion from the Song of Songs, as does much medieval mysticism, but rather from images of spiritual preparedness like the story of the Five Wise and the Five Foolish Virgins. Thus, Richard Woodman wrote to Mistress Roberts of Hawkhurst, 'Now is the time come that we must go and meet the Bridegroom with oil in our lamps.' Similar views were also expressed by Richard Roth in the letter written in his own blood to certain brethren and sisters in Christ who were about to be burnt at Colchester.[31] In this muted form, Bridegroom imagery was as available to male as to female martyrs.

---

[28] See pp. 203–4.   [29] Pratt (ed.), *Acts and Monuments*, vol. 7, pp. 742–3.
[30] Ibid., vol. 7, p. 320, vol. 8, p. 392.
[31] Ibid., vol. 8, p. 375; ibid., p. 420: 'O blessed virgins! ye have played the wise virgins' part, in that ye have taken oil in your lamps, that ye may go in with the Bridegroom when he cometh into the everlasting joy with him. But as for the foolish, they shall be shut out, because they made not themselves ready to suffer with Christ neither to go about to take up his cross.'

A variation of this pattern, which took the martyr's identification with Christ much further than was usual, and further than in the description of Bartlet Green, occurs in the account of the martyrdom of Anthony Peerson. As he embraced and kissed the stake at Windsor in 1543 he said, 'Now welcome mine own sweet wife! for this day shall thou and I be married together in the love and peace of God.'[32] With these words, Peerson appears to see himself in the place of Christ being married to the cross, instead of his soul becoming one with the Bridegroom through death by persecution. For Peerson, the total identification of the christian with Christ precedes martyrdom, and in the act of martyrdom the christian replicates the action of Christ. Peerson's view is unusual, at least in Foxe's accounts of the martyrs. It may be no coincidence that Peerson was also more radical in breaking down the clerical–lay divide by rejecting communion in favour of scripture. In his sermons at Wingfield (Berkshire) he maintained that scripture was the word, the bread and the body of Christ, and that when Christ broke bread and said to his disciples, take and eat, he meant us to take the scripture of God and break it to the people.[33] When Christ's injunction to celebrate communion in remembrance of him was translated into a demand to share the scriptures, it was more possible for the protestant layman to conceive of his actions replicating those of Christ. In so doing, he reversed the gender assumptions of the standard image of the relationship between Christ and christian soul or christian conscience.

Peerson's interpretation was however exceptional. In general, Bridegroom imagery, rather than a literal conception of *imitatio Christi*, was dominant. This imagery was not only powerful in the context of death and martyrdom, but also provided a supportive framework for the lives of the godly who were not approaching the heretic's stake. In fact, a significant part of the power of the accounts of martyrdom could lie precisely in the perceived overlap between the two circumstances. It was possible to use similar Bridegroom imagery in a non-martyrdom context, and to draw a close parallel between the two experiences. John Careless wrote to his brother T.V. to comfort him for his lack of confidence that he could be close to Christ:

But in the mean space (I say) most happy are you, that so heartily mourn for the absence of the Bridegroom. If you were not a wedding child you could never do it. Only Christ's true disciples do mourn for his absence. therefore shall they doubtless rejoice at his presence, which will be so much the more joyful by how much the absence is more sorrowful.

But my good Bridegroom is present, and biddeth me cast away my mourning garments, and therefore I must needs be merry with him: and so he biddeth you to be, by my mouth; for he is present with you, although for sorrow you cannot know him, as Magdalen could not in the garden, until he spake to her.[34]

---

[32] Ibid., vol. 5, p. 493.   [33] Ibid., p. 487.   [34] Ibid., vol. 8, pp. 183–4.

Such interpretations offered comfort to the godly during the Marian persecutions, and may have had an even greater resonance in the later Reformation, when the possibility of martyrdom had receded, but the dilemma
of assurance persisted. Every christian could be a 'wedding child', and like
the Magdalen should expect Christ's response, even when circumstances appeared hopeless.

III

The changed emphasis in the use made by protestants of the martyrs in the
later Reformation can be illustrated most clearly with the example of Anne
Askew. The ballad 'I am a woman poor and blind', entered in the Stationers'
Register in 1624, contrasts sharply with Bale's version of Anne's texts and
with her Newgate ballad (Fig. 40). The title of the later ballad signals what
we are to expect. Since Anne was actually a gentlewoman, it is clear that
'a woman poor and blind' is meant to be taken metaphorically: Anne is
a poor, helpless woman, blind to true doctrine, who is dependent on the
assistance of others to find the right way. The idea of Anne's vulnerability
pervades the ballad, especially in the double meaning of 'work his will' in
relation to Gardiner's flattery, which harks back to medieval clerical–seducer
songs. None of this would work so well if Anne was presented as the artic-
ulate, determined young gentlewoman of her own narratives. Instead, the
idea of Anne as 'poor and blind' is reinforced by her own admission that
'little knowledge remains in me'.

This idea of woman as a receptive vessel is fused with garden imagery.
Anne is figured as a garden in whom others can plant things. This garden
motif is encouraged by a convenient play on words. Bishop Gardiner, her
inquisitor, is also the prelate who fails in his duty as pastor when Anne seeks
instruction. Instead of cultivating her garden, he sows 'pestilential seed'.
His advice to Anne contains no word of Christ's passion, but only corrupt
popish ceremonies. Anne's garden, unlike the *hortus conclusus* of the Virgin
Mary, can be invaded by tares. As Anne realises later, in following Gardiner's
counsel, 'thus Christ of his merits I did deprave', and she was worse than a
Jew or a Turk.

The ballad is more concerned with the corruption of popish ceremonies,
and the consequent effacing of Christ, than with Anne's protestant beliefs,
and reads much more like a 'repentant sinner' ballad than an account of
martyrdom. Indeed, the ballad author asserts that he has no space to show
the true cause of her death, and is prepared to trust that by God's grace
all faithful people will know. Such confidence may not have been too optimistic. Anne's story clearly was well known in the protestant community

Figure 40 Woodcut accompanying the ballad of Ann Askew 'I am a woman poor and blind'

in the early decades of the Reformation, but the priorities of the ballad author also indicate the changed context of the early seventeenth century. Not only was the witness of martyrdom no longer central, but the author felt able to take liberties with her story to make a very different point. The defence of eucharistic doctrine no longer seemed of prime importance, but rather the difficulties encountered by the frail christian dependent on specialised religious advice which cannot be trusted to advocate true practice and belief. Anne Askew, in fact, has become a model of Mary Magdalen. The spiritual garden metaphors set up this association. As the medieval Digby Mary Magdalen play explained, when Mary Magdalen mistook Christ for the gardener the confusion was appropriate, since Christ is the gardener of the soul. The same idea persisted in later interpretations. Southwell in his *Marie Magdalens Funerall Teares* (1594) saw the connections between Christ and Adam in terms of their shared role as gardeners, and defined Christ as 'the gardiner that hath planted the tree of grace, and restored us to the use and eating of the fruits of life', and such views were clearly possible in a protestant context.[35] The problem for the Magdalen, as for every christian, is recognising the identity of the true gardener, and avoiding being misled by those who preach doctrines which efface Christ. In protestant, as in catholic, tradition Mary Magdalen is not wilfully evil, but needs guidance.

[35] Furnivall (ed.), *The Digby Plays*, p. 96; Southwell, *Marie Magdalens Funerall Teares*, pp. 53–54v.

In this framework the idea of Anne being able to judge and control her own fate is minimised. Although in retrospect Anne is able to state that she should have been more actively in control ('where I should have sown, / The seed of Christ's true verity'), this is not seen as a real option. Similarly the transition from being a person following Gardiner's advice to becoming a martyr is not explored. The treatment is closer to ballad of the poor, repentant sinner who is easily led astray, but it still lacks the dramatic force of conversion usually found in these ballads. A parallel with repentant criminal ballads is also inexact: Anne has fallen by seeking assistance, not by her special depravity. In the end, the Lord has mercy upon her and strengthens her so that she will not recant despite the threats of prison, fire, faggot and sword. She can ask the Lord to strengthen her and for forgiveness, but she cannot extend that request to Gardiner because he has sown so much pestilential seed. This contrasts with Bale's account, in which Anne's ability to ask for forgiveness and conversion for her persecutors is one of the two reasons why Anne is Christ's faithful servant, a saint and a true martyr. There could perhaps be no clearer indication of the significance of the transformation of the martyr into the Magdalen: the martyr acts with conviction, the Magdalen's fate depends on the company into which she falls.

I V

The transformation of Anne Askew, from the confident saint with her martyr's palm in the woodcut accompanying Bale's edition to the vulnerable Magdalen and frail christian needing guidance, shows the range of interpretations possible within the protestant hagiographical tradition. A similar spectrum might be expected in the catholic context. After all, Bale's woodcut of Askew is clearly modelled on standard depictions of female martyr saints in pre-Reformation catholicism, and the story of the Magdalen could be interpreted with similar empathy by protestant and catholic authors in the later sixteenth century. Moreover, since the protestant and catholic traditions could share Christocentric devotional emphases, there was potential for overlap in the conceptualisation of the gendered experience of martyrdom, depending on the significance of becoming Christ's spouse and of participating in the Crucifixion.

Historians note as an aside that the portrayal of the catholic Margaret Clitherow is similar to that of protestant martyrs such as Anne Askew. So far though, due to the protestant bias of current Reformation historiography, there has been no sustained comparison, and the question is not addressed in the most recent study of Clitherow.[36] Such a comparison is complicated by the different nature of the surviving texts: we see Clitherow entirely through the eyes of the priest John Mush, not in her own words.[37] It is unclear how far Mush's conceptions of martyrdom and of model female catholic behaviour, acquired at Douai and the English College at Rome, were internalised by Margaret herself, although it is evident that the idea of martyrdom was important to her long before she herself had to confront the possibility. The fact that she had to be restrained by priests in her desire to go on 'pilgrimage', as she called it, to Knavesmire, the site just outside York where six seminary priests were executed between 1582 and 1585, is testimony to the importance of martyrdom in her religious conceptions even before the death of Marmaduke Bowes, the first lay martyr, made death by martyrdom for her own actions seem a realistic possibility. It is, perhaps, less certain that Mush's vision of the submissive, dependent catholic laywoman corresponds entirely with the strength of character of a woman who was able to convert to catholicism in defiance of her family, and to resist all blandishments which might have saved her life in her steadfast refusal to plead.

For the modern reader, the most striking aspect of Mush's description of Margaret Clitherow's conduct is her absolute submission to the direction of her priests and her decision to 'forsake her own judgement and will in all actions', as 'it seemed to her the only safe way to please God, humbly to submit herself in all things to follow the advice and direction of his priests', who were provided by God to govern inferior creatures such as herself.[38] With this description we enter the world of the seventeenth-century ballad of Anne Askew: Clitherow's priests are equivalent to Askew's 'gardener'. In both cases the woman is a helpless, dependent, inferior creature. Clitherow being a convert from a protestant upbringing such dependence on the priests, the instruments of her conversion, may be psychologically plausible in her case; but her tale, like that of the ballad version of Askew, highlights her vulnerability to advice and her inability unaided to discern what is right. In the words of Mush, she believed 'that since God of His infinite mercy had sent His priests already to call her to His grace, by delivering her from error in faith and ungracious affections of the will, he would also with like goodness that by their helps she should continue in the same'.[39]

---

[36] C. Cross, 'An Elizabethan martyrologist and his martyr: John Mush and Margaret Clitherow', in D. Wood (ed.), *Martyrs and Martyrologies*, Studies in Church History, 30 (Oxford, 1993), pp. 271–81.

[37] J. Mush, *A true report of the life and martyrdom of Mrs Margaret Clitherow*, repr. in J. Morris (ed.), *The Troubles of our Catholic Forefathers Related by Themselves*, ser. 3 (London, 1877), pp. 360–440.

[38] Ibid., pp. 378–9.   [39] Ibid., p. 378.

It is notable, however, that in describing her dependence and rejection of the 'peril' of her own will and judgement, Mush is careful not to describe this as something particularly remarkable or desirable for a member of the female sex, even though elsewhere in his text he is happy to describe the astonishment that a woman should be so virtuous.[40] For Mush, dependence on priests indicates catholic obedience to God, whom such priests represent. But at the same time, and parallel with the godly protestant woman and the godly minister, the spiritual relationship is not portrayed as totally one-sided.[41] Mush claims that he admired Margaret even before her martyrdom, and that her virtues inspired in him a fervent, and spiritually profitable, remorse for his own sins. Margaret in her frailty surrendered her will to him and his fellow priests, but her successful cultivation of virtue serves as both a rebuke and a spur to them. Viewed from the outside, the relationship now seems more even, but to Margaret herself the centrality of the virtue of humility requires that such reciprocity remain unacknowledged. A spiritual reciprocity similar to that outlined in a protestant context is therefore submerged by stricter expectations of humility and obedience.

The differences between the two religious traditions are even more evident when we consider Mush's relationship with the martyr as distinct from the godly laywoman. Even though Mush cautions strongly against disconnecting these two stages of Margaret's life – the martyr is made not only by death for the cause, but also by the preceding virtuous preparation of a godly life – his relationship with Margaret is profoundly transformed by her martyr's death, and in his written account he invites his audience to follow his reassessment of roles. The transition is signalled by a change of identity: in the first section Margaret is referred to as 'she'; in the second part, the discussion of her apprehension, arraignment and death, she becomes 'the martyr'. At the same time she begins to be portrayed as acting autonomously, forced by necessity to act without reference to priests. This creates a transition for the ultimate reversal of roles. Mush, once her ghostly father, now casts Margaret in the role of mother able by her intercession to recompense him for his earlier efforts, paltry by comparison, to assist and guide her. Addressing her as 'sacred martyr', Mush styles himself as 'in times past thine unworthy Father, and now thy most unworthy servant', and appeals to her as if to the Virgin Mary:

> I was not so able to help thee as thou art now to procure mercy and grace for me; for thou art now all washed in thy sacred blood from all spots of frailty, securely possessing God himself; whereas I am yet a woeful wretch, and clothed with impiety,

[40] For example, 'They [others of 'no small judgement'] never saw the like prudency in any woman, and that they learned more wisdom by her behaviour than ever they had done by the conversation and example of men in any degree': ibid., p. 402.

[41] D. Willen, 'Godly women in early modern England: Puritanism and gender', *JEH* 43/4 (1992), 568–76.

as now thou seest, and not so able to break the loathsome bonds of my own sensuality as I shall be when, by thy gracious intercession, I receive more help. Be not wanting therefore my glorious mother, in the perfection of thy charity, which was not little towards me in thy mortality, to obtain mercy and procure the plenties of such graces for me, thy miserable son, as thou knowest to be most needful for me, and acceptable in the sight of our Lord, which hath thus glorified thee; that I may honour Him by imitation of thy happy life, and by any death, which He will give me, to be partaker with thee and all holy saints of His kingdom, to whom be all glory and honour, now and for ever. Amen.[42]

Such a conclusion was clearly unthinkable in a protestant context due to the rejection of such forthright appeals for saintly intercession, although both traditions shared ideas of the saintly martyr as an inspirational exemplar and a reassurance of God's grace. The opportunities of reversal in Margaret's story, which hinge on intercessory, hierarchical roles (priest-father becomes son; daughter becomes martyr-mother), mean that it is oversimplistic to view the histories of catholic and protestant female martyrs as entirely parallel in their gender implications.

V

Clitherow's story emphasises her maternal and wifely roles, and imagines her transformation through martyrdom in terms of the interchangeability of physical and spiritual images of maternal nurture. Her poor neighbours lose a mother at her death with loss of her alms, but in the end they may benefit from her edifying example. Clitherow embraces martyrdom as willingly as she put her children to her paps, an image which combines notions of a natural propensity to embrace martyrdom with the early modern medical understanding of the cyclical transformation of blood and milk. She rebuts her opponents' charges that she is unmaternal in her care for her family: it is sufficient if she has brought up her children to be virtuous, and she can wish death (martyrdom) for them too.[43] Such continuities of maternal imagery are

---

[42] Mush, *A true report of the life and martyrdom*, p. 440.

[43] Ibid., pp. 384–5, 426–7. 'As for my husband, know you that I love him next unto God in this world, and I have care over my children as a mother ought to have; I trust I have done my duty unto them as a mother ought to have: I trust I have done my duty unto them to bring them up in the fear of God, and so I trust now I am discharged of them. And for this cause I am willing to offer them freely to God that sent them me, rather than I will yield one jot from my faith. I confess death is fearful, and flesh is frail; yet I mind by God's assistance to spend my blood in this faith, as willingly as ever I put my paps to my children's mouths.' A similar idea was also used by Mush earlier in his account to describe the persecuted Church: 'In the primitive Church they persecuted her that she should remain barren and bring forth no increase; now they labour also to the same effect, but principally to subvert and destroy her already born children; and as she then cast her seed of blood to the generation of many, so now she fighteth with blood to save those that she hath borne, that the lily roots being watered with the fruitful liquor of blood, may keep still and yield new branches hereafter

not irrelevant, rather they are part of a mutually reinforcing transformation. As Mush emphasised in his introduction, only by acquiring such virtues is spiritual progress and martyrdom possible. The continuity also means that martyrdom, unlike the cloister, which she rejects, does not entail a severing of obligations, or a rejection of maternal and wifely duty. This explains the symbolic gifts to husband and daughter: 'Her hat before she died she sent to her husband, in sign of her loving duty to him as to her head. Her hose and shoes to her eldest daughter Anne, about twelve years old, signifying that she should serve God and follow her steps of virtue.' The martyr, although she dresses herself in ribbons for her death as if for a marriage, does not renounce her earthly family ties whilst anticipating becoming the bride of Christ.[44]

Her claim to be an exemplary mother and wife is however contested by her persecutors, but this is a standard response. Margaret's concern to defend the reputation of herself and husband in face of sexual slander and innuendo corresponds to that of female protestant martyrs who were faced with similar strategies by their persecutors, operating in a context where defamation was gendered: female honesty was primarily sexual, male honesty primarily financial. The protestant martyr Elizabeth Young was habitually addressed as 'whore' by her questioners, who also assumed that, as a woman, she must have gained her knowledge of the scriptures by sleeping with a priest.[45] Agnes Prest was seen by her interrogators as a 'prattling' woman who should return to her husband and her domestic duties.[46] Similarly, Clitherow was told: 'It is not for religion that thou harbourest priests, but for harlotry', and was accused of offering daintier cheer (food and sexual) to priests than to her husband, who was left alone with bread and butter and a red herring.[47]

Such examples lead Macek to conclude, with reference to Foxe, that after the period of persecution the accounts of female martyrs provided little support for the evolving protestant concern that women should be encouraged to seek salvation through the patriarchal institution of the family.[48] This view needs closer examination: apparent neglect of family duties could be, as we have seen in the case of Margaret Clitherow, compatible with support for patriarchal family ideals. The same is true of Foxe's narratives, and

with so much more plentiful increase by how much more abundantly such sacred streams flow among them.' (pp. 362–3).
[44] Ibid., pp. 432, 430.
[45] O'Sullivan, 'Women's place', 251–6; Pratt (ed.), *Acts and Monuments*, vol. 8, pp. 536–48.
[46] Ibid., p. 498. ' "Thou foolish woman," quoth the bishop, "I hear say, that thou hast spoken certain words against the most blessed sacrament of the altar, the body of Christ. Fie for shame! Thou art an unlearned person and a woman. Wilt thou meddle with such high matters, which all the doctors of the world cannot define? Wilt thou talk of such high mysteries? Keep thy work and meddle with that thou hast to do. It is no woman's matters at cards and tow to be spoken of." '
[47] Mush, *A true report of the life and martyrdom*, pp. 414, 427.
[48] Macek, 'The emergence of feminine spirituality', 79.

in both cases, since the reader is assumed to be on the side of the 'heretic', some accounts may be subversive of the conventional patriarchal order, but others seem designed to project this family ideal. There are case histories which advocate that household authority is only to be followed where it is godly, but other examples laud wifely obedience and support which put the woman's practice of her faith, and her life, in jeopardy.

Women are praised by Foxe for shielding their husbands and preserving their undeserved good reputation. Alice Benden of Staplehurst (Kent) protects the reputation of her husband, who accepted money from the constable as payment to assist in her arrest, by giving herself up voluntarily to the authorities. Foxe similarly praises William Calloway's wife's perjury to save her husband, and also notes unquestioningly in the case of Joan Seaman that it is a wife's 'duty' to return to her husband when he is sick or in need, despite the risk of arrest and the loss of her own life. His obituary of Joan Seaman and her husband summarises the model conduct of godly yoke fellows: 'Her husband and she kept a good house, and had a good report amongst their neighbours, willing always to receive strangers, and to comfort the poor and sick; and lived together in the holy estate of matrimony very honestly for above forty years.'[49] Even more strikingly, the story of Mother Benet of Wetheringset by Mendlesham seems to be included simply to demonstrate protestant domestic virtues. The point of the story ostensibly is that Mother Benet was refused christian burial by the commissary during the reign of Mary, but this seems to be an excuse for a homely dialogue extolling her freedom from the vice of covetousness: she cannot firkin up her butter and keep her cheese in the parlour to wait for a good price, and let the poor want and so displease God.[50]

Nevertheless, despite these attempts to present the female martyr as the ideal, self-sacrificing housewife, Foxe's narratives also had to deal with women who seemed to shirk their marital duties and chose to live apart from their husbands in pursuit of the gospel. From one perspective such cases were straightforward: Christ's injunction, 'he that leaveth not father or mother, sister or brother, husband . . .', could be invoked in support of such actions, as Agnes Prest did in her defence in 1558. She also maintained that 'in the cause of Christ and his truth, where I must either forsake Christ or my husband, I am contented to stick only to Christ my heavenly spouse, and renounce the other'.[51] In this formulation the stance of the martyr broke the rules of earthly patriarchal authority, but only in the context of obedience to a higher authority. This could be seen as a licence for women to evade

---

[49] Alice Benden of Staplehurst (Kent), Pratt (ed.), *Acts and Monuments*, vol. 8, p. 327; Wife of William Calloway, ibid., vol. 5, pp. 525–6; Joan Seaman of Mendlesham (Suffolk), ibid., vol. 8, pp. 466–7.
[50] Ibid., p. 467.   [51] Ibid., p. 498.

the demands of wifely obedience, but it could not generally be considered in this way, since wifely obedience itself was understood as fulfilling the terms of divine obedience. Similarly, although at first sight martyrdom seems to involve submission to an unjust patriarchal authority, it does so only in the context of obedience to God.

Authors of accounts of martyrs, like those of household advice literature, had to confront the recurring dilemma facing every christian when the demands of divine and secular obedience conflicted, and obedience to both was divinely sanctioned. In this respect, martyrs' accounts addressed issues of continuing relevance even when the Church was no longer under the cross. Moreover, authors like Foxe were concerned to make sure that the ideal of domestic conduct was advocated clearly. The inclusion of the letters written by godly martyrs to their family and friends was particularly useful for this purpose. John Bradford's farewell letter (1555) exemplifies such summaries of the female duty: 'I require you Elizabeth and Mary my sisters, that you will fear God, use prayer, love your husbands, be obedient unto them as God willeth you; bring up your children in God's fear, and be good housewives.' This advice was not all one-sided. The husband's duty was not neglected. As John Philpot told Master Robert Harrington, 'Since you have married a wife, whom God bless, I cannot excuse you from this mart, but you must bring your wife for an usury to the Lord, whose pleasure is in godly yoke-fellows.'[52] The martyrs spoke to their godly readers not simply of a superhuman sacrifice in defence of the faith, but also as 'godly yoke-fellows' familiar with the burdens and responsibilities of a godly marriage.

Martyrs fundamentally were members of the godly and the weak made strong by faith, and female martyrs therefore had a special place in their ranks. But the demands of protestant understanding also created countervailing pressures to the attractiveness of portraying a feeble, weak female martyr. The need to defend doctrine had to be reconciled with the idea that the female disputant transgressed gendered assumptions of decorum. This was not insurmountable, as the example of Askew shows: it was possible for women to dispute with their interrogators, whilst using the arguments for female non-participation in this sphere as their weapons. Such strategies assisted the erosion of gendered associations. This was carried further by the need to show that Christ acted in the martyr, and that consequently the gender deficit in strength was less significant than human frailty, whether male or female. As such, the message of the accounts of martyrs had perennial relevance in the Reformation, even after the danger of actual persecution had receded, and can be seen as ameliorating women's position. The role of the

---

[52] Ibid., vol. 7, pp. 265, 699.

martyr as a bearer of witness, and a confounder of the pretensions of her persecutors, seems to be less important than the transformation of the martyr into the Magdalen, or into a human individual attempting to negotiate a good passage through the conflicting demands of faith and the world. In this process there were differences in catholic and protestant expression, especially in terms of the degree of submission acknowledged and the emphasis on maternal roles and intercession; but the similarities seem more striking, and consistent with the ease with which Southwell's view of the Magdalen could be absorbed into the protestant tradition.

12

Adam's Fall

Conceptualisations of the position of women in terms of an oscillation between pit and pedestal suggest that the reformers' attempts to prevent the veneration of Mary would result in the greater prominence of Eve as the representative of the female. Such ideas are, as we have seen, based on a false understanding of late medieval devotion: on the eve of the Reformation both Eve and Mary lacked the commanding clarity and prominence which could have made them effective models for female parishioners. In addition, proponents of such ideas fail to consider the fact that the reformers did not reject Mary entirely and that they were markedly reluctant to discuss the implications of the Fall, especially in gender terms. It is far from clear that the changes wrought by the events of the Reformation meant the destruction of the Marian ideal of the female and a corresponding rise in the negative figure of Eve. The period saw the modification of both female images, resulting in a closer identification with human experience whilst diminishing the sharpness of gender distinctions. Moreover, protestant support for the ideas of the patriarchal family and of Christ as the new Adam gave encouragement to Adam-centred interpretations of the Fall.

The redefinition of the roles of Adam and Eve was not a central part of the reformers' agenda. In drama and popular literature the Reformation caused a movement to comparatively safe Old Testament and moral topics, but it did not seem appropriate to dramatise the story of the Fall. The exception, a revision of a mystery play to ensure its continuance in a protestant context, ultimately failed to achieve its aim.[1] Protestant reluctance to address this issue seems surprising, given the importance of human frailty and sinfulness in protestant interpretations of man's relationship with God, but the issue also

---

[1] Blackburn, *Biblical Drama under the Tudors*, pp. 125, 155. Watt, *Cheap Print and Popular Piety*, traces an identical chronology in wall paintings and printed pictures. The Norwich Grocer's play of the Fall and Expulsion was revised and expanded in 1565: Waterhouse (ed.), *The Non-Cycle Mystery Plays*, and repr. in N. Davis (ed.), *Non-Cycle Plays and Fragments*, EETS suppl. texts 1 (1970).

raised complex questions concerning predestination, and the relationship between the Old and New Testaments.

Continental reformers were less reticent. For Luther, partly due to his concern to distance himself from the Old Testament fundamentalism of men like Karlstadt, defining the relationship between the Old and the New Law could not be avoided. From the late 1520s his views received powerful visual expression in the altarpieces of his follower Cranach, but it was one in which the Fall played only a subsidiary role. In the centre a tree divides the Old and New Testament sides of the image, but bears leaves only in response to the coming of Christ. Chronologically, the Temptation and the Crucifixion seem to be juxtaposed, but in fact the central concern in these complex images was the relationship between the law of the Ten Commandments and the availability of saving grace through Christ's passion. The Fall, like the Annunciations to Mary and to the Shepherds, was relegated literally to the picture's historical and background.[2]

Even in the early more Lutheran decades of the Reformation, such images do not seem to have been adopted in England, except for a modified version on the title page of the Matthew Bible of 1537, and became less appropriate as the reformers adopted more Calvinist ideas (Fig. 41). In fact, despite the circulation of the Pentateuchs of Luther and Tyndale amongst early evangelicals in England, the New Testament became the main focus when the Reformation reached the parishes. Tyndale's more influential *Obedience of a Christian Man* (1528) was based on the New Testament, and mainly used the Old to correct quotations that might seem to support papal power.[3] Moreover, when English reformers specified what books should be acquired by parishes, they were prepared to state that only the provision of the New Testament, and not the Old, was essential. Practical pressures clearly had a role here – all reformers could have drawn up a longer wish list – but the choices made also indicate their priorities.[4]

---

[2] C. C. Christensen, *Art and the Reformation in Germany* (Athens, Ohio, 1979), pp. 124–8.

[3] D. Daniell, *William Tyndale: A Biography* (New Haven and London, 1994), pp. 223–249, 283–315.

[4] The second Henrician Injunctions (1538) ordered that a complete Bible of the largest size should be acquired by each parish, the cost to be equally divided between pastor and parishioners. A year earlier, Bishop Latimer's injunctions for the diocese of Worcester urged that each cleric should own 'a whole Bible, if ye can conveniently, or at the least a New Testament, both in Latin and English'. Archbishop Lee's injunctions for York diocese *c.* 1538 specified that every curate and priest should have a New Testament in English or Latin as well as a copy of *The Institution of a Christian Man*. The Injunctions of 1547 and 1558 specified the acquisition of the whole Bible in English and Erasmus' *Paraphrases on the New Testament*. Bishop Hooper differed, in this as in so much else, from his fellow bishops in the emphasis he placed on Genesis. His injunctions for the dioceses of Worcester and Gloucester, 1551–2, stated that vicars and curates were to study one book of the Bible each quarter of the year and

The low profile of the Old Testament in the parish churches of Reformation England partly accounts for the rarity of detailed discussions of the Fall, but is not a complete explanation. As important was the issue of how the doctrine of original sin fitted with the reformers' ideas of predestination and election. At parish level these hard doctrines, which could be seen to offer little hope and comfort, seem to have been largely avoided until the development of Arminianism in the 1620s forced clarification and commitment. Green's analysis of the content of catechisms demonstrates that even authors concerned to supplement the basic teaching of prescribed catechisms did not consider inculcating doctrines of predestination to be an important part of their task.[5] A similar reluctance to embrace ideas of predestination can be seen in the isolated, but nevertheless striking, fact that it was possible for the Caroline puritan parishioners of St Andrew's Norwich to censure their minister for denying that Christ died to save all men.[6] Uncertainty about the doctrine of predestination, or perhaps more plausibly its acceptance as a background feature conveying not much more than a general notion of divine power and providence, thus helps to explain the apparent reluctance of popular authors to tackle the topic of the Fall.

A further difficulty, and one of greater significance for our enquiry, was the reconciliation of the gender implications of the Fall with the idea of the spiritual equality of all believers. That the doctrine of spiritual equality was never fully worked out in early Reformation England was due, in part, to the connection between this doctrine and that of the priesthood of all believers. The latter obviously had implications for the position of the clergy, which could seem dangerously radical to the promoters of an officially led Reformation. The development of such a doctrine was also hampered by the legacy of opinions concerning the nature of women, which can be summed up in the view of the woman as the weaker vessel.

These factors meant that detailed discussions of the Fall were comparatively infrequent, but they do not entirely explain why so little emphasis was placed on the role of Eve. The official homilies of 1547 and 1563 do not mention Eve once by name, despite the inclusion of numerous allusions to the Fall. The writers of the homilies were not, of course, prepared to exonerate Eve. They were too concerned with the need to be faithful to the scriptural text to contemplate such a thing easily. However, their overriding interest in

be examined on this by the bishop's officials. The four books chosen were Romans, Deuteronomy, Matthew and Genesis. Bray (ed.), *Documents of the English Reformation*, pp. 179, 250, 336–7; Frere and Kennedy (eds.), *Visitation Articles and Injunctions of the Reformation*, vol. 2, pp. 15, 44, 281.

[5] I. Green, ' "For children in yeeres and children in understanding": the emergence of the English catechism under Elizabeth and the early Stuarts', *JEH* 37/3 (1986), 397–425.

[6] Sharpe, *The Personal Rule of Charles I*, p. 300.

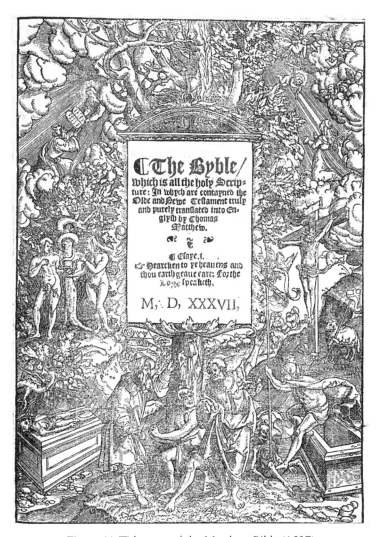

Figure 41 Title page of the Matthew Bible (1537)

the text of the New Testament meant that the references of St Paul to the Fall of mankind being by the sin of 'only Adam' could strongly influence their interpretation of the scene. Indeed, the 1563 sermon 'On the death and passion of our Saviour Christ' declared that 'by the offence of onely Adam, death came upon al men to condemnation'.[7]

[7] 'Homily on the death and passion of our Saviour Christ', *Second Tome of Homelyes* (London, 1563), p. 410. As Sommerville comments, considering a range of sixteenth- and

This surprising admission that responsibility for the Fall rests entirely with Adam was rarely expressed in the late medieval sources, which relied principally on the Genesis and apocryphal accounts. Even *Dives and Pauper*, which does use Paul's reference, only drew from it the still quite radical conclusion that Adam was more responsible than Eve.[8] However, the emphasis on Adam in the Homilies cannot be explained completely by the idea that the text of the New Law could cancel that of the Old. Preference for the Pauline texts did promote the Adam–Christ antithesis whilst ignoring the now more problematic one of Eve and Mary, but only if used selectively, since 1 Timothy 2.14 blames Eve for the transgression. It is also evident that a similar Christocentric focus had also underpinned late medieval interpretations, but that this had been less able to displace Eve from the centre of attention. In the Reformation existing tendencies in favour of an Adam–Christ emphasis were strengthened by protestant claims about the responsibility of the father for the religion and morals of his family: Adam's responsibility for the Fall was that of the patriarchal head of the family of mankind. It was the strength of this view, rooted in social conventions, combined with the comparative weakness of the doctrine of spiritual equality, which discouraged the equal attribution of responsibility between the sexes.

This patriarchal solution seems, however, to have been largely limited to theological writings and to the official homilies, and even in the latter it may have had limited impact, conflicting as it did with pastoral concerns. The reviser of the Norwich Grocers' play of the Fall clearly aimed to produce a version that would pass muster in the newly hostile context of a scripturally based Reformation, but he did not see the need to change the interpretation of the Fall itself in New Testament terms. Concessions to the new religious climate were limited to the emphasis in the prologue that the play was scripturally based and could be a useful teaching aid, and more significantly a new conclusion. The revised ending did not seek to apportion responsibility between Adam and Eve, but celebrated the doctrine of the possibility of salvation by faith because of Christ's role in taking mankind's sins upon his back.[9] More remarkably, although Calvin maintained that

---

seventeenth-century theological literature, 'When crucial theological points were at issue, Adam's sin was the decisive one. Even when sinning – the only thing she was remembered for – Eve had less impact than Adam': M. R. Sommerville, *Sex and Subjection: Attitudes to Women in Early Modern Society* (London, 1995), p. 32. Catechisms also played down Eve's role. As Green comments, 'Adam became sinful by listening to the whispers of "the devil", "a tempting spirit"; in most of the works in our sample Eve did not incur the proportion of blame she later did. Adam broke "an easy commandment, which God gave him as the first trial of his obedience" ': I. Green, *The Christian's ABC: Catechisms and Catechising in England, c. 1530–1740* (Oxford, 1996), pp. 307–8.

[8] See p. 138.

[9] Waterhouse (ed.), *The Non-Cycle Mystery Plays*, pp. 11–18. The revised version dates from 1565 and the audience is assured in the prologue that the stories in the pageant 'with the

'truly Paul... states that sin came not by the woman, but by Adam himself', the Geneva Bible, which was arguably more influential amongst the English protestant community, left the crucial New Testament passages (especially Romans 5.12) supporting this point unglossed.

In view of this, it is perhaps less surprising that the Adam-centred interpretation found little favour in works of the Elizabethan period which discussed the Fall. These works are firmly based on the text of the Genesis account, and despite the limitations of the scriptural text their authors are able to present an account of the Fall in which responsibility is distributed between the sexes. Three texts of very different forms can be used to demonstrate the similarity of interpretation. Gervase Babington, Bishop of Llandaff, produced in 1592 his *Certaine plaine, briefe and comfortable Notes upon everie Chapter of Genesis*, which is in fact a rather lengthy detailed commentary on the book. Perhaps more accessible, and certainly shorter, was an early

---

Skriptures most justly agree' (line 14). The conclusion, in which Man (Adam) is comforted by the Holy Ghost, expounds the protestant view of salvation:

HOLY GHOST Be of good cheare, Man, & sorowe no more.
This Dolor & Miserie that thou hast taste,
Is nott in respect, layd up in store,
To ȝe joyes for the that ever shall last.
Thy God does not this the away to cast,
But to try the as gold is tryed in the fyer;
In the end, premonyshed, shalt have thy desyre.

Take owt of the Gospell ȝat yt the requyre,
Fayth in Chryst Ihesu & grace shall ensewe.
I wyl be thy guyde & pay the thy hyer
For all thy good dylygence & doenge thy dewe.
Gyve eare unto me, Man, & than yt ys trewe,
Thou shalt kyll affectes ȝat by lust in the reygne
And putt Dolor & Mysery & Envy to payne.

Theis armors ar preparyd, yf thou wylt turn ageyne
To fyght wyth, take to the, & reach woman the same;
The brest plate of rightousnes Saynte Paul wyll the retayne;
The shylde of faythe to quench, thy fyrye darts to tame;
The hellmett of salvacion the devyles wrath shall lame;
And ȝe sworde of ȝe Spright, which is ȝe worde of God, –
All theis ar nowe the offred to ease thy payne & rodd.

ADAM Oh! prayse to The, Most Holye, ȝat hast with me abode,
In mysery premonyshynge by this Thy Holy Spright
How fele I such great comforte, my syns they be unlode
And layde on Chrystes back, which is my joye and lyght.
This Dolor and this Mysery I fele to me no wight;
No! Deth is overcum by forepredestinacion,
And we attayned wyth Chryst in heavenly consolacion.
Therfor, myne owne swett spous, withouten cavylacion,
Together lett us synge, & lett our hartes reioyse,
& gloryfye ower God wyth mynde, powre & voyse.
                                                    Amen. (lines 123–53)

reform text entitled *Storys and prophesis out of the holy scriptur garnysched with faire ymages and with devoute praiers and thanksgevings unto God*, which was published in Antwerp for the English market in 1535. Finally, as an example of a text aimed at a more popular audience rather than a work of exegesis or devotion, there is the work of William Hunnis, who was one of the gentlemen of the royal chapel. This text, entitled, in an obvious reference to the author, *A hyve full of Hunnye; Contayning the Firste Booke of Moses, called Genesis*, was published in 1578 and consists of a verse rendition of the story, together with marginal notes explaining the true significance of particular incidents.

These different works are strikingly similar in their treatment of the Fall, and especially in their desire to diminish the gender significance of Eve's action. Thus, for example, Hunnis, in following the Biblical story, adds the marginal note to point out that Adam was present when Eve first took the fruit and was therefore associated in the act from the beginning. This point is further elaborated in his description of the responses of Adam and Eve to God. Adam is stated to have sinned by pride before Eve ever gave him the apple to eat. A proud ambition is Eve's fault too, but her later acknowledgement that she was deceived is seen as a partial confession of guilt, whilst Adam persists in his sinful pride and in effect blames God for causing his fall by providing him with Eve. The Fall in this interpretation may not be Adam's sin alone, but his behaviour is seen as more reprehensible.[10]

Bishop Babington is similarly concerned to assert an equality of responsibility, since neither yielding to the persuasions of the serpent nor yielding to Eve is seen as sufficient excuse. However, Babington's main concern lies elsewhere. The Fall demonstrates the devil's practice of attacking people where they are weakest. Satan attacked Adam through Eve because 'he knewe there is no easyer way to deceyve the man then by his wife, the husband yeelding to her often what hee will to none'. Babington does not hesitate to draw the obvious, but notably evenhanded, lesson from this and counsels, 'good wyves will learne by this what they perswade their husbands too, and wise men what they consent unto'. Moreover, he is concerned to broaden the application of the story: the counsel of a friend can be as deceptive as that of a wife. We all have different weaknesses where we need to be on our guard to prevent the devil's entrance: in the case of David, for example, the devil began with adultery and from there was able to bring him to commit murder.[11]

This concept of individual responsibility for the Fall and the need for vigilance against the onslaughts of the devil is, in fact, the key to the

---

[10] W. Hunnis, *A hyve full of Hunnye; Contayning the Firste Booke of Moses, called Genesis* (London, 1578), f. 5r–5v.

[11] G. Babington, *Certaine plaine, briefe and comfortable Notes upon everie Chapter of Genesis* (London, 1592), f. 16v–17r.

interpretation of the story of Adam and Eve in all these texts. All the authors are concerned less with the significance of the Fall in protestant religious doctrine than with the lessons that can be drawn from the story to guide the daily conduct of the individual christian. Thus the burden of the prayer appended to the Bible story in *Storys and prophesis* is that God should give the christian the wisdom to tell good counsel from bad and to be able to recognise the works of the devil. This stress on the individual involvement of Adam and Eve, and on the clear parallels with the dilemmas in the daily lives of contemporary individuals, represents a significant transformation of the view of the Fall and of its gender implications. As Babington's work demonstrates, this new interpretation is still compatible with much of the original stereotype, but the emphasis on individual choice means that the possibility of weakness is no longer automatically linked to the female. Instead, the emphasis is on the vulnerability of mankind as a whole and the difficulty everyone faces in being certain of making the right choice between good and evil.

These new attitudes were not confined to the world of religious texts and, at least by the early seventeenth century, it is clear that they had been adopted in the culture of rural society. A rare survival of a wall painting of Adam and Eve in a farmhouse at Meadle (Buckinghamshire) demonstrates by its crude, and presumably local, composition the percolation of these attitudes (Fig. 42).[12] The painting is a simplified version of John Speed's 'Genealogy', which was commonly bound into copies of the Authorised King James Bible from its first publication until *c.* 1640[13] (Fig. 43), and represents a significant development from the standard pre-Reformation depiction of the scene. At Meadle, as in the 'Genealogy', Adam and Eve stand on either side of the tree, each resting a hand on its trunk as if to associate themselves equally in the trespass. More remarkable is the conspicuous absence of the serpent in the Meadle painting, though it was included in Speed's image, coiled around the tree in the traditional manner. Such a surprising omission can only be deliberate and would seem to imply that Adam and Eve fell through the exercise of their own will rather than as a result of the strength of the devil's power.

The absence of an actively persuading serpent at Meadle is unusual, and reminds us that the gender significance of the serpent needs to be examined more closely. Although the Genesis account does not link the serpent with the

---

[12] Reader, 'Tudor mural paintings in the lesser houses of Buckinghamshire', pl. 23. The painting is dated *c.* 1627(?).

[13] D. K. McColley, *A Gust for Paradise: Milton's Eden and the Visual Arts* (Urbana and Chicago, 1993), p. 58, p. 66 n. 55, fig. 44. McColley suggests that the depiction of Adam and Eve in the Speed Genealogies was 'probably the most familiar image of Adam and Eve in the early seventeenth century'. In 1610 John Speed obtained the right to insert his genealogies into every edition of the Authorised Bible for ten years, and this practice continued until at least 1640.

Figure 42 Domestic wall painting of Adam and Eve *c*. 1627, from The Spring,
Meadle (Bucks.)

devil or Lucifer, this was the standard assumption in the medieval period. It
also became usual to depict the serpent with a human female head, a practice
that has been seen as encapsulating medieval misogyny.[14] Such readings
are, however, oversimplifications, since the initiating power was recognised
as male.[15] The appearance of the serpent with a female head was a tactic
adopted by the male devil in order to secure his aim more easily, and thus a
strategy parallel to his decision to tempt Eve, a member of the weaker sex,
rather than Adam. The choice of the female head for the serpent, and of
Eve as its target, rendered female qualities emblematic of both the temptress
and the easily tempted, or the seducer and the seduced. Consequently, the

[14] Bonnell, 'The serpent with the human head'; H. A. Kelly, 'The metamorphoses of the Eden
serpent during the Middle Ages and Renaissance', *Viator* 2 (1971), 301–327.
[15] Kelly, ibid., 324, points out that in the medieval mystery plays, with the exception of the
Chester cycle, the serpent is addressed as male despite having the face of a virgin.

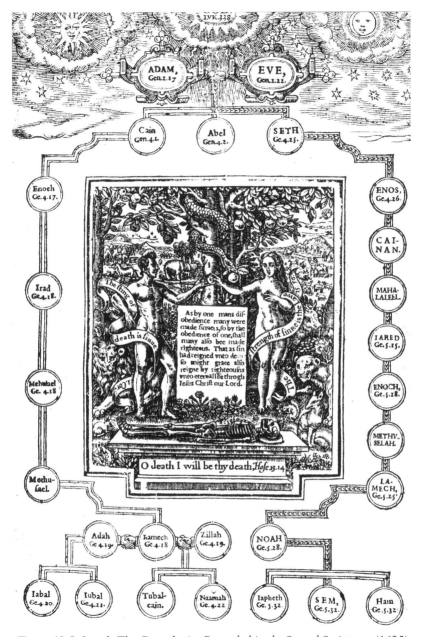

Figure 43 J. Speed, *The Genealogies Recorded in the Sacred Scriptures* (1625)

Figure 44 Illustration for Genesis 3.1 in the Matthew Bible (1537)

decision in most English Reformation Bible illustrations to depict the serpent without human features reduced the emphasis on woman's role as
seducer.

This tendency was developed even further by the decision of the artist at
Meadle to omit the serpent completely, especially since Eve's persuasion of
Adam to eat the fruit was not, and could not easily be, the focus of attention.
The idea of male strength and rationality made it hard for contemporaries
to be as completely comfortable with the idea of Adam seduced by Eve the
temptress as they could be with a female pairing of these roles. Of course, visual representations always left some room for ambiguity here, but Eve's role
as temptress seems understated. The illustration for Genesis 3 used in both
the Coverdale and the Matthew Bibles provides a good example (Fig. 44).
The active figure is Adam himself: he leans forward to take the apple
from Eve, who appears to be engaging the serpent, rather than Adam, in
conversation. Even when, unusually, a protestant English Bible illustration
depicted the serpent with a female head as in the image for Genesis 3 in the
Great Bible, the same assumptions seem to apply (Fig. 45). Although complicated by the simultaneous representation of chronologically distinct parts
of a narrative, the striking feature of this image is that the female-headed
serpent offers Adam the apple directly whilst Eve appears to indicate this
episode to the viewer.[16] Although it is possible that the Great Bible Genesis

---

[16] Adam and Eve are shown covering their nakedness after the Fall whilst the serpent offers
Adam the apple.

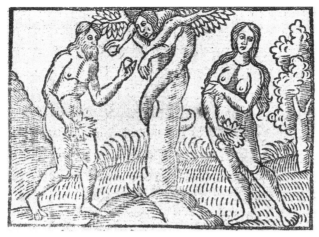

Figure 45 Illustration for Genesis 3.1 in the Great Bible

illustration represents a physical conflation of the roles of the serpent and Eve as seducers, the general trend in visual representations for an English audience seems to have been to reduce the emphasis on Eve as temptress, and it is likely that this illustration would also have been read in that way.

That this was so is also suggested by another unusual Reformation image of Adam and Eve, which includes an anthropomorphic depiction of the serpent: the domestic wall painting recently discovered at Knightstone Manor, Ottery St Mary (Devon) (Figs. 46 and 47).[17] Perhaps the most striking feature of this painting is its depiction of the serpent with a male head. This seems to have been inconceivable as an iconographic solution in medieval art, but in the later sixteenth century some Continental examples are known. This change can be partly explained by a greater concern for Biblical literalism (perhaps bolstered by the fact that the Hebrew for serpent, *nahash*, is a masculine word), and a tight identification of the serpent with Satan. Of greater interest, though, is the gender implication of such a shift, especially since the female-headed serpent is often seen by modern commentators as emblematic of medieval misogyny. Following the interpretation offered above, it is clear that the masculinisation of the serpent serves to further diminish the significance of the Fall as a purveyor of the idea of the female as temptress. The iconography of the whole image also supports this view. The Ottery depiction offers a chronologically condensed image of the Fall: Eve receives the fruit from the serpent, whilst both Adam and Eve cover their nakedness

---

[17] L. Shekede and S. Rickerby, *Knightstone Manor, Ottery St Mary: Report on the Conservation of the Wall Painting* (March 1998). A copy of this report can be consulted at the Wall Painting Archive, The Courtauld Institute, London.

Figure 46 Wall painting of the Fall, Knightstone Manor, Ottery St Mary (Devon)

with fig leaves. In this context Adam's gesture of stretching his hand towards Eve is ambiguous, but it seems significant, in view of the reduced accent on woman as temptress that, as in the Bible illustrations discussed earlier, Eve is not offering the fruit to her husband. The Ottery painting does not make as clear a statement about shared responsibility as the Meadle one does, but both images share a concern to play down the gendered messages of female weakness and culpability.

Figure 47 Detail of the male-headed serpent and of Eve, Knightstone Manor, Ottery St Mary (Devon)

The Ottery wall painting also shows that, despite the virtual disappearance of a human-headed serpent from Reformation visual culture, the concept still persisted.[18] It surfaced both on the wall of a prosperous Devon yeoman's house and in the culture of the radical sects of the mid-seventeenth century. In both contexts the absence of a visually dominant paradigm may have facilitated freedom of interpretation. It is, of course, very unlikely that the owner of Knightstone Manor considered himself to be a Muggletonian, or a member of a similar religious group, but we need to examine how far their views of the story of Adam and Eve could have been compatible. The radical tradition, influenced by the ideas of Jakob Boehme and early Jewish interpretations of the Fall as the sexual seduction of Eve by a fallen angel, produced a clear identification of the serpent as a masculine sexual seducer and saw Eve's persuasion of Adam as a similarly sexual seduction.[19] Such views were clearly compatible with the depiction of the serpent as male at Ottery, but the omission of the parallel seduction of Adam by Eve suggests that the sexual interpretation was not predominant. The function of the male serpent at Ottery was to diminish, not to accentuate, the sexual content of the story, at least in terms of the female's role as temptress. Woman's punishment for the Fall in terms of the pains of childbirth could be seen simply as appropriate to the nature of her vocation, rather than as a precise indicator of the sexual nature of her fall. This was especially the case in Lutheran views, which took the divine command before the Fall to increase and multiply as the key instruction for marriage, and saw procreation as a blessing and the way in which even in a fallen state humans could fulfil God's purpose in making up the number of the elect.[20] Calvin also rejected a sexual Fall, and considered an emphasis on the consciousness of sexuality to be a far too narrow interpretation of its consequences.

The Fall in Elizabethan and Jacobean England was therefore viewed neither as the prime responsibility of a feeble, easily persuaded Eve nor as the lapse of the supposedly responsible patriarchal figure of Adam. The consequence of the move away from these gendered emphases was the weakening

---

[18] Philip Almond notes that the literal sense of the Genesis story became increasingly dominant in the seventeenth century. Thomas Browne thought that the idea that Satan appeared with a virgin's head so that 'thereby he might become more acceptable, and his temptation find the easier entertainment, is a conceit not to be admitted, and the plain and received figure, is with better reason embraced' (*Pseudodoxxia Epidemica* 5.4), but other authors such as John Salkeld and Thomas Milles maintained the old tradition. P. C. Almond, *Adam and Eve in Seventeenth Century Thought* (Cambridge, 1999), p. 184.

[19] Ibid., pp. 173–9. Such conclusions also interconnected with debates about the nature of pre- and post-lapsarian sexuality as analysed in J. G. Turner, *One Flesh: Paradisal Marriage and Sexual Relations in the Age of Milton* (Oxford, 1987), especially Ch. 4, pp. 124–73.

[20] Ibid., pp. 58–9. Luther did, of course, retain the Augustinian distinction between sexuality and lust.

of sexually based explanations. Even in the radical sects where the language of this interpretation persisted most strongly, it could often be transposed into allegorical terms, and for protestants in general the perils of sexual temptation were seen as simply one of many potential human vulnerabilities to sin. The result of these reassessments was to create a situation in which Adam and Eve, like Mary and the saints, were more humanised than their medieval predecessors in the sense of being portrayed as individuals making decisions and mistakes like any other person. As such Eve could be the 'grandmother', as in many prayers written for women to repeat during the pains of childbirth, and every christian could be admonished to be aware of the 'old Adam' within. In both cases the Fall was seen as being both an inheritance and also continually repeated in the life of the individual. Thus, for example, the prayer to be said by a woman in childbirth written by the Puritan Samuel Hieron includes the plea, 'O Lord, I now find by experience the truth and certaintie of thy word, and the smart of ye punishment which thou laidst upon me beeing in the loynes of my Grandmother Eve for my disobedience towards thee.'[21]

However, since such reflections were squarely placed in a framework of a changed situation since the coming of Christ, they need not be seen as a grave cause for despair. That this was so is clearly shown by the inscriptions accompanying the Meadle painting which followed, and slightly condensed, those in Speed's illustration in the Authorised Version of the Bible.[22] These texts place the Fall in the broader context of christian history, juxtaposing Adam's fall with the victory over death offered by Christ. Thus the central panel bears the quotation 'As by the disobedience of one mane many weare made sinners so by the obedience of one shall many be made righteous', and the scrolls twisted round the bodies of Adam and Eve carry the text of 1 Corinthians 15.56, '[The sting of] deth is sinne. The strength of sinne is the lawe.' The lower border carries the text of Hosea 13.14, 'O death I will be thy [death.]'

The same idea was a recurring feature of the title pages of English Bibles.[23] The Coverdale Bible juxtaposes fallen Adam and Eve with the resurrected Christ, and goes on to visually explain that, despite mankind's continued

---

[21] Samuel Hieron, *All the Sermons of Samuel Hieron* (London, 1614), p. 283, cited in Almond, *Adam and Eve*, p. 204.

[22] The artist at Meadle omitted the second sentence in the central panel of Speed's 'Genealogy'. Instead of writing 'That as sin had raigned unto deth so might grace also raigne by ryghteousnes unto eternal life throgh Iesus Christ our Lord', he decided to elaborate the sprigs of flowers at the base of the panel, perhaps as an allusion to transience and mortality.

[23] The exception is the title page of the *Great Bible* (1539), which is dominated by the handing down of the Word of God from the King to his subjects and their approving cries of 'God Save the Kynge' and 'Vivat Rex'.

disobedience in not following the Mosaic law which prompted Esdra's rebuke, the vernacular gospel is offered by God for the benefit of all who will follow and apply it to their own lives. The Matthew Bible title page, which was based more closely on Lutheran Law and Gospel iconography, develops the same theme more elaborately, setting up a series of contrasts between the giving of the Ten Commandments and the Incarnation of Christ, the Fall and the Crucifixion, Death and Christ's Resurrection, which are divided by a tree in full leaf on the side of the gospel and in winter on the side of the Law (Fig. 41). Such illustrations may not quite fit the idea of a 'fortunate Fall', but they do remind the viewer that the coming of Christ has mitigated the consequences of the Fall of mankind's first parents. This is spelled out even more explicitly in the frontispiece to Genesis in the Geneva Bible (Fig. 48). Eve and Adam stand some distance away from the tree, in a paradise teeming with animals, and hold explanatory scrolls. Those in their left hands, which also hold an apple, explain the Fall: 'Desire to knowe hath wrought our woe / By tasting this th'exile of blisse.' The scrolls held in their right hands curl heavenwards and announce, 'By promis made restord we be / to pleasures of eternity'. Finally, just in case the connection is not clear, the words printed across the breasts of Adam and Eve explain that this is 'through faith in Christs death'.

This stress on viewing the Fall in the context of a Christocentric view of christian history does not serve to exonerate Eve by emphasising the Adam–Christ antithesis. Instead, it allows the gender implications of the scene to be overridden by directing attention to the relationship between fallen humanity and Christ. Perhaps surprisingly, given the protestant emphasis on the wretchedness of sinful mankind, it admits the possibility of seeing the Fall as a *felix culpa*.[24] For Baxter, if not for all seventeenth-century commentators, it was possible to maintain the idea of a fortunate Fall. As he argued, 'If Man had kept his first Rest in Paradise, God had not had

---

[24] McColley argues against this possibility, but this seems to be mainly due to her adoption of a narrower chronological focus. When the immediate pre- and post-lapsarian positions are compared, ideas of *felix culpa* necessarily become harder to sustain than is the case when a Christocentric framework is in mind. She also comments (*A Gust for Paradise*, p. 160) that 'Protestant Bible illustrations rarely show the Fall as fortunate even in a teleological sense. Title pages changed to avoid the implication; that of the 1535 English [Coverdale] Bible counterposes the Fall to the Resurrection, but even this hint of a *felix culpa* was absent from the 1537 edition [Matthew Bible], where the Fall is paired with the Crucifixion and Death with the Resurrection. Either pairing provides a redemptive view, but the latter treats the Fall as the cause of pain to humanity and suffering to Christ.' This view ignores the composite impact of the Matthew Bible's title page in favour of a narrower partial pairing which seems inappropriate, and the rejection of a sense of optimistic improvement in the possibilities open to mankind with the coming of Christ goes against the iconography of the living and dead tree and the advice being offered to the representative christian seated at its roots (ibid., p. 154ff).

Figure 48 Geneva Bible, title page of Book of Genesis (1583)

opportunity to manifest that far greater Love to the World in the giving of
his Son. If Man had not fallen into the depth of misery, Christ had not come
down from the height of Glory, nor died, nor risen, nor been believed on in
the World.' Without the Fall there would have been no redemption in Christ,
and the redeemed world is better than man's existence in paradise.[25]

Baxter's argument shows the possibility of celebrating the Fall within a
protestant Christocentric understanding. This differed from the medieval
position. There is a parallel for ideas of the Fall as a *felix culpa* in pre-
Reformation elaborations of the Eve–Mary antithesis, but the nature of late
medieval Christocentric piety, which emphasised empathy with Christ's suffering for mankind's fault and continued faults, made it harder for the Fall to
be hailed as beneficial and desirable. For Baxter the context was different. In
the Reformation, devotion to the passion of Christ was more subdued. There
was more emphasis on Mary Magdalen's agonies of belief than on imagining
the wounds, even if there were overlaps and continuity. This different set of
Christocentric priorities facilitates the development of the idea that the Fall
is beneficial because it brings Christ and, most importantly, the possibility of
faith and belief. Implicit here is the idea that the knowledge and realisation of
good and evil which was acquired at the Fall created an understanding of God
which, although imperfect, can be seen as in some ways superior to the Edenic
position, since it contains awareness, realisation and active faith. Or, in
the sense of the Meadle text, it allows disobedience to be replaced by
obedience.

This treatment of the Fall also meant that other aspects of the model
of Eve could have more positive prominence, since she was less tainted
than Eileen Power's formulation might lead us to expect by responsibility for the Fall. In particular, this meant that the relationship of Eve and
Adam could be unproblematically incorporated into the image and eulogy of
the godly marriage and household. Of course, this was not entirely new. The
idea that the creation of Eve as Adam's helpmeet from a bone from his
side (rather than his head or his foot) demonstrated the appropriate role of
the wife as companion was not an innovation. But it was also accompanied
by arguments designed to place Eve's significance in the life of the aspiring
godly woman rather than in the cycle of christian history. Thus, Henry Smith
in his *Preparative to mariage* (1591) develops 1 Timothy 2.15 to argue that
the promise that the woman who bears children and continues in faith and
patience will be saved turns Eve's curse of pain in childbirth into a blessing.
Patterning oneself on Eve, and acknowledging her as one's 'grandmother',
could be envisaged as parallel to the emulation of the series of models of

---

[25] Richard Baxter, *The Saints Everlasting Rest* cited in Almond, *Adam and Eve*, pp. 197–8.

godly women.[26] Eve, like Bathsheba, may not have been as unproblematic as Susanna as a name to give one's daughter, but despite their 'fall' both could be exemplars of the godly wife.

In this framework the Eve who span and bore children while Adam delved was as important as the Eve created as Adam's helpmeet and as the first woman to be joined in matrimony according to God's holy ordinance. Those who bewail early modern authors' inconsistency in arguing for the nature of women by an indiscriminate fusion of pre- and post-lapsarian Biblical evidence are mistaken in seeing this simply as intellectual sloppiness.[27] Rather, it has to be understood in terms of a conception of scripture as ongoing revelation in which the Fall and the crucifixion are important turning points which do not fundamentally revise the nature of mankind, but instead change the terms on which it is possible for humans to relate to God. The Fall, and the role of Adam and Eve within it, are emblematic of human frailty, but are less significant in defining it than is often assumed when they are considered in isolation. As a consequence, although it would be naive to envisage a response to the Fall devoid of gendered associations, the contribution of the protestant Reformation was to make these more muted, and especially to discard ideas of the active female sexual seducer, in favour of seeing both Adam and Eve as representative vulnerable christians. Reformation reinterpretations rendered the distance between Eve and Mary, or sinner and saint, much closer than in medieval conceptions, and offered a much more realistic and acceptable understanding of the range of human possibilities.

---

[26] Henry Smith, *Preparative to mariage The summe where of was spoken at a contract, and inlarged after* (London, 1591), pp. 7–8. A similar view can be found in Latimer's 'Last Sermon preached before Edward VI' (1550): 'Yes, she was now a good woman: when she believed the serpent, she was not good. But now she had repented that deed, and had taken hold of the promise of God . . . and was now a good woman, and a godly woman.' Corrie (ed.), *Sermons by Hugh Latimer*, pp. 242–3.

[27] Turner, *One Flesh*, pp. 3, 118–19.

13

Godly marriage

That which maketh a wives yoake heavy and hard, is an husbands abuse of his authority: and more pressing his wives dutie, than performing his owne: which is directly contrary to the Apostles rule ... if both of them be conscionable and carefull to performe theire owne duty, the matrimoniall yoke will so equally lie on both their necks as the wife will be no more pinched therewith then the husband, but that it will be like Christs spirituall yoke, *light* and *easie*: and that on the other side it may be manifest that there is commonly as much failing by husbands in their duties, as by wives in theirs. (William Gouge, *Of Domesticall Duties*, 1622, 4–4v.)

Clarifying his thoughts for the printed edition of the sermons delivered to his parishioners at Blackfriars, the preacher William Gouge responded directly to the protests of the female members of his congregation who had been outraged by his depiction of the extent of women's subjection to their husbands. In particular, in Gouge's interpretation, these women had been appalled by the stipulation of absolute obedience to the husband's 'uttermost' demands, and the prohibition on alienating the family's common goods without, or against, his consent. Whether Gouge had in fact been so unguarded in his preaching cannot now be known, but this well-known confrontation of female voices with one of the most influential of puritan preachers and authors of advice literature captures the vibrancy of early modern debate, and should also remind us of the dangers inherent in compartmentalising too sharply lived experience and the literature of religious aspiration. Not only were the comments of such authors informed by their own experiences of married life, but their guidance mattered to many, although of course not all, of their contemporaries.

The mining of such texts by historians of women, feminism or gender for suitable extracts and apposite quotations to include in anthologies of early modern writing about women has all too often perpetuated the distorted view in Gouge's account of the reaction of the women of Blackfriars to his sermons. These misunderstandings have two main causes: a misinterpretation of the concept of subjection, which had different and less negative resonances in the early modern period than in the language of modern feminism and critiques of patriarchy; and a refusal to take the deliberate plural in Gouge's title seriously as an indicator of the agenda of early modern discussions. 'Domesticall Duties' are the duties of the wife *and* of the husband. As Gouge told his readers, and probably also his hearers, 'It is a generall mutuall dutie appertaining to all Christians, to submit themselves one to another.'[1] Such mutual subjection did not dissolve hierarchy. Gouge, like the rest of his contemporaries, saw hierarchy as absolutely essential for the well ordering of the family as much as of the state. Rather, mutual subjection involved distinguishing between two types of subjection: subjection of reverence and subjection of service. The former entails the appropriate respect shown by an inferior to a superior; the latter 'is that whereby one in his place is ready to doe what good he can to another. This is common to all christians: a dutie which even superiors owe to inferiors.'[2] In this framework, criticism of the inconsistency of early modern metaphors of the couple as yoke fellows, or as rowers in the same boat, misses the point. The inclusion of a gendered hierarchy of strength and authority does not make the boats and oxen 'go around in circles' as Gowing suggests.[3] Rather, the mutuality of subjection, and the gendered difficulties of both kinds of subjection, mean that equal 'strength' is required by both yoke fellows, albeit partly of a different nature, so that the yoke of marriage can be *'light* and *easie'*.

Discussing the subjection of wives to their husbands, Gouge describes willing subjection as 'salt to season every duty'.[4] This homely image of preservative and flavouring brings out clearly the essential, sustaining nature of wifely subjection in marriage. For Gouge 'subjection is no servitude', contrary to the view of many wives who have been corrupted and tainted by ambition. Subjection does not give the husband absolute authority, and therefore does not make the wife a slave. Rather, it is a requirement established by God and has the beneficial consequence of preventing 'womanish weaknesse' leading to another fall.[5] Wifely subjection is devised by God for the wife's own good, rather than for her husband's benefit, and should not be exploited by him. Indeed, the concept of 'subjection of service' suggests that the subjection of a wife to a husband should be viewed by him as a heavy and difficult responsibility.

To the modern reader, Gouge's definition of the husband's *duty* as that of love reads rather awkwardly, especially when directly contrasted with the wife's duty of obedience. But this is a direct rendition of Colossians 3.18–19, and elsewhere in his text Gouge softens this contrast. Love is required of the wife as well as the husband since 'under *love* all other duties are comprised'

---

[1] Gouge, *Of Domesticall Duties*, B2.   [2] Ibid., B3.
[3] L. Gowing, *Domestic Dangers: Women, Words and Sex in Early Modern London* (Oxford, 1996), p. 188.
[4] Gouge, *Of Domesticall Duties*, p. 271.   [5] Ibid.

and 'without it no duty can be well performed'.[6] Love as the distinctive duty of husbands is not simply sexual attraction or affection, but represents the husband's willingness to bear with the weaknesses of his wife, which are assumed to be inherent in her female nature. It is therefore appropriate that the same images of salt and seasoning should be applied to the husband's love for his wife as to the wife's willing subjection. Both are viewed as difficult, but essential, tasks in which perfunctory performance is inadequate. It is also appropriate that in discussing the husband's duty of love Gouge can switch from salt to sugar, thus offering a more attractive interpretation of love than of subjection. Love sweetens the husband's, otherwise onerous, task of offering guidance and of responding with forbearance to his wife.

The effective performance of the mutual duties of married partners makes them not only comfortable yoke fellows, but also godly exemplars to other members of the household. Breach of duty thus has wider ramifications than simply wronging the other spouse, since it also sets a poor example and thus encourages children and servants to sin. This 'double fault' represents the failure of the family as the 'seminary of the Church and Commonwealth'.[7] In such a conception the correct rowing of the marital boat takes on a heightened importance in which equal stress must be laid upon the correct performance of the duties of both the husband and the wife. The essential willingness of the wife's subjection to her husband is threatened if he does not carry out his duties appropriately. Similarly, wilful withdrawal of the duties of subjection by the wife encourages the husband to exceed his authority. Given contemporary assumptions of exemplary hierarchy, the stability of family and society depends primarily upon the success of this core relationship.

Fear of instability explains the concern in advice literature for care in choosing a marriage partner, and the insistence on parity of piety, wealth, status and age as safeguards against dissension. Of course, even if they were followed, such counsels could only mitigate the widest causes of disagreement. Practical concerns therefore served to reduce ideas of conjugal equality and to make scriptural arguments for a hierarchy of authority within the marriage more attractive. This search for harmony also meant that the potentially radical implications of parity had to be qualified with ideas of complementarity. The husband was the head of the wife, and Eve drawn from Adam's rib was his 'helpmeet'. Favourite New Testament texts reinforced this position, figuring the husband as Christ and his bride as the Church. Nevertheless, although commentators agreed that in general the nature of men was such that they were likely to possess judgement and understanding superior to

[6] Ibid., p. 227.   [7] Ibid., pp. 20, 17.

that of women, they acknowledged that this was not always the case. Men who surrendered their better judgement to the temptations of drink or illicit sex could forfeit their authority, and even amongst the most godly the flexibility of scriptural interpretation was such that conflicts of conscience between spouses were possible.

The clearest case for displacing male authority was economic. When the actions of the husband appeared to undermine the economic resources of the household, changing the hierarchy of authority to preserve the household could be envisaged. In response to the husband's dissipation of the family's goods by drinking, dicing or card playing, there was a moral consensus which could justify the wife assuming authority. The husband, by neglecting his duty to maintain his wife and family as best he could, forfeited the right to manage the family resources.[8] The ability of the wife to take over this task was facilitated by her existing role as joint governor and manager of the female sphere of the household economy, and was underpinned by concerns about rising poor-rate costs. However, even if such conduct could justify the wife's assumption of practical authority, Gouge wished to maintain that she should still reverence her husband as her superior. In answer to the question, 'But what if a man of lewd and beastly conditions, as a drunkard, a glutton, a profane swaggerer, an impious swearer, and blasphemer, be maried to a wise, sober, religious Matron, must she account him her superior and worthy of an husbands honour?', he ruled, 'Surely shee must.'[9]

Even with this fundamental qualification, other commentators were unwilling to go as far as Gouge in advocating a change in practical authority where the husband was ineffective. R. C. saw the complementary economic roles of husband and wife as immutable. 'The dutie of the husband is to get goods; and of the wife to gather them together, and save them.'[10] The difficulties of the wife who has 'an idle and unthrifty husband' are not minimised: it is as if she 'draweth a Carte havie loden, through a sandy way without a horse'. But the solution envisaged, even when the husband is also an alehouse haunter, is not for the wife to take over the husband's economic duties. Instead, her only remedy is patience and discreet admonition. This, though, is due to a strong attachment to the gendered nature of economic roles, rather than a specific consequence of the wife's duty of subjection. The husband with 'a prodigall and slouthfull wife' 'casteth his labours into a bottomles sacke', but patience and discreet admonition are similarly seen as the only appropriate response.[11]

[8] Ibid., p. 294.   [9] Ibid., p. 275.
[10] R. C., *A Godly Forme of Household Government: For the ordering of private families according to the direction of Gods word* (London, 1603), p. 170.
[11] Ibid., p. 187.

For the authors of godly advice literature, economic relationships were the least of their concerns. Other areas in which male authority could be cast in doubt were more problematic, but they were not completely avoided. According to Davies, there was a 'lack of guidance' in puritan texts on how to reconcile the reciprocal duty of spouses to care for each other's salvation with the demand of wifely obedience, which she sees as the total subordination of the wife's mind and judgement.[12] But this overstates the case. It is not true to say that authors such as Gouge made no attempt to reconcile the two aspects, or to offer guidance, even if their success in doing so may have been limited. It is also questionable whether these authors saw wifely obedience as a total subordination of mind and judgement. Even Whately's image of the wife as a well-broken horse need not imply this: the well-broken horse responds to being well ridden, but may respond differently to a less accomplished rider.[13] However, Davies's surprise that the resolution of crises of conscience does not figure more prominently in these discussions is apposite since, as she reminds us, Reformation ideas increasingly made this a real practical problem for many. Moreover, spiritual support formed the foundation of the ideology of the *godly* household, and authors, such as Gouge, maintained that the duty of spouses to edify each other spiritually was the best use of the marriage bond.[14]

Nevertheless, spiritual support did not define marriage. However much Puritan commentators emphasised its importance, the fundamental definition of the purposes for which marriage was ordained remained sexual. There may have been an increased stress on companionship, alongside procreation and the avoidance of fornication, but such companionship or mutual support was not envisaged as primarily spiritual. Indeed, despite Gouge's opinion that spiritual edification was the best use of the marriage bond, this aspect is not referred to directly in his discussion of the mutual aid which was the third reason for which marriage was prescribed.[15] The ill-defined place of spiritual support in the understanding of the divine nature of marriage highlights the difficulty of authors in advising couples how to proceed when religious conscience appeared to conflict with domestic authority. Their problem here was greater than in the economic sphere. The improvident spouse neglected the duty of maintenance, but did not threaten the existence of the marriage in principle. However, deviation from true religion could be defined

---

[12] Davies, 'Continuity and change in literary advice on marriage'.

[13] W. Whately, *A Bride-Bush or A Wedding Sermon* (London, 1617), p. 43. In using the image of the wife as a well-broken horse, Whately makes it clear that she should only obey instructions which do not involve disobeying God. The imagery of horse and rider was a common feature of medieval body and soul dialogues, and was similarly understood in terms of mutual dependence and common attraction: Matsuda, *Death and Purgatory in Middle English Didactic Poetry*, p. 141.

[14] Gouge, *Of Domesticall Duties*, p. 242.   [15] Ibid., pp. 211–12.

as spiritual adultery, which, like physical adultery, could lead to divorce or separation.

The initial solution to this problem was therefore to stress that there should be 'an especiall respect to parity in piety' in choosing a marriage partner, but this, as with all other demands for parity in the nature of spouses, only reduced the problem and did not remove it. This requirement also fitted awkwardly with views of gender hierarchy in marriage, and produced inconsistent statements which exposed the tangle of assumptions. Thus, immediately after asserting the need for parity in piety, Gouge declares that this applies '*especially* [my emphasis] [to] females, because they are in subjection to their husbands'.[16] Since parity of piety was the essential underpinning of mutual spiritual support, this cannot be more necessary for one sex than for the other, but Gouge appears to be trying to emphasise the need to safeguard women as obedient wives from the possibility of having to follow their less well-qualified husbands in matters of religion. A similar concern can be seen in the next sentence when he turns his attention to men: 'Yet ought not men to be carelesse herein: for wives, if the feare of God possesse not their hearts, though they be the weaker vessels, doe oft make their husbands plaine vassals to them'.[17] Parity of piety was an elusive ideal, and in practice the idea of mutual support was often vitiated by the fact that the partner with the greatest authority or influence was not always spiritually superior. The recognition that true religion would not necessarily triumph, and that the battle between good and bad influences was unequal and unpredictable, permeated all discussions of the godly couple. In addition to the realisation that superior godliness and superior authority did not always coincide, commentators also had to reckon with the strong possibility that individuals would yield to baser desires.

The example of conversion presented these issues in the starkest form. Although the sanctification of the unbelieving spouse by the believer was a possibility, Gouge argued that this did not sanction marriage with an unbeliever, even though it did mean that a marriage could not be broken by the subsequent conversion of one of the spouses to a different religious position.[18] Henry Smith, in his *Preparative to mariage* (1591), presented the case more starkly: one's marriage partner is like Christ's spouse and therefore cannot be a harlot, heretic or atheist. Seeking the hand of such a person in marriage was equivalent to having recourse to the assistance of witches. In both cases, the individual was guilty of seeking evil before good.[19] Eschewing vivid parallels with the seeking out of witches, Gouge employed more homely metaphors to support his case and to explain why it was wrong to

---

[16] Ibid., pp. 191–2.   [17] Ibid., pp. 192–3.   [18] Ibid., p. 193.
[19] Smith, *Preparative to mariage*, p. 51.

marry an unbeliever on the pretext of hoping to convert him or her. Reminding his readers that evil was of a more infectious nature than good, he described how 'A little sowre leaven will soon make a great batch of dough sowre: but a great deal of sweet dough will not sweeten a little leven', and concluded that 'It is therefore an unwarrantable pretext for any to marie one of a contrary religion or disposition, on hope to convert them.' Conversion was a divine, not a human, work, and God's blessing for conversion was unlikely to be forthcoming when individuals disregarded God's instruction by marrying with an unbeliever.[20]

The incompatibility of the believer and unbeliever as marriage partners was a logical consequence of the stress on godly marriage and the mutual spiritual support of man and wife. As Henry Smith remarked, 'How should my marriage speede well, when I marrie to one to whome I may not say *Godspeede*, because she is none of Gods friendes? Doth not hee marrie with the Devill, which marrieth with the tempter?' As the identification of the unbelieving spouse with the devil here suggests, the risk of the influence of evil was great even for the most godly. Since Solomon turned into an idolater under the influence of his idolatrous concubines, no godly person can be sure that they will not be seduced 'where such a Cedar fell'.[21] This emphasis on the vulnerability of the godly to the evil influence of a spouse did, however, make it more difficult to sustain the view that religious apostasy during marriage did not dissolve the union, or at least sanction separation. After all, it was easy to propose that spiritual adultery was a graver offence than physical adultery, for which divorce could be permitted. As Smith remarked, 'If adulterie may separate marriage, shal not idolatry hinder marriage which is worse than it?'[22]

The awkwardness of this position was met by evasion. Gouge poses the question whether 'the professor of the true religion may depart from the Infidell or Idolater?', and gives a clearly negative answer based on 1 Corinthians 7.12–14 and 1 Peter 3.1.[23] This involves a much more optimistic assessment of the possibility of the unbelieving spouse being sanctified by the believer than he had offered when discussing the choice of marriage partner. Moreover, the clarity of this conclusion is only reached by not considering the verses from 1 Corinthians which immediately follow those cited. Verse 15 does not demand the separation of the couple, but it does allow the unbeliever to leave, and states that if he or she does so then the believer is no longer bound to the marriage. In omitting this possibility, Gouge appears to be taking extensive liberties in his interpretation of Corinthians. However,

---

[20] Gouge, *Of Domesticall Duties*, p. 194. The image of the leaven is based on 1 Corinthians 5.6–8.
[21] Smith, *Preparative to mariage*, pp. 49–50.   [22] Ibid., p. 49.
[23] Gouge, *Of Domesticall Duties*, p. 197.

since the text does not overtly give the believer the same right of departure as the unbeliever, this can be seen as a judicious omission by a preacher concerned to limit opportunities for divorce or marital separation.[24] Verse 16 stresses that individuals cannot know whether they will be able to save their spouses, and thus returns to arguments used by Gouge to declare that marriage with an unbeliever is against God's will. Its position in the Corinthians chapter suggests the more obvious reading that it is meant to justify separation when the religious beliefs of the couple are incompatible. For Gouge, although conversion was a divine work and individuals should not presume that they would be able to effect it, it remained the duty of spouses to cohabit and, as part of the duty of mutual care for each other's salvation, to try to win the unbeliever for the faith.

It also remained the wife's duty to be in subjection to her unbelieving husband, since Peter had told christian wives to remain in subjection to their infidel husbands (1 Peter 3.1–2). For Gouge this instruction was to be explained in the same way as the wife's continued duty of subjection to a drunken, gluttonous or blaspheming husband:

> For the evill quality and disposition of his heart and life, doth not deprive a man of that civill honour which God hath given unto him. Though an husband in regard of evill qualities may carry the Image of the divell, yet in regard of his place and office, he beareth the Image of God: so doe Magistrates in the Common-wealth, Ministers in the Church, Parents and Masters in the Family.'[25]

The idea of the king's two bodies was as problematic in the sphere of godly marriage as in that of the state, since in both contexts obedience was only to be expected in accordance with the word of God. Gouge's explanation that 'spirituall blindnesse disableth not from civill government' offers a surprisingly secular reading of the husband's authority, and highlights the extent to which the need to maintain subjection had pushed him into a difficult position.[26]

It is particularly hard to see how this relates to the idea that the wife's obedience was limited by her obedience to Christ, her husband in heaven. However, whilst warning wives that they should fear offending Christ more than they feared offending their earthly husbands, Gouge is certain that even

---

[24] Nicolas Byfield, commenting on this verse, drew a similar conclusion. The wilful departure of the infidel was not a case of divorce but of nullity, since the believer did not put away the unbeliever. Moreover, to shore up the interpretation of this verse in the interests of contemporary social stability, Byfield added that it was important to realise to what kind of unbeliever this verse referred: 'not everie wicked man or woman, nor everie person that professeth a false religion, but such an unbeleever as is a profest enemie to the Name of Christ.' N. Byfield, *A Commentary upon the first three chapters of the first Epistle generall of St. Peter* (London, 1637), p. 637.

[25] Gouge, *Of Domesticall Duties*, p. 275.   [26] Ibid., p. 290.

if the husband is an enemy of Christ, subjection should be yielded to him as
to Christ himself 'because in his office he is in Christ's stead, though in his
heart an enemy'. It is a cross to have a bad husband, but to be a bad wife is
a sin. This stance did have a practical clarity to commend it. A wife's willing
subjection should not be measured out according to her assessment of her
husband's failings.[27] After all, as Gouge realised, that might mean that she
offered no subjection at all.[28] Subjection was based on reciprocity, but not
necessarily in equal measure. Each partner was to take especial care over
their own duties, since

> It is more acceptable before God and more commendable before men to doe duty
> than to exact duty. As in matters of free charity, so also of bounden duty. *It is more
> blessed to give than to receive.* In particular, it is better for an husband to bee a good
> husband, then to have a good wife: so for a wife. To have others faile in duty to us,
> may be an heavy crosse; for us to faile in our duty to others, is a fearefull curse.[29]

In contrast to Gouge's view, Whately in his *Bride-Bush* (1617) envisaged the
possibility that wilful desertion by the unbeliever (1 Corinthians 7.15) dissolved the marriage. Nevertheless, this did not license the believer to take the
initiative. The departure of the unbeliever was unlawful and was therefore
not an option available to the believer. For Whately, as for many of his contemporaries, adultery was the only justifiable, and scripturally sanctioned,
reason for leaving one's spouse. Even in this form, the case for desertion on
religious grounds was contentious, and in the advertisement to the reader
prefacing *A Care-Cloth or the Cumbers and Troubles of Marriage* (1624),
Whately, the 'roaring boy of Banbury', felt obliged to retract his argument
that wilful desertion dissolved matrimony. That it was necessary to do so
shows the degree of sensitivity towards any extension of the grounds for
dissolving marriage. It may also suggest that the need to separate religious
position from allegiance to hierarchy (as also manifested in the Crown's
treatment of catholics) could be more powerful than the demands for mutual spiritual edification and parity of piety. It is thus less surprising that
the more radical arguments for the dissolution of marriage should have been
proposed by a preacher who also, rather optimistically, advocated the ability
of spouses to solve all marital difficulties by merely praying together. Mutual
spiritual support implied the use of prayer, but its effectiveness in securing
marital harmony obviously required a close similarity in piety which would
be severely undermined by the conversion of one partner to another faith.
Whately had no place for Gouge's distinctions between doing and exacting

---

[27] Ibid., p. 334: 'Let wives therefore remove their eyes from the disposition of their husbands
person, to the condition of his place: and by vertue thereof, seeing he beareth Christs image,
be subject to him as unto Christ.'
[28] Ibid., p. 131.   [29] Ibid., pp. 130–1.

duty: the heavy cross and the curse both implied the absence of effective mutual spiritual support.

In issues of smaller matters of conscience, which fell short of complete apostasy, commentators followed the same principles, since these examples similarly entailed one party maintaining a position against God's will. Such discussions, however, highlighted the gender dimension more clearly. Although historians have focussed on cases where the wife's conscientious interpretation was pitted against that of her husband, and was complicated by her acknowledgement of her religiously based duty of obedience to him (e.g. Lake's discussion of Mrs Ratcliffe's dress),[30] authors of advice literature placed the burden of judgement in matters of conscience on both partners. The husband had a duty of spiritual nurture and training and was to cultivate his wife so that she might grow into a fruitful vine.[31] But, as Nicholas Byfield explained, this did not mean that the wife's conscience was completely subordinate to that of her husband

in matters of her soul and religion where his will is contrary to God's will... The unbeleeving husband must not compell the beleeving wife to change her religion, or to neglect the meanes of her salvation. And againe, she is not so subject but she may admonish and advise her husband with certaine cautions, as, if she be sure the thing she speakes against be sinfull and hurtfull: and withall that she speake without passion or contempt, with reverence, and without frowardnesse or imperiousnesse.[32]

Alongside this even-handed recognition of responsibility inherent in a notion of mutual support, there was however a strong current which mistrusted women's interpretation, questioned the reliability of women's judgement, and cautioned against their undue influence. This mistrust gained polemical strength, if not entirely consistent support, by association with the scriptural prohibition of women speaking in church, despite the role of the godly wife as an exemplar. Thus Gervase Markham in his *The English Huswife* (1615) could maintain that it was the wife's responsibility to urge her family to 'an upright and sincere religion' through her example, but that she should not 'utter forth that violence of spirit which many of our (vainely accounted pure) women do, drawing a contempt upon the ordinary Ministrie, and thinking nothing lawefull but the fantazies of their owne inventions, usurping to themselves a power of preaching and interpreting the holy word, to which

[30] Lake, 'Female piety and personal potency', 151.
[31] Smith, *Preparative to mariage*, pp. 68–9: 'when he takes a wife he takes a Vineyard, not grapes, but a vineyard to bear him grapes: therefore he must sow it and dresse it, and water it, and fence it, and think it a good vineyard if at last it bring forth grapes. So hee must not looke to finde a wife without a fault, but think that she is comitted to him to reclaime her from her faults; for all are defectives: and if he finde the Proverbe true, that in space commeth grace, hee must reioyce as much at his wife when she mendeth, as the Husbandman reioyceth when his Vineyard beginneth to fructifie.'
[32] Byfield, *A Commentary upon the three first chapters*, pp. 582–3.

onely they ought to be but hearers and beleevers.' Brathwait concurred, and
inveighed against women commenting on scripture: 'the strange opinions of
Shee-clarkes, which, as they understand them not themselves, so they labour
to intangle others of equall understanding to themselves'. Both cases rested
on an elaboration of scripture. As Brathwait summarised: 'Women as they
are to be no speakers in the Church so neither are they to be disputers of
controversies of the Church.'[33]

Nevertheless, it was also recognised that a wife's scruples of conscience
could be justified, and some commentators attempted to define what scruples
were admissible against the husband's authority. A clear attempt to lay down
some guidelines can be found in Whately's *Bride-Bush*. The author argues
that if a wife pretends conscience, but cannot show any reason for this in
the Word of God, then she is to be persuaded by her husband to abandon
her obstinacy. However,

> when shee grounds upon the word of God, though mis-interpreted and mistaken,
> she must be resolved and not compelled. Not every scruple of conscience makes a
> thing sin to a man, but that which is grounded upon God's Word, by which alone
> conscience must be informed and guided: which when it is, though it bee mis-informed
> through want of iudgement, yet it retaines its owne authority; and then to enforce
> the wife against it were to force her to sinne, the most unrighteous thing that can
> be in a Governour. None is Lord, but onely the Lord of Heaven and earth. Bee not
> therefore so unrighteous towards thy wife, as to urge her either to displease G O D,
> or her conscience leaning on his word.[34]

The husband, as governor, had to tread a fine line in seeking to guide his
wife while not forcing her to sin.

From this perspective Gouge's opinion that although 'wives may most
complaine of their burden, because it is a *Subjection*, whereunto by nature
we are all loath to yeeld: yet I am sure that the heaviest burden is laid
upon the husband's shoulders: and much more easie it is to perform the
part of a good wife, then of a good husband' makes sense.[35] Authority
is harder to maintain than subjection, because it requires a more careful
exercise of judgement. The wife might find the duty of reverence hard to
square with the behaviour of her husband, but it was at least clear what she
was supposed to do. As Gataker put it, the difference between a wife and a
wife indeed was that the latter acknowledged her subjection to her husband,
and was a help and a comfort to him.[36] Obedience to some commands,

---

[33] Cited in A. R. Jones, 'Nets and bridles: early modern conduct books and sixteenth-century
women's lyrics,' in N. Armstrong and L. Tannenhouse (eds.), *The Ideology of Conduct:
Essays on literature and the history of sexuality* (New York and London, 1987), pp. 60–1.
[34] Whately, *A Bride-Bush*, p. 34.   [35] Gouge, *Of Domesticall Duties*, p. 424.
[36] T. Gataker, *A Good Wife Gods Gift and A Wife Indeed. Two Marriage Sermons* (London,
1623), *A Wife Indeed*, pp. 6–16.

such as to attend mass or stage plays, to sell with false measures, and to commit whoredom, was forbidden, but the wife was still to remain subject to the husband who demanded such things and stood in Christ's stead.[37] For the husband, the demand that the exercise of authority should be tempered with love was less easily measured. All authors were clear that overmuch insistence on his authority rendered a man a tyrant rather than a husband. More subtly, Gouge developed the idea of authority as a sword: in the hands of the swaggerer it was drawn from its sheath upon the slightest cause, and soon failed to make a serious impression. Infrequent use kept the blade sharp and effective, but even on these occasions the husband was counselled 'for loves sake' to entreat his wife to amend her behaviour rather than to draw his sword. At the same time, the husband was warned not to be so feeble and ineffective that he forfeited his authority and failed to fulfil his duty.[38]

Not only was it hard to get the balance right, but the husband's responsibility was great. In reminding the husband that even if his wife was 'a very lewd and wicked woman' he should still consider her as the best wife, Gouge offered two explanations:

It may be shee was good enough when first she was brought to thee, but thou by thine evill example, or negligent government, or hard usage, hast made her as bad as she is. Which if it be so then she is to be considered not as thou hast marr'd her, but as thou diddest mary her. Alternatively she may have been provided by God not for thine ease and quiet, yet for triall of thy wisedome and patience: and so as a schoole of vertue she may be unto thee. As a skilfull pilots sufficiency is tried & knowne by tempestuous seas, so a man's wisedome by a troublesome wife.

Moreover, even in this case the husband was thought to have brought this trial of his virtue upon himself: such a wife was a punishment for former sins or a means to dissuade him from following his sinful inclinations.[39] In contrast, the wife was not considered to be responsible for her husband's conduct, despite the duty of mutual support and correction of faults and the possibility that the wife might exercise undue influence over her husband, as Eve did over Adam. This appears inconsistent, but only if we fail to understand Gouge's distinction between 'common mutuall duties' and specific principal duties, which underpins the structure of his text. The common mutual duties described in the second treatise blur the gender roles, but each sex is held accountable for the performance of its specific principal duty of subjection or love, as outlined in the third and fourth treatises. In setting these

---

[37] Gouge, *Of Domesticall Duties*, p. 332. 'If an Husband shall command his Wife to go to Masse, to a Stage play, to play at Dice, to prostitute her body to uncleannesse, to go garishly and whorishly attired, to sell by scant weights, short measures, or the like, she ought not to do so.'

[38] Ibid., pp. 382–3.   [39] Ibid., pp. 363–4.

ideals, Gouge, as a married man himself, was well aware that he was offering
a counsel of perfection, but, despite the emphasis in both contemporary popular literature and modern historiography on the problems of unruly wives,
it is also important to note that he saw both sexes as being equally deficient
in their attainments: 'If triall be made of Husbands love by their practise and
performance of the forenamed duties, it will be found that they for the most
part come as farre short in *love*, as Wives in *subjection*.'[40]

This framework of understanding does not mean that the idea of wifely
obedience or subjection was insignificant, but that it could be understood
in a way that was more acceptable and less one-sided than historians often assume. It does not need to be seen in terms of misogynistic oppression,
whether conscious or unconscious, but rather as part of a balance of duties.[41]
Moreover, although the women of Blackfriars chafed at some of Gouge's
statements, it is notable that the female name which grew most in popularity
in the seventeenth century was Sarah, the model of the submissive and obedient behaviour of wives to their husbands.[42] According to the influential New
Testament reference 1 Peter 3.6, women, as daughters of Sarah, should make
themselves beautiful not with jewellery, clothes and braided hair, but in their
inner self by being submissive to their husbands.[43] For R. C. the example
of Sarah was similar to the model of Christ and the Church in advocating
subjection. A wife should submit herself to her husband because 'she oweth
her subiection to him, like as the Church doth to Christ; and because the
example of *Sarah*, the mother of the faithfull, which obeyed Abraham and

---

[40] Ibid., p. 419.

[41] Lucas interprets these texts as more sinister and cleverly manipulated instruments of male
control. But passages taken out of context may be misleading. The quotation from R. C.'s
A godly forme of household government, 'The husband ought not to bee satisfied, that he
hath robd his wife of her virginitie, but in that he hath possession and use of her will'
sounds like a prescription for extreme male control. However, the sentence continues 'for
it sufficeth not that they be married, but that they be well married, and live Christianly
together, & be very wel contented.' A husband 'who is not beloved by his wife' is vulnerable
to the loss of his goods, credit, reputation, and even his life. In this context the idea that the
husband should have 'possession and use of' his wife's will should not be seen as advocating
husbandly tyranny; rather, that love involves each partner subjecting their will to the other.
R. V. Lucas, 'Puritan preaching and the politics of the family', in A. M. Haselkorn and
B. S. Travitsky (eds.), *The Renaissance Englishwoman in Print: Counterbalancing the Canon*
(Amherst, 1990), pp. 224–35 (discussion of R. C. text p. 233).

[42] Smith-Bannister, *Names and Naming Patterns in England*, p. 144 and Appendix C.

[43] Commenting on this verse, Nicolas Byfield explained that godly women were the daughters
of Sarah if they followed her example and reverenced their husbands. They would have
the same reward from God, but only if they imitated her in her well-doing, and not in her
frowardness concerning Hagar (Gen. 16.5), or in her willingness to risk her chastity by
going to Pharaoh's house even though this was done to protect her husband's life and on
his instruction (Gen. 12.11–20). Galatians 4 identified Sarah as the New Jerusalem, and her
children as the children of the Spirit, in contrast to the fleshly offspring of the bondwoman
Hagar. Byfield, *A Commentary upon the first three chapters*, pp. 628–30, 623.

called him Lord moveth them thereunto.'[44] The popularity of Sarah, a name lacking any significant medieval tradition in England, is strong testimony to the powerful influence of preachers and authors of godly advice. Unlike the case of Susanna, whose story was told in ballads and drama, the promotion of Sarah was limited to the drier world of pious prescription. Yet, at least in terms of parents' aspirations in naming their daughters, the obedience of Sarah increasingly vied with the chastity of Susanna.

Both qualities – chastity and obedience – were, of course, central to the understanding of marriage, and especially of women's roles. Commentators who were unable to countenance the dissolution of marriage for apostasy were able to envisage the possibility of divorce for adultery. In part, of course, this simply reflected the legal position, but it is notable that the stillborn attempt of the *Reformatio Legum Ecclesiasticarum* to redesign marriage law according to protestant principles retained this emphasis. However much sermons preached the importance of spiritual support, marriage was still fundamentally defined as a remedy for fornication. Even if formal divorce for adultery remained infrequent, the gendered assumptions underpinning this possibility provided one of many reference points for the contemporary understanding of marriage which interacted with the different emphases of sermons, and with the customary social expectations of honour and reputation as dramatised in charivaris or defamation cases. These different sources offered various perspectives on gender roles and responsibilities in marriage, and especially on the extent to which a double standard applied.

In legal terms, a judicial separation, which allowed the couple to live apart but not to remarry, was available in England to the husband who could prove his wife's adultery, and to the wife who could prove her husband's excessive physical cruelty.[45] This distinction clearly enshrined a double standard, but it is less evident that these assumptions prevailed in sixteenth- and seventeenth-century society. The principle that the adulteress was more reprehensible than the adulterer, which was based on the fact that the woman's action could

---

[44] R. C., *A Godly Forme of Household Government*, p. 224. The model of Sarah was also stressed in the Homily of the State of Matrimony (1563), which, quoting 1 Peter 3, explained that 'holy matrons' adorned themselves '*in putting their whole hope in God* and in *obeying their husbands, as Sara obeyed Abraham, calling him Lord, whose daughters ye be* (saith he) if ye follow her example. This sentence is very meet for women to print in their remembrance.' See J. Larsen Klein (ed.), *Daughters, Wives and Widows: Writings by Men about Women and Marriage in England, 1500–1640* (Urbana and Chicago, 1992), p. 18. Thomas Gataker argued that only those women who were true wives willingly acknowledging their subjection were daughters of Sarah, and would gain a similar divine reward. 'Such as they be *Daughters of faithfull Sara*; so shall they have their part and portion with her. But for the rest since they refuse to doe the work, thay have no reason to expect or looke for the wages' Gataker, *A Wife In Deed* (1623), p. 26.

[45] Gowing, *Domestic Dangers*, pp. 180–3.

saddle her husband and family with a false heir, had already been questioned in the medieval period.[46] Moralists and social reformers saw the outcome of adultery as being less important than the degree of sin involved. From this perspective, men who, unlike weak and emotional women, were assumed to possess superior judgement and self-control, fell further from their natural abilities, sinned more grievously, and set a more serious example of bad conduct. This interpretation asserted a reversal of the double standard, and also encouraged a widening of the definition of what acts of marital infidelity constituted adultery. The prevailing legal definition confined adultery to a sexual relationship with a married woman, which meant that the married man who limited his promiscuity to single women and widows was merely guilty of fornication. The newer interpretation included sexual relationships involving a married person of either sex, and was more consistent with the idea that adultery was a serious undermining of the marriage that had made the couple one flesh.

As these views gained ground, they facilitated calls for harsher penalties to be imposed on adulterers, and for adultery to entail the dissolution of the marriage bond. These attitudes featured strongly in the early years of the Reformation, and should not be seen simply as a puritan concern. Thomas Becon's 'homilie of whoredome and unclennesse' in the official Book of Homilies of 1547 was virulent in its condemnation of adultery, unusually severe in its advocacy of Old Testament punishments, and clear that its warnings of damnation applied to 'unlawful conjunction' of a man with a woman who was not his wife and vice versa. Even the story of Christ telling the adulteress to go her way and sin no more was used as proof that adultery is sinful, rather than to extend mercy to the adulteress.[47] The homilist was not alone in his concern. Latimer bewailed the extent of whoredom in London, which, in his view, had not been reduced by the closure of the Bankside stews. To avoid the fate of Nineveh, Sodom and Gomorrah, he advocated the death penalty for adultery, allowing the husband or wife to plead for the reprieve of their spouse, but only for the first offence.[48]

Such extreme positions were not shared by all, but attempts to strengthen punishments for adultery were a recurring feature of Elizabethan and early Stuart parliaments, and there may have been significant sympathy for the complaint of a Norfolk parson that it was shameful that in so godly a country

---

[46] See pp. 145–9.
[47] R. B. Bond, ' "Dark deeds darkly answered": Thomas Becon's *Homily against Whoredom and Adultery*, its contexts, and its affiliations with three Shakespeare plays', *Sixteenth Century Journal* 16/2 (1985), 191–205. *Certain Sermons or Homilies, appointed by the King's Majesty to be declared and read by all parsons, vicars, or curates every Sunday in their churches, where they have cure* (London, 1547), Piii.r, Piv.v.
[48] Corrie (ed.), *Sermons by Hugh Latimer*, pp. 196, 244.

as England, there was no penalty for adultery but a white sheet.[49] Advocating death for adultery could also be attractive because it unequivocally gave the innocent spouse the right of remarriage. Nevertheless, when the death penalty was finally translated into law in the Adultery Act of 1650 the provisions were hardly implemented, and, as Thomas argues, this was as much the result of parliamentary actions, which demanded impossible testimony to secure a conviction, as an indication of popular attitudes.[50] The details of policy also show that expanding the definition of adultery did not necessarily entail a rejection of the double standard. The proposals in the *Reformatio Legum Ecclesiasticarum* of 1552 involved the adulterous husband restoring his wife's dowry, forfeiting half his goods to her, and incurring either life imprisonment or perpetual banishment. Similar punishments were to be imposed on an adulteress. However, the 1650 Act prescribed the death penalty for a husband who was twice convicted of adultery with a single woman, but sentenced an adulteress to death for the first offence.[51]

Authors who advocated mercy and encouraged penitence were, perhaps unsurprisingly, more likely to reject the double standard. Gouge recognised that there was scriptural warrant for divorce for adultery (Matthew 5.32 and 19.9), but, even though the adulterer became one flesh with his harlot, this did not automatically dissolve the marriage. Christ's words to the adulteress, and God's practice of retaining churches after they had committed spiritual adultery, were evidence that divorce should not follow, if the innocent spouse was prepared to offer forgiveness to the repentant offender. The innocent spouse, whether the husband or the wife, takes on the husband's role of Christ, and can determine the fate of the marriage. Following the model of Christ does, of course, carry with it a strong presumption in favour of mercy, but the heinousness of adultery means that readmission is still envisaged as a real choice: it is 'not meet in this case to impose it as an inviolable law upon the innocent party.'[52]

Allowing the wife the role of Christ in deciding whether the marriage could continue was a significant step. Gouge also argued that the fault in adultery was not greater in the case of the wife. Whilst recognising the 'inconvenience' of uncertain paternity, this should carry no weight in assessing the sinfulness of the transgressors. Rather, since both are made one flesh, they should be punished equally. Moreover, Gouge argued, and in this he followed Augustine, if one party was to be considered the more guilty, it should be the husband: 'If difference be made, it is meet that adulterous husbands be so

[49] K. Thomas, 'The Puritans and adultery: The Act of 1650 reconsidered', in D. Pennington and K. Thomas (eds.), *Puritans and Revolutionaries: Essays in Seventeenth Century History Presented to Christopher Hill* (Oxford, 1978), pp. 273–7, 264.
[50] Ibid., pp. 278–80.
[51] Sommerville, *Sex and Subjection*, p. 143.   [52] Gouge, *Of Domesticall Duties*, p. 220.

much the more severely punished by how much the more it appertaineth to them to excell in vertue, and to governe their wives by example.'[53] Whately in his *A Bride-Bush* (1617) also argued that the wronged party could be readmitted to the marriage if repentant, since the love of a married couple should be fervent and abundant. However, if the sin was persistent, the injured party should separate, 'for no man must make himselfe a member of an harlot, nor woman of an whore-master'.[54] Such arguments were controversial in implying that adultery dissolved marriage, and in the preface to *A Care-Cloth* (1622) Whately retracted them, together with his views on desertion. Arguments for divorce, and for the equivalence of spiritual and physical adultery, were hard to sustain. This was presumably largely because such ideas were seen as a licence for sexual infidelity and separation. Even for the authors of godly advice literature, although the idea of repentance and placing the decision in the hands of the innocent spouse had its attractions, there was a fundamental religious objection: marriage was based on the consent of the couple, but they formed a covenant not with each other but with God. Consequently, the injunction that what God had joined together man should not put asunder applied. The Old Testament condemnation of adultery and idolatry indicated the grievousness of these offences in God's sight, but did not sanction the use of the punishments which were prescribed in the Old Law.

In many ways of greater interest, and perhaps impact, than proposals advocating changes in legal practice was the discussion in these texts of why adultery occurred. In considering this, authors had the opportunity to address more directly issues of gender and the double standard. What is notable in these discussions is the separation of adultery from lust, and in particular from arguments about the greater inherent lustfulness of the female sex. Instead, Whately can compare the adulterer to the man 'that having a great store of Deere in his owne Parke, would yet needs steale a Buck out of his neighbours ground, because hee was so foolish as to glorie in his shame, and to bragge, that he durst steale one.'[55] The attraction of adultery is a misplaced pride in the ability to steal property when one already has sufficient.

Female adultery, on the other hand, was envisaged as a continuum of behaviour, which began with any rejection of one's husband's authority, including acts without any specific sexual content. What kept the wife faithful was her reverence for her husband, which would be eroded as his authority increasingly became ineffective. The straying wife would chat with her

---

[53] Ibid., p. 221.   [54] Whately, *A Bride-Bush*, p. 2.
[55] W. Whately, *A Care-Cloth, or a treatise of the cumbers and troubles of marriage* (London, 1624), p. 39.

gossips and ultimately end up in another man's bed. As Whately put it, the wife who despises her husband and causes him to fear her behaves in an unwomanly manner and 'tracks the way to the harlots house'.[56] The wife becomes an adulteress not because her husband cannot satisfy her sexually, but because his lax authority gives her the opportunity and does not restrain her.

What is odd about these explanations is not so much the arguments used as the fact that explanations of failed sexual satisfaction, and innate sexual characteristics, are not central to them. This is surprising because, as Fletcher reminds us, these authors are not prudish about sex. The Pauline injunction about spouses rendering one another due benevolence, and the institution of marriage as a means to avoid fornication, gave authors plenty of scope to discuss the duties of sex within marriage. Moreover, they were prepared to go beyond a basic tolerance of sex as a means of procreation to argue that sexual pleasure could also be an adequate justification.[57] That the sexual debt was owed to the barren woman, and to the woman who was past childbearing age, was adduced by Gouge in support of this position.[58] A few limits remained. Sex with a menstruating woman was generally seen as unlawful, but Gouge was prepared to argue that the custom that men should abstain from their wives whilst they were breastfeeding need not be observed.[59] The latter may have been partly stimulated by the desire to encourage couples not to employ wetnurses, but, since breastfeeding inhibits conception, it was also compatible with a positive assessment of the value of sexual pleasure.

Nevertheless, moderation in sexual activity was required. Due benevolence could be identified by Gouge as a remedy against adultery, and 'defect or excesse therein' as potentially problematic, but he hesitated in developing this line further. Fear of God was a much more acceptable and overarching remedy, and this had the additional advantage of preventing the author being drawn into assertions of the inherent greater lustfulness of women. Athough such views could be seen as scriptural, being subsumed in the notion of the woman as the weaker vessel, they were unattractive because Gouge was well aware that both defect and excess could be the failing of either the husband

---

[56] Whately, *A Bride-Bush*, p. 38.
[57] A. Fletcher, 'The Protestant idea of marriage in early modern England', in A. Fletcher and P. Roberts (eds.), *Religion, Culture and Society in Early Modern Britain: Essays in Honour of Patrick Collinson* (Cambridge, 1994), pp. 176–9.
[58] Gouge, *Of Domesticall Duties*, p. 226.
[59] P. Crawford, 'Attitudes to menstruation in seventeenth-century England', *P & P* 91 (1981), 60–2. Leviticus 15.20–4 states that the menstruating woman is unclean, and also any man that lies with her. Leviticus 20.18 prescribes the death penalty for sex with a menstruating woman. 2 Esdras v. 8 stated that 'menstruous women bring forth monsters', and early modern medical opinion concurred with this view.

or the wife. As elsewhere in his text, Gouge's concern to respond to everyday life and to avoid gender stereotypes resulted in a loss of clarity, but it also provided his readers with material for a more practical assessment which corresponded to the realities of their lives.

The accent of godly advice literature on patriarchal authority and wifely subjection has been seen by historians as reinforcing, or strengthening, gender stereotypes. A more careful reading of influential authors like Gouge, however, suggests that although such authors defined authority in very gendered terms, they were much more open to the idea that characteristics of behaviour were not gendered. In this respect they may have offered a more nuanced interpretation than the harsher world of slander and defamation, which demanded male authority as the norm and defined female reputation primarily in sexual terms. As R. C. told his readers,

> Most true it is, that women are as men are, reasonable creatures, and have flexible wittes, both to good and evill, the which with use, discretion and good counsell may be altered and turned. And although there be some evill and lewde women, yet that doth no more prove the malice of their nature then of men. And therefore the more ridiculous and foolish are they, that have enveighed against the whole sex for a few evill: and have not with like fury vituperated and dispraised all mankind, because part of them are theeves, murtherers, and such like wicked livers.[60]

This was not simply an appeal for a more even-handed observation of the contemporary world. It was also a perspective in which gender stereotypes were bound to suffer, as readers were reminded that women inherited the frailty of Eve and men the corruption of Adam, and that they should therefore bear with each other's infirmities.[61]

Bearing with infirmities is manifestly what participants in slander and defamation cases were not doing, and caution is therefore required in taking such gender stereotypes as the norm. As Stretton has emphasised, considering pleading strategies in matrimonial litigation, the process of confrontation accentuated gender stereotypes.[62] Consequently, to hold that attitudes can be read directly from the content of such litigation is to misunderstand the nature of this material. Slander, like humour, deals in stereotypes which to be effective have to be somewhat larger than life. This does not, of course, mean that such expressions lack impact, but they were vivid tools of attack, which were wrenched from the more careful consideration of context that characterised ordinary social interaction.

The relationship between prescriptive literature and the contents of defamation suits should not, therefore, be seen in terms of a contrast between ideal and reality. Not only did the prescriptive material speak more directly

---

[60] R. C., *A Godly Forme of Household Government*, p. 160.   [61] Ibid., p. 192.
[62] Stretton, *Women Waging Law in Early Modern England*, pp. 178–215.

to its audience than this view suggests, but the evidence of slander requires a more subtle interpretation which has much in common with the engagement with lived experience found in the conduct literature. In analysing both types of material we need to be careful not to assume that chastity and sexual reputation defined female honour. For Gowing the connection between conduct literature and defamation is precisely in these terms. We are told that

> Prescriptive literature . . . communicated a vision of morality in which women, not men, bore the load of guilt for illicit sex, and in which women's virtue was premised entirely on sexual chastity. The literature of household advice sought to infuse every element in the domestic hierarchy with a moral value; and at the heart of this project was the distinction between men's morals and women's which, discussing women's virtues in terms of silence, obedience, submissiveness, and restraint, placed the most stress on chastity.[63]

Sexual chastity was clearly important in the prescriptions of authors of godly advice, in the sense that adultery could destroy a marriage, but to argue that most stress was placed on it requires a selective reading of these texts. In the tables summarising the duties and aberrations of husbands and wives that accompany Gouge's *Domesticall Duties* as a guide to the reader, sexual fidelity is not explicitly mentioned. For these authors, the wife's duty, as we have seen, is generally encapsulated in the notion of subjection, which entails an exclusive sexual obligation but is by no means predominantly defined by it. Moreover, as Gowing herself notes, Gouge's discussion of adultery stressed male culpability as well as women's, and her argument that this was somehow more superficial than the emphasis on female chastity carries little conviction.[64] Moralists and scriptural commentators were concerned to be even-handed for obvious reasons, and occasionally we can even watch them thinking this out. Nicholas Byfield, discussing 1 Peter 3.2, remarked:

> Some observe, that a chaste conversation is especially charged upon the woman: which must be warily understood; for God hates whoredome in men as well as women. But yet it is true, that some sins as they are abominable in any, so they are much more in women, as we see in swearing and drunkennesse: so it is true of filthinesse in the woman: and therefore the whorish woman is called a strange woman in the *Proverbs*. But I think it is not safe to restraine the sense of this place, or other like places, so: but I take the meaning of the Apostle to be, so to commend chastitie in the wife, as that which is necessary in all, both men and women.[65]

Advice literature is, of course, not Gowing's main concern, except to dispute the idea 'that gender was worked out from the prescriptive texts that made the ideal conjugal household the foundation of society and social order.'[66]

---

[63] Gowing, *Domestic Dangers*, p. 2.   [64] Ibid.
[65] Byfield, *A Commentary upon the first three chapters*, p. 596.
[66] Gowing, *Domestic Dangers*, p. 7.

That influence flowed exclusively in one direction is obviously untenable, but it does not follow that all influence should be discounted. Rather, we should envisage a mutual interaction. Gowing's study is based upon suits for defamation, and from this evidence she argues, echoing the views of others but expressing the polarity more strongly, that women's reputation was defined in sexual terms and men's by other forms of honesty and credit. Moreover, in her view, this material suggests that 'women's sexual culpability was not just greater than, but incomparable with, men's'.[67] Clearly, both viewpoints, if sustainable, suggest that much of the message of the Church on morality had passed unheeded, and that the strength of the double standard remained unscathed.

Much of Gowing's case rests on the predominance of women amongst those bringing defamation suits in the church courts, and on the absence of any male equivalent for the accusation of 'whore'. Female participation is indeed striking, especially given the low profile of women in other spheres of legal action, and this does suggest a particularly female sensitivity about reputation and the use of words, which is also consistent with the identification of the scold as a woman. However, as Gowing realises, it would be naive to assume that female litigation straightforwardly reflects female concerns, or that defamation cases were not often the pursuit of other conflicts by additional means.[68] Nevertheless, these considerations weaken arguments about sensitivities more than they do those about gendered ideas of reputation. The latter depend on our interpretation of the meaning of the slanderous words used.

In defamation cases 'whore' was the most common slander against women, but its significance in defining female reputation in sexual terms seems to be undermined by its possible detachment from any suggestion of actual sexual misconduct. This could be seen, as Gowing wishes us to see it, as evidence of the pervasiveness of the identification of the female with potential whoredom, but it is arguably more plausible to see it as evidence of the dilution of the sexual association, as the word 'whore' no longer carries incontrovertible damaging power. The circumlocution of some defendants ('I will not call you

---

[67] Ibid., p. 4. A more judicious view is offered by Ingram, who recognises that 'women were more sensitive, and probably more subject, to sexual slander' and that 'The nature of slanders alleged by men in the common law courts, concerning probity in business dealings, social rank and status, and "honesty" in its modern sense, were probably a fair reflection of the central issues around which male reputation revolved. The pattern of cases in the church courts reflected the fact that for women the central issue was that of "honesty" in its now obsolete sense of "chastity" – was she an honest woman or a whore? However, it is clear that the notion of a double standard must not be pressed too far: it was in this period a matter of degree rather than an absolute dichotomy between the ways in which male and female reputations were regarded.' M. Ingram, *Church Courts, Sex and Marriage in England, 1570–1640* (Cambridge, 1987), pp. 302–3.

[68] Ibid., pp. 314–16; Gowing, *Domestic Dangers*, pp. 111, 118.

whore...') could buttress either case. Precision in the choice of defamatory terms could suggest that 'whore' could never be used in a diluted manner. However, it is more likely that such remarks represent a prudent response of individuals in particular situations of heightened tension in which an unwanted escalation to litigation appeared imminent. Generally, 'whore' was a potentially vague term of abuse, as shown by such combinations as 'witch whore', which suggest both the pervasiveness of the language of sex, and its dilution.

Furthermore, it is simply not true that 'There was no way of calling a man a whore, or condemning his sexual promiscuity.'[69] Between a quarter and a third of defamation cases in Gowing's London Consistory Court material were brought against men, and of these slanders a third were clearly sexual ('thou lay with me', pox, and other specific sex acts), and others arguably so. As significant may be the low incidence of the term 'cuckold' in the defamation of men. Given arguments about the popular sensitivity to this state, as witnessed by ridings or charivaris, it would seem logical that if there was no way of calling a man a whore, but only a cuckold, such slanders would be predominant in defamation cases brought by men to preserve their reputations. In the London Consistory Court imputation of cuckoldry only constituted 19 per cent of slanders on men in 1572–94, and 17 per cent in 1606–40.[70] Ingram's statistics for Wiltshire, York and Ely in the late sixteenth and early seventeenth centuries produce a figure of only 10 per cent of slanders on men being for cuckoldry.[71] That the overwhelming majority of defamation cases were brought against women, rather than men, is still significant, but when male reputation needed to be defended it was similarly most likely to be in terms which related to their own sexual activity.[72]

The meaning of such terms as 'whoremonger' and 'whoremaster' also needs more careful consideration.[73] It should not be assumed that they mean that the man is being called a pimp: they could also refer to his promiscuity, and therefore be a male equivalent of 'whore'. Thus Whately can assert that 'no man must make himselfe a member of an harlot, nor woman of an whore-master', and Latimer considered the appropriate translation of the Latin 'non fornicaberis, non adulteraberis' to be 'Thou shalt not be a

[69] Ibid., p. 63   [70] Ibid., p. 64.
[71] Ingram, *Church Courts, Sex and Marriage*, p. 301.
[72] Foyster, *Manhood in Early Modern England*, pp. 86–7, 156–7, similarly notes the rarity of suits brought to clear the reputation of a man who had been called a 'cuckold', and explains this in terms of the power of the insult, which limited its use and also made it embarrassing to counter in the courts. That it was often wives who appeared in court to clear their husband's reputation of being a cuckold was a way of demonstrating to the community that the husband had reassumed control over his household.
[73] Gowing, *Domestic Dangers*, p. 114, inaccurately asserts that words like 'whoremaster' were 'not by definition about men's own sexual behaviour'.

whoremonger, thou shalt not be a wedlock-breaker.'[74] In a sense, of course, 'harlot' and 'whoremaster' were not equivalent, but gendered, terms: they could not be applied to members of the opposite sex. It is also true that the male terms describe the offence in relation to women, and to women of dubious sexual morality, whilst the term 'whore' defines female nature. But this distinction disguises the underlying similarity. It may be more significant to focus on the continuity of 'mastery' and its debasement in the role of the whoremaster. Real male mastery occurs in the successful performance of the role of the male household head, and involves a wider range of duties and responsibilities than the mere sexual and/or financial satisfaction of a woman. The whoremaster opts out of adult manhood.[75] He retains mastery, but does not perform effectively or prove himself as a wife-master or husband. Dominated by passion, rather than by a mature acceptance of duty and responsibility, the whoremaster in this sense, no less than the harlot, is defined by sexual urges which lead him to neglect what society views as his true, and more difficult, role.

Gowing's assertion that 'There was no way of calling a man a whore, or condemning his sexual promiscuity; nor of calling a woman a cuckold, or calling her to account for her spouse's misconduct. Women remained the focus of sexual guilt and responsibility' must therefore be clarified.[76] There was no way of calling a woman a cuckold, since ultimately her duty of mutual support and counsel was not assumed to extend to control. There was no way of calling a man a whore, since ultimately the whore was mastered, and even the defamed man did not surrender the association with control. Words such as 'whoremaster' did not in themselves condemn sexual promiscuity, but they did censure men for only being able to exercise mastery in the sexual control of a whore rather than in the governance of a wife. It is therefore less true to say that 'women remained the focus of sexual guilt and responsibility'. Although notions of male chastity were clearly weaker than the demands placed upon women, the issue of responsibility and the evasion of responsibility was more complex. In labelling men as 'whoremongers' or 'whoremasters', and in mocking men as cuckolds, there was an acknowledgement of male responsibility, which was understood beyond the pulpit. In their views of conjugal morality, puritan preachers and authors of advice literature were largely preaching to the converted. Their texts provided more precise delineations of the nuances of this gender system, but they echoed lay assumptions about the location of sexual guilt and responsibility.

[74] Whately, *A Bride-Bush*, p. 2; Corrie (ed.), *Sermons by Hugh Latimer*, p. 464.
[75] C.f. Roper's analysis of the culture of male adolescents in Augsburg. L. Roper, *Oedipus and the Devil: Witchcraft, Sexuality and Religion in Early Modern Europe* (London, 1994), pp. 107–24.
[76] Gowing, *Domestic Dangers*, p. 63.

The spectacle of women accusing other women of being their husbands' whores, rather than attacking their own husbands for their adultery, might however seem to suggest that wives viewed male sexual fidelity as of little account. Adultery might be the most effective solvent of a marriage, but it was something that male reputation could withstand, and perhaps even brag about, with impunity. The fault lay with the loose woman who broke the female code of conduct and enticed other wives' husbands. But implicit in this was a recognition by the wife of the weakness of her husband in being unable to resist seduction. Even this version therefore relates more closely than first appears to the fundamental notions of authority and control, and provides a possible link with the pastoral and moral concerns of preachers.

The view that responsibility correlated to the degree of inability to control, and that woman's assumed inherent weakness and greater natural lust made her less culpable in sexual lapses, was not simply confined to the pious preaching of a few who were largely unheard. The figure of the cuckold, and the possibility that he, as much as the adulterous wife, would be the target of popular ridicule by both men and women in a charivari reminds us that the responsibility for sexual transgression crossed gender boundaries. Men's failure to control, and sexually satisfy, their wives rendered them a target of ridicule as being manifestly unable to effectively carry out husbandly duties. Lay culture had internalised gendered notions of the need to control, which partially exonerated the married woman, whilst also reinforcing ideas of inherent sexual weakness.

However, the message seems to have been much less effectively transmitted in the other direction. Contemporaries were more reluctant to assimilate the moralist's argument that sexual lapses were more reprehensible in the sex that was assumed to be better able to control and also to be subject to weaker sexual urges. The failure to confront this may be related to the strength of anxieties about male sexual potency within marriage, as illustrated by ballads. These anxieties could be countered by exploring and fantasising about male sexual control in other circumstances. Most obviously, male sexual power is reasserted in tales of rape, but such strategies were ultimately inadequate.[77] Male power based on brute force does not automatically confer authority, and, as ballads of the physical chastisement of the unruly wife demonstrate, did not even necessarily result in the taming of the shrew.

These reflections remind us that an understanding of sexual reputation and gender cannot be separated from issues of authority and control. To do so violates the early modern understanding in which domestic gender relations

[77] Wiltenburg, *Disorderly Women*, p. 206; Roper, *Oedipus and the Devil*, p. 60, describes the uneasy transition from the culpability of female temptress to the final assertion of male control in the sexual act.

were a microcosm of the commonwealth. Moreover, as Gowing points out, the vocabulary of 'occupation' to describe the sexual act accentuated ideas of possession and control,[78] even if such notions were less evidently fore-grounded in the alternative language of 'carnal knowledge' and 'copulation'. Similarly, the conceptualisation of the act of the man who had sex with a married woman as theft from her husband meant that to be slandered as a 'knave' could imply general dishonesty or sexual misconduct.

Once again, what is striking here is the similarities in the framework of interpretation underpinning both the evidence of defamation suits and the message of godly advice literature. The explanation of adultery in terms of the disruption and disintegration of household order, and the intercon-nectedness of the husband's concern about his loss of sexual and verbal authority, form part of the essential context in which the promiscuous male was conceptualised in terms of mastery, and the word 'whore' could be used diffusely. The language of sex forms the central focus of conceptions of the disruptive, dishonest woman, but in this broader association of ideas it is linked less narrowly to ideas of women's innately more lustful nature. The threat posed by women to male society, and especially to the position of husbands, is thus only partly sexual. Women's mastery has wider connota-tions, which mean that the domineering wife can be seen as at least equally threatening. The status of a husband as a cuckold, wittall (contented cuck-old) or a spouse of a physically and verbally domineering wife represented differing degrees of social humiliation, and it is far from clear that cuckoldry involved the greatest degradation. Despite her emphasis on the centrality of sex, Gowing identifies the position of the domineered husband as the most shameful state.[79] If this was the case, it would seem to suggest that sexual transgression was less significant since it was more natural, less within the scope of the husband to control, and involved deceit (which women are as-sumed to be good at), whilst the domineered husband lost mastery in a direct contest and confrontation, and thus exposed a greater failing.

This interpretation gains some further support from the nature of chari-varis and ballads. Charivaris seem more likely to be directed against wives who beat their husbands than against sexual misconduct, and ballads seem to tell more brutal, or unsettling, tales of mastering domineering wives than adulterous ones.[80] Although ballads of adulteresses frequently end in the hor-ror of the murder, or attempted murder, of the husband, this is not envisaged

---

[78] Gowing, *Domestic Dangers*, p. 271.

[79] Ibid., pp. 192, 228–9. Gowing gives no clear evidence to support why the degrees of humil-iation should follow this sequence.

[80] The current state of research means that these conclusions must still be seen as largely impressionistic: M. Ingram, 'Ridings, rough music and the "reform of popular culture" in early modern England', *P & P* 105 (1984), 79–113.

Figure 49 *A New yeares guift for shrews, c.* 1620

as being carried out by the wife single-handedly, but in alliance with her lover, and the outcome is the reassertion of justice with the imposition of the death penalty for the unnatural murder. In contrast, ballads of domineering wives are more ambivalent. Despite the efforts of the husband to tame his wife, it is not clear that he is able to do so. In *A New yeares guift for shrews* (*c.* 1620) a week of marriage is described (Fig. 49):

Who marieth a Wife uppon a Moneday. If she will not be good uppon a Tewesday. Lett him go to ye wood uppon a Wensday. And cut him a cudgell uppon the Thursday. And pay her soundly uppon a Fryday. And she mend not ye Divil take her a Saterday. Then may he eate his meate in peace on the Sunday.

The husband beats his unruly wife, but his attempt at discipline is only partly successful, since it does not shape her into a model wife. Instead, the devil takes her away, and the husband is left with a quiet, solitary life dining at the alehouse. The devil's intervention represents the failure of the husband. It also contrasts with treatments of the same theme in German ballads, which either attribute more success to the husband's efforts, or depict the wife as a blacker character. In a parallel German 'week' of marriage, the beaten wife is penitent, but sickens, and on her deathbed she urges wives to be obedient to their husbands, and bequeaths all her goods to her husband.[81] When taming does not succeed, the German shrew wins over the devil, and is thus worse than he, whilst in England she is the devil's victim through her failure to heed her husband's justified discipline. The English version clearly relates more closely to the priorities and concerns of advice literature. The struggle is not with the devil, but is a matter of the correct, and effective, balance of chastisement and obedience. The husband, in the place of Christ, competes with the devil for control of his wife.

The mid/late-sixteenth century *A merry Ieste of a shrewde and curst Wyfe, lapped in Morrelles Skin, for her good behavyour* also offers a similarly understated parallel between the role of the husband and Christ. The scolding wife who would play the master is subdued by her husband's judicious brutality. To make her obey his commandments the husband beats his wife with birch rods until she bleeds, and then wraps her in the salted skin of his dear horse (Morel) until she begs for grace.[82] This sacrifice of a much-valued and faithful horse to restore domestic order, and to encourage obedience to commandments, can also be seen as a thinly disguised parable of God's sacrifice of his precious son for the redemption of mankind. A similar message is more clearly articulated in the adaptation of the stories of Griselda in which the marquess's apparently cruel testing of his wife is given a Christological gloss. Here, of course, the female protagonist is figured as essentially obedient and longsuffering, even if a little more spirited in the early modern than in some medieval versions.[83] Despite their differences, both stories of conjugal relations and the establishment of order share an acceptance of the modelling of the role of the husband on Christ. As such, they suggest that the message of advice literature and sermons could find a receptive audience, and dovetailed with the concerns of popular culture. They also suggest that rather sterile, didactic ballads such as 'A mery balade, how a wife entreated her husband to have her own will', which insisted on a wife's subjection rather than her having her will, may not have been so alien or ineffective as they appear when considered in isolation.[84]

---

[81] Wiltenburg, *Disorderly Women*, p. 125.

[82] Gowing, *Domestic Dangers*, pp. 225–6; Wiltenburg, *Disorderly Women*, pp. 126–7; E. V. Utterson, *Select Pieces of Early Popular Poetry, Re-published Principally from Early Printed Copies in the Black Letter*, 2 vols. (London, 1817), vol. 2, pp. 173–221.

[83] Bronfmann, 'Griselda, Renaissance woman', pp. 211–23; Bliss, 'The Renaissance Griselda'; Comensoli, *Household Business*, pp. 49–64.

[84] J. Lilly (ed.), *A Collection of Seventy-nine Black-letter Ballads and Broadsides, Printed in the Reign of Queen Elizabeth, between the Years 1559 and 1597* (London, 1870), pp. 129–32. The wife who asks her husband to let her have her will is told that she can have her will in

Despite the obvious divergence between prescriptive literature and practice, these texts show how the godly could rationalise the conflicting gender messages of Reformation religious culture, notions of patriarchal authority and lived experience. Scriptural precepts and an acknowledgement of male dominance were combined to form a more flexible concept of subjection which would accommodate the idea of spiritual equality or, more precisely, the idea of mutually supportive spiritual capacities. Such views could not be integrated fully. The expansion of the sexual interpretation of Pauline 'due benevolence' to include a more prominent role for companionship did not consistently make spiritual support central to this. Difficulties in dealing with questions of authority and support in religiously mixed marriages encouraged the continuance of the view that the only fundamental reason for marriage was the avoidance of fornication. Despite this, the assumption that responsibility and ability to control were gendered could encourage subversion of the sexual double standard and male authority within a continuing framework of subjection. The discussion in these texts of adultery, divorce, conversion and incapacity to manage the household due to drunkenness shows that the subjection of wives to their husbands was seen as being threatened not only by female insubordination or mechanistic obedience, but also by male inadequacy. The possibility of male culpability was clearly recognised, and this strengthened the need for parity of partners to facilitate a successful and godly marriage.

The conclusions of the authors of godly advice literature therefore had more connections with the assumptions of popular literature, shaming rituals and slanders than is often thought. That this has not been clearly realised is due to the narrow identification of female reputation with sexual conduct. In fact, all three sources shared a concern with responsibility for sexual activity, which was not so starkly polarised. The whore was mastered and the whoremonger exercised mastery, but both, whilst acting in conformity with their gender roles, neglected their true responsibilities as wife and wifemaster. If popular culture was less ready to absorb the idea that innately superior male qualities meant that the man who fell was more culpable, the same impulse to shore up male authority was shared by godly authors. Moreover, they, like the ballad writers, saw the greatest specifically female threat to lie in the conduct of the unruly wife who exercised mastery over her husband. Such conduct could give rise to adultery, but the weak point was in the first successful contest for authority within the household. If a man fails to reassert his authority and his ability to command respect when

doing good. She is confined to her domestic duties and not allowed to wear fine clothes, or to visit her gossips and the alehouse.

directly challenged by his wife, the game is lost. Cuckoldry, envisaged as a later development when a wife no longer feels constrained by her husband's authority, at least involved female independence being tempered by male mastery, albeit another man's.

The fusion of popular and godly assumptions about domestic relations was also encouraged by the telling of exemplary stories. The Christologi-cal resonances of the histories of the wife wrapped in Morel's skin, or of Griselda, chimed with the preacher's depiction of marriage as the relation-ship between Christ and his Church. Stories of Susanna, Bathsheba and Eve explored issues of male culpability and responsibility, and offered the possi-bility of exonerating the unconscious temptress. Such ideas also co-existed with narrower, and more controlling, representations of woman's role: the emblematic depictions of the virtuous, chaste woman confined to her house, and the inverse image of the Whore of Babylon. However, for individuals negotiating their way through the complexities of everyday life and human relations, these conceptions were a more distant reference point. They shaped behaviour, but did not define it. In assessments of fallen humanity, sin had to be contextualised, and the admission of grey areas could favour women's position. It remained the case that only the truly virtuous woman could as-pire to parity in subjection, but also that only the most incorrigible offender could be placed in the company of the Whore of Babylon.

Conclusion

In a window-splay of the small Oxfordshire church of Shorthampton, an image of St Sythe was painted against a red ochre background. A stocky figure in homely peasant costume, she still stands as an emblem of the housewife holding an oversize bunch of keys, in reference to her presumed ability to find lost house keys (Fig. 25). Originally an Italian servant, by the later medieval period this saint had been fully domesticated in the English context. She encapsulates the process of humanisation of the saints and their role in testifying to the possibility of a domesticated female sanctity that, despite Sythe's halo, would always remain more human than divine. Labelled as idolatrous by protestants, such images were obliterated by whitewash in the Reformation, and a different interpretation of the godly housewife emerged in the domestic sphere. At Elmdon (Essex) in the mid-seventeenth century a large, and almost gaunt, figure of a woman in starched contemporary costume was painted on the staircase as if going upstairs. Unapproachable and determined, she carries a single lighted candle in her hand, perhaps signifying her prudent watchfulness and dedication to her household duties (Fig. 50).[1]

In the 'merrier world' that was looked back to with nostalgia by religiously conservative Elizabethans, groups of women held ales or dances to raise funds for the church or particular altars, were feasted at parish expense at Hocktide, and their contribution was immortalised in the serried ranks of minute donor figures, as in the glass at St Neot (Cornwall) (Fig. 5). These images of communal conviviality, in which women had their own place and made a recognised contribution, contrast sharply with the orderly Reformation congregation sitting in their pews at sermon time, and with the pew disputes played out in the church courts that attempted to prevent married women sitting in church with their unmarried friends.

Such juxtapositions of patterns of piety, whether of exemplary role models or of the practice of religious devotion, seem to lend support to a rather bleak

---

[1] Carrick, 'Sixteenth and seventeenth century wall painting in the county of Essex', p. 13, fig. 17.

343

Figure 50 Domestic wall painting of a woman going upstairs carrying a candle,
Church Farm, Elmdon (Essex), middle of the seventeenth century

picture of the Reformation process. The loss of Duffy's 'traditional religion'
appears to spell the end of female religious sociability and the potential
sanctification of the housewife, and its replacement with a sober sense of
household roles.[2] Such juxtapositions are, however, formed from misleading
fragments. Those lamenting the passing of a 'merrier world' focussed more
on the loss of cakes and ale, the outward manifestations of a communal

[2] Duffy, *The Stripping of the Altars*.

sociability that was symbolised as much by maypoles as by the gild feast. They tell us little about the continuities in religious understanding. There was no 'traditional religion', just as there was no 'reformation', but there were reformations of both. That this was so was not due simply to the changing nature of royal policy that constitutes Haigh's 'Reformations'.[3] More fundamentally, it can be explained by the development of a Christocentric piety in the late medieval period that focussed on the passion of the adult Christ. It was this devotional trend, regionalised in the extent of its fifteenth-century impact, that provided for many a bridge to protestantism, but also subsequently created new tensions as Reformation policy moved away from Lutheran towards Calvinist ideas.

By the eve of the Reformation this increasingly Christocentric parish piety had transformed the nature of catholic devotion, including the cult of the saints that is often seen as the hallmark of 'traditional religion'. In this context the figure of St Sythe had more resonance as an assistant in finding lost keys than as a saintly role model. The humanisation of the saints coincided with a growing realisation of the gulf between mankind and the incarnate Christ, and this emphasis on distance affected the cult of the saints. Depictions of saints, especially female ones, on the lowest panels of the rood screen graphically illustrated the possibility of transition between human and divine, as well as its limits. In this framework the mystical idea of the saint as the bride of Christ could have no real place in the religious understanding of late medieval parishioners.

Devotion to the wounds of Christ in the parishes was similarly far from the mystic's fantasy of fusion with the Son of God, although it was from this tradition that it had originated. The wounds and blood could only be understood in terms of the 'warnings to swearers' in which man's ill-considered and sinful actions harmed Christ, and thus reinforced the idea of the gulf between the human and divine. The process of emblematic meditation, focussing on the wounds or the instruments of the passion in isolation, further weakened the sense of Christ's humanity. It was this stress on the sinfulness of mankind in the face of Christ that rendered the nuances of gender almost meaningless. The paradox of the humanisation of the divine was an intensification of the sense of human inferiority and fallibility combined with an appreciation of the extent of divine mercy. For the same reasons, gender had comparatively little role in defining devotion to the saints: women did not identify more closely with female saints than with male ones. Despite the usefulness of female saints as markers of transition, their inferiority was more human than female.

---

[3] Haigh, *English Reformations*.

The figure of Eve might be thought to have counterbalanced this trend and to have placed women, as daughters of Eve, in a different category. However, as a more Christocentric devotion permeated the parishes, unambiguous condemnation of Eve became less common and the story of the Fall itself less prominent. The Eve–Mary antithesis also became less central as the focus shifted from the Nativity to the passion of Christ. The changing emphasis in Marian devotion from the tender images of Virgin and Child to a concern with the crucified adult Christ, as typified by the popularity of the image of the Pietà, similarly served to reduce the possibility of gendered identifications. The Pietà did not sanctify the virtues of maternal domesticity, but promulgated the idea of Mary as a universal witness. The Virgin Mary holding the body of the dead Christ and mourning for her son was a powerful emblematic figure that combined the possibilities of empathy and comprehension, but also illustrated the limits of the human in the presence of the divine, even when linked by bonds of blood. In the fifteenth and early sixteenth centuries, but for different reasons and probably more clearly than in the previous, more gendered, phase of Madonna and Child devotion, the Virgin Mary appealed, and spoke, to male and female parishioners alike.

This does not mean that gender was unimportant in structuring late medieval religious experience. Rather, we need to recognise that, to a surprising extent, clearly defined gender divisions were an optional extra. This was so even in expressions of the parish community where the intersection of social and religious order could be most clearly visualised, in the segregation of men and women in the congregation and in the formation of more informal parish gilds of young men, maidens and wives. Gendered models of conduct could still be strongly advocated, most obviously the expectation that women should be chaste, silent and obedient. But such constructs were at odds with the pastoral concerns of clerics who wished, for example, to counter the lay view that male lechery was a moral offence of less gravity than female unchastity. Since the prevailing gender stereotypes characterised men as rational and self-controlled and women as weak and emotional, grading sin according to the ideas of responsibility inherent in the patriarchal system created a situation that destabilised rigid conceptions of gender. The weak, emotional temptress could be seen as less culpable than both the man who succumbed to her sexual charms, and her husband who had failed in his duty to guide and control her. Moreover, that both interpretations were present to varying degrees in late medieval culture added to the ambiguities of gendered experience, as too did the apparently contradictory stereotype of the godly woman.

In late medieval catholicism the assumed female propensity for piety was translated into the role of the wife as the household's ritual specialist, and it might seem that it was the loss of this ritual role, more than the supposed 'loss' of female saints, that constitutes the most significant Reformation change for women. Certainly, historians charting the fate of catholicism have pointed to the important role of women in sustaining the faith by maintaining such practices as fasting. However, not only is it possible that such observations say more about control of the kitchen than about propensity for piety, but the notion of the godly household and the protestant conception of the godly woman offered female roles which were potentially just as attractive. There is in fact little difference between the domestic appeal of the figure of St Sythe, whose concern for keys epitomises housewifely thrift, and the watchful, godly housewife at Elmdon. Authors of polemic identified women as particularly prone to catholicism, lollardy, protestantism and puritanism. This doctrinal and devotional eclecticism might seem to lend support to the view that such comments represent opportunistic attempts to tar the opposition with emotional female gullibility rather than being descriptive. This was certainly an effective strategy, but such rhetorical considerations do not give the whole picture. Women, in whatever proportions, found comfortable niches in all these religious movements and positive grounds for commitment to them.

Paradoxically, it was the extent to which late medieval Christocentric piety had reduced the significance of gendered patterns of devotion, whilst retaining the notion of the laywoman as the religious specialist, that allowed women to experience the Reformation not as an alien male environment, but as one in which quite literally they could feel at home. The same trends of Christocentric piety that provided a bridge to Reformation for many were also those that were responsible for reducing its gender impact. They meant that there was no real 'loss' of female models like the Virgin Mary, and that the late medieval reinterpretation of her, and of the associated figure of Mary Magdalen, was carried over into protestantism. When the representative frail christian was a woman devoted to Christ, protestantism could not be a hostile environment for the weaker sex.

The greatest threat to the willing involvement and numerical dominance of women as members of congregations was, therefore, not the supposedly decisive break of the Reformation, but tendencies within an increasingly dominant Calvinistic strain of protestantism. These advocated, in place of a Christocentric devotion, an austere focus on a distant awesome God, who was only apprehendable as rays of light emanating from the mysterious Hebrew characters of the tetragrammaton. However, such an abstract and uncompromising view of the deity and divine precepts did little to satisfy devotional needs, or to help the christian to navigate life in society. In the same way that the stern didacticism of the scriptural texts painted on the walls of parish churches was inadequate on its own, so an abstract, awesome deity could not nurture faith. In the first case, the prescriptive scriptural texts in the house of God were complemented by the subtle discussions of the ambiguities of the relationship between gender and responsibility in stories from the Old Testament and Apocrypha. In the second, the result of reducing God to an impersonal unapproachable word was to intensify the emotional Christocentric strands in godly protestant devotion.

The resilience of Christocentric devotion was largely due to the way in which both catholicism and protestantism defined the christian (and hence the laity) in female terms. The frail, uncertain figure of the struggling christian was identified in both faiths with the weak, emotional figure of the female stereotype. This was a natural outcome of a later medieval affective piety that focussed on Christ's bloody wounds, but exposed an emotional void when that same frail christian was left facing an awesome distant God. Envisaging the deity as a shining tetragrammaton provided no human consolation that could nurture fragile faith. Thus, although in Hooker's engraving it is these divine rays that illumine the figure of the devoted and faithful Magdalen, it was equally important that her story should direct christians back to an intimate relationship with the incarnate Christ (Fig. 1).

The threat that protestantism would strengthen the discipline of patriarchy was therefore averted. The controlling presence of a distant masculine deity was tempered by the continuing acceptance of devotion in emotional, feminine terms. Similarly, rather than protestantism enclosing women within rigid and prescriptive gender boundaries in their daily lives, the recognition that the stereotype of the weak, feeble woman was also that of the christian encouraged a more flexible understanding of gender roles. This process was strengthened by the development of a vigorous visual and literary culture that questioned the link between gender and responsibility, and advocated a godly household in which parity and complementarity were the watchwords. Whether discussing wife-beating, the responsibility for adultery or the duties of spiritual edification and obedience, no preacher or author of godly advice literature in Reformation England assumed that applying gender definitions to the complexities of individual lives was easy.

Thus, even if the incidence of scolding, cuckoldry and the communal remedy of the charivari or skimmington ride may have peaked during the early modern period, the 'crisis of gender relations', identified by some historians as characteristic of it, was not in fact a 'crisis' in terms of a battle between the sexes for mastery.[4] Such behaviour was simply the most disruptive aspect of a wider process in which the former certainties of gender were increasingly

---

[4] D. E. Underdown, 'The taming of the scold: The enforcement of patriarchal authority in early modern England', in A. Fletcher and J. Stevenson (eds.), *Order and Disorder in Early Modern England* (Cambridge, 1985), pp. 116–36; M. Ingram, ' "Scolding women cucked or washed": a crisis in gender relations in early modern England?', in G. Walker and J. Kermode (eds.), *Women, Crime and the Courts in Early Modern England* (London, 1994), pp. 48–80.

being reassessed. The Reformation period witnessed a growing recognition of gender as a social construct that could fit awkwardly with individual capacities and pastoral concerns. This understanding was an integral part of the motif of the frail christian and was not created by protestantism. However, because of their closer engagement with scripture and the Apocrypha, and with actual married life, it was increasingly articulated by its supporters and promoters. It was, paradoxically, the Christocentric piety of the late medieval parish that, in reducing the religious significance of gender, and in attaching it more closely to a view of general human frailty and propensity to sin, paved the way for a more subtle understanding of gender in the early modern period.

APPENDIX

CHURCHWARDENS' ACCOUNTS
BEFORE 1570

The compilation of this list has been assisted by the work of earlier historians. In particular, the lists in J. C. Cox, *Churchwardens' Accounts* (London, 1913) and J. F. Williams (ed.), *Hampshire Churchwardens' Accounts* (London, 1913) have been invaluable. In tracing the current place of deposit of these documents, I am indebted to the assistance of staff in record offices throughout the country.

In the following list the date (1570) in brackets indicates that the accounts continue to later dates.

Parish and dates	Current location	References
Bedfordshire		
Clifton, 1543	Beds. RO	*Beds. Hist. Rec. Soc.* 33 (1953)
Northill, 1561–(70)	Beds. RO	As above
Berkshire		
Brightwalton, 1481–(1570)	Berks. RO	
Reading, St Lawrence, 1432–59, 1498–(1570)	Berks. RO	Rev. Charles Kerry, *History of the Municipal Church of St Lawrence* (1883), extracts
Reading, St. Giles, 1518–(70)	Berks. RO	Rev. W. L. Nash (1881)
Winkfield, 1521–(70)	Berks. RO	
Reading, St Mary, 1550–(70)	Berks. RO	B. Stubbs (1893)
Stanford-in-the-Vale, 1552–(70)	Berks. RO	*Antiquary* 17 (1888)
Abingdon, St Helen's, 1555–(70)	In parish	*Archaeologia* 1, extracts
Thatcham, 1561–(70)	Berks, RO	Barfield, *Thatcham*, vol. 1, 121–6; vol. 2, 92–125
Childrey, 1568–(70)	Berks. RO	

(*cont.*)

Parish and dates	Current location	References
Buckinghamshire		
Wing, 1527–	Bucks. RO	*Archaeologia* 36 (1855)
Amersham, 1539–41	Bucks. RO	
Burnham, 1549	Bucks. RO	*Records of Bucks.* 10 (1913); privately printed, W. H. Guthrie and W. H. Williams (1913)
Aston Abbotts, 1562–(70)	Bucks. RO	*Records of Bucks.* 10 (1910)
Ludgershall, 1565–(70)	Bucks. RO	
Cambridgeshire		
Bassingbourn, 1498–1540	Camb. RO	*East Anglian N & Q* 4 (1871), extracts
Cambridge, Gt. St. Mary's, 1504–(70)	Camb. RO	
Cambridge, Holy Trinity, 1504–(70)	Camb. RO	
March, Edw VI		
Cheshire		
Chester, Holy Trinity, 1532–(70)	Cheshire RO	*Journal of the Chester Archaeological Society* ns 38 (1951).
Chester, St Mary, 1536–(70)	Cheshire RO	J. P. Earwaker, *History of St Mary on the Hill* (London, 1898), a few extracts
Wilmslow, 1555–(70)		J. P. Earwaker, *East Cheshire*, vol. 2, pp. 111–17
Chester, St Michael, 1558–(70)	Cheshire RO	
Prestbury, *c.* 1561–(70)	In private hands	
Cleveland		
None		
Cornwall		
Launceston, St Thomas, 1479, 1523–48, 1559	Cornwall RO	
Bodmin, 1484	Cornwall RO	Sir J. Maclean, *History of the Parish and Borough of Bodmin* (1870), extracts
North Petherwin, 1490–(1570)	Cornwall RO	
Stratton, 1512–(46)	BL Addl. MS 32, 243–4	*Archaeologia* 46 (1881)

(*cont.*)

Parish and dates	Current location	References
Poughill, 1525–59	Cornwall RO	
St. Breock, 1529–54, 1566–(70)	Cornwall RO	
Camborne, 1535–(70)	Cornwall RO	
Cumbria None		
Derbyshire Derby, All Saints, 1465–	Derby Cathedral	J. C. Cox and W. H. St. John Hope, *Chronicles of the Church of All Saints, Derby* (1881); microfilm at Derbyshire RO (Matlock)
Devon Exeter, St John's, 1422, 1425, 1467, 1547–(70)	Devon RO	
Exeter, St Petrock's, 1425–(1570)	Devon RO	*Trans. Devon Assoc.* 14 (1882)
Tavistock, 1470–1, 1493, 1537–9, 1543–4, 1552–3, 1556, 1561, 1563–4, 1566–7	Devon RO	
Ashburton, 1479–(1570)	Devon RO	*Devon & Cornwall Rec. Soc.* ns 15 (1970)
Chagford, 1480–1547	Devon RO	F. M. Osborne (ed.), *CWA of St Michael's Church, Chagford 1480–1600* (Chagford, 1979)
Dartington, 1483–(1570)	Devon RO	
North Molton, 1549–(70)	N. Devon RO (unfit for production)	Typescript of accounts by N. Annett (1960) in RO
Modbury, 1505, 1543–8	Devon RO	
Winkleigh, 1518–(70)	N. Devon RO	
Morebath, 1520–(70)		Ed. J. E. Binney (Exeter 1904); *Som. Arch. & Nat. Hist. Soc.* 29 (1883); *Som. Rec. Soc.* 4 (1890)
South Tawton, 1524–40, 1550?–(70)	Devon RO	*Trans. Devon Assoc.* 38–41 (1906–9)
Woodland, 1527–(70)	Devon RO	
Iddesleigh, 1536–43	N. Devon RO	
Woodbury, 1536–(70)	Devon RO	
Crediton, 1551–(70)	Devon RO	Transcr. by B. F. Cresswell
Coldridge, 1552–(70)	Devon RO	

(cont.)

Parish and dates	Current location	References
Exeter, St Mary's Steps, 1553–8	Devon RO	
Braunton, 1554–(70)	N. Devon RO	
Kilmington, 1555–(70)	Devon RO	Ed. R. Cornish (Exeter, 1901)
Molland, 1557–(70)	Devon RO	*Trans. Devon Assoc.* 35 (1903)
Chudleigh, 1561–(70)	Devon RO	Jones, *History of Chudleigh* (1852)
Dean Prior, 1567	Devon RO	
Dorset		
Wimborne Minster, 1475–(1570)	Dorset RO	Extracts in C. Mayo, *History of Wimborne Minster* (London, 1860)
Durham		
None		
Essex		
Saffron Walden, 1439–90	Essex RO	R. Lord Braybrooke, *History of Audley End and Saffron Walden* (1836)
Great Dunmow, 1526–(70)	Essex RO	
Great Hallingbury, 1526–55, 1566–(70)	Essex RO	*Trans. Essex Arch. Soc.* 23 (1942)
Heybridge, 1532–1564	Essex RO	Rev. W. J. Pressey, *Churchwardens' Accounts of Heybridge* (n.d.) (incl. missing accounts 1509–32); Nichols, *Illust. of Manners*
Broomfield, 1540–4, 1552, 1558,1563–(70)	Essex RO	
Harwich, 1550–(70)	Essex RO	
Chelmsford, 1557–(70)	Essex RO	
Ashdon, 1560–(70)	Essex RO (in p. reg.)	
Wivenhoe, 1562–(70)	Essex RO	
Boreham, 1565–(70)	Essex RO	
Felsted, 1566–(70)	Essex RO	
Canewdon, 1568–(70)	Essex RO	
Gloucestershire		
Gloucester, St Michael, 1545–6, 1549–51, 1556–(70)	Glouc. RO	
Minchinhampton, 1555–(70)	Glouc. RO	*Archaeologia* 35 (1853), extracts

(*cont.*)

Parish and dates	Current location	References
Gloucester, St Aldates, 1565–(70)	Glouc. RO	
Tewkesbury, 1563–(70)	Glouc. RO	
Dursley, 1566–(70)	Glouc. RO	
Lechlade, 1567–(70)	Glouc. RO	
Hampshire		
Andover, 1470–4		J. F. Williams (ed.), *Hampshire Churchwardens' Accounts* (1913)
Bramley, 1522–(70)	Hants. RO	As above
Stoke Charity, 1541–(70)	Corpus Christi, Oxford	As above
Crondall, 1543–(70)	Surrey RO (Guildford)	As above; *Hants. Rec. Soc.* (1890)
Ellingham, 1543–(70)	Hants. RO	J. F. Williams (ed.), *Hampshire Churchwardens' Accounts* (1913)
Weyhill, 1543–(70)	Hants. RO	As above
St John's, Winchester, 1548–(70)	Hants. RO	As above
Wootton St Lawrence, 1559	Hants. RO	As above
Portsmouth, St Thomas, 1564–6	Hants. RO	As above; *JBAA* 44 (1888), extracts
St Peter Chesil, Winchester 1566–(70)	Hants. RO	J. F. Williams (ed.), *Hampshire Churchwardens' Accounts* (1913)
Herefordshire		
Stoke Edith, 1532–1546, 1566–70	Heref. RO	
Hertfordshire		
Bishops Stortford, 1482–1583	Herts. RO	J. L. Glasscock, *The Records of St. Michael's Parish Church* (London, 1882), 1431–40 in extenso, good extracts from other rolls
Baldock, *c.* 1540–53		*Herts. Rec. Soc.* (1985)
Barkway, 1558–(70)	Herts. RO	
Ashwell, 1563–(70)	Herts. RO	
Huntingdonshire		
Ramsey, 1511–52	Huntingdon RO	
Holywell, 1547–(70)	Huntingdon RO	

(cont.)

Parish and dates	Current location	References
Kent		
Hythe, 1412–3, 1480–1	Hythe	*Arch. Cant.* 10 (1876), in extenso
Canterbury, St Dunstan's, 1484–(1570)	Kent RO (Canterbury)	*Arch. Cant.* 16–17 (1886–7); J. M. Cowper, *CWA's of St. Dunstan's* (1885)
Folkestone, 1487–(1570)	Kent RO (Canterbury)	Transcr. E. L. Holland (1924)
Sandwich, St Mary's, 1444–(1570)	Kent RO (Canterbury)	
Bethersden, 1508–(70)		*Kent Records* 5 (1928)
Pluckley, 1509–(70)	Kent RO (Maidstone)	
Fordwich, 1510–40		*Historical Manuscripts Commission* 5th Report, 607; summary and extracts
Hawkhurst, 1515–(70)		*Arch. Cant.* 5 (1863)
Rainham, 1517–19, 1565–9	Kent RO (Maidstone)	*Arch. Cant.* 15 (1883)
Lydd, 1520–58	Unknown	A. Finn (ed.), *Records of Lydd* (Ashford, 1911)
Smarden, 1536–(70)	Kent RO (Maidstone)	*Arch. Cant.* 9 (1874), extracts
Dover, St Mary's, 1536–58	BL Eg. 1912	
Eltham, 1554		Halsted, *History of Kent*, vol. 1 (London, 1886), extracts; *Archaeologia* 34, extracts
Strood, 1555	BL Addl. MS 36,937	*Kent Records* 5 (1927)
All Hallows Hoo, 1555–(70)	Kent RO (Maidstone)	*Kent Records* 22–5
Chiddingstone, 1565		*Kent Records* 35–6
Lancashire		
Prescot, 1522 68	Lancs. RO (Preston)	*Transactions of the Historical Society of Lancashire and Cheshire* 92 (1940), 95 (1943)
Wigan, 1561–(70)		
Leicestershire		
Leicester, St Mary de Castro, 1490–1	Leics. RO	Nicholls, *History of Leicestershire* (1795), extracts 1491–1571

(cont.)

Parish and dates	Current location	References
Cossington,1534–(70)	Leics. RO	*Leics. Arch. Soc. Trans.* 19 (1936–7), extracts
Leicester, St Martin's, 1547	Leics. RO (transcript)	T. North (ed.), *The Accounts of St. Martin's, Leicester, 1489–1844* (1844)
Melton Mowbray, 1547–	Leics. RO	*Leics. Arch. Soc. Trans.* 3 (1874)
Castle Donington, 1550–(70)	Leics. RO	
Leicester, St Margaret's, 1553–(70)	Unknown	Extracts in *Antiquities of the County of Leicester* (1795)
Lincolnshire		
Sutterton, 1483–1536	Bodl. MS Rawl. D786	*Arch. Jnl.* 39 (1882)
Kirton in Lindsey, 1484	Unknown	*Antiquary* 19 (1889)
Wigtoft, 1487–1558	Unknown	Nichols, *Illust. Hist. of Manners*
Leverton, 1492–(1570)	Lincs. RO	*Archaeologia* 41 (1867)
Louth, St James, 1500–24 1527–(70)	Lincs. RO	*Archaeologia*, 10 (1792); R. C. Dudding (ed.), *The First Churchwardens' Book of Louth* (Oxford, 1941)
Horbling, 1533–(70)	Lincs. RO	
Addlethorpe, 1542–(70)	Lincs. RO	
Ingoldmells, 1542–(70)	Lincs. RO	
Witham on the Hill, 1548–(70)	Lincs. RO	
Heckington, *c.* 1560–(70)	Lincs. RO	
Norfolk		
East Dereham, 1413–70 (intermittent); 1478–98, 1538–40	Norf. RO	
Tilney All Saints, 1443–(1570)	Wisbech and Fenland Museum, Wisbech	Ed. A. D. Stallard (London, 1922)
Snettisham, 1468–(1570)	Norf. RO	
Swaffham, *c.* 1484, 1504–(70)	Norf. RO	
Denton, 1507–38	Norf. RO	
Shipdham, 1511–(70)	Norf. RO	
Anmer, 1522–58	Norf. RO	
Gt Witchingham, 1528–(70)	Norf. RO	*Norfolk Arch.* 13/2 (1896)

(*cont.*)

Parish and dates	Current location	References
Necton, 1536–(70)	Norf. RO	
Gissing, 1537–(70)	Norf. RO	
North Elmham, 1539–(70)	Norf. RO	A. G. Legge (ed.), *CWAs of North Elmham* (Norwich, 1891)
Wymondham, 1544–61	In parish	
Narborough, 1544–(70)	Norf. RO	
Norwich, St Benedict, 1547	BL Harl. MS 604	*East Anglian N & Q* 4 (1871)
Norwich, St Margaret, 1552–(70)	Norf. RO	
Brockdish, 1553–	Norf. RO (modern extracts)	
Loddon, 1554–(70)	Norf. RO	
Norwich, St John Madder market, 1556–(70)	Norf. RO	
Watton, 1560–(70)	Norf. RO	
Pulham, St Mary Magd., 1557–(70)	BL Addl. MS 23010	*East Anglian N & Q* 4 (1871), extracts
East Tuddenham, 1564–(70)	Norf. RO	
Reymerston, 1567–(70)	Norf. RO	
Northamptonshire		
Peterborough, St John, 1467–(1570)	Northants. RO	*Northants. Rec. Soc.* 9 (1939)
Culworth, 1530–(70)	Northants. RO	
Norton, 1548–(70)	Northants. RO	
Burton Latimer, 1559–(70)	Northants. RO	
Kingsthorpe, 1565	Northants. RO	J. H. Glover (ed.), *Kingsthorpiana* (1883)
Northumberland		
None		
Nottinghamshire		
Worksop Priory, 1544–(70)	Notts. RO	
Holme Pierrepoint, 1560–(70)		*Old Nottinghamshire* 2nd ser. 93–104
Oxfordshire		
Oxford, St Aldates, 1410, 1536	Oxf. RO	

(*cont.*)

Parish and dates	Current location	References
Oxford, St Michael, 1404, 1416–18, 1425, 1427–8, 1430, 1434–6, 1444–5, 1457–8, 1468–73, 1476, 1478–80, 1482, 1484, 1490–2, 1500, 1512, 1515–17, 1519, 1523, 1525–7, 1529–33, 1535–6, 1538, 1544, 1547, 1549, 1551–3, 1556–8, 1561, 1563–7, 1569–(70)	Oxf. RO	*Trans. Oxf. Arch. Soc.* (1933)
Thame, 1442–1524, 1528–(70)	Oxf. RO	*BBOAJ* 7–14, 16, 19, 20 (1902–14)
Oxford, St Peter's in the East, 1444, 1462, 1466, 1475, 1481–3, 1489, 1495, 1499?, 1503–5, 1507–10, 1512–13, 1518, 1520–1, 1523–4, 1527, 1531, 1541, 1545–6, 1553	Oxf. RO	
Oxford, St Peter le Bailey, 1453, 1461–2, 1464–9, 1471–80, 1499–1500, 1506–7, 1529–32, 1534–43, 1545–8, 1556–7, 1560–1, 1563–4	Oxf. RO	
Spelsbury, 1525–(70)	Oxf. RO	*Oxf. Rec. Soc.* 6 (1925)
Oxford, St Martin's, 1540, 1544–7, 1557–60, 1564–9	Oxf. RO	
Pyrton, 1547–(70)	Oxf. RO	*Oxf. Rec. Soc.* 6 (1925)
Marston, 1529–(70)	Oxf. RO	*Oxf. Rec. Soc.* 6 (1925)
South Newington, 1553–5, 1560–(70)	Oxf. RO	*Banbury Hist. Soc.* 6 (1964)
Witney, 1569–(70)	Oxf. RO	
Somerset		
Glastonbury, 1366–		*Jnl. Som. Arch Soc.* 48 (1902)
Bridgwater, 1373, 1383, 1385, 15th cent		
North Curry, 1443, 1460–1	Som. RO	
Yatton, 1445–1567	Som. RO	*Som. Rec. Soc.* 4 (1890); *Somerset and Dorset N & Q* 32 (1986)

(*cont.*)

Parish and dates	Current location	References
Tintinhull, 1453–1569	Som. RO	*Som. Rec. Soc.* 4 (1890)
Yeovil, 1457–8	Som. RO	Nichols, *Collectanea* (1836)
Croscombe, 1475–1548	Som. RO	*Som. Rec. Soc.* 4 (1890)
Pilton, 1498–1530	Som. RO	*Som. Rec. Soc.* 4 (1890)
Stogursey, 1502–47	Som. RO	
Nettlecombe, 1507–49	Som. RO	
Banwell, 1516–(70)	Som. RO	
Trull, ?1524–?1549	Som. RO	
Ilminster, 1542–	Som. RO	
Goathurst, 1545, 1553–4	Som. RO	
Lydeard St Lawrence, 1550–9	Som. RO	
Langford Budville, 1550–	Som. RO	
Winsford, 1551–	Som. RO	
Shropshire		
Worfield, 1500–(70)	Shrops. RO	*Trans. Shrops. Arch. Soc.* 3rd ser. 3–9 (1903–9)
Ludlow, 1469–71	Unknown	*Trans. Shrops. Arch. Soc.* 2nd ser. 1 (1889)
1540–(70)	Shrops. RO	*Camden Society* (1869)
Cheswardine, 1544–(70)	Shrops. RO	Extracts in *Shropshire Parish Docs.*
Shrewsbury, St Mary's, 1544–		
Staffordshire		
Walsall, 1462–1531	Walsall Local History Centre	*Collections for a History of Staffs.* (1928)
Wolverhampton, 1518–(70)	Shaw Hellier Coll., Womburne Woodhouse, Wolverhampton	
Yoxall, 1541–5	Staffs. RO	
Suffolk		
Mildenhall, 1446–54, 1504–33	Suffolk RO (Bury St Edmund's)	*East Anglian N & Q* 1 (1864)
Walberswick, 1450–99	Suffolk RO (Ipswich)	T. Gardener, *History of Dunwich* (1754), extracts
Brundish, 1474–1545	Suffolk RO (Ipswich)	
Cratfield, 1490–(1570)	Suffolk RO (Ipswich)	W. Holland and Raven, *Cratfield Parish Papers* (1895)

Appendix

(*cont.*)

Parish and dates	Current location	References
Chevington, *c.* 1513–43	CUL Hangrave Hall	MSS 17 (1) fragmentary
Bungay, St Mary, 1523–(70)	Suffolk RO (Lowestoft)	*East Anglian N & Q* 1 (1864)
Boxford, 1529–(70)	Suffolk RO (Bury St Edmunds)	*Camb. Antiq. Soc.* 1 (1859); *Suffolk Rec. Soc.* 23 (1982)
Huntingfield, 1529–47	Suffolk RO (Ipswich)	*Proc. Soc. Antiq.* 2nd ser. 1 (1861), extracts
Elmsett, 1530–(70)	Unknown	*East Anglian N & Q* 1 (1864)
Horham, 1531, 1564, 1569	Suffolk RO (Ipswich)	
Mickfield, 1538–48	Suffolk RO (Ipswich)	
Dennington, 1539–(70)	Suffolk RO (Ipswich)	
Burgate, 1540, 1558–9	Suffolk RO (Ipswich)	
Mendlesham, 1541–(70)		*Historical Manuscripts Commission* 5th report, 593, extracts
Metfield, 1547–(70)	Suffolk RO (Ipswich; unfit for production)	
Bungay, Holy Trinity, 1557–(70)	Suffolk RO (Lowestoft)	*East Anglian N & Q* 1 (1864)
Framlingham, 1557–8, 1567–70	Suffolk RO (Ipswich)	
Earl Soham, 1561–(70)	Suffolk RO (Ipswich)	
Ipswich, St Peter's, 1563–(70)	BL Addl. MS 25,344	
Bardwell, 1564–70	Suffolk RO (Bury St Edmunds)	
Surrey		
Kingston on Thames, 1498, 1503–38, 1561–(70)		
Shere, 1500–(70)	Surrey RO (Guildford)	
Horley, 1507–(70)	BL Addl. MS 6173	*Surrey Arch. Coll.* 8 (1883) extracts
Wandsworth, 1545–58		*Surrey Arch. Coll.* 15 (1900), 17 (1902)
Bletchingley, 1547		*Surrey Arch. Coll.* 15, 17 (1903)

(cont.)

Parish and dates	Current location	References
Seale, 1559–64	Surrey RO (Guildford)	*Surrey Arch. Coll.* 2 (1864)
Sussex		
Arlington, 1456–80	BL Addl. MS 33192	
Cowfold, 1460–85	W. Sussex RO	*Sussex Arch. Coll.* 2 (1849)
Rotherfield, 1509–(70)	E. Sussex RO	*Sussex Arch. Coll.* 41 (1898)
Rye, 1513–70	E. Sussex RO	
West Tarring, 1515–(70)	W. Sussex RO (transcript)	*Sussex Arch. Coll.* 41 (1898), p. 68
Steyning, 1519–(70)	W. Sussex RO	
Billingshurst, 1520–(70)	W. Sussex RO	
Ashurst, 1522–(70)	W. Sussex RO	
Lewes, St Andrew, 1522–46	E. Sussex RO	
Worth, 1528–1570	W. Sussex RO	
Bolney, 1536–(70)	W. Sussex RO	*Sussex Arch. Coll.* 6 (1853), extracts
Maresfield, 1543–(70)	E. Sussex RO	
Lewes, St Michael and St Andrew, 1546–(70)	E. Sussex RO	
Warwickshire		
Solihull, 1526–(70)	Warw. RO	
Warwick, St Nicholas, 1547–	Warw. RO	
Gt. Packington, 1551(?)–(70)	Warw. RO	
Rowington, 1554–(70)	Warw. RO	J. W. Rowland, *Records of Rowington* (1922)
Wiltshire		
Salisbury, St Edmund, 1443–	Wilts. RO	*Wilts. Rec. Soc.* (1896)
Calne, 1527–(70)	Wilts. RO	
Winterslow, 1542–61	In parish	*Wilts. Arch. Mag.* 36 (1909)
Steeple Ashton, 1542–50, 1558–60, 1569–(70)	Wilts. RO	
Mere, 1556–(70)	In parish	*Wilts. Arch. Mag.* 35 (1907)
Worcestershire		
Halesowen, 1487–(1570)	In parish; microfilm Birmingham Ref. Lib.	*Worc. Hist. Soc.* 40 (1952–7)
Worcester, St Helen's, 1519–20		*Worc. Hist. Soc.* 6 (1896)

(*cont.*)

Parish and dates	Current location	References
Badsey, 1529–58, 1566–(70)	Worcs. RO	W. H. Price and E. A. Barnard (eds.), *Churchwardens' Accounts of Badsey* (1913)
South Littleton, 1548–(70)		*Trans. Worc. Arch. Soc.* 3 (1925–6)
Worcester, St Michael in Bedwardine, 1539–(70)		*Worc. Hist. Soc.* 6 (1896)
Bewdley, 1569–(70)		Burton, *Bewdley* xii–xxxv
Yorkshire Hedon, St James, 1350–1476		J. R. Boyle, *History of Hedon* (Hull, 1895).
Hedon, St Nicholas, 1370–1537		As above
York, St Michael Spurrier Gate 1518–46		
Ecclesfield, 1520–(70)	Sheffield Archives	A. S. Gatty, *Registers of Ecclesfield* (1878)
Sheriff Hutton, 1524–68		*YAJ* 36 (1944)
Hedon, St Augustine's, 1549–(70)	Humberside RO	

BIBLIOGRAPHY

Manuscript sources

(For churchwardens' accounts see Appendix)

PUBLIC RECORD OFFICE

PRO E 117 2/17, E 117 8/22 Inventories of church goods, Dorset, Devon and
   Worcestershire.
PRO S P 1/102

LINCOLNSHIRE RECORD OFFICE

Consistory Court wills of the diocese of Lincoln (Leverton) to 1570

WORCESTERSHIRE RECORD OFFICE

Consistory Court wills of the diocese of Worcester to 1570
Visitation of the diocese of Worcester *c.* 1540, 802.0

THE QUEEN'S COLLEGE, OXFORD

A. Stafford, 'A iust Apology or a vindication of a booke entituled The Femall Glory
   from the false, and malevolent aspersions cast uppon it by Henry Burton of
   late deservedly censured in the Starr Chamber', The Queen's College, Oxford,
   MS Barlow 227.

PRINTED PRIMARY SOURCES

Abbott, R., *A wedding sermon preached at Bentley in Darbyshire*, London, 1608
   (STC 55).
Anon., *Maria Triumphans being a Discourse, wherin (by way of Dialogue) the B.
   Virgin Mary Mother of God, is defended and vindicated from all such
   Dishonours and Indignities, with which the Precisians of these our dayes, are
   accustomed uniustly to charge her*, St Omer, 1635 (STC 18331).
Anon., *Storys and prophesis out of the holy scriptur*, Antwerp, 1536 (STC 3014).

Anon., *The Song of Mary the Mother of Christ: containing the story of his life and passion*, London, 1601 (STC 17547).

Aylett, R., *Susanna; or the arraignment of the two uniust elders*, London, 1622 (STC 1003).

Babington, G., *Certaine plaine, brief and comfortable notes upon everie chapter of Genesis*, London, 1592 (STC 1086).

Bale, J., *The Actes of Englysh Votaryes*, London, 1560 (STC 1274).

Becke, E., *A brefe confutacion of this most detestable & anabaptistical opinion that Christ did not take flesh of the blessed Vyrgyn Mary nor any corporal substaunce of her body*, London, 1550 (STC 1709).

Bentley, T., *The Monument of Matrones: conteining seven severall lampes of virginitie*, London, 1582 (STC 1892).

Brice, T., *A compendious register in metre conteining the names, and pacient suffryngs of the members of Iesus Christ*, London, 1559 (STC 3726).

Bullinger, H., *The golden boke of christen matrimonye*, London, 1543 (STC 1724).

Byfield, N., *A Commentary upon the three first chapters of the first Epistle generall of St Peter*, London, 1637 (STC 4212).

C., R., *A Godly Forme of Household Government: For the ordering of private families according to the direction of Gods word*, London, 1603 (STC 5385).

Erasmus, D., *The First Tome or Volume of the Paraphrases of Erasmus upon the Newe Testament*, London, 1548 (STC 2854).

Gataker, T., *A Good Wife Gods Gift and A Wife Indeed. Two Marriage Sermons*, London, 1623 (STC 11659).

Goodman, G., *The Fall of Adam from paradice proved by naturall reason*, London, 1629 (STC 12026).

Greene, R., *The Myrrour of Modestie*, London, 1584 (STC 12278).

Gouge, W., *Of Domesticall Duties*, London, 1622, 1634 (STC 12119 and 12121).

Hunnis, W., *A hyve full of Hunnye: Contayning the First Booke of Moses, called Genesis*, London, 1578 (STC 13974).

Markham, G. (attrib.), *Marie Magdalens Lamentations for the losse of her master Iesus*, London, 1601 (STC 17569).

Shaw, J., *The Blessednes of Marie the mother of Iesus*, London, 1618 (STC 22391).

Smith, H., *Preparative to mariage – The summe whereof was spoken at a Contract, and inlarged after*, London, 1591 (STC 22685).

Southwell, R. [S. W.], *Marie Magdalens Funerall Teares*, London, 1594 (STC 22951).

Stafford, A., *The Femall Glory: or the Life and Death of our blessed lady, the holy virgin Mary, God's own immaculate mother*, London, 1635 (STC 23123).

Taylor, J., *The Life and Death of the most blessed among women, the Virgin Mary Mother of our Lord Iesus*, London, 1620 (STC 23770).

W. Whately, *A Bride-Bush or A Wedding Sermon*, London, 1617 (STC 25296).

A Care-Cloth, or a treatise of the cumbers and troubles of marriage, London, 1624 (STC 25299).

Edited primary sources

Babington, C. (ed.), *The Repressor of Over Much Blaming of the Clergy by Reginald Pecock, DD., sometime Lord Bishop of Chichester*, Rolls Series, vol. 19/1 and 2 (1860).

Bannister, Rev. Canon A.T., 'Visitation returns for the diocese of Hereford', *EHR* (1930).

Barnum, P. H. (ed.), *Dives and Pauper*, EETS orig. ser. 275 (London, 1976).

Beadle, R. (ed.), *The York Plays*, London, 1982.

Block, K. S. (ed.), *Ludus Coventriae or The Plaie called Corpus Christi*, EETS extra ser. 120 (London, 1922).

Brown, S. (ed.), *Women's Writing in Stuart England: The Mother's Legacies of Dorothy Leigh, Elizabeth Joscelin and Elizabeth Richardson* (Stroud, 1999).

Bruce, J. (ed.), *The Works of Roger Hutchinson*, Parker Society (Cambridge, 1842).

Burton, E. (ed.), *Three Primers Put Forth in the Reign of Henry VIII*, Oxford, 1834.

Campbell, W. E. (ed.), *Thomas More's 'The Dialogue Concerning Tyndale'* (London, 1927).

Cardwell, E. (ed.), *The Two Books of Common Prayer, Set Forth by the Authority of Parliament in the reign of King Edward VI* (Oxford, 1841).

Christmas, Rev. H. (ed.), *Select Works of John Bale D.D., Bishop of Ossory Containing the Examinations of Lord Cobham, William Thorpe and Ann Askew and The Image of Both Churches*, Parker Society (Cambridge, 1849).

Corrie, Rev. G. E. (ed.), *Sermons by Hugh Latimer, Sometime Bishop of Worcester, Martyr, 1555*, Parker Society (Cambridge, 1844).

Corrie, Rev. G. E. (ed.), *Sermons and Remains of Hugh Latimer*, Parker Society (Cambridge, 1845).

Davies, R. T. (ed.), *Medieval English Lyrics* (London, 1963).

Deimling, H. (ed.), *The Chester Plays*, EETS extra ser. 62 (London, 1892).

Dowling, M. and Shakespeare, J. (eds.), 'Religion and politics in mid Tudor England through the eyes of an English protestant woman: the recollections of Rose Hickman', *BIHR* 55 (1982), 97–102.

Ellis, F. S. (ed.), *The Golden Legend, or Lives of the Saints as Englished by William Caxton*, 7 vols. (London, 1928).

Erbe, T. (ed.), *Mirk's Festial: A Collection of Homilies by Johannes Mirkus*, EETS extra ser. 96 (London, 1905).

Fincham, K. (ed.), *Visitation Articles and Injunctions of the Early Stuart Church*, 2 vols. (Woodbridge 1994, 1998).

Frere, W. H. and Kennedy, W. M. (eds.), *Visitation Articles and Injunctions of the Period of the Reformation*, Alcuin Club Collection 14–16 (1910).

Furnivall, F. J. (ed.), *Early English Poems and Treatises on Manners and Meals in Olden Time*, EETS orig. ser. 32 (London, 1868).

(ed.), *The Digby Plays with an Incomplete Morality*, EETS extra ser. 70 (London, 1896).

(ed.), *Robert of Brunne's 'Handlyng Synne', AD 1303 with Those Parts of the French Treatise on which it was Founded, William of Waddington's 'Manuel des Pechiez'*, EETS orig. ser. 119 and 123, repr. as one vol. (New York, 1973).

Queene Elizabethes Achademy, A Booke of Precedence etc., EETS extra ser. 8 (London, 1969).

Garmonsway, G. N. and Raymo, R. R. (eds.), 'A Middle English prose life of St Ursula', *Review of English Studies* new ser. 9 (1958), 355–61.

Garter, T., *The Commodye of the moste vertuous and Godlye Susanna, never before this tyme Printed* (London, 1578), Malone Society Reprints, 1936.

Greg, W. W. (ed.), *A new enterlude of Godly Queene Hester edited from the quarto of 1561*, Materialen zur Kunde des älteren englischen Dramas (Louvain, 1904).

Harland, J. (ed.), 'Custom roll and rental of the manor of Ashton-under-Lyne, 1422', *Chetham Society* 74 (1868), pp. 112–16.

Hoskins, E. (ed.), *Horae Beatae Mariae Virginis or Sarum and York Primers with Kindred Books and Primers of the Reformed Roman Use* (London, 1901).

Keatinge Clay. Rev. W. (ed.), *Liturgical Services: Liturgies and Occasional Forms of Prayer Set Forth in the Reign of Queen Elizabeth*, Parker Society 27 (Cambridge, 1847).

Knox, Father R. and Leslie, S. (eds.) *Miracles of Henry VI* (Cambridge, 1923).

Lilly, J. (ed.), *A Collection of Seventy-nine Black-letter Ballads and Broadsides, Printed in the Reign of Queen Elizabeth, between the Years 1559 and 1597* (London, 1870).

Louis, C. (ed.), *The Commonplace Book of Robert Reynes of Acle: An Edition of Tanner Ms 407*, Garland Medieval Texts (London, 1980).

Masters, B. R. and Ralph, E. (eds.), *The Church Book of St Ewen's, Bristol, 1454–1584*, Bristol & Gloucestershire Arch. Soc. – Records Section 6 (1967).

Matthews, Dr. (ed.), *The Chester Plays, part 2*, EETS extra ser. 115 (London, 1916).

Morris, J. (ed.), *The Troubles of our Catholic Forefathers Related by Themselves*, ser. 3 (J. Mush, *A true report of the life and martyrdom of Mrs Margaret Clitherow*), London, 1877, pp. 360–440.

Mustanoja, T. (ed.), *The Good Wife Taught her Daughter, The Good Wyfe Wold a Pylgremage, The Thewis of Gud Women*, Annales Academiae Scientarum Fennicae в 61/2 (Helsinki, 1948).

Neale, Rev. J. W. and Webb, Rev. B. (eds.), *The Symbolism of Churches and Church Ornaments: A Translation of the First Book of the Rationale Divinorum Officiorum, Written by William Durandus Sometime Bishop of Mende* (London, 1843).

Nichols, J. G. (ed.), *The Diary of Henry Machyn*, Camden Society orig. ser. 42 (1847–8).

Nichols, J. G. (ed.), *Narratives of the Days of the Reformation*, Camden Society orig. ser. 77 (1859).

Norris, E. (ed.), *Ancient Cornish Drama*, vol. 1 (Oxford, 1859).

Palmes, W. (ed.), *Life of Mrs Dorothy Lawson of St Antonys near New Castle on Tyne* (Newcastle upon Tyne, 1851).

Powicke, F. M. and Cheney, C. R. (eds.), *Councils and Synods with other Documents Relating to the English Church, AD 1205–1265*, Oxford, 1964.

Pratt, Rev. J. (ed.), *The Acts and Monuments of John Foxe*, 8 vols. (London, 1877).

Purvis, J. S. (ed.), *Tudor Parish Documents of the Diocese of York* (Cambridge, 1948).

Raine, J. (ed.), *Depositions and other Ecclesiastical Proceedings from the Courts of Durham Extending from 1311 to the Reign of Elizabeth I*, Surtees Society 21 (1845).

Raine, J. (ed.), *Testamenta Eboracensia*, Surtees Society 53 (1868).

Robbins, R. H. (ed.), *Secular Lyrics of the Fourteenth and Fifteenth Centuries*, 2nd edn (Oxford, 1955).

Ross, W. O. (ed.), *Middle English Sermons Edited from BM MS Royal 18B xxiii*, EETS orig. ser. 209 (London, 1940).

Sparks, H. F. D. (ed.), *The Apocryphal Old Testament* (Oxford, 1984).

Spector, S. (ed.), *The N-town Play: Cotton MS Vespasian D.8*, EETS, 2 vols. (London, 1991).

Utterson, E. V. (ed.), *Select Pieces of Popular Poetry, Re-published Principally from Early Printed Copies in the Black Letter*, 2 vols. (London, 1817).

Waterhouse, O. (ed.), *The Non-Cycle Mystery Plays*, EETS extra ser. 104 (London, 1909).

Weatherly, E. H. (ed.), *Speculum Sacerdotale*, EETS orig. ser. 200 (London, 1936).
Whitfield White, P. (ed.), *Reformation Biblical Drama in England: The Life and Repentance of Mary Magdalene – The History of Esau and Jacob* (London, 1992).

Secondary sources

Almond, P. C., *Adam and Eve in Seventeenth Century Thought* (Cambridge, 1999).
Alsop, J. D., 'Religious preambles in early modern English wills as formulae', *JEH* 40 (1989), 19–27.
Amussen, S. D., *An Ordered Society: Gender and Class in Early Modern England* (Oxford, 1988).
 'Gender, family and the social order, 1560–1725', in A. Fletcher and J. Stevenson (eds.), *Order and Disorder in Early Modern England* (Cambridge, 1985), pp. 196–217.
Ashley, K. and Sheingorn, P. (eds.), *Interpreting Cultural Symbols: Saint Anne in Late Medieval Society* (Athens, Georgia, and London, 1990).
Aston, M., 'Segregation in church', in W. J. Shiels and D. Wood (eds.), *Women in the Church*, Studies in Church History 27 (Oxford, 1990), pp. 237–94.
 'Lollard women priests?' in her *Lollards and Reformers: Images and Literacy in Late Medieval Religion* (London, 1984).
 England's Iconoclasts: Laws against Images (Oxford, 1988).
 'The Bishops' Bible illustrations', in D. Wood (ed.), *The Church and the Arts*, Studies in Church History 28 (Oxford, 1992), pp. 267–85.
Atkinson, C. W., *Mystic and Pilgrim: The Book and the World of Margery Kempe* (Cornell, 1983).
Atkinson, C. W., 'Precious balsam in a fragile glass: the ideology of virginity in the later Middle Ages', *Journal of Family History* 8/2 (1983), 131–43.
Aveling, H. [J. C. H.], *Northern Catholics: The Catholic Recusants of the North Riding of Yorkshire, 1558–1790* (London, 1966).
 The Handle and the Axe: The Catholic Recusants in England from Reformation to Emancipation (London, 1976).
Bainbridge, V., *Gilds in the Medieval English Countryside: Social and Religious Change in Cambridgeshire, c. 1350–1558* (Woodbridge, 1996).
Bakere, J., *The Cornish Ordinalia: A Critical Study* (Cardiff, 1980).
Barron, C. M., 'The parish fraternities of medieval London', in C. M. Barron and C. Harper-Bill (eds.), *The Church in Pre-Reformation Society: Essays in Honour of F. R. H. Du Boulay* (Woodbridge, 1985).
Baskins, C. L., ' "La festa di Susanna": virtue on trial in Renaissance sacred drama and painted wedding chests', *Art History* 14/3 (1991), 329–44.
Beatie, B. A., 'Saint Katherine of Alexandria: traditional themes and the development of a German hagiographic narrative', *Speculum* 52 (1977), 785–800.
Beckwith, S., 'A very material mysticism: The medieval mysticism of Margery Kempe', in D. Aers (ed.), *Medieval Literature: Criticism, Ideology and History* (Brighton, 1988), pp. 34–57.
 Christ's Body: Identity, culture and society in late medieval writings (London & New York, 1993).

Beilin, E. V., 'Anne Askew's self portrait in the *Examinations*', in M. P. Hannay (ed.), *Silent but for the Word: Tudor Women as Patrons, Translators and Writers of Religious Works* (Ohio, 1985), pp. 77–91.

    Redeeming Eve: Women Writers of the English Renaissance (Princeton, 1987).

Benton, Rev. G. H. 'Wall paintings formerly in the churches of Dovercourt and Hazeleigh', *Trans. Essex Arch. Soc.* 20 (1930–31), 243–7.

Beit-Hallahmi, B. and Argyle, M., *The Psychology of Religious Behaviour, Belief and Experience* (London, 1997).

Binski, P., *Medieval Death: Ritual and Representation* (London, 1996).

    'The English parish church and its art in the later Middle Ages – a review of the problem', *Studies in Iconography* 20 (1999).

Bird, W. H., *The Ancient Mural Paintings in the Churches of Gloucestershire* (Gloucester, 1933).

Blackburn, R. H., *Biblical Drama under the Tudors* (The Hague, 1971).

Blair, J. 'Saint Beornwald of Bampton: Further references', *Oxoniensia* 54 (1989), 400–3.

Blamires, A., 'Women and preaching in medieval orthodoxy, heresy and saints' lives', *Viator* 26 (1995), 135–52.

Blaylock, S. R. and Bishop, P. J. F., 'St Mary's church, Bratton Clovelly, Devon: recording of wall paintings, 1993', *Exeter Museums Archaeological Field Unit Report* no. 93.31 (Exeter, 1993).

Bliss, L., 'The Renaissance Griselda: a woman for all seasons', *Viator* 23 (1992), 301–43.

Bond, F. Bligh, *Wood Carvings in English Churches*, 2 vols. (London, 1910).

Bond, F. Bligh, and Camm, Dom. Bede, *Roodscreens and Roodlofts* (London, 1909).

Bond, R. B., "Dark deeds darkly answered": Thomas Becon's *Homily against Whoredom and Adultery*, its contexts and its affiliations with three Shakespeare plays', *Sixteenth Century Journal* 16/2 (1985), 191–205.

Bonnell, J. K., 'The serpent with the human head in art and mystery play', *American Journal of Archaeology* new ser. 21 (1917), 255–91.

Bossy, J., 'Blood and baptism: kinship, community and Christianity in Western Europe from the fourteenth to the seventeenth century', in D. Baker (ed.), *Sanctity and Secularity: The Church and the World*, Studies in Church History 10 (Oxford, 1973), pp. 129–43.

    The English Catholic Community, 1570–1850 (London, 1975).

    Christianity in the West, 1400–1700 (Oxford, 1985).

    'The mass as a social institution, 1200–1700', *P & P* 100 (1983), 29–61.

Bowman, W. M., *England in Ashton-under-Lyne* (Altrincham, 1960).

Breeze, A., 'The Virgin's rosary and St. Michael's scales', *Studia Celtica* 24/25 (1989–90), 91–8.

Brigden, S., 'Youth and the English Reformation', *P & P* 95 (1982), 37–67.

    'Religion and social obligation in early sixteenth-century London', *P & P* 103 (1984), 67–112.

    London and the Reformation (Oxford, 1989).

Bronfmann, J., 'Griselda: Renaissance woman', in A. M. Haselkorn and B. S. Travitsky (eds.), *The Renaissance Englishwoman in Print: Counterbalancing the Canon* (Amherst, Mass., 1990).

Brooke, C., 'Religious sentiment and church design in the later Middle Ages', in C. Brooke (ed.), *Medieval Church and Society* (London, 1971), pp. 162–82.

Brown, A., *Popular Piety in Late Medieval England: The Diocese of Salisbury, 1250–1550* (Oxford, 1995).

Brownlow, F. W., *Robert Southwell* (New York, 1996).

Bulwer, Rev. J., 'Notice of a mural painting in the south transept of Cawston church', *Norfolk Archaeology* 3 (1852), 36–9.

Burgess, C., ' "For the increase of divine service": chantries in the parish in late medieval Bristol', *JEH* 36/1 (1985), 46–65.

    ' "A fond thing vainly invented": an essay on purgatory and pious motive in later medieval England', in S. Wright (ed.), *Parish, Church and People: Local Studies in Lay Religion, 1350–1750* (London, 1988), pp. 56–84.

    'Late mediaeval wills and pious convention: testamentary evidence reconsidered', in M. Hicks (ed.), *Profit, Piety and the Professions in Later Medieval England* (Gloucester, 1990), pp. 14–30.

Byman, S., 'Ritualistic acts and compulsive behaviour: the pattern of Tudor martyrdom', *Am. Hist. Rev.* 83/3 (1978), 625–43.

Bynum, C. W. *Holy Feast and Holy Fast: The Religious Significance of Food to Medieval Woman* (Berkeley and London, 1987).

    Fragmentation and Redemption: Essays on Gender and the Human Body in Medieval Religion (New York, 1991).

Caiger-Smith, A., *English Medieval Wallpaintings* (Oxford, 1963).

Camden, C., *Elizabethan Women: A Panorama of English Womanhood, 1540–1640* (London, 1952).

Capp, B., 'Separate domains? Women and authority in early modern England', in P. Griffiths, A. Fox and S. Hindle (eds.), *The Experience of Authority in Early Modern England* (London, 1996), pp. 117–45.

Carey, H. M., 'Devout literate laypeople and the pursuit of the mixed life in later medieval England', *Journal of Religious History* 14 (1987), 361–81.

Casey, P. F., *The Susanna Theme in German Literature: Variations of the Biblical Drama*, Abhandlungen zur Kunst-, Musik-, und Literaturwissenschaft 214 (Bonn, 1976).

Cautley, H. M., *Royal Arms and Commandments in our Churches* (Ipswich, 1934).

Cheetham, F., *English Medieval Alabasters, with a catalogue of the collection in the Victoria and Albert Museum* (Oxford, 1984).

Christian, W. A., *Local Religion in Sixteenth Century Spain*, Princeton, 1981.

Christensen, C. C., *Art and the Reformation in Germany*, Ohio, 1979.

Clayton, M., *The Cult of the Virgin Mary in Anglo-Saxon England*, Cambridge Studies in Anglo-Saxon England 2 (Cambridge, 1990).

Clegg, C. S., *Press Censorship in Elizabethan England*, Cambridge, 1997.

Collinson, P., 'A magazine of religious patterns: an Erasmian topic transposed in English protestantism', in D. Baker (ed.), *Renaissance and Renewal in Christian History*, Studies in Church History 14 (Oxford, 1977), pp. 233–49.

    From Iconoclasm to Iconophobia: The Cultural Impact of the Second English Reformation, Stenton lecture (Reading, 1986).

    The Birthpangs of Protestant England: Religious and Cultural Change in the Sixteenth and Seventeenth Centuries (New York, 1988).

    ' "Not sexual in the ordinary sense": women, men and religious transactions', in his *Elizabethan Essays* (London, 1994), pp. 119–50.

Collinson, P. and Craig, J. (eds.), *The Reformation in English Towns, 1500–1640* (Basingstoke, 1998).

Comensoli, V., *Household Business: Domestic Plays of Early Modern England* (Toronto and London, 1996).

Cox, J. C., *Churchwardens' Accounts from the Close of the Fourteenth Century to the Close of the Seventeenth Century* (London, 1913).

Crawford, P., *Women and Religion in England, 1500–1720* (London and New York, 1993).

Crewe, S., *Stained Glass in England, 1180–1540* (RCHME, 1987).

Cross, C., 'An Elizabethan martyrologist and his martyr: John Mush and Mrs Margaret Clitherow', in D. Wood (ed.), *Martyrs and Martyrologies*, Studies in Church History 30 (Oxford, 1993), pp. 271–81.

Cullum, P. H., ' "And hir name was Charite": Charitable giving by and for women in late medieval Yorkshire', in P. J. P. Goldberg (ed.), *Woman is a Worthy Wight: Women in English Medieval Society, 1200–1500* (Stroud, 1992), pp. 182–211.

Davies, K. M., 'Continuity and change in literary advice on marriage', in R. B. Outhwaite (ed.), *Marriage and Society* (London, 1981), pp. 58–80.

Davis, J., 'Joan of Kent, Lollardy and the English Reformation', *JEH* 33/2 (1982), 225–33.

   Heresy and the Reformation in the South East of England, 1520–1559 (London, 1983).

Devereux, J. A., 'Reformed doctrine in the collects of the First Book of Common Prayer', *Harvard Theological Review* 58 (1965), 49–68.

Dewar, S., 'St Katherine of Alexandria and her cult at Abbotsbury', *Proceedings of the Dorset Natural History and Archaeological Society* 90 (1969), 261–3.

Dickens, A. G., *Lollards and Protestants in the Diocese of York, 1509–58* (Oxford, 1959).

Dodgson, C., 'English devotional woodcuts of the late fifteenth century, with special reference to those in the Bodleian Library', *Walpole Society* 17 (1929), 95–108.

Dolan, F. E., *Dangerous Familiars: Representations of Domestic Crime in England, 1550–1700* (Ithaca and London, 1994).

Douglas, M., *Natural Symbols: Explorations in Cosmology* (London, 1970).

Drury, G. Dru, 'Three Dorset effigies with unusual individual details', *Proceedings of the Dorset Natural History and Archaeological Society* 75 (1953), 86–90.

Duffy, E., 'Devotion to the crucifix and related images in England on the eve of the Reformation', in R. Scribner (ed.), *Bilder und Bildersturm im Spätmittelalter und in der frühen Neuzeit* (Wiesbaden, 1990), pp. 21–36.

   ' "Holy maidens, holy wyfes": the cult of women saints in fifteenth and sixteenth century England', in W. J. Shiels and D. Wood (eds.), *Women in the Church*, Studies in Church History 27 (Oxford, 1990), pp. 175–96.

   The Stripping of the Altars: Traditional Religion in England, 1400–1580 (New Haven and London, 1992).

   'The parish, piety and patronage in late medieval East Anglia: the evidence of rood screens', in K. L. French, G. G. Gibbs and B. A. Kümin (eds.), *The Parish in English Life, 1400–1600* (Manchester, 1997), pp. 133–62.

Eales, J., 'Gender construction in early modern England and the conduct books of William Whately (1583–1639)', in R. N. Swanson (ed.), *Gender and Christian Religion*, Studies in Church History 34 (Oxford, 1998), pp. 163–174.

Fairfield, L. P., *John Bale: Mythmaker for the English Reformation* (Indiana, 1976).

Fletcher, A., 'The Protestant idea of marriage in early modern England', in A. Fletcher and P. Roberts (eds.), *Religion, Culture and Society in Early Modern Britain: Essays in Honour of Patrick Collinson* (Cambridge, 1994), pp. 161–81.

Gender, Sex and Subordination in England, 1500–1800 (London, 1995).

Foister, S., '*Paintings and other works of art in sixteenth-century English inventories*', Burlington Magazine CXXIII no. 938 (May 1981), 273–82.

Fowler, D. C., 'The date of the Cornish "Ordinalia" ', *Medieval Studies* 23 (1961), 91–125.

Foyster, E. A., *Manhood in Early Modern England: Honour, Sex and Marriage* (Longman, 1999).

Freeman, T., ' "The good ministry of godlye and vertuouse women": the Elizabethan martyrologists and the female supporters of the Marian martyrs', *Journal of British Studies* 39/1 (2000), 8–33.

French, K. L., *The People of the Parish: Community Life in a Late Medieval English Diocese* (Philadelphia, 2001).

Friedl, E., 'The position of women: appearance and reality', in J. Dubisch (ed.), *Gender and Power in Rural Greece* (Princeton, 1986).

Gardiner, A., *English Alabaster Tombs of the Pre-Reformation Period in England* (Cambridge, 1940).

Garth, H. M., *Saint Mary Magdalene in Medieval Literature*, Johns Hopkins University Studies in Historical and Political Science 67/3 (Baltimore, 1950).

Gaskill, M., 'Witchcraft in early modern Kent: stereotypes and the background to accusations', in J. Barry *et al.* (eds.), *Witchcraft in Early Modern Europe: Studies in Culture and Belief* (Cambridge, 1996).

Gittings, C., *Death, Burial and the Individual in Early Modern England* (London, 1984).

Goldberg, P. J. P., *Women, Work and Lifecycle in a Medieval Economy: Women in York and Yorkshire c.1300–1520* (Oxford, 1992).

Gowing, L., *Domestic Dangers: Women, Words and Sex in Early Modern London* (Oxford, 1996).

Green, I., ' "For children in yeeres and children in understanding": the emergence of the English catechism under Elizabeth and the early Stuarts', *JEH* 37/3 (1986), 397–425.

The Christian's ABC: Catechism and Catechising in England, c. 1530–1740 (Oxford, 1996).

Guldan, E., *Eva und Maria: Eine Antithese als Bildmotiv* (Graz and Cologne, 1966).

Hackett, H., *Virgin Mother, Maiden Queen: Elizabeth I and the Cult of the Virgin Mary* (Basingstoke, 1995).

Haigh, C., *English Reformations: Religion, Politics and Society under the Tudors* (Oxford, 1993).

Hanawalt, B., 'Keepers of the lights: late medieval English parish gilds', *Journal of Medieval and Renaissance Studies* 14 (1984), 21–35.

Hardy, W. J., 'Remarks on the history of seat reservation in churches', *Archaeologia* 53 (1892), 95–106.

Hart, A. T., *The Man in the Pew, 1558–1660* (London, 1966).

Heales, A. C., *The History and Law of Church Seats or Pews* (London, 1872).

Hobhouse, Dr. 'Hogglers and hoglinge money', *Somerset & Dorset N & Q* 20 (1930), 62–3.

Hodnett, E., *English Woodcuts, 1480–1535* (Oxford, 1973).

Holbrook, S. E., 'Margery Kempe and Wynkyn de Worde', in M. Glasscoe (ed.), *The Medieval Mystical Tradition in England*, Exeter Symposium IV, Papers Read at Dartington Hall, July 1987 (Woodbridge, 1987), pp. 27–46.

Horst, I. B., *The Radical Brethren: Anabaptism and the English Reformation to 1558* (Nieuwkoop, 1972).

Houlbrooke, R. A., 'Women's social life and common action in England from the fifteenth century to the eve of the Civil War', *Continuity and Change* 1/2 (1986), 171–89.

   Death, Religion and the Family in England, 1480–1750 (Oxford, 1998).

Hudson, A., *The Premature Reformation: Wycliffite Texts and Lollard History* (Oxford, 1988).

Hudson, E. K., 'English protestants and the *Imitatio Christi*, 1580–1620', *Sixteenth Century Journal* 19/4 (1988), 541–58.

Huizinga, J., *The Waning of the Middle Ages: A Study of the Forms of Life and Art in France and the Netherlands in the Fourteenth and Fifteenth centuries* (London, 1955).

Hull, S. W., *Chaste, Silent and Obedient: English Books for Women, 1475–1640* (San Marino, 1982).

Husenbeth, Rev. F. C., 'Mural paintings at Drayton', *Norfolk Archaeology* 3 (1852), 24–8.

Hutton, R., *The Rise and Fall of Merry England: The Ritual Year 1400–1700* (Oxford, 1994).

Ingram, M., *Church Courts, Sex and Marriage in England, 1570–1640* (Cambridge, 1987).

   'Ridings, rough music and the "reform of popular culture" in early modern England', *P & P* 105 (1984), 79–113.

   '"Scolding women cucked or washed": a crisis in gender relations in early modern England?', in G. Walker and J. Kermode (eds.), *Women, Crime and the Courts in Early Modern England* (London, 1994), pp. 48–80.

James, M., *Family, Lineage and Civil Society: A Study of Society, Politics and Mentality in the Durham Region, 1500–1640* (Oxford, 1974).

James, M. R., 'The iconography of Buckinghamshire', *Records of Bucks.* 12 (1932), 281–98.

Jennings, M., 'Tutivullus: The literary career of the recording demon', *Studies in Philology* 74 (1977), 1–87.

Jones, A. R., 'Nets and bridles: early modern conduct books and sixteenth-century women's lyrics', in N. Armstrong and L. Tannenhouse (eds.), *The Ideology of Conduct: Essays on Literature and the History of Sexuality* (New York and London, 1987), pp. 39–72.

Jordan, W. K., *Philanthropy in England, 1480–1660* (London, 1959).

Karras, R. M., 'Two models, two standards: moral teaching and sexual mores', in B. Hanawalt and D. Wallace (eds.), *Bodies and Disciplines: Intersections of Literature and History in Fifteenth Century England* (Minneapolis and London, 1996), pp. 123–38.

Kendon, F., *Mural Paintings in English Churches during the Middle Ages* (London, 1923).

Kelly, H. A., 'The metamorphoses of the Eden serpent during the Middle Ages and Renaissance', *Viator* 2 (1971), 301–27.

Kelly-Gadol, J., 'Did women have a Renaissance?', in R. Bridenthal and C. Koonz (eds.), *Becoming Visible: Women in European History* (New York, 1977), pp. 137–64.

Keyser, C. E., *A List of Buildings Having Mural Decorations* (London, 1883).
'On some mural paintings recently discovered in the churches of Little Horwood and Padbury, Buckinghamshire', *Records of Bucks.* 7 (1897), 215–228.
'On the panel paintings of saints on the Devonshire screens', *Archaeologia* 56/1 (1898).

King, J. N., *English Reformation Literature: The Tudor Origins of the Protestant Tradition* (Princeton, 1982).
'The godly woman in Elizabethan iconography', *Renaissance Quarterly* 38 (1985), 41–84.

Kinnear, M., *Daughters of Time: Women in the Western Tradition* (Ann Arbor, 1982).

Knott, J. R., *Discourses of Martyrdom in English Literature, 1563–1694* (Cambridge, 1993).

Kreider, A., *English Chantries – The Road to Dissolution* (Cambridge, Mass., 1979).

Kümin, B., *The Shaping of a Community: The Rise and Reformation of the English Parish, c. 1400–1560* (Aldershot, 1996).

Kunoth-Leifels, E., *Über die Darstellung der "Bathseba im Bade": Studien zur Geschichte des Bildthemas 4. bis 17. Jahrhundert* (Essen, 1962).

Lack, W., Stuchfield, H. M. and Whittemore, P., *The Monumental Brass Society County Series*: Bedfordshire, Berkshire, Buckinghamshire, Cambridgeshire, Cheshire, Cornwall, Cumberland and Westmorland, Derbyshire, Devonshire (London, 1992–2000).

Lake, P., *Moderate Puritans and the Elizabethan Church* (Cambridge, 1982).
'Feminine piety and personal potency: the emancipation of Mrs Jane Ratcliffe', *The Seventeenth Century* 2/2 (1987), 143–65.

Lewis, F., 'From image to illustration: the place of devotional images in the Book of Hours', in G. Duchet-Suchaux (ed.), *Iconographie médiévale – Image, texte, contexte* (Paris, 1990), pp. 29–48.
' "Garnyshed with gloryous tytles": indulgences in printed books of hours in England', *Transactions of the Cambridge Bibliographical Society* 10 (1995), 577–90.
'The wound in Christ's side and the instruments of the passion: gendered experience and response', in L. Smith and J. H. M. Taylor (eds.), *Women and the Book: Assessing the Visual Evidence* (London and Toronto, 1996), pp. 204–229.

Lillie, Rev. W. W., 'Medieval paintings on the screens of the parish churches of mid and southern England', *JBAA* 2nd ser. 9 (1944), 33–47.

Litzenberger, C., 'Local responses to changes in religious policy based on evidence from Gloucestershire wills (1540–80)', *Continuity and Change* 8/3 (1993), 417–39.
The English Reformation and the Laity: Gloucestershire, 1540–80 (Cambridge, 1997).

Lucas, R. V., 'Puritan preaching and the politics of the family', in A. M. Haselkorn and B. S. Travitsky (eds.), *The Renaissance Englishwoman in Print: Counterbalancing the Canon* (Amherst, 1990), pp. 224–35.

McColley, D. K., *A Gust for Paradise: Milton's Eden and the Visual Arts* (Urbana and Chicago, 1993).

MacCulloch, D., *Suffolk and the Tudors: Politics and Religion in an English County, 1500–1600* (Oxford, 1986).

McGuinn, B., 'Teste David cum Sibylla: the significance of the Sibylline tradition in the Middle Ages', in J. Kirshner and S. F. Wemple (eds.), *Women of the Medieval World: Essays in Honour of John H. Mundy* (Oxford, 1985), pp. 7–35.

McIntosh, M. K., *A Community Transformed: The Manor and Liberty of Havering, 1500–1620* (Cambridge, 1991).

McMurray Gibson, G., *The Theater of Devotion: East Anglian Drama and Society in the Late Middle Ages* (Chicago, 1989).

'Blessing from sun and moon: churching as women's theater', in B. Hanawalt and D. Wallace (eds.), *Bodies and Disciplines: Intersections of Literature and History in Fifteenth-Century England* (Minneapolis and London, 1996), pp. 139–54.

McSheffrey, S., *Gender and Heresy: Women and Men in Lollard Communities, 1420–1530* (Philadelphia, 1995).

Macek, E., 'The emergence of feminine spirituality in the *Book of Martyrs*', *Sixteenth Century Journal* 19 (1988), 63–80.

Maltby, J., *Prayer Book and People in Elizabethan and Early Stuart England* (Cambridge, 1998).

Malvern, M. M., 'An earnest "Monyscyon" and "thinge Delectabyll" realized verbally and visually in "A Disputacion Betwyx the Body and Wormes", a Middle English poem inspired by tomb art and northern spirituality', *Viator* 13 (1982), 415–43.

Marks, R., *Stained Glass in England during the Middle Ages* (London and Toronto, 1993).

Marshall, P., *The Catholic Priesthood and the English Reformation* (Oxford, 1994).

Matsuda, T., *Death and Purgatory in Middle English Didactic Poetry* (Cambridge, 1997).

Mayo, C., *A History of Wimborne Minster* (London, 1860).

Miles, M. R., *Image as Insight: Visual Understanding in Western Christianity and Secular Culture* (Boston, 1985).

Milton, A., *Catholic and Reformed: The Roman and Protestant Churches in English Protestant Thought, 1600–1640* (Cambridge, 1995).

Moore, S. H., 'Sexing the soul: Gender and the rhetoric of puritan piety', in R. N. Swanson (ed.), *Gender and Christian Religion*, Studies in Church History 34 (Oxford, 1998), pp. 175–186.

Mueller, J. M., 'Pain, persecution and the construction of selfhood in Foxe's *Acts and Monuments*', in C. McEachern and D. Shuger (eds.), *Religion and Culture in Renaissance England* (Cambridge, 1997), pp. 161–87.

Nair, G., *Highley: The Development of a Community, 1550–1880* (Oxford, 1988).

Nichols, A. E., *Seeable Signs: The Iconography of the Seven Sacraments, 1350–1544* (Woodbridge, 1994).

Neale, J. M., *The History of Pues* (Cambridge, 1843).

Nussbaum, D., 'Reviling the saints or reforming the calendar? John Foxe and his "Kalendar" of martyrs', in S. Wabuda and C. Litzenberger (eds.), *Belief and Practice in Reformation England: A Tribute to Patrick Collinson from his Students* (Aldershot, 1998), pp. 113–36.

O'Sullivan, O., 'Women's place: gender, obedience and authority in the sixteenth century', *Reformation* 3 (1998), 225–58.

Owst, G. R., *Literature and Pulpit*, 2nd edition (Oxford, 1961).

Palliser, D. M., 'The parish in perspective', in S. Wright (ed.), *Parish, Church and People* (London, 1988), pp. 5–28.

Pantin, W. A., *The English Church in the Fourteenth Century* (Cambridge, 1955).

'Instructions for a devout and literate layman', in J. J. G. Alexander and M. T. Gibson (eds.), *Medieval Learning and Literature* (Oxford, 1976), pp. 398–422.

Parish, H. L., *Clerical Marriage and the English Reformation: Precedent, Policy and Practice* (Aldershot, 2000).

Park, D., 'The "Lewes group" of wall paintings in Sussex', in R. Allen Brown (ed.), *Anglo-Norman Studies 6*, Proceedings of the Battle Conference 1983 (Woodbridge, 1984), pp. 200–35.

Parker, R., *The Subversive Stitch: Embroidery and the Making of the Feminine* (London, 1984).

Petroff, E. A., *Body and Soul: Essays on Medieval Women and Mysticism* (Oxford, 1994).

Pfaff, R. W., *New Liturgical Feasts in Later Medieval England* (Oxford, 1970).

Phillips, J., *The Reformation of Images: Destruction of Art in England, 1535–1660* (Berkeley and London, 1973).

Power, E., 'The position of women', in C. G. Crump and E. F. Jacob (eds.), *The Legacy of the Middle Ages* (Oxford, 1926).

Purdie, E., *The Story of Judith in German and English Literature* (Paris, 1927).

Ravenshaw, T. F., *Antiente Epitaphes, from AD 1250 to AD 1800, Collected by T. F. Ravenshaw* (London, 1878).

Reader, F. W., 'Tudor mural paintings in the lesser houses in Buckinghamshire', *Arch. Jnl.* 89 (1932), 368–98.

'Tudor domestic wall paintings', *Arch. Jnl.* 92 (1935), 243–86 and 93 (1936), 220–62.

Rex, R., 'The crisis of obedience: God's Word and Henry's Reformation', *Historical Journal* 39/4 (1996), 863–94.

Riddy, F., 'Mother knows best: reading social change in a courtesy text', *Speculum* 71 (1996), 66–86.

Roper, L., 'Luther: Sex, marriage and motherhood', *History Today* 33 (Dec. 1983), 33–8.

Ross, E. M., *The Grief of God: Images of the Suffering Jesus in Late Medieval England* (Oxford, 1997).

Rosser, G., 'Communities of parish and gild in the Middle Ages', in S. Wright (ed.), *Parish, Church and People* (London, 1988), pp. 29–55.

Roston, M., *Biblical Drama in England from the Middle Ages to the Present Day* (Evanston, 1968).

Rouse, E. C., 'Wall paintings in the church of St. John the evangelist, Corby, Lincs.', *Arch. Jnl.* 100 (1943), 150–76.

'Wall paintings in Radnage church, Buckinghamshire', *Records of Bucks.* 15 (1947–52), 134–38.

'Wall paintings in the church of St. Pega, Peakirk, Northants.', *Arch. Jnl.* 110 (1954), 135–49.

'The Penn Doom', *Records of Bucks.* 17/2 (1962), 95–104.

'Wall paintings in St Mary's church, Padbury', *Records of Bucks.* 18 (1966–70), 24–33.

'Elizabethan wall paintings at Little Moreton Hall', in G. Jackson Stops (ed.), *National Trust Studies 1980* (1979), pp. 112–18.

'Domestic wall and panel paintings in Hertfordshire', *Arch. Jnl.* 146 (1989), 423–50.

Rowlands, M. B.,'Recusant women, 1560–1640', in M. Prior (ed.), *Women in English Society, 1500–1800* (London, 1985), pp. 149–80.

Rubin, M., *Corpus Christi: The Eucharist in Late Medieval Culture* (Cambridge, 1991).

'Choosing death? Experiences of martyrdom in late medieval Europe', in D. Wood (ed.), *Martyrs and Martyrologies*, Studies in Church History 30, (Oxford, 1993), pp. 153–83.

Rushforth, G. McN., 'The windows of the church at St. Neot, Cornwall', *Transactions of the Exeter Diocesan Architectural and Archaeological Society* 15 (1927), 150–90.

Scarisbrick, J. J., *The Reformation and the English People*, (Oxford, 1984).

Scase, W., 'St. Anne and the education of the Virgin: literary and artistic traditions and their implications', in N. Rogers (ed.), *Harlaxton Medieval Studies III: England in the Fourteenth Century* (Stamford, 1993), pp. 81–96.

Schmitz, G., *The Fall of Women in Early English Narrative Verse*, (Cambridge, 1990).

Sharpe, K., *The Personal Rule of Charles I* (London, 1992).

Sheingorn, P., *The Easter Sepulchre in England* (Kalamazoo, 1987).

'The wise mother: the image of St. Anne teaching the Virgin Mary', *Gesta* 32/1 (1993), 69–80.

Shekede, L. and Rickerby, S., *Knightstone Manor, Ottery St Mary: Report on the Conservation of the Wall Painting* (March 1998).

Shen, C. S., 'Women and the London parishes, 1500–1620', in K. L. French, G. G. Gibbs and B. A. Kümin (eds.), *The Parish in English Life, 1400–1600* (Manchester, 1997), pp. 250–68.

Shiels, B., 'Household, age and gender amongst Jacobean Yorkshire recusants', in M. B. Rowlands (ed.), *English Catholics of Parish and Town, 1558–1778*, Catholic Record Society Publications Monograph Series (London, 1999), pp. 131–52.

Shorrocks, D. M. M., 'The custom of hogling', *Somerset & Dorset N & Q* 28 (Sept. 1967).

Shuger, D. K., *The Renaissance Bible: Scholarship, Sacrifice and Subjectivity* (Berkeley and London, 1994).

Slater, P., 'Ancient mural painting, lately discovered in Lindfield church', *Sussex Archaeological Collections* 2 (1849), 129–31.

Slatter, J., 'Description of the paintings discovered on the north wall of Swanbourne church, Buckinghamshire', *Records of Bucks.* 3 (1870).

Smith-Bannister, S., *Names and Naming Patterns in England, 1538–1700* (Oxford, 1997).

Sommerville, M. R., *Sex and Subjection: Attitudes to Women in Early Modern Society* (London, 1995).

Spufford, M., 'The scribes of villagers' wills in the sixteenth and seventeenth centuries and their influence', *Local Population Studies* 7 (1971), 28–43.

Contrasting Communities: English Villagers in the Sixteenth and Seventeenth Centuries, (Cambridge, 1974).

Small Books and Pleasant Histories: Popular Fiction and its Readership in Seventeenth-Century England (London, 1981).

St. John Hope, W., 'On the sculptured alabaster tablets called St John's heads', *Archaeologia* 52/2 (1890), 669–708.

Stokes, J., 'The hoglers: evidence of an entertainment tradition in eleven Somerset parishes', *Somerset & Dorset N & Q* 32 (March 1990).

Strachan, J., *Early Bible Illustrations: A Short Study Based on Some Fifteenth and Early Sixteenth Century Texts* (Cambridge, 1957).

Stretton, T., *Women Waging Law in Elizabethan England* (Cambridge, 1998).

Sutcliffe, S., 'The cult of St. Sitha in England: An introduction', *Nottingham Medieval Studies* 37 (1993), 83–9.

Sutherland, S., ' "Not or I see more neede": the wife of Noah in the Chester, York and Towneley cycles', in W. R. Elton and W. B. Long (eds.), *Shakespeare and Dramatic Tradition: Essays in Honour of S. F. Johnson* (London and Toronto, 1989), pp. 181–93.

Thomas, K., 'The Puritans and adultery: The Act of 1650 reconsidered', in D. Pennington and K. Thomas (eds.), *Puritans and Revolutionaries: Essays in Seventeenth Century History Presented to Christopher Hill* (Oxford, 1978), pp. 257–82.

Todd, M., *Christian Humanism and the Puritan Social Order* (Cambridge, 1987).

Trill, S., 'Religion and the construction of femininity', in H. Wilcox (ed.), *Women and Literature in Britain, 1500–1700* (Cambridge, 1996), pp. 30–55.

Tristram, E. W., *English Wall Paintings of the Fourteenth Century*, (London, 1955).

Turner, D., 'Mural paintings in Catfield church', *Norfolk Archaeology* 1 (1847), 133–9.

Turner, J. G., *One Flesh: Paradisal Marriage and Sexual Relations in the Age of Milton* (Oxford, 1987).

Turner, V. and Turner, E., *Image and Pilgrimage in Christian Culture – Anthropological Perspectives* (Oxford, 1978).

Underdown, D. E., 'The taming of the scold: The enforcement of patriarchal authority in early modern England', in A. Fletcher and J. Stevenson (eds.), *Order and Disorder in Early Modern England* (Cambridge, 1985), pp. 116–36.

Fire From Heaven: Life in an English Town in the Seventeenth Century (London, 1993).

Vallance, A., *English Church Screens* (London, 1936).

Wall, J. C., *Medieval Wall Paintings* (London, 1914).

Waller, J. G., 'On wall paintings discovered at Raunds and Slapton, Northamptonshire', *Arch. Jnl.* (1877), 219–41.

Warner, M., *Alone of all her Sex: The Myth and the Cult of the Virgin Mary* (London, 1976).

Waterton, E., *Pietas Mariana Britannica: A History of English Devotion to the Most Blessed Virgin Marye* [sic] *Mother of God* (London, 1879).

Watt, D., *Secretaries of God: Women Prophets in Late Medieval and Early Modern England* (Woodbridge, 1997).

Watt, T., *Cheap Print and Popular Piety, 1550–1640* (Cambridge, 1991).

Wayment, H., *The Stained Glass of St Mary, Fairford, Gloucestershire* (London, 1984).

Webb, D. M., 'Women and home: The domestic setting of late medieval spirituality', in W. J. Shiels and D. Wood (eds.), *Women in the Church*, Studies in Church History 27 (Oxford, 1990), pp. 159–174.

Wenzel, S., *The Sin of Sloth: Acedia in Medieval Thought and Literature* (Chapel Hill, 1967).

Westlake, H. F., *The Parish Gilds of Mediaeval England* (London, 1919).

White, H. C., *Tudor Books of Saints and Martyrs* (Wisconsin, 1963).

Whiting, R., *The Blind Devotion of the People: Popular Religion and the English Reformation* (Cambridge, 1989).

Wiesner, M. E., 'Beyond women and the family: towards a gender analysis of the Reformation', *Sixteenth Century Journal* 18/3 (1987), 311–21.

Wiesner, M. E., 'Luther and women: the death of two Marys', in J. Obelkevich, L. Roper & R. Samuel (eds.), *Disciplines of Faith: Studies in Religion, Politics and Patriarchy* (London, 1987), 295–305.

Wilkins, E., *The Rose Garden Game: The Symbolic Background to the European Prayer Beads* (London, 1969).

Willen, D., 'Godly women in early modern England: Puritanism and gender', *JEH* 43/4 (1992), 561–80.

Williams, E. C., 'Mural paintings of St. Catherine in England', *JBAA* 19 (1956), 20–33.

Willis, D., *Malevolent Nurture: Witch-Hunting and Maternal Power in Early Modern England* (Cornell, 1995).

Wiltenburg, J., *Disorderly Women and Female Power in the Street Literature of Early Modern England and Germany* (Charlottesville and London, 1992).

Winstead, K. A., *Virgin Martyrs: Legends of Sainthood in Late Medieval England* (Ithaca and London, 1997).

Woodbridge, L., *Women and the English Renaissance: Literature and the Nature of Womankind, 1540–1620* (Brighton, 1984).

Woodeforde, C., *Stained Glass in Somerset, 1250–1830* (London, 1946).
  The Norwich School of Glass Painting in the Fifteenth Century (Oxford, 1950).

Woolf, R., *The English Religious Lyric in the Middle Ages* (Oxford, 1968).
  The English Mystery Plays (London, 1972).

Wright, S. (ed.), *Parish, Church and People* (London, 1988).

Yeatman-Biggs, W. H., 'Wall paintings in Sherrington church', *Wilts. Arch. & Nat. Hist. Mag.* 50 (1942–4), 63–5.

Young-Bruehl, E., *Subject to Biography: Psychoanalysis, Feminism and Writing Women's Lives* (Cambridge Mass., 1998).

Yule, G., 'James VI and I: furnishing the churches in his two kingdoms', in A. Fletcher and P. Roberts (eds.), *Religion, Culture and Society in Early Modern Britain: Essays in Honour of Patrick Collinson* (Cambridge, 1994), pp. 182–208.

Zell, M. L., 'The use of religious preambles as a measure of religious belief in the sixteenth century', *BIHR* 50 (1977), 246–9.

Theses

Ashby, J. E., 'English medieval murals of the Doom', M.Phil. thesis, University of York (1980).

Brown, A., 'Lay piety in late medieval Wiltshire', D.Phil. thesis, University of Oxford (1990).

Carrick, M., 'Sixteenth and seventeenth century wall painting in the county of Essex', M.Phil. thesis, University of Essex, 3 vols. (1989).

Dillow, K. B., 'The social and ecclesiastical significance of church seating arrangements and pew disputes, 1500–1740', D.Phil. thesis, University of Oxford (1990).

Geuter, V. R., 'Women and embroidery in seventeenth century Britain: The social, religious and political meanings of domestic needlework', Ph.D. thesis, University of Wales (Aberystwyth) (1996).

Gill, M. C., 'Late medieval wall painting in England: content and context (*c.* 1350–*c.*1530)', Ph.D. thesis, Courtauld Institute of Art (2001).

Lewis, K. J., ' "Rule of lyf alle folk to serve": lay responses to the cult of St. Katherine of Alexandria in late medieval England, 1300–1530', Ph.D. thesis, University of York (1996).

McIntosh, J., 'English funeral sermons, 1560–1640: the relationship between gender and death, dying and the afterlife', M.Litt. thesis, University of Oxford (1990).

Martin, J., 'The people of Reading and the Reformation 1520–70: leadership and priorities in borough and parishes', Ph.D. thesis, University of Reading (1987).

Peters, C., 'Women and the Reformation: social relations and attitudes in rural England, c.1470–1570', D.Phil. thesis, University of Oxford (1992).

Sutcliffe, S., 'Piety and the cult of saints in fifteenth century Yorkshire from testamentary evidence and surviving church art', MA thesis, University of York (1990).

Tudor, F. P., 'Changing private belief and practice in English devotional literature, c.1475–1550', D. Phil. thesis, University of Oxford (1984).

Wooding, L., 'From humanists to heretics: English catholic theology and ideology, c.1530–c.1570', D.Phil. thesis, University of Oxford (1994).

INDEX

Personal names and places mentioned only in the footnotes are not included in this index.

Titles in the series